Taming the Taxonomy

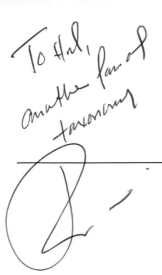

Taming the Taxonomy

Toward a New Understanding
of Great Lakes Archaeology

edited by
Ronald F. Williamson
Christopher M. Watts

Published in association with
The Ontario Archaeological Society, Inc.

eastendbooks
Toronto 1999

Design and Production by Caroline Thériault
Copy Editing by David Robertson
Printed in Canada by Métrolitho.

Cover illustration: Carte du Canada ou de la Nouvelle France, & des Découvertes, Qui y ont été faites, Dressée sur les observations les plus nouvelles, & sur divers memoires tant manuscrits qu'imprimez, 1719, Guillaume Delisle, Paris, Zacharias Chatelain (Publisher). Reproduced courtesy of the Joe C. W. Armstrong Canadiana Collection in *From Sea Unto Sea: Art & Discovery Maps of Canada*, edited by J. C. W. Armstrong, Fleet Books, Toronto.

Canadian Cataloguing in Publication Data

Main entry under title:

Taming the taxonomy : toward a new understanding of Great Lakes archaeology

Papers presented at the 1997 Ontario Archaeological Society-Midwest Archaeological Conference symposium.
Co-published by the Ontario Archaeological Society.
Includes bibliographical references.
ISBN 1-896973-18-3

1. Archaeology – Great Lakes Region – Classification – Congresses. 2. Great Lakes Region – Antiquities – Congresses. 3. Indians of North America – Great Lakes Region – Antiquities – Congresses. I. Williamson, R.F. (Ronald F.). II. Watts, Christopher M., 1972- . III. Ontario Archaeological Society. Symposium (1997 : Toronto, Ont.). IV. Midwest Archaeological Conference (1997 : Toronto, Ont.).

E78.G7T35 1999   977'.01   C99-932606-6

eastendbooks is an imprint of Venture Press
45 Fernwood Park Avenue
Toronto, Canada M4E 3E9
(416) 691-6816 [telephone]
(416) 691-2414 [fax]
Visit our website at www.eastendbooks.com

PREFACE AND ACKNOWLEDGEMENTS

This volume is the product of a joint Ontario Archaeological Society–Midwest Archaeological Conference symposium, held in Toronto, Ontario, Canada, over the weekend of October 24– 26, 1997. The Toronto Chapter of the Ontario Archaeological Society with help from Robert Salzer and Lynne Goldstein of the Midwest Archaeological Conference organized the symposium. The organizing committee included Ellen Blaubergs, Dena Doroszenko, Annie Gould, Peter Hamalainen, Norma Knowlton, Martha Latta, Pierre Lavoie, Eva MacDonald, Wayne McDonald, Roberta O'Brien, Melanie Priestman, Jane Sacchetti, Jim Shropshire, Robert von Bitter and Ron Williamson.

The symposium's theme, as suggested by the title of this book, revolved around the issue of taxonomy as it relates to the process of understanding cultural interaction and change among neighbouring populations in the archaeological record of the Great Lakes region. The symposium was organized into one plenary session on October 25 and two open sessions, one on October 24, and the other on October 26. A number of researchers were invited to prepare papers for the plenary session outlining culture change in their area of interest without reference to the existing taxonomy. In many cases, these participants were paired together with distant colleagues in an attempt to make the implications of each topic as far-reaching as possible. This approach produced a number of useful and at times novel analyses, and we are grateful to the authors for embracing a somewhat unconventional format. We equally wish to thank the other symposium participants for their time and effort.

The papers in this volume were chosen from those presented at the conference although almost all of the plenary session papers have been reproduced. Due to other commitments, only the ceramics paper by Robert Pihl and another paper concerning interaction among Upper Great Lakes populations, by Grace Rajnovich, were unavailable. Ron Mason and David Brose did not submit their comments for publication. For those who missed the symposium, the plenary session was filmed and tapes may be obtained from the office of the Ontario Archaeological Society (oas@globalserve.net).

Financial support for the publication of these proceedings was provided by the Ontario Archaeological Society, Inc. We also thank David Robertson, Andrew Stewart, and Caroline Thériault who were all very helpful in bringing this project to fruition. Finally, we are grateful to the staff at eastendbooks, in particular Randall White, for their support in ensuring that the results of this conference reach the widest audience possible.

Ronald F. Williamson
Christopher M. Watts

NOTES ON CONVENTIONS

In recognition of the fact that our terminology has a political context and that many of the authors in this volume have proposed the replacement of prehistory with precontact history, we have implemented that recommendation. While pre- and post-contact appear to work well, at least one author has asserted that protohistoric remains the most accurate term for the period subsequent to the introduction of European goods to the region and prior to the first written records.

The radiocarbon dates have been presented where possible as B.P. years or "before present" in an effort to present a standard, basic chronological system throughout the volume. In specific instances, however, such as the case of a calibrated date or when presenting tabular data in a manner following previous convention, Christian calendrical dates have been provided.

CONTENTS

Contents

Section III: Taming the Tamers

Section IV: Synthesis

List of Figures

Contents

List of Tables

Introduction

TOWARD A GROUNDED ARCHAEOLOGY

7

Ronald F. Williamson
Archaeological Services Inc.

T he student of Great Lakes archaeology is currently confronted with an extraordinary number of traditions, co-traditions, horizons, phases and cultural referents. In some cases, different terms are applied to precontact communities that were situated only a few miles apart, across what are now state or international boundaries. Moreover, the number of these taxonomic referents is growing rather than diminishing, exacerbating the already difficult and complex process of understanding cultural interaction and change among these neighbouring populations.

It was hoped that the 1997 joint Ontario Archaeological Society-Midwest Archaeological Conference symposium, at which versions of the following papers were presented, would provide an opportunity to address this problem. The objective was to invite a number of Great Lakes researchers, who are investigating precontact peoples from a wide variety of temporal and spatial contexts, not to eliminate the existing taxonomic scheme, but to question the usefulness of current archaeological constructs and to identify new directions that would enhance rather than obscure communication across our research area.

We invited archaeologists from all employment contexts since it is now important, in light of the vast quantity of data to emerge in the past two decades, for researchers to examine the "new archaeological record" in order to demonstrate the actual level of socio-political integration and co-operation among regionally based social systems rather than force these new data into old taxonomic structures. And make no mistake, there is a "*new* archaeological record". Awareness and understanding of the data collected by cultural resource management (CRM) programs have become the keys to identifying and understanding the past, both in Canada and in the United States. There has been a revolution in data collection in the last decade; over 80 percent of the 3,000 sites added to the Ontario provincial database from 1991 to 1997, for example, were documented by consultants and there has been a three-fold increase in the number of annually documented sites from fifteen years ago. These changes are also reflected more generally in the 1994 census of American archaeology analysed by Melinda Zeder (1997),where she identified private firms and independent consultants as the fastest growing sector of the archaeological workforce.

While this is not the place to engage in a debate concerning the predictable response that the data are unpublished and are therefore inaccessible, current trends suggest a publication structure in which consultants publish in regional journals and newsletters while university-based researchers publish in national and international journals. In a survey of articles published between 1991 and 1997, for example, university based archaeologists were responsible for 86 percent of the articles in *American Antiquity*, 75 percent in the *Canadian Journal of Archaeology*, but only 30 percent in *Ontario Archaeology*, a peer-reviewed regional journal published by the Ontario Archaeological Society. Consultants, on the other hand, have published 50 percent of the articles in both *Ontario Archaeology* and in *Kewa*, the most referenced newsletter published by the society. These tendencies reflect both the consultant community's frequent contributions to the design and refinement of regional and local culture histories, based on the vast body of newly emerging site data, but also their relative absence in contemporary theoretical debates, which are for the most, played out by university-based archaeologists in national and international forums.

Provincial publications such as the *Annual Archaeological Report of Ontario* play an important role, however, in informing the entire archaeological community of the extent and nature of annual archaeological research in the province and so should be mandatory reading for all researchers. A considerable amount of this annual archaeology does indeed go unpublished, and while acknowledging the occasional personality conflict, most consultants have learned to share unpublished data from projects undertaken in CRM contexts and to consult each others' collections of grey literature. This is an especially important research task at a time when governments are often unable to act as the keepers and distributors of reports. All one has to do is ask. To understand and synthesize all of the archaeological record, it is necessary to actively seek the data in new ways and places and to realize that the old practice of conducting research in offices and libraries with only published documents will now lead to ill-informed summaries of the past.

We should be clear, however, about what is involved in this attempt to reach a new understanding of the archaeological record of the Great

Lakes region. In the context of the current questioning of North American archaeological research paradigms, it is no less than a search for a new method for reconstructing the past. Some have argued, for example, that culture history has failed in the late twentieth century for want of an explicit archaeological theory of cultural evolution (Lyman et al. 1997:231). Others, including many of the authors in this volume, define our major problem as one of reaching a clear understanding of the distinction between constructs based on archaeological data, largely derived from material culture, and socio-cultural constructs, based largely on ethnological data. Over the past decade, it has been this basic struggle that has defined the discomfort with current models of culture change in the Great Lakes region (e.g., Krakker 1983; Niemczycki 1984; Timmins 1997; Williamson and Robertson 1994a). Indeed, the primary shared concern to emerge from the papers in this volume relates to the problems created when researchers confuse taxonomic referents with actual social groups.

This is most evident when archaeologists construct complex histories of cultural interaction and change on the basis of selected constituents of the precontact past. In a recent article, for example, it was argued that in order to fully realize the potential of the archaeological record, archaeologists must begin to consider archaeological culture "types" in the context of a discrete attribute approach with these attributes being considered in isolation (Bursey 1997:42). This is of course the tired supremacy of ceramics argument, the trait chase, whose abandonment in the mid-twentieth century in most places was unfortunately never completely realized in Ontario. While the collection of detailed empirical ceramic and lithic artifact data is useful in the context of well-developed explanatory theory, a frequent problem is analogous to that of the unsatisfactory autobiography where you suspect the author yielded to the temptation to edit their past, where what they chose to forget might be as important as what they elected to remember. In fairness, Bursey went on to argue that we must pay closer attention to obtaining adequate samples of all classes of archaeological data. In light of the "ceramic syndrome", however, I am not so sure that *collection* of all of the data is the problem as much as it is *consideration* of all of the data. The objective of considering *all* of the data in the archaeological record, in part explains the way in which the plenary session of the conference was structured. Not only was an attempt made to invite participants from all employment contexts from across the Great Lakes region, but also to ensure that

5

consideration was given to concomitant change in environment, socio-political organization, regional interaction, language, biological structure, ideology and material culture. It is important to note that these subject areas were not considered exhaustive. It was simply a matter of what could be accommodated within a single day session, thereby still allowing for freedom for the Friday and Sunday papers, although those selected for the Friday session were focussed on the conference theme. Indeed, most of the Friday papers, many of which are presented in Section I, deal with taxonomic issues in light of real archaeological data.

The objective of reconsidering current taxonomic referents led to the explicit request of plenary session participants to prepare their papers without reference to the existing cultural taxonomy since it was thought it might be an interesting—although admittedly difficult—task to examine the archaeological record to determine, given some understanding of a constantly evolving natural environment, when there was concomitant and profound change in the economic, social, political, and religious life of precontact peoples that might signal new stages of cultural development. From these observations, it was thought that it might be possible, at the very least, to alter the existing lexicon for Great Lakes culture history. That this would happen in Ontario was predicted many years ago by J. V. Wright, when he recognized that, in the fullness of time and with accumulation of data, many of his interpretations would be "subject to marked alterations" (1966:101).

Some of the plenary session papers, most of which are presented in Section II, successfully met the challenge of presenting their interpretations of culture change free of the existing taxonomy, while others found it impossible to avoid using at least some aspect of the existing taxonomic scheme. Even when the challenge was met, many of the reviewers of the papers, recommended confrontation with the existing taxonomy, suggesting for example, that explicit dialogue is required to reduce the duplication and ambiguity in the typological classifications of certain artifact classes (e.g., Clovis-Gainey; cf. Morrow this volume). This was not our intention with the plenary session, but we hope that these papers will stimulate researchers to address such issues.

While as program convenor, I was free to organize the events of the day within a certain structure, imposing guidelines on participants and making unreasonable requests such as asking them to work with far-distant strangers (Timmins and Staeck, for example, had never met), there was a limit to my influence. What I would have liked to have also asked of the participants is to consider how the change that they recognized in the archaeological record had manifested itself "on the ground". This is a question too often avoided by researchers in their theoretical musings of branches, traditions, phases, complexes and cultures, yet it goes to the heart of the issue of collecting empirical data such as ceramic or lithic attribute frequencies and addressing our inability to understand how they might have been employed in precontact technological and social environments. It is inane, for example, to consider artifact stylistic data in the context of a model of socio-cultural evolution that you are trying to demonstrate with those data. It is considerably more fruitful to assume that contemporaneous communities within a single geographical region are autonomous until an examination of the interaction between them sheds some light on shared political institutions, shared ideological systems, shared economic systems and conventionalized patterns of material culture that suggest that these communities together constituted a more broad and recognizable social or political group. The sharing of one or more ceramic decoration attributes may indeed form part of such a pattern, but it would be foolish to postulate a social evolutionary scheme on those data alone. It is necessary to ask, among other questions, how those two or more communities came to share those ceramic attributes or more precisely, how did it work on the ground? Michael Spence (this volume), for example, has refocussed our attention on the exchange of marriage partners as one of the primary social mechanisms through which these changes occurred.

Intermarriage and other socio-political mechanisms must have played a role in the case of migration and linguistic metamorphosis. Many Iroquoianists have been contemplating Dean Snow's (1992a,b,1995a) argument that a founding population of Iroquoian speakers, originating from Pennsylvania, migrated into the Northeast at a much later date than previously thought. He now dates that migration to the sixth century (1996), having revised his earlier estimate of 1050 B.P. on the basis of the results of Crawford and Smith's (1996) research with Princess Point sites in southern Ontario. Regardless of when they arrived, Snow has hypothesized a language change of the most extraordinary kind, presuming that until this time, the area was populated by Algonquian speakers (cf. Feidel this volume). How did this language change work on the ground? While I was reflecting on this question, I came across the story of a fifteenth century linguist having compiled a book of Spanish grammar to send with Columbus for his journey to the New World. When the volume was presented to Queen Isabella, she was puzzled and asked what it was for. "Your Majesty" the Bishop of Avila replied, "language is the perfect instrument of empire" (Geary 1997). The understanding of how language change is effected rests with an understanding of how languages, like all living things, depend on their natural and cultural environments to survive. They may be absorbed by competitor tongues or displaced from their natural habitats by more successful adversaries. In this type of "linguistic natural selection", the economic might, military muscle, social inclusiveness, and/or influence of the culture in which a language is spoken all play significant roles in its future (Geary 1997; cf. Engelbrecht this volume). How did these factors play out on the ground in the Algonquian-Iroquoian case, specifically in the context of largely band level social and political organization and interaction?

The ability to propose answers to how these changes worked on the ground is, for me, a necessary prerequisite to proposing far reaching cultural change and represents an initial test of the workability of a theoretical position. While I confess to an incomplete understanding of the archaeological record, there appears to me to be too many theories as well as branches and complexes in Great Lakes archaeology in need of grounding.

Section I: Problems in Taxonomy

THE WAY WE WERE: SIXTY YEARS OF PARADIGM SHIFTS IN THE GREAT LAKES REGION

2

Martha A. Latta

Department of Anthropology, University of Toronto at Scarborough

This symposium developed around themes of *taxonomies of history*, classifications of lifeways and cultural evolution in the Great Lakes region. Many participants were concerned with the definitions of taxa—what groups (of people, of languages, of technologies, of beliefs) can be recognized in the past and how these groups interacted spatially and chronologically.

A second parallel theme may be termed *histories of taxonomy*. Many of these papers are concerned with the evolution of taxa—how archaeologists defined taxa in the (archaeological) past and how archaeological definitions interacted—spatially and chronologically.

Thus this conference may be very generally summarized as "Why are taxa as they are?", "What is the practical result of using a particular taxon?" and "What alternative taxa exist?" These three questions are central to the archaeologist's cognitive world.

The term *taxonomy* was defined in the seventh edition of the Encyclopedia Britannica (1832) as "...that branch of botany which has for its object the combination of all our observations on plants, so as to form a system or classification." To a biologist, taxonomy means the systematic arrangement of plant and animal organisms, according to accepted diagnostic criteria, which allow them to be placed into a ranked hierarchy of increasingly inclusive stages. Generally, taxonomy is the science of the laws and criteria of classification.

To a nineteenth century scientist, individual taxa were defined normatively on the basis of characteristic and distinctive traits. Even at the lowest level, biological taxa—known as *species*—could be clearly distinguished on the grounds of mutual infertility. For the most part, this infertility required no proof: carrots and fruit flies could not interbreed. For a few species, notably horses and donkeys, cross-breeding produced infertile descendants; this was considered sufficiently distinctive for species status. Cases were known where individuals of different assigned species (such as timber wolves and domestic dogs) might interbreed to produce fertile offspring, but these were usually avoided as "unproven" or "mistakes in taxonomic definition".

In the latter part of the twentieth century, biologists have increasingly changed their focus from the norms to the variability of their taxa. Rather than a condition defined for all time, a species has become a marker along an evolutionary string which leads from the past to the future:

> Modern taxonomy is the product of an increasing awareness among biologists of the uniqueness of individuals, and of the wide range of variation which may occur in any population of individuals. The taxonomist is, therefore, primarily concerned with the measurement of variation in series of individuals which stand as representatives of the species in which he is interested [Kinsey et al 1948].

From a hierarchical "tree" composed of unique, discrete entities, taxonomy has adopted a broader approach which recognizes that variability, not identity, is the usual state of reality.

Modern taxonomists recognize that data are real; taxa are constructs. In this perspective, individual taxa can be multiplied as needed to increase the sophistication of the model. Associated information, such as age, geographical appearance, ecology and behaviour, derive from the data *in each case*. Data should never be altered to fit the taxa.

To the archaeologist and palaeontologist, whose data possess no mechanical tests for taxonomic integrity, this problem is greatly magnified. We cannot introduce a *Tyrannosaurus rex* to an *Albertosaurus* to test mutual fertility. We certainly cannot persuade ceramic pots to breed. Almost invariably, the taxa of the past are historical accidents, based on the information available to, and the personal opinions of, one or a few individuals. It is useful to remember that accidents of history have shaped our perception of the past.

Once established, taxonomies tend to be self-replicating. Researchers compare present work to past work; thereby, they confirm the existing taxonomy. Individuals become psychologically entangled with their own taxa, defending them against intruders like howler monkeys; this is particularly true of human palaeontologists, but archaeologists are not immune to taxonomic territoriality. A sadly repetitive occurrence in archaeological history is the refusal of a former innovator to accept the fact that his pet taxon has failed to mirror reality in a way which is useful to his colleagues.

Finally, evolutionary taxonomies do not usually have sharp boundaries; they are separated by ecotones of various sorts. The appearance of *Homo erectus* does not mean that every *Homo habilis* in the world disappeared. Likewise, people did not wake up one morning and say, "Gee, Mel, I feel really Woodland today!" Boundary dates become less and less meaningful as we deal with larger taxa. Instead, we should look at the variability within taxa, seeking the inevitable overlaps, intrusions or coexistences in our data.

It is widely held that the changes which took place in North American archaeological theory in the late 1930s represent a *paradigm shift* (Custer 1981; Meltzer 1979, 1981; cf. Meltzer and Dunnell [editors] 1992; Spaulding 1953; Swartz 1977; Willey and Sabloff 1982). By this term I mean not only a change in theory but a change in the cognitive structures on which theory subsequently builds. A mark of a paradigm shift is not just that people are persuaded but that everyone says, "But of course... that feels right!" Orientation changes supraconsciously after which theory emerges to codify and justify the change, not the other way around. Whatever its cultural origins, this paradigm shift is clearly documented in the archaeological publications of the Great Lakes.

Chronology and History

It is as difficult for us to understand the minds of archaeologists in the years before radiocarbon dating as it is to understand the medieval European peasant's view of the universe. We are so accustomed to the scope and range of the carbon-dated past that our cognitive map of the human past has been moulded to fit these dates. A universe without radiocarbon dates is like a flat earth, whose borders can only be traced by imagination.

The chronometric breakthrough of the 1920s, dendrochronology, had provided a yardstick for the development of the First Nations of the American Southwest. In so doing, dendrochronology put an end to speculations that native history was of very short duration and entirely derivative from Eurasian cultures. In the Great Lakes region, where wood was poorly preserved, there were few data with which to build a master dendrogram.

Stratigraphy, the workhorse of the Near East, was also of limited utility in the Great Lakes. Caves are relatively uncommon in this region and few stratified sites had been excavated before 1936.

There was ethnohistory, particularly in the eastern part of the Great

Lakes. Much of it dealt solely with the Huron, an Iroquoian-speaking group living in southcentral Ontario. The 73 volumes of the Jesuit Relations and Allied Documents (Thwaites [editor] 1896-1901) plus the memoirs of Cartier (Biggar [editor] 1924), Champlain (Biggar [editor] 1922-1936), Sagard (Wrong 1939), Lafitau (1724), Charlevoix (1923), Chaumonot (1869) and Gendron (1868) provide the most extensive early-contact description of any First Nation north of Mexico.

In the late nineteenth century, the Bureau of American Ethnology began to collect copious data on surviving First Nations in the United States. This generated an upsurge of interest in the New York Iroquois (Clarke 1870; Connelley 1899; Hewitt 1907; Morgan 1901; Parker 1910; Stites 1905). Two topics which sound surprisingly modern, in concept if not in execution, are Iroquois women (Beauchamp 1900; Carr 1887; Hewitt 1932) and Iroquois food (Carr 1895; Parker 1910: Waugh 1916).

A body of anthropometric studies of human skeletal remains offered insights derived from skull size and shape. These innocently racist studies traced a development from early, primitive Archaic peoples ("dolichocranial, hypsicranial, leptorrhine, leptoprosopic, mesoseme" [Ritchie 1932:409]), through a developed population ("brachycranial, hypsicranial, platyrrhine, chamaeprosopic, microseme" [Ritchie 1932:409]), to the "well-known early Iroquoian (Proto-Negroid, dolichocranial, hypsicranial and platyrrhine" [Ritchie 1932:413]).

Glottochronology suggested that the origin of the Iroquois language was linked with that of the Cherokee in the southeast United States (Chafe 1964). Since glottochronology equated degree of linguistic divergence with duration of separate linguistic development, this method offered a means of establishing at least one date in Iroquois precontact history—that of the physical separation of Iroquois and Cherokee and the movement of either or both groups to their historic locations. The observed fact that Iroquoian speakers were surrounded by speakers of languages which belonged to the great Algonquian family was thought to indicate that the Iroquois had migrated north to reside in the Great Lakes region and intruded into formerly Algonquian territory (cf. Parker 1923).

Researchers in New York (Beauchamp 1894, 1897, 1898; Parker 1916) combined glottochronology with anthropometry to produce speculative "histories" of the Iroquois. In the final statement of the old paradigm, Ritchie (1932) added archaeological data to these histories. He linked the ceramic sites in New York with the Iroquois and equated the middle, "brachycranial..." people with "the Algonkin", a group which he neglected to define. These people, following Parker (1923), had intruded into New York "from the west, the direction of the apex of the fan, some thousands of years ago, being eastern detachments of some of the tribes which were milling out from the upper plains" (Ritchie 1932:407-408).

The oldest, "dolichocranial", group were Archaic peoples of unknown language. The initial invasion by the "Algonkins" was hostile but "apparently subsided into a more amicable relationship, for the skeletal remains found on several sites in central New York portray the results of some degree of amalgamation of the dolichycranial and brachycranial populations" (Ritchie 1932:411).

I have outlined Ritchie's presentation of Parker's theory in some detail both because it is the clearest statement of the old paradigm and because it impacted on later taxonomic studies. In 1932, archaeological taxonomy consisted of migrating populations. As Ritchie concludes his article, "The virile character of the Iroquois wrought the gradual acculturation of the more retarded Algonkin, who progressively yielded, retiring toward the north and east" (Ritchie 1932:414).

Classificatory Taxonomies

Something happened in the middle 1930s. In part, it reflected changes in other parts of the world, notably in the southwest United States and in the Near East, where chronological taxonomies were being developed on the basis of specific ceramic styles. In part, it seems to have represented a philosophical rejection of the simplistic historical thinking of the past. Perhaps the facts of the Great Depression forced archaeologists to rethink their implicit assumptions about white Euro/North Americans as the pinnacle of human evolution. Certainly, the development of massive make-work archaeological programs brought in a vast amount of new data.

It is hard to put a name on the centre for this new thought, but it seems to have emerged from a nexus of activity which involved Professor Fay-Cooper Cole at the University of Chicago, Will C. McKern, Curator of Anthropology at the Milwaukee Public Museum, and Carl Guthe, Curator at the Museum of Anthropology, University of Michigan. In later years, James Griffin could not remember exactly who had first put forth the concepts which were later to be published as "The Midwestern Taxonomic Method" (McKern 1939). It had resulted from a number of formal and informal discussions at the University of Chicago, in December 1932; at the meeting of the American Anthropological

Association, Central Section, in Indianapolis, in 1934; and at meetings of the National Research Council's Committee on State Archaeological Surveys in Indianapolis (1935), and in Washington D.C. (1937).

Present at these meetings were a number of graduate students, including James B. Griffin, Albert Spaulding, Carlyle S. Smith (my own undergraduate mentor) and William Ritchie. They embraced the concepts with enthusiasm (Griffin, personal communication, 1986).

The impact of the Midwestern Taxonomic Method (MTM) was far greater in a philosophical than a practical sense. The rather tedious distinctions between *focus, aspect, phase* and *pattern* became blurred by subsequent use, so that these terms are often treated by modern analysts as roughly equivalent. A quick survey of graduate students a few years ago showed that most of them understood "pattern" as the most particular and local category, whereas the MTM used this term for the broadest, most general category (McKern 1939:308-309).

Philosophically, however, the MTM had a tremendous impact. It provided a method for the systematic creation of local taxonomies based on material culture from observed archaeological contexts rather than on speculations drawn from history, language, or skull shape.

Although McKern denied any inherent chronological implication in the MTM taxa, most analysts used it in conjunction with a direct historic approach: that is, the archaeologist began with the historic peoples and created taxa which extended the definition of the same peoples into the past until they were no longer recognizable.

The New Paradigm

The first results of the MTM paradigm shift actually preceded McKern's definitive article (1939), though the authors made it clear that the sources of their thinking were the same as those credited by McKern. It began with the definition of two distinct taxa: the Mississippi Basic Culture and the Woodland Basic Culture (Deuel 1935). After 60 years, we would make many changes in Deuel's criteria for definition but his taxa remain solidly intact.

The paradigm shifted rapidly—it was the New Archaeology of its day. By 1938, Ritchie had discarded his glottochronology and craniometry in favour of a taxonomy based on archaeological criteria which remains essentially intact today. As other papers in this volume will demonstrate, the role of population migrations in this taxonomy remains an issue of vigorous theoretical debate.

To this atmosphere of creativity, Richard Ford and Gordon Willey (1941) added a new set of taxa—*component, site, tradition, stage*—which were explicitly chronological as well as spatial. This provided a framework for in situ development of historic traditions and at the same time it provided a unifying umbrella taxonomy for the entirety of eastern North America (Ford and Willey 1941; Willey 1966), indeed of the entire New World (Willey and Phillips 1958; Willey 1966, 1968).

Although the Ford/Willey taxonomy has almost completely replaced the MTM in use, it was built upon the MTM model. Data were translated, in many cases intact, from "phase" to "tradition" and subsequent generations of archaeologists have mixed the taxa of the two systems in a fairly free fashion.

Like the MTM, the Ford-Willey taxonomy relied on diagnostic *types* (Ford 1954) With the addition of a quasi-mathematical framework (Brainard 1950; Spaulding 1953), archaeologists began confidently to plot the traces of precontact culture processes. By the time radiocarbon dating arrived in the early 1960s, it was possible to attach dates to established taxa in a way which involved very little reorganization of precontact history.

In New York, archaeologists rushed to define and name ceramic types (Ritchie and MacNeish 1949; MacNeish 1952), lithic types (Ritchie 1961), settlement and burial types and so forth. To Ritchie's chronological taxonomy (Ritchie 1944, 1969), MacNeish (1952, 1959) added a focus upon the concept of in situ continuity of ceramic type sequences from historic First Nations to precontact sites in New York and Ontario. Later archaeologists crossed Ritchie's chronological taxa with MacNeish's geographical ones, creating or recognizing quasi- or non-historical First Nations such as the Wendat, the Erie and others to account for sites outside the territories equated with historic members of the League Iroquois.

Ontario

The aboriginal peoples of Ontario were widely studied in the years before World War I (Barbeau 1912, 1913, 1917; Gerin 1900; Goldenweiser 1912, 1913, 1914; Hewitt 1907; Jones 1910; Orr 1921; Wilson 1885). Archaeological research began around 1870 in southern Ontario (Latta 1985) and was put on a solid footing through the works of David Boyle and his assistants Andrew Hunter, William Wintemberg, George Laidlaw and Roland Orr (Killan 1983). By 1900, the archaeological resources of southern Ontario had been extensively surveyed and published through the *Annual Archaeological Reports of Ontario*, addenda to the report of the Minister of Education.

At the same time, popular interest became focussed on the seventeenth French Jesuit missionaries who were canonized as saints in 1920. A highly successful publicity campaign utilized dubious archaeological research to support this process (Latta 1985) and interest in pre-European archaeology dwindled. Popular and scholarly interest was drawn into debates about sites mentioned by the French writers—the mission of St. Ignace, where Brebeuf and Lalemant died in AD 1649 (Fox and Jury 1949; Latta 1985) and the village of Cahiagué which was visited by Champlain in AD 1615 (McIlwraith 1947; Fitzgerald 1986). One tangible result of this focus was the excavation (Kidd 1949) and massive reconstruction (Jury and Jury 1954) of the seventeenth century Jesuit home mission dedicated to the Virgin Mary (now Sainte Marie Among the Hurons).

With a few notable exceptions such as the work of Wintemberg (cf. 1940, 1942, 1946, 1948), Ontario archaeology during the period of the Great Depression and World War II was historical archaeology and it drew its taxonomy from history, seeking to define more and more precise subdivisions of the forty-year period of European presence in Huronia and lumping all of the pre-European past into a general "non-European" category.

In the post-war period, this orientation changed through the contributions of W.S. MacNeish and J. N. Emerson. MacNeish (1952) defined ethnic sequences based on seriations of ceramic types and created the first artifact-based taxonomy which linked the Iroquois of New York with those of Ontario. In so doing, he expounded the "in situ hypothesis" which was derived, in essence, from the taxonomies of the 1930s. Massive population movements were rejected in favour of internal processes of culture change, though diffused traits were generally viewed as the work of captive women.

In Ontario, the work of J. Norman Emerson returned to old-paradigm hypotheses of massive population movements. One of the last students of Fay-Cooper Cole at the University of Chicago, Emerson created the first taxonomy of Ontario precontact history (Emerson 1954) based on artifact assemblages from eleven sites in southcentral Ontario. The sites were seriated using MacNeish's ceramic types and with castellation and pipe types of his own (Emerson 1954); a later version of this study incorporated the Brainard-Robinson coefficient of similarity (Emerson 1966). The late sites in this sequence were located in Huronia and the earlier sites were from the Toronto region. Emerson concluded that this represented a northward migration of the Huron from the Lake Ontario area of modern Toronto.

The dangers of seriation as an analytic tool are well known. Data can be ordered in linear fashion with relative ease, and the straightforward mathematics of most procedures give a feeling of solidity to the results which cannot be validated by any measure of confidence. Unfortunately, the difficult parts of seriation are those of determining sample adequacy, of appropriateness of seriated traits, and of interpretation of results: the resulting order can reflect chronology, spatial distance and/or other dimensions of culture change. In this case, Emerson's database was flawed, and ten years of vituperative controversy ensued.

Frank Ridley, a highly skilled avocational archaeologist, surveyed widely in and around Huronia and carried out systematic investigation of several stratified sites in which he traced a gradual in situ development of Huron traits. His conclusion was that the Huron had evolved in Huronia, perhaps from a generalized Archaic base, and that later Iroquoians had migrated south to Lake Ontario (Ridley 1952). The conflict between Emerson and Ridley, termed the "Ontario Iroquois Controversy" (Emerson 1959, 1961; Emerson and Popham 1952; Ridley 1958, 1963), drew other researchers into unproductive conflict throughout the 1950s and early 1960s.

The question was finally laid to rest by the dissertation of James V. Wright of the newly-created Archaeological Survey of Canada, published by the National Museum as *The Ontario Iroquois Tradition* (Wright 1966). Wright's study reconciled Emerson's and Ridley's approaches by arguing that Early Iroquoians (not Hurons) had spread north from the Great Lakes into Huronia and had then developed in situ in that region.

A much more important aspect of Wright's research, though it was perhaps less appreciated at the time, was its presentation of the first broad taxonomy of pre-European archaeological traditions in southern Ontario. This study, which added radiocarbon dates to seriated sequences, incorporated the researches of many early archaeologists, and it systematized these data through a series of focal stages, sub-stages and branches. Wright's use of terminology has been criticized, but the effect of his study was dynamic: it opened new archaeological vistas by spreading the focus of precontact history beyond the Toronto-Huronia corridor and provided the first chronological taxonomy for southern Ontario precontact history. For researchers in Ontario, Wright's taxonomy produced a paradigm shift comparable in scope to that of the MTM. Its success is reflected in the degree to which it forms the base upon which all of the Ontario papers in this conference were developed.

Following the success of the *Ontario Iroquois Tradition*, Wright turned his attention to the upper Great Lakes regions of northern Ontario and produced the first syntheses of the precontact history of this region—*The Laurel Tradition* (1967a) and *The Shield Archaic Tradition* (1972). These were the first comprehensive studies of archaeological cultures in these regions and they raised taxonomic questions which have only begun to be examined in a systematic fashion.

Wright's taxonomies reject Fordian (and particularly MacNeish/ Emersonian) *types* as constructs which shape, rather than derive from, the data. Instead, Wright has repeatedly advocated "attributes", minimalist traits which assort independently, rather like genes, to form clusters which are the phenotypic artifacts of history. Such taxa were amenable to statistical analysis using the electronic computers which first became widely accessible in the 1960s. In theory, this process removes subjectivity from the taxonomic process and renders all analyses mutually comprehensible.

In the longer run, this optimistic innovation has proved something of a disappointment. It is far more difficult to define completely objective attributes than was previously anticipated; most archaeologists still insist on carrying out their own assessment of the data because they do not agree on basic definitions. Further, the ease with which modern personal computers can generate tables has led to a proliferation of interpretive noise, full of numbers and signifying very little. On the whole, one might argue, the adoption of attribute-level taxa has made it more difficult—not easier—to extract meaning from the past.

As well, Wright's taxa are curiously Postmodernist in their tendency toward multiple-reality states. Not exactly chronological categories, not exactly horizons, not exactly linguistic groups, Wright's taxa have challenged and frustrated a generation of archaeologists, most of whom have ultimately accepted his definitions because they work. Although his terminology draws upon traditional studies, researchers are advised to tread carefully. I would suggest that "stage" and "tradition" mean something rather different to Wright than they did to Willey and Phillips (1958).

With the adoption of Wright's thesis, then, the Ontario Iroquois Controversy found itself outflanked and gradually fizzled to a close. As late as 1967, Emerson still fulminated on the weaknesses of Ridley's hypothesis but everyone else was glad to drop the issue and move on to the larger perspectives provided by Wright's synthesis.

Newer Paradigms

Arguably, the primary influence of the New Archaeology in Ontario (and indeed in all of Canada) has been the widespread acceptance of environmental adaptation as the overriding mechanism leading to culture change and of environmental reconstruction as a valid, indeed a necessary, concomitant of archaeology. In this paradigm, culture history consists of adaptation by specific peoples to specific environments; innovation and diffusion are generally regarded as of minor importance compared with environmental factors, and population movements take place only in gradual response to environmental change. Great stress has been laid on the shift of biotic borders such as the prairie/woodland edge and the treeline. A widespread corollary which has emerged is an assumption that cultures within environmentally homogeneous regions, no matter how large, will themselves be relatively homogeneous (cf. Wright 1972:62). Unfortunately, poor organic preservation in the highly acidic soils of the Boreal Forest has seriously hampered paleoecological reconstruction and radiocarbon dating in the north; even in southern Ontario, environmental interpretation relies heavily on modern analogy.

The New Archaeology has had limited influence upon Ontario taxonomy. Trigger (1970b, 1978d, 1980) and Wright (1985) agree that culture history remains the dominant approach in Canadian archaeology: "Canadians have a strong focus on culture history and hypothesis testing is generally viewed as a method of inducing culture history rather than as an end in itself" (Wright 1985:428). Whether or not the present paradigm can be properly termed scientific (cf. Trigger 1978d:19-52, 1980:672), it still demonstrates the philosophical dichotomy between history, which seeks to explain specific phenomena and anthropology which seeks to formulate and test general laws (Trigger 1978d:20). This probably reflects the relative youth of the discipline and the vast amount of undigested raw data which have been produced in the past decade. Questions of culture theory wait for data to be obtained and structured to test them.

Archaeologists, in Canada at least, continue to employ the methods of both sides (Trigger 1980:670; Wright 1985). Culture history provides a flexible framework for the acquisition and initial interpretation of limited data and, on the one hand, Canadian archaeologists profit from this flexibility:

> Archaeology, straddling as it does both the sciences and the humanities, has so many and varied contributions to make to society that it is ill-served by any restrictive, doctrinaire schools of thought. Also it is most fortunate that the eclectic nature of archaeology places it in an ideal position to exploit the theoretical stocks of many other disciplines for its own purposes [Wright 1985:428].

On the other hand, it might be argued that this absence of clearly defined theoretical structure has produced a discipline which lacks internal cohesion and a clear sense of purpose. Too many reports lack the basic anthropological insight demonstrated seventy years ago by Wintemberg.

Analyses which consist of computer-generated tables of measurements and naive environmental reconstructions give little sense of the range of precontact culture choices and the ability of populations to make non-adaptive culture changes. As social/cultural anthropologists note, much of this stuff bears little resemblance to the multifaceted reality of living cultures.

Even less forgivably, much of it is dull and this represents a serious threat to heritage. Museums and electronic media have replaced published reports and books to provide a link between research and the public, and neither community is intrinsically well informed about archaeological issues. A quick scan of internet discussion groups reveals that questions of "Lost Arks" and "Biblical Creation" are widely accepted as legitimate archaeological concerns by members of the public. Archaeologists need to reconsider their research goals. If we lose the interest and the support of the nonarchaeological community, we may lose the past.

The Newest Paradigm

Postprocessual/postmodernist perspectives have made a strong impression on Great Lakes taxonomy in two areas: feminist studies and the rights of First Nations in regard to their own heritage.

Feminist archaeology has become generally accepted, both through the ongoing participation of women in the archaeological profession and through concern for the roles and contributions of women in the past (Latta et al. 1998). If some areas of inequity still remain, and if some archaeologists remain unconvinced of the need for change, there have indeed been profound changes in our profession. Whatever he might privately think, no male archaeologist today would refuse to hire a woman on the grounds that she might "disturb the scholars".

Archaeologists in both Canada and the United States are learning to be sensitive to the concerns and interests of the living descendants of precontact First Nations, particularly in the handling of burials. Canada does not yet have a formal equivalent of the Native American Graves Patriation and Recovery Act, on either the federal or provincial level, but First Nations in Canada are well aware of NAGPRA and press for similar ends. Archaeologists and museologists have been encouraged to establish working agreements with First Nations to satisfy the concerns of both sides without invoking the inflexibility of legislation. While it would be premature to say that this process has produced total accord, it is generally accepted as an honourable goal.

The taxonomic implications of postmodernist archaeology remain, for the most part, unformulated. It is even fair to say that some postmodernists reject taxonomy altogether.

Conclusion

Throughout the past century, paradigms of archaeological taxonomy have expanded our understanding of the past. This is the basic stuff of science. In the words of a biological taxonomist:

> Taxonomy is often regarded as the dullest of subjects, fit only for mindless ordering and sometimes denigrated within science as mere "stamp collecting". If systems of classification were neutral hat racks for hanging the hats of the world, this disdain might be justified. But classifications both reflect and direct our thinking. The way we order represents the way we think. Historical changes in classification are the fossilized indicators of conceptual revolutions [Gould 1983:72].

INTEGRATIVE TAXA IN MIDWESTERN ARCHAEOLOGY   *3*

William Green
Office of the State Archaeologist and *Department of Anthropology, University of Iowa*

The term *systematics* refers to the means people use to classify things, the ways we organize observations and interpretations. Systematics, an essential concern of any historical science, is still important in archaeology. The past few decades of new and newer archaeology have not freed us from having to care about such seemingly mundane matters. Of course, we should strive to avoid creating ideal, essentialist taxa (Lyman et al. 1997:4–6) and then shoe-horning sites and groups of materials into such static, etic entities. Our systematics should not strangle our imaginations. But neither should we accept a confusing or anarchic systematics merely because we have been stuck with it. Even the many scholars who have helped move archaeology beyond culture history would agree with the fundamental need to address the when and where questions for these are the building blocks of understanding the past:

> The study of cultural evolution does not end with a reconstruction of the 'genealogies' of cultures. But without such a reconstruction it can never begin.... [I]t is culture history and its ostracized 'space-time systematics' that are required if we are interested in the evolution of culture [Tschauner 1994:89, 90].

Systems of organizing archaeological information should be flexible, to accommodate and promote future research. As James V. Wright noted: "closed systems like so many beads on a string...disrupt or mask continuities in both time and space. As archaeology is a dynamic and cumulative discipline it is mandatory that it use open-ended systems" (1974:207–208) of taxonomy. But any taxonomy—including a flexible one—requires precision in nomenclature. You do not have to be a proponent of Sapir-Whorf to agree that the ways we classify and name things not only reflect but also affect how we think about those things (Gould 1983:72; Krause 1998:77). Sloppy systematics promotes or at least accompanies sloppy thinking.

In the 1950s, Willey and Phillips decried the interchangeable use of terms such as period, culture, and stage, "depending on the exigencies of the moment" (1958:46). That this situation continues today is sad but true. On the verge of the twenty-first century, with all the advantages of careful excavations and radiometrically-based chronologies, we seem to be in the same boat that Willey and Phillips were in 40 years ago, despite their hope that "deliverance from this kind of semantic ambiguity will come" with more dependable techniques of absolute dating (1958:46). As Krause has pointed out, "if taxonomic issues continue to be ignored, if the ad hoc labelling practices that are so much a part of our past are continued, the growth of understanding will be inhibited more than stimulated" (1989:289).

In much of North America, most archaeologists have come to employ a modified Willey and Phillips (1958) systematics accompanied by lingering undercurrents of the Midwestern Taxonomic Method (McKern 1939). The Midwestern Taxonomic Method (MTM) was designed to illustrate degrees of formal similarities among archaeological groupings, analogous to the way the Linnaean system hierarchically indicates similarities among species, genera, etc. Neither the MTM nor Linnaean systematics attempts to account for the temporal dimension: form alone is to be the criterion for establishing and distinguishing between groupings (Fisher 1997; Kehoe 1990; Latta, this volume). In contrast, the Willey and Phillips system explicitly incorporated time and space along with formal criteria (Lyman et al. 1997:177–205), making it a useful classificatory tool for both culture-historical and processual archaeology.

Overall, the Willey and Phillips system works well in the Midwest. The concept of the phase within that system has been particularly useful in defining local and regional archaeological taxa. A phase in the Willey and Phillips system is comprised of recurring artifact types and classes, "spatially limited to the order of a locality or region and chronologically limited to a relatively brief interval of time" (1958:22). The phase, therefore, is a group of artifact types, not a group of people or even a group of sites or other type of "social reality" (1958:49–51). Social meaning may be attributed to a phase by the archaeologist(s) who define and modify it (Johnson 1986). "A phase is assumed to have some sociopolitical reality, although the assumption requires considerable faith in the social and/or political significance of potsherds, lithics, features or other material remains" (Brain 1978:312). But whether the phase is also an ethnographic reality is a point which has been the subject of much discussion.... [I]n archaeological practice, a certain sociopolitical reality is *assumed* for the artifactual complexes and their physical dimensions in time and space without further testing or validation [Brain 1978:311; emphasis in original].

For example, Phillips termed his lower Mississippi Valley phases "alleged demographic realities", reflecting his hope that those phases are the equivalents of "local units of a specific socio-political group" (1970:524). In that case, subsequent work successfully matched many of the late precontact phases with ethnohistorically 'real' social units (Brain 1978). But it is doubtful whether such high correspondence between archaeological and ethnographic units can be achieved for earlier periods (Duke 1988). Rarely is the connection even testable. As Trigger remarked in regard to Iroquoian archaeology:

Nothing but needless difficulties can be gained by confusing political entities with 'ethnic divisions' and, by this muddled process, further confusing them with archaeological cultures....If historical data were lacking, the political divisions of the Iroquois could not be reconstructed in terms of coefficients of similarity in material culture using the evidence that is presently available [Trigger 1978c:305].

Most midwestern phases rightfully will remain constellations of artifact forms limited in time and space despite a frequent wish that phases represent tribes or other social groups. Reifying phases into societies or other ethnic units is usually insupportable, and it also obscures the real value of these archaeological taxa, which I believe is to help identify and compare the range of material variation that existed among groups. Within most regions, coeval groups also were *interacting* groups. Discrete tribal or ethnic identification within intergroup networks may have been uncommon both in pre- and postcontact times and extremely difficult to discern even when present (Mason 1976). As in much of the world, those clear distinctions that existed among related neighbouring groups often were established more for the convenience of colonial powers than applied by the people themselves. As Wright stated in regard to the early historic Upper Great Lakes:

The broad mosaic of politically independent bands, loosely related at the specific level through clan and/or marriage and, at a more general level, through language and way of life, limits, in part, the reality of discrete tribal designations to taxonomic units of anthropological convenience [Wright 1965:190].

And many archaeologists can attest that the very search for archaeological echoes of stable ethnic groups or tribes will often be problematical because of the inherently ideational and situational nature of ethnicity (Barth 1969; Emberling 1997; Jones 1997; Trigger 1977):

Ethnic identity is one of many identities available to people. It is developed, displayed, manipulated, or ignored in accordance with the demands of particular situations....Individuals, within certain constraints, will use ethnic identity how and when it suits them [Royce 1982:1, 3].

Therefore, much as we might hope for "archaeoethnic" equivalences (Mason 1997) between phases and known, named groups, the majority of the archaeological record is not amenable to meaningful testing of such hypotheses (Pettipas 1997). Ethnographically, homogeneity in material classes, which archaeologists would use to define phases, often actually reflects stable networks of regional interaction and exchange more than it expresses ethnic group identification (MacEachern 1998). The degree of material culture similarities does not necessarily correlate with the intensity or extent of interaction (Hodder 1982), but it is clear—even axiomatic—that intersocietal interaction is a critical process in the sharing of many elements of material and expressive culture. Interactive events and processes rarely occur at the scale of the entire community or society; rather, segments and individuals are the actors, leading to complex patterns of cultural change (Schortman 1989). As an example of the recognition of such processes, Mark Seeman, noting that many Ohio Hopewell "technological, social, and ideological relationships do not correspond with one another, nor with recognized political or ethnic boundaries", suggests that some social relationships "must have transcended our typological 'phase' constructions" (Seeman 1996:306).

Clearly, it is not safe to assume that phases represent bounded ethnic units. Yet these points do not negate the utility of the phase concept for characterizing local, relatively short-term archaeological contexts. Phases effectively integrate similar components into taxa of manageable scale, supplying useful bases for discussion and comparison, as long as the defining criteria are clear.

Subsequent to phase definition, archaeologists often identify similarities among roughly coeval phases as indicating some form(s) of relationship within a region or area. What taxonomic unit is comprised by several (or many) seemingly related, roughly contemporary phases in a region or area? And what unit can be used to characterize regional homogeneity above the phase level if phases have not been defined? The *tradition* of both Willey and Phillips (1958) and Wright (1974) integrates units along a temporal axis and thus consists of a sequence of units, not a set of contemporary phases. Likewise, but at smaller spatial scales, the local sequence and regional sequence integrate phases temporally (Willey and Phillips 1958).

Horizons can link coeval phases in the Willey and Phillips model, but definition of a horizon depends upon identifying "cultural traits and assemblages whose nature and mode of occurrence permit the assumption of a broad and rapid spread" (Willey and Phillips 1958:33). Sets of phases related by shared elements that do not necessarily imply rapid spread of horizon styles would be difficult to define as horizons.

Archaeologists commonly use *culture* as a unit that is meant to integrate related, contemporary phases, often citing the Willey and Phillips model in support of this usage. However, Willey and Phillips suggest using *culture* to denote the "maximum units" within their culture-historical scheme (1958:48), indicating that cultures are not simply groups of phases but are instead formed by groups of traditions. As a "maximum unit", the culture in this sense represents the largest-scale integrative device in the Willey and Phillips system and should not be employed to join phases when the traditional, regional sequence, or other unit is more appropriate.

European archaeology has employed the terms *archaeological culture* and *culture group* extensively, from V. Gordon Childe through David Clarke to the present. Clarke defined the archaeological culture as "a polythetic set of specific and comprehensive artefact-type categories which consistently recur together in assemblages within a limited geographical area" (Clarke 1968:285). Trigger offered a similar definition: "a geographically contiguous set of artefact types that may occur in differing combinations in different functional contexts"; but he went one step further and suggested that the archaeological culture forms "the surviving material expression of a distinctive way of life sufficiently comprehensive to permit its bearers to perpetuate themselves and their behavioural patterns over successive generations" (Trigger 1978b:76). In essence, Clarke's *culture* is a taxonomic unit similar to Willey and Phillips' *phase*, making Clarke's *culture group* the equivalent of Willey and Phillips' *culture* (J. B. Stoltman, pers. comm., 1997).

According to Trigger, European archaeologists generally assume "archaeological and ethnographic cultures are alike, in that the former are in some sense the remains of once living cultures" (Trigger 1978b:76). Nobody can deny that artifact assemblages comprise the remains of cultures. Nor can one disagree with Trigger's subsequent point that the putative connections between modern and precontact Europeans has led to greater confidence in archaeology's ability to identify precontact (archaeological) cultures in Europe than in North America. Yet the assumption that assemblage differences—even accounting for functional differences—signal cultural differences should not imply that they also necessarily distinguish among societies or ethnic groups: "Even in his earliest works, [Childe] stressed that the correlation of archaeological cultures with known ethnic and linguistic groups was a speculative and hazardous undertaking" (Trigger 1978b:86). This crucial point is what others emphasize in this volume: the difference between culture and society, and between a culture and a society. We might be able to identify *archaeological cultures* that consist of shared artifact assemblages, but how confident can we be that such units—defined by technological and economic criteria—equate with social groups? How do we even know what kinds of social groups to look for in precontact history?

Having "discovered" or defined an archaeological culture (or, as noted above, a phase), archaeologists often expect or permit the unit to signify a partitive culture (in the ethnographic sense) on one hand or a society or ethnic group on the other. In most cases, neither equivalence seems warranted. Unfortunately, it is easy to speak of "(the) Hopewell culture" or "(the) Effigy Mound culture" or to identify local or regional "cultures" that comprised such formations. *Culture*, of course, means many things, and archaeologists understandably use the term when it seems useful or convenient; what easier way for a North American archaeologist to signal allegiance to anthropology than by frequently referring to *culture* and *cultures*? Yet terminology helps the archaeological culture take on an unwarranted life of its own by fostering a misleading, ethnographic-like appearance.

Culture carries so much baggage (e.g., Freilich 1972; Kroeber and Kluckhohn 1952) that it seems counterproductive to attempt to carve a specifically archaeological definition out of its myriad meanings. I argue that it is precisely the *wrong* word to use when seeking to integrate phases or assemblages, which are themselves co-occurring artifact and feature types, not people or societies. Although phase, horizon, tradition, and other words with multiple meanings received Willey and Phillips's approbation, these do not retain the potential power of *culture*. For McKern, in fact, "the indefinite use of the word 'culture'" to denote a wide variety of archaeological formations constituted one of the problems necessitating establishment of an orderly archaeological systematics (1939:303).

In the late 1960s archaeologists working in the Missouri Valley faced a mass of data that needed synthesis and integration. They realized there was "no classificatory unit in the Willey and Phillips system which precisely answers the need for expressing the fact that groups of phases appear to be localized and contemporary expressions of the same culture complex" (Lehmer and Caldwell 1966:515). Such multi-phase groupings were neither traditions nor horizons, nor were they cultures in the Willey and Phillips sense. So Plains archaeologists developed the unit of the *variant* to bridge this chasm in scale between the local or regional and short-lived phase and the expansive, long-lived tradition (Krause 1969, 1977, 1989; Lehmer 1971).

A variant is "a unique and reasonably uniform expression of a cultural tradition which has a greater order of magnitude than a phase, and which is distinguished from other variants of the same tradition by its geographic distribution, age, and/or cultural content" (Lehmer 1971:32). "Variants were designed to be mid-range integrative taxa" (Krause 1989:289) squarely within the Willey and Phillips framework. A variant was conceptualized as a network of related though not necessarily precisely coeval phases. A tradition then can be understood as comprising several—perhaps many—regional variants. If necessary, *culture* can still be used for the maximum unit as Willey and Phillips intended as long as it is applied carefully. That this scheme works for much of late precontact history in central and eastern North America is seen by its widespread and effective application on the Plains (e.g., Butler 1986, 1988; Johnson 1973; Krause 1989:286; Tiffany 1983) and its increasing acceptance in the interior and Gulf-coastal Southeast (e.g., Jenkins and Krause 1986; Mikell 1992).

31

Leigh Syms (1977) and other Canadians working on the northeastern Great Plains and in the Lake Superior basin employ a taxonomic system similar to the Willey and Phillips model in many respects but divergent in others (cf. Lenius and Olinyk 1990; Meyer and Russell 1987; Reid and Rajnovich 1991; Ross 1995). Rough equivalences in scale between units in the two systems are shown in Table 3.1.

Table 3.1
Comparison of Taxonomic Units

Willey and Phillips (1958), modified by Lehmer (1971)	Syms (1977)
Culture	Pattern
Tradition	Configuration
Variant	Composite
Phase	Complex
Component	Assemblage

Syms' *composite* represents an integrative unit similar to the *variant* in the sense that it groups smaller scale units—complexes—that are themselves composed of materials from individual sites. Syms notes that a complex, as he defines it, encompasses "vast areas across several biomes" (1977:71), more space than the locality or region occupied by a Willey and Phillips phase, in recognition of the large territories used by the post-contact era groups that occupied the northeastern Great Plains. A more important difference between the two schemes derives from their conceptual bases. Willey and Phillips define the component simply as "a site or a level within a site" (1958:22), presumedly representing a community or a segment thereof (1958:49). Syms uses *assemblage* "in the same sense as the term component"; both terms, he states, represent "the remains of a single occupation or multiple occupations that are so closely spaced that no differentiation can be made between the occupations" (1977:70). Yet he specifies the *assemblage* as the "surviving materials, features, and evidence of activities of a *single residential group* over a short period of time at one site" (1977:70; emphasis added). This differs from the Willey and Phillips *component* in a way that is rather subtle but that gains in importance in the higher, integrative units.

Willey and Phillips assign spatial, temporal, and formal dimensions to each of their taxonomic units, knowing that these units often do not correspond with sociocultural "reality" (e.g., 1958:49–52). In contrast, Syms makes a unit's ethnographic meaning part of its definitional criteria; viz., the assemblage's "single residential group" requirement, and the definition of the complex as "the total expression of a number of assemblages *left by the same group*" over a short time span (1977:70; emphasis added). The *composite* consists of a number of complexes with apparent "common and recent ancestry" (1977:71), and the *configuration* and *pattern* also are defined in reference to ethnographic and historical cases.

Syms' system is internally consistent, and its eschewing of *culture* as a taxonomic unit is laudable. The *composite* is an attractive integrative unit because of its intermediate scale, serving a role similar to that of the *variant*. However, the degree to which Syms' framework imputes social reality to its taxa requires conflation of unknowable ethnological data with describable and quantifiable archaeological data. The system assumes particular social formations equate with particular archaeological patterns and builds these prejudices into the archaeological taxonomy. I suggest we should strive to refrain from using sociocultural attributes in defining units of archaeological taxonomy and also from ascribing sociocultural correlates *a priori* to archaeological taxa. The modified Willey and Phillips system meets these criteria more effectively.

We may shed a clarifying light on many midwestern archaeological units by severely limiting the archaeological *culture* as a taxonomic unit and by conceiving of regional and sub-areal integrative units as *variants*. In Iowa, for example, several Woodland variants have been defined that integrate local phases and draw attention to formal similarities across regions (Benn 1990:16–17; Benn and Green 1997; Tiffany 1986:244). Building from this work, we can redefine several unwieldy collections of midwestern phases, groupings that are often and improperly called phases, cultures, or traditions. For example, "Weaver" encompasses several regions in the Illinois and Mississippi valleys and exhibits local and regional variability that clearly calls for several phase-level distinctions, yet Weaver itself has been called a phase (McConaughy 1993). By conceptualizing Weaver instead as a regional variant, we recognize the differences between—yet close relatedness of—its constituent elements, and we encourage researchers to explore and interpret that variability. We can conceptualize other Woodland units in the same light: Tampico and Adams following Weaver in west-central Illinois (Green and Nolan 1997), and Marion, Crab Orchard, Adena, Black Sand, Havana, and Effigy Mound, among others, in various parts of the midcontinent. The variant or, more usefully, *regional variant* modifier indicates that each of these terms denotes several related or interacting Woodland phases, all of which appear more similar to each other than to the phases of other Woodland variants. Each regional variant can be conceptualized as a network of related though not necessarily precisely coeval phases or local sequences. A tradition then can be understood as comprising several—perhaps many—regional variants. Often, the constituent phases within a particular variant are well defined, but a regional variant also can be defined prior to definition of local phases. Available data might justify definition of a regional variant prior to definition of local phases. Thus, the taxonomy does not force usage of a smaller-scale unit than is warranted.

Earlier I noted that phases are not necessarily societies or cultures; and so regional variants clearly are not necessarily tribes or "ethnic groups." Still, the regional variant as an integrative archaeological unit has some intriguing reflections in ethnoarchaeological work, where, as noted earlier, examples of homogeneity in the regional material record have been determined to reflect stable, regional interaction and exchange networks to a far greater degree than they express ethnic group identification (MacEachern 1998). This recognition reinforces the desirability of not using *culture* as a modifier for regional multi-phase units. By calling such integrative units *cultures* we misrepresent them as identifiable ethnic or social groups rather than perceive them as constellations of interacting and potentially culturally distinctive communities. Viewing phases, regional variants, and other integrative units as open systems promotes the latter, more realistic, viewpoint.

Is it really important to conceptualize Weaver or Effigy Mound, for example, as regional variants rather than as cultures or even not caring what we called them? I believe so, if only because how we label things and ideas shapes how we think about them. We should not capriciously append to "Effigy Mound(s)" whatever taxonomic term is handiest. Loose application of archaeological systematics—a tendency to which I am no less susceptible than anyone else—suggests we often give relatively little thought to what our groups and classes really represent. Lack of taxonomic clarity hinders our ability to understand the past in a scientific way. Without careful classification there can be no comparisons, no basis for determining variability, and no means for developing or testing propositions about cultural change and continuity. Of course, it is unproductive to attempt to apply inflexible taxonomic systems that are unsuited to the archaeological record. To avoid reversion to a pure trait-list approach, we should not forget we are trying to understand ancient peoples, not just classify artifacts and sites. But for the sake of precision in communication—a prerequisite for progress in the field—we need a commonly understood systematics (McKern 1939).

Undoubtedly there may be drawbacks to using the concept and term of the variant in the Midwest. Chief among them is the word itself, which Ronald Mason pointed out (pers. comm., 1996) connotes "something not typical or normal" (*sensu* Griffin 1964:244, 247; cf. Mason 1970), even though it is meant to denote just the opposite. Perhaps *regional variant* as used here and elsewhere (e.g., Butler 1986, 1988) may alleviate some concerns. For those who prefer the Syms system and its nomenclature over the Willey and Phillips framework, *composite* is a serviceable unit. It is important mainly to recognize the utility of this integrative taxon, whatever it is called, as long as it is not *culture*. We do archaeology to understand people and their cultures, but we do not excavate culture or cultures (Deetz 1967:7). As anthropologists who commonly employ the culture concept (Flannery 1982), we should respect that term and reserve its use for appropriate contexts.

It is true, as James A. Brown has noted that:

> midwestern archaeologists have not been overly concerned with ambiguities of their application of systematics. Most of us have been content with defining minimal units of membership—at the phase level. Work at the tradition and horizon [i.e., integrative] level has been minimal [1986].

I hope in the future we will devote more thought to mid-range integrative taxa and that we will more frequently scrutinize, modify, and reconceptualize our space-time systematics so our ways of thinking will promote rather than hinder our understanding of the past.

Acknowledgements

I thank Dave Benn, Jim Brown, Dale Henning, Scott MacEachern, Ron Mason, Jim Stoltman, Joe Tiffany, and an anonymous reviewer for useful discussions or comments on earlier drafts of this paper or portions thereof, but I am responsible for misusing or ignoring any of their advice. I also thank Ron Williamson for the invitation to participate in the Symposium and to contribute to this volume.

THE MAGIC OF NAMES: CULTURAL CLASSIFICATION IN THE WESTERN LAKE ERIE REGION

4

Christopher M. Watts
Department of Anthropology, University of Toronto

> *There is magic in names. Once let a hatful of miserable fragments of fourth-rate pottery be dignified by a 'Name', and there will follow inevitably the tendency for the name to become an entity, particularly in the mind of him who gives it. Go a step further and publish a description and the type embarks on an independent existence of its own. At that point the classification ceases to be a 'tool', and the archaeologist becomes one [Phillips et al. 1951:62].*

Given that one of the aims of this symposium was to revisit the rather divisive and ambiguous taxonomic labels employed in Great Lakes archaeology, this paper focuses on the current state of ceramic classification and ideas pertaining to cultural development in the western Lake Erie region ca 1350 to 750 B.P.

The objectives of this paper are threefold: (1) to present a brief review of ceramic typology, its use and development in the western Lake Erie region for the initial Late Woodland period (ca 1350 to 750 B.P.); (2) to argue that our understanding of cultural development during this time, and in this area, suffers from a dangerous complacency on the part of researchers towards applying ill-suited typological schema in ceramic classification; and (3) to suggest that a more unencumbered approach, attribute analysis, can be an effective tool in comparative ceramic studies within the region.

As the dominant archaeological paradigm in ceramic classification over the last 40 years, typology or the type-variety approach (Wheat et al. 1958; Gifford 1960), when used to construct the temporal and spatial dimensions of past cultural groups, encourages insular sequences, favours diversity, and rewards the creation of new taxa where such designations are not necessarily warranted. Traditional approaches to cultural construction, by which actual "peoples" or bounded ethnic groups are created, appear too often applied to spatial-temporal areas represented ceramically by broader, clinal variation in a suite of decorative attributes.

Furthermore, such spurious cultural structures, if considered "true" archaeological cultures (as defined by Childe 1939) appear, more often than not, to be referenced solely by the ceramic types claimed as their products.

As regards the study area, the initial Late Woodland ceramic chronology in the western Lake Erie region is partitioned into two phases known as Riviere au Vase and Younge. Borrowing from the work of Greenman (1937, 1939), Fitting defined these phases in the early 1960s largely on the basis of general differences in decorative techniques and motifs, with the former phase occurring from 1150 to 950 B.P., and the latter from 950 to 750 B.P. (Fitting 1965b:153). Both Riviere au Vase and Younge fit within a temporal sequence beginning with the close of the Middle Woodland Period and ending with the Late Woodland.

Classification and the Typological Approach

Ceramic classification is a process aimed at bringing order to a myriad of structural and decorative attributes through the use of artificial classificatory devices (e.g., wares and types). Central to this notion is the idea that classification should be problem-oriented and ever evolving. In the drive, however, to construct regional culture histories in the 1950s and 1960s, these tenets became rigid directives, aimed at uncovering "real" cultural entities in space and time. Many regions underwent an unprecedented number of archaeological surveys, excavations and analyses within a paradigm intent on articulating cultural development through time (Lyman et al. 1997:229). The results, while pioneering, have led to a series of substantive chronologies which often cite differing degrees of ceramic relatedness between (sub)areas as evidence of substantive cultural variation. Indeed, variation in certain types and varieties within ware groups have led researchers to propose that acts of migration, interaction and warfare are responsible for chronological changes in type frequency. The fact is that we, as researchers, impose a classificatory structure on this artifact class to fit specific research objectives, not all of which are related to cultural chronology. The data contribute to a ceramic tradition and not necessarily a cultural trajectory.

One detrimental aspect of such an approach, as alluded to above, lies in the tendency for many researchers to either equate small-scale differences between ceramic assemblages with evidence of distinct populations or to use those differences to contrstuct or modify culture-histories. This can involve the revision and "fissioning" of existing ceramic sequences to support the creation of new, culturally-bounded "ethnic" entities. Such phenomena are particularly apparent in many portions of the western Lake Erie region, where the original ceramic sequence advanced by Fitting (1965b), has been claimed by researchers in neighbouring areas, sometimes uncritically (see below).

Here, however, ceramics fit a geographic pattern of clinal variation in a specific suite of ceramic attributes which stretch from the east coast to the midwest. During the initial Late Woodland, this horizon cross-cuts typologically bounded cultural units such that general similarities in vessel form, tool use, and decorative attributes are apparent within the various wares assigned to each subarea (cf. Lizee 1995:9). As one might expect, regional similarities are common and are often referred to qualitatively, although the reasons for such homogeneity are rarely addressed (cf. Brashler [1981] and Brose [1997a] for exceptions).

In the western Lake Erie region, the gradual nature of ceramic change through time makes it difficult to differentiate between the late Riviere au Vase and early Younge phase ceramics (Murphy and Ferris 1990:199; Watts 1997), while in southcentral Ontario, much the same is true of Princess Point ceramics as decorative attribute frequencies appear to flow gradually into Early Iroquoian times (Bekerman 1995:40-41; Smith and Crawford 1995:67). The following section illustrates these points by providing a brief review of the historical development of the culture constructs within the western Lake Erie region.

Culture-Histories in the Western Lake Erie Region

The first ceramic typology to be created for the western Lake Erie region came from James Fitting (1965b) whose synthesis of Late Woodland cultural development in southeastern Michigan was based on two ceramic traditions known as the Wayne Tradition (characterized by Wayne Ware) and the Younge Tradition (characterized by Riviere Ware). According to Fitting (1965b), the Wayne ceramic tradition represented the Middle to Late Woodland transition in southeastern Michigan which eventually gave way to the more elaborately decorated Riviere Ware of later phases. Fitting later revised this interpretation and concluded that the Wayne and Riviere ceramic traditions developed as separate sequences, yet overlapped in time (Fitting 1970).

Adhering to the Wayne typology as proposed by Fitting (1965b), both

Brose (1966) and Wobst (1968) applied these taxa to initial Late Woodland ceramics from the Saginaw Valley region. Brose (1966) added an additional type, Wayne Textile Marked, to the Wayne classification. A fissioning of the Wayne typology occurred when Fischer (1972:182) suggested that Saginaw Thin, a new ware identified at the Schultz site, should be considered a northern variant of Wayne Ware. This was later discounted as a separate ware by Brashler (1981:276) when she demonstrated higher frequencies of this type in southern Michigan (Brashler 1981:333). Instead, Brashler (1973) suggested Fitting's (1965b) typology was valid and the geographic scope of Wayne could be extended to include the Saginaw region of Michigan. This was later confirmed in subsequent analyses by Brashler (1981:239-240) and the regional term "Saginaw Wayne" was born (Brashler 1981:340).

This "regionalization" of Wayne Ware has led to certain taxonomic problems for the Saginaw Valley. Stothers and Graves (1985) have suggested that ceramic development there would be better understood within a separate construct known as the "Saginaw Tradition". In this scheme, Wayne ware was seen as a ceramic assemblage brought by migrating populations from southeastern Michigan, although the authors' focus on determining the ethnohistoric terminus for the tradition suggests that they were less than keen on the intricacies of ceramic development. Others, such as Halsey (1976) and Brashler (1981), believed in an initial Late Woodland "Saginaw Phase", a local in situ development which existed contemporaneously with the Younge Tradition. Both Fitting (1970) and Brashler (1981:335) argued that Wayne ware had a longer duration in the Saginaw Valley (cf. Lovis 1990) owing to the absorption of Wayne by Younge-related peoples further south ca 950 B.P. In his definition of the Saginaw Phase, Halsey (1976:445) suggested that:

> This phase closely resembles the Riviere au Vase phase and is not far distant from it geographically. Future discoveries may show these two phases to be even more closely related. At the present time, the distinction between a Riviere au Vase phase and a Saginaw phase is mainly a geographical convenience.

The difficulty in separating these two traditions remains to this day as is apparent from recent statements describing them as "culturally similar but distinct" (Murphy and Ferris 1990:191).

Due to its rather amorphous nature, and dual status alongside that of the Younge tradition, the validity of the Wayne Tradition has recently been challenged by Stothers (1994) and his colleagues (Stothers et al. 1994). Stothers (1994:110) has argued that a lack of single component Wayne Ware sites, in addition to the gradual evolution of Wayne Ware into later Riviere Ware, implies that a separate Wayne Tradition is little more than a falsity sustained by academic citation and taxonomic convenience. Stothers and his colleagues (1994:136) have instead suggested that Wayne should be replaced by the term "Gibraltar" for the period ca 1450 to 1250 B.P. in southeastern Michigan. Offered as defining characteristics of this new construct are the types "Gibraltar Cordmarked" and "Vase Cordmarked". The authors describe these as "plain cord roughened wares" yet offer little in the way of additional archaeological signatures (Stothers et al. 1994:136) or any justification for the use of new terminology.

Originally intended for use in northern Ohio, Prahl et al. (1976) created a regional companion to the Wayne Tradition known as the "Western Basin Tradition". This new tradition, which existed for that portion of western Lake Erie south of Detroit and west of Cleveland, around Sandusky Bay, has come to subsume the taxonomic terms Wayne and Younge within the western Lake Erie region (cf. Murphy and Ferris 1990). Initially, however, the authors believed the Wayne and Western Basin Traditions were distinct and "chronologically sequential, forming a base from which the Younge Tradition emerged" (Prahl et al. 1976:262), yet they did not identify any wares or types unique to this new tradition. Regional ties to points further north, particularly the Niagara (Princess Point) region were noted (Prahl et al. 1976:281).

Since the early 1980s, Stothers and his colleagues (e.g., Stothers and Pratt 1981; Stothers and Graves 1983, 1985; Stothers et al. 1984; Stothers and Abel 1990) have lobbied for an autonomous tradition known as the Sandusky Tradition. This tradition, originally conceived of as a Late Woodland manifestation by Bowen (1980), has now been "shown" to have antecedents in the localized Late Archaic "Firelands Complex" of northcentral Ohio and the "Maumee River Complex" (Feeheley Phase) of the lower Maumee River Valley and Maumee Bay area. New post-Middle Woodland taxa known as "Green Creek" ca 1450-950 B.P. and "Eiden" ca 950-750 B.P. (Stothers and Abel 1990:39), therefore, replaced Wayne, Riviere au Vase and Younge. Finally, the Sandusky Tradition is believed to terminate in the ethnohistorically-documented *Assistaeronon* (Fire Nation) (Stothers and Abel 1990:39), essentially suggesting a 4,000 year uninterrupted in situ cultural lineage within the area.

As illustrated, the quest for regional culture-histories which are intimately tied to ceramic typology, has led many archaeologists working in the western Lake Erie area to create ceramic traditions of questionable merit and "real-life" relevance. The regional fissioning of Fitting's (1965b) Wayne-Riviere sequence has resulted in overlapping and ambiguous umbrella taxa such as the Wayne Tradition, the Younge Tradition, the Western Basin Tradition (which encompasses the Younge Tradition), the Sandusky Tradition and the Saginaw Tradition for the period between 1350-750 B.P. (cf. Lovis 1990:37) (Figure 4.1). In light of these conflicts, and in response to new issues raised by Stothers (1994) and Stothers et al. (1994) regarding initial Late Woodland ceramic development, it seems appropriate to revisit the efficacy of using ceramic typologies as the sole informant of cultural development both within this region and beyond.

Figure 4.1: Ceramic traditions in the Lower Great Lakes region, ca A.D. 600-900.

Another Approach to Chronology

The use of typology (specifically type-variety) in initial Late Woodland ceramic classification schemes has contributed towards a series of traditions suggesting discrete cultural development in regionally-defined areas. The proliferation of these types and the implications of such an approach suggest each ware within the region represents a cultural, "ethnically-unique" expression (e.g., Stothers and Graves 1985; Stothers and Abel 1990; Stothers et al. 1994, cf. Brose 1994, 1997a). Like Wright (1967b), I would argue that such approaches manufacture archaeological cultures which do not necessarily approximate real cultural manifestations in the precontact past.

Ironically, the type-variety system (as envisioned by Wheat et al. 1958) can accommodate three facets of variety: (1) technological; (2) areal; and (3) temporal. Moreover, Wheat et al. (1958) made explicit the notion that varieties were meant to be used for denoting small scale regional or temporal departures from the type standard. Basically, varieties need not be subtypes in that they can signify geography (cf. Green, this volume), an approach which seems ideally suited to the current debate in the Saginaw Valley (e.g., the Wayne Cordmarked Saginaw variety). Instead, we remain with the more ornery tradition and type status (e.g., the types associated with Saginaw Wayne).

As the dominant methodology for chronological ordering of components in the western Lake Erie region, it is not that typological approaches are totally inadequate to the task, but that they are meant to be bounded in time and space and have little bearing on coeval developments and fine-scale chronological control. It seems a more suitable strategy would be to recognize patterns of discontinuity in ceramics at a finer scale, focussing on the clinal variation of attribute frequencies through space and time, while avoiding the ethnic "identity crises" given by some typological constructions. Such an approach is hardly innovative (cf. Wright 1967b, 1981; Ramsden 1977; Smith 1983, 1987), but its application within the study area appears to have few antecedents.

The following case study provides an example of such an approach. In order to ascertain the nature and degree of ceramic change during the initial Late Woodland period, I recently examined a series of ceramic assemblages attributed to the initial Late Woodland in southwestern Ontario (Watts 1997). Attribute frequency counts contained in earlier works by Keenlyside (1977, 1978) from two stratified sites in the Point

Pelee region (11H2 and 11H8) were compared to the recently excavated initial Late Woodland Silverman site (AbHr-5) near Windsor (MHCI 1996) (see Figure 4.2). Radiocarbon determinations from both Point Pelee sites span the Riviere au Vase temporal continuum ca 1350-1050 B.P. (Keenlyside 1977:68 and see Figure 4.3). Since neither the Wayne nor

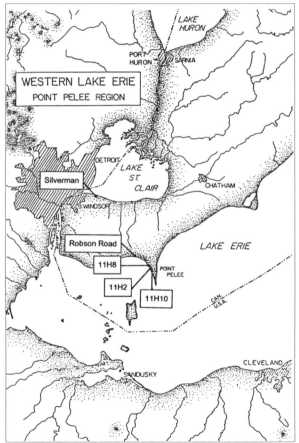

Figure 4.2: Map of southwestern Ontario showing the locations of several initial Late Woodland sites referred to in the text (after Keenlyside 1977).

Riviere ware constructs are recognized in southwestern Ontario, using attributes rather than attribute clusters or types, averted the need for types to be created within the samples. This further obviated the need to compare types assigned to one assemblage with those created for another, where type descriptions can be ambiguous or altogether absent.

When the data were examined for a simple presence/absence of decoration (Table 4.1), some clear temporal patterns began to emerge. From a review of interior and exterior decoration on the first band below the lip, several trends emerge.

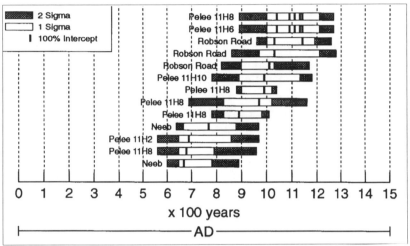

Figure 4.3: Graphic representation of radiocarbon date ranges for several initial Late Woodland sites in southwestern Ontario.

Table 4.1

Presence/Absence Decorative Data from Watts (1997)

	11H8-2 (Lower)	11H8-1 (Upper)	Silverman	11H8 (Area B)	11H2
Interior Decoration Absence	38%	41%	32%	29%	15%
Exterior Decoration Absence	50%	50%	44%	39%	26%

There was a clear increase in both interior and exterior Band 1 decoration, with the exception of 11H8a components 1 and 2 which were statistically identical. This exercise implies that relatively little ceramic decorative change occurred during the occupation of this site, which is consistent with contemporary observations made for southern Michigan (cf. Rodgers 1972:94; Brashler 1981:328). Assemblages based solely on a unilinear presence/absence of interior and exterior decoration suggested an order consistent with that of other single attribute and attribute combination data, particularly from the first two bands of interior decoration, and the first two bands of exterior decoration (Watts 1997:84, 212-222). With respect to the first band of interior decoration, all assemblages showed high frequencies of plain interiors (approx. 30-40 percent) excluding the later 11H2 sample with approximately 15 percent. In terms of tool-use within this band, cord-wrapped designs were common in each assemblage, but dentate-based designs were primarily confined to the 11H8b and 11H2 assemblages, which are interpreted as later 'Younge' phase assemblages. The preference for cord-wrapped decoration during the initial Late Woodland (ca 1450-1050 B.P.), has long been recognized among contemporary archaeological manifestations such as Blackduck (Lugenbeal 1981; Mason 1981:313; McPherron 1967:101) and Princess Point (Stothers 1977; Bekerman 1995; Smith and Crawford 1997) but has been either erroneously associated with the later Younge Phase (cf. Stothers and Pratt 1981) or largely absent in discussions involving southwestern Ontario (cf. Murphy and Ferris 1990). Where decorative motifs are concerned, Band 1 on the interior suggested a pattern of increased use of non-continuous design elements (e.g., verticals, obliques right and obliques left) through time (Watts 1997:55). While previous studies (Fitting 1965b; Brashler 1973; Hoxie 1980; Krakker 1983) have largely focussed on the patterned change in exterior decoration as part of a type combination, frequencies of attribute data gleaned from the interior of the assemblages suggest it too may be a valid chronological indicator. With respect to the exterior, similar trends were observed regarding tool-use and decoration from the first two exterior bands of decoration (Watts 1997:57-58).

The overall efficacy of the above case study, however, lies in its comparative capabilities and quantitative nature. These data suggest that ceramic development during the initial Late Woodland is gradual and is markedly different from later design sequences. Similar conclusions were reached by Brashler (1981:324-325, 328) for this period in southeastern Michigan. The quantification presented in this study is also important in that it validates earlier notions presented by Fox (1990a) that initial Late Woodland (Riviere au Vase) ceramics would be better understood within the Western Basin Tradition rather than as a focus of the Princess Point

Complex as had been originally suggested by Stothers (1977).

In addition to the quantification and seriation, a small component of this research was also concerned with comparing the patterned change observed in the Riviere au Vase sample with that of the neighbouring Princess Point Complex from southcentral Ontario. Sites attributed to the Riviere au Vase Phase were, at one time, claimed to be part of the "Pelee Focus"; one of three regional "foci" assigned to the Princess Point Complex (Stothers 1977). The "Pelee Focus" was later thought to be more closely allied with cultural manifestations in Michigan and Ohio, and thus was reassigned to the southwestern Ontario expression of the Riviere au Vase Phase (Fox 1990a; Murphy and Ferris 1990).

The comparison of ceramic attributes between the initial Late Woodland in these two areas was facilitated primarily by comparing the results of this study with one undertaken by André Bekerman (1995). Bekerman's (1995:33-34) examination of Princess Point exterior decoration suggested a general trend of more extensively-decorated specimens giving way to undecorated specimens as time progressed. Plain specimens recorded by Bekerman suggested that this design attribute increased in frequency through time, while this study suggested it decreased. The co-occurrence of right obliques on Band 1 with horizontal lines on Band 2 in the Princess Point Complex assemblages appeared to Bekerman (1995:34, 53, 60) to be indicative of temporal patterning in the sense that they were frequent in earlier assemblages and declined at later sites. The opposite appears true of the Riviere au Vase sample. Also of note in Bekerman's (1995) study was the temporal significance of horizontal lines on Band 2, which was not observed within the Riviere au Vase assemblages. Finally, the lack of triangular zone motifs from Bekerman's (1995) Princess Point study suggests the two study areas differ in terms of certain ceramic motifs. The frequencies of certain design attributes (particularly plain specimens, right obliques, and horizontal lines), might be interpreted in a manner to suggest that different attributes in the Riviere au Vase assemblages, and the Princess Point collections, are chronologically sensitive.

Comparative endeavours, such as the case study presented above, are not beyond the scope of typological analysis. The traditional application of ceramic typology in the western Lake Erie region, however, as illustrated above, makes this a challenging task. Determining the criteria necessary for inclusion within a ware/type, in addition to ascertaining the exact relationship *between* ware and type, represent potential pitfalls in the comparative analysis of ceramic change. Moreover, the variation of a particular attribute through time and space within the type may be overlooked in favour of the covariance of attributes contained within the type itself.

Conclusions

The historical development of culture-historical constructs in the western Lake Erie region has been influenced, to a large extent, by typological methods of ceramic classification. Although I am somewhat critical of this approach, I do not necessarily believe that an ornery taxonomic system of related traditions, co-traditions, and phases will result from the creation and use of ceramic types and varieties. I would suggest, however, that the tendency to uncritically associate ceramic type with archaeological culture in this part of the world has advanced ill-informed notions of interaction and ethnicity in the precontact past.

As regards the inferential aims in ceramic analysis, we must understand that typological approaches carry implications in how we construct ceramic traditions. Such traditions are often substituted for cultural developments which invariably terminate with early historic tribal manifestations. As such, it is important to consider the methodological frameworks behind ceramic classification when dealing with chronology or any other consideration. It is not so much a question of type versus attribute in formulating such designs, but rather what is the best approach given the question at hand?

Finally, with respect to advancing an answer to the problems identified above, I believe it is necessary to revisit the methodological frameworks for many of our current classifications. We must recognize that the initial Late Woodland period within the greater Northeast is characterized by a pattern of clinal variation in a defined suite of ceramic attribute frequencies, not hard and fast differences in design and decoration. The effects of typological approaches with respect to ware designations such as "Wayne" and "Riviere", have erected barriers in the form of archaeological terminology, which hinders attempts to recognize and describe this variation, and which ultimately impacts on our understanding of ceramic relationships and cultural interaction within the region.

Acknowledgements

I would like to thank David Brose, Carl Murphy, Robert Pihl, David Robertson and Ron Williamson for reading and commenting upon earlier drafts of this paper. I am also very grateful to David G. Smith for his assistance with many aspects of my research. I alone am responsible, however, for the ideas expressed in this paper.

IROQUOIAN ETHNICITY AND ARCHAEOLOGICAL TAXA

5

William Engelbrecht
Department of Anthropology
Buffalo State College, State University of New York

This paper criticizes the use of ethnic labels like "Seneca" and "Iroquois" as if they were archaeological taxa. Treating ethnic labels as static, bounded entities has hindered our understanding of Iroquoian cultural development. The formation of the archaeological record and the formation of ethnic identity are separate processes. Because of the differing nature of these processes, archaeologists should not assume a concordance between ethnicity and archaeological remains. Attempts by archaeologists to project ethnicity onto the archaeological record are at best problematic (Hodder 1979; Starna and Funk 1994).

The determination of ethnic identity in non-state level societies is neither clear cut nor simple. Individuals may be involved in "...multiple, overlapping spheres of community, authority, and interdependency" (Anaya 1997:64). One might simultaneously identify with an extended family, a community, a tribe, and a confederacy. To Richard Hill, a contemporary Iroquois, "...identity is internal" (1997). Cohen notes: "ethnic group formation is a continuing and often innovative cultural process of boundary maintenance and reconstruction"(1978:397). This process involves both the manner in which a group identifies itself and how others identify it.

Archaeological study of shifts in population distribution and material culture over time presents a dynamic rather than static picture of Iroquoian cultural development. One may infer that the ethnic landscape was in flux as well. From historic sources, we know that many native groups ceased to exist in the seventeenth and eighteenth centuries. However, the Haudenosaunee, or Iroquois, not only survived, they thrive to this day. This success relates in part to the inclusive nature of Iroquoian ethnicity, in which both adoption and intergroup alliances have played important roles.

Ethnogenesis of Iroquois Groups

When Europeans encountered the Seneca, Cayuga, Onondaga, Oneida, and Mohawk in what is now New York, they were geographically and linguistically differentiated populations which constituted separate ethnic groups. An implicit assumption has been that these units had considerable time depth, but an examination of site distribution over time suggests that the nucleation characteristic of the seventeenth century Iroquois was a relatively recent phenomenon (Tuck 1971:225; Sempowski et al. 1988). Had Europeans encountered the Iroquois 200 years earlier, the distribution of population would have been different, and one can infer that the nature and distribution of political and ethnic units would have been different as well.

In 1952, Richard MacNeish formulated a series of pottery types for Iroquoian groups. He assumed that each group was ceramically unique and had a distinctive history of ceramic development (MacNeish 1952:88; 1976:82). Using ceramic seriation, he linked historic sites associated with these groups with earlier sites. This technique allowed MacNeish to argue for a considerable time depth for the Iroquois in New York. As a result, the Owasco culture (ca 1050-600 B.P.) is no longer seen as the product of Algonquian speakers, but rather as ancestral to Iroquoian culture.

What does it mean, however, to refer to the Owasco culture as "Iroquoian"? Owasco as an archaeological taxon contains elements of later Iroquoian culture, but the Iroquoian cultural pattern is not yet established. Owasco population was widely scattered in small groups. As William Ritchie (1980:300) noted, Owasco ceramics have been recovered from areas associated with Algonquian speakers at contact, suggesting that the Owasco culture was shared by both Algonquian and Iroquoian speakers. While groups making Owasco style pottery were no doubt in direct or indirect contact with one another, there is no indication that they constituted a cohesive social group or that they would have shared a common ethnic identity. It seems unlikely that the archaeological taxon, Owasco, would have corresponded with any past socio-cultural or ethnic unit.

MacNeish (1952:87) presented a dendritic (branching) or cladistic model of the development of Iroquoian nations based on his pottery types. In this view, Seneca and Cayuga sites are traced back to a probable common ancestral site, as are sites in other groups. Through time, groups are seen as becoming increasingly differentiated. This scheme of cultural development is analogous to a phylogenetic tree illustrating the evolution of species from a common ancestor. Nearly thirty years ago, Jim Tuck (1971:225) suggested that such a model was inappropriate for characterizing Iroquois cultural development. Instead, Tuck opted for a model of community fusion which resulted in the development of Iroquois nations from widely dispersed earlier communities (Tuck 1971:225). Similarly, in a recent critique of cladistic theory, John Moore (1994) argues that a dendritic model is not appropriate for describing the evolution of cultural groups, which may merge with other groups, split, and reform. He advances the term ethnogenesis which emphasizes "...the extent to which each human language, culture, or population is considered to be derived from or rooted in several different antecedent groups" (Moore 1994:925).

This paper also argues that an ethnogenetic model for the emergence of Iroquoian groups fits the available data better than the traditional dendritic or cladistic model. That is, each historically known group can be seen as the product both of multiple ancestral groups and of diverse contacts. Linguistically, northern Iroquoian languages evidence a series of splits and recontacts (Chafe and Foster 1981; Lounsbury 1978:336). Similarly, study of ceramic attributes suggests that both fission and fusion occurred among Iroquoian groups, with populations sometimes moving considerable distances. I have suggested elsewhere that some sixteenth century Iroquoians split from a population just south of Buffalo and moved over 60 miles south to Ripley, New York, while Iroquoians from Jefferson County, New York (near Watertown) joined the Mohawk, a move of approximately 100 miles (Engelbrecht 1991:7-8; 1995:49).

A comparison of ceramics between areas using attributes rather than types suggests greater ceramic similarity between areas than MacNeish's study (Engelbrecht 1978). This is because similar ceramics in different areas were often given different type names by MacNeish. MacNeish's types were devised to trace connections through time in an area, not assess similarity between contemporaneous groups in different areas. While the specific mechanisms producing ceramic similarity between groups is the subject of debate, these groups were clearly open systems in terms of ceramic style.

Using Seneca ethnogenesis as an example, one can see the historically known pattern of two large contemporaneous villages established sometime before 350 B.P. (Sempowski et al. 1988; Wray, et al. 1987). Two distinct traditions concerning Seneca origins may reflect this process

(Niemczycki 1984:14). Before the establishment of these two large villages, the population was scattered in small sites throughout the region, and it seems unlikely that these small scattered populations shared a common identity. The large communities which appear prior to 350 B.P. are, in all likelihood, the result of the fusion of the smaller, scattered communities in the region, rather than the movement of "Seneca" into the area, after having split from the "Cayuga" as seen in MacNeish's cladistic model.

The fact that two large communities located near one another suggests that some form of agreement or alliance existed between them. Such an alliance may be considered a form of inter-ethnic social organization (Sharrock 1974:103). If one assumes that there were marriages between individuals of the two large contemporaneous communities, then this would have led to longhouses consisting of individuals of differing backgrounds. However, children growing up in such longhouses would come to view themselves as Seneca or Notowa'ka:', Great Hill People. The participation of individuals in medicine societies (Tuck 1971:213) and rituals such as the Condolence Ceremony (Sempowski 1997) would have helped integrate these new, larger social groups.

Attribute analysis of pottery is consistent with this general scenario. Ceramics from the Adams site, an early large Seneca village, are more heterogeneous than those of the smaller earlier sites, presumably reflecting the differing backgrounds of the female potters (Engelbrecht 1985:168; Sempowski et al. 1988:101-103). More females than males are buried at Adams, and osteological data suggests a non-local origin for some of these females who may have been war captives or refugees (Sempowski et al. 1988). Ceramics from later large Seneca sites are once again homogeneous, indicating a shared ceramic tradition. By mid-seventeenth century, metal European kettles replace ceramics of native manufacture.

Also during the mid-seventeenth century, the process of amalgamation continued as individuals of diverse backgrounds were adopted and incorporated into the Seneca. Adoption of individuals into clans provided them with a defined place in the society. The *Jesuit Relations* state that by mid-seventeenth century there were individuals from 11 different nations living among the Seneca (Thwaites 1896-1901: 43:265). The seventeenth century Seneca were a hybrid group, as was true of the other Iroquois nations at this time.

Iroquoian Ethnicity

During the early contact period, there is no evidence that northern Iroquoian speakers shared a common ethnic identity. Palisaded villages on hill tops throughout Iroquoia suggest widespread conflict. Alliances between nations resulted in the growth of Iroquoian confederacies, some of which fought one another. As confederacies increased in importance, there would have been a growing tendency for individuals to identify with these, in addition to identification with a nation, a community, and a kin group. Eventually, only one confederacy of northern Iroquoian speakers was left, in what is now New York State, that of the Five Nations. It is from this political organization that the ethnic identity of "Iroquois" or Haudenosaunee can be derived.

Adoption is a common strategy for augmenting population among matrilineal groups and the adoption of captives is well documented for the Five Nation Iroquois. During the seventeenth century, large numbers of former enemies were incorporated into the Five Nations, in part compensating for the loss of population from warfare and disease. "Within one or two generations thousands of prisoners had come to regard themselves as Iroquois, and were socially and culturally indistinguishable from their captors" (Trigger 1990b:141). Iroquois adoptions continued during the eighteenth century, the most famous example being that of Mary Jemison, who has many descendants among the Iroquois today. Also in the eighteenth century, the Tuscarora were adopted into the League, the Five Nations becoming the Six Nations. The metaphor of the longhouse is an important integrative symbol for the Iroquois confederacy, with the Seneca referred to as door keepers (Ho-nan-ne-ho-ont).

The incorporative nature of Iroquois ethnicity, as well as its spiritual dimension, is reflected in the following statement:

> If any nation or individual from outside adopted the Great Law, then upon learning it or by tracing the roots to the Great Tree, they would discipline their minds and spirits to obey and honour the wishes of the Council of the League. Then they will be made welcome to take shelter under the branches of this tree [Chief Jacob Thomas 1994:17].

This inclusive nature of Iroquoian ethnicity can be seen in early documents. In 1645, for example, the Mohawk concluded a peace treaty with the French and their allies. On that occasion, a Huron said:

It is done, we are brothers. The conclusion has been reached; now we are all relatives—Iroquois, Huron, Algonquin and French; we are now one and the same people [Thwaites 1896-1901:27:289-291].

This treaty was short lived, and the sentiments expressed in this statement were never realized. Regardless of the motives of the speaker, however, these ideals serve as a reminder that for some people the sharing of a common identity may be dictated by factors other than language or physical type.

In Situ Development versus Migration: A Dubious Dichotomy

Dean Snow (1992a, 1994, 1995a, 1995b) has suggested a migration of Iroquoians into New York and Ontario from Pennsylvania. Robert Funk, on the other hand, argues that "the Point Peninsula—Owasco developmental continuum is very strongly supported by the evidence" (Funk 1997:26). Because of these differing views, some have felt compelled to choose between in situ development and migration as an explanation for Iroquoian origins. However, building on Starna and Funk's critical examination of the in situ hypothesis (1994), this paper argues that framing the issue of Iroquoian origins in terms of a choice between in situ development or migration is simplistic. It stems from thinking of Iroquoians as a taxonomic unit characterized by a list of traits including language, maize horticulture, longhouses, ceramics, and matriliny.

Snow originally argued for an ancestral version of Iroquoian culture spreading north from the Clemson's Island culture in Pennsylvania about 1050 B.P., replacing Algonquians in much of New York and Southern Ontario. In response to new evidence for maize as early as 1300 B.P. in Ontario, as well as evidence of cultural continuity in Ontario after that (Crawford and Smith 1996, Crawford et al. 1997), Snow (1996) revised his hypothesis and now postulates that a migration occurred 300 years earlier. However, this then leads to questions concerning the similarity of this earlier culture to later Iroquoian culture.

This "Out of Pennsylvania Model", like the "Out of Africa Model" for modern humans, assumes the arrival of an intrusive population. An important difference is that any migrants into New York and Ontario would have been fully capable of finding mates and interacting in other ways with resident populations in the area. While Snow (1992b:34; 1995a:76) acknowledges that absorption of non-Iroquoians was possible and that the migration may not have been a single event, his argument emphasizes population replacement.

To date, evidence from physical anthropology does not provide clear support for Snow's hypothesis. A recent study attempting to differentiate northern Iroquoian and Algonquian peoples on the basis of metric attributes proved equivocal, and the author stated that "the apparent phenotypic similarity among northeastern groups regardless of linguistic association suggests that Algonquian and Iroquoian speakers may share a common biological origin" (Langdon 1995:369).

Like physical traits, cultural traits are not differentially distributed between the Iroquoian and Algonquian language families, nor are these traits of equal antiquity. Flannery (1939) noted many cultural traits shared by both Algonquian and Iroquoian speakers. The Algonquian-speaking Mahican in the Hudson Valley were matrilineal and matrilocal with a three clan system similar to the adjacent Mohawk (Brasser 1978:200). In Ontario, there was an economic symbiosis between Huron farmers and the more northerly Nipissing which may go back to early Iroquoian times (Trigger 1976:170). This resulted in the sharing of ceramic style and possibly other cultural traits. Even MacNeish (1952:85) noted Iroquoian pottery on Algonquian sites and Brumbach (1975, 1995a) and others have cautioned against a one-to-one equation between ceramics and ethnicity. Archaeologists now realize that finding Iroquoian pottery on a site does not mean that the makers were Iroquoian speakers.

These studies also imply that social boundaries between Iroquoian and non-Iroquoian speakers were not rigid. In assessing similarities between archaeological cultures in Ontario and Pennsylvania between 1450-950 B.P., Crawford and Smith suggest that they were "...participating in more general changes and developments that affected communities throughout the Northeast"(1996:789).

Recently, researchers have considered various models for the spread of Iroquoian archaeological culture, including regional interaction (Jamieson 1992), peer polity interaction (Williamson and Robertson 1994a), and a transformative social movement formalizing architecture and rituals (Kapches 1995). Clermont (1995a) argues for the spread of the

Owasco culture into Québec as an example of acculturation, rather than replacement by migration. Brumbach (1995b:64-65) suggests that Iroquoian ceramic style diffused to Algonquians in the Upper Hudson drainage along with the diffusion of maize and maize preparation. These diverse processes provide alternatives to population replacement as an explanation of the widespread distribution of Iroquoian archaeological culture.

Snow's revised migration scenario gives priority to linguistic evidence. In the Northeast, Iroquoian speakers were surrounded by Algonquian speakers and were separated from Iroquoian speakers to the south. A replacement of Algonquians by northward-moving Iroquoian speakers as Snow suggests is not the only possible explanation for this distribution. Floyd Lounsbury (1978:336) suggests a long occupation of Iroquoian speakers in central New York and north-central Pennsylvania with subsequent expansions to both the south and north. Hetty Jo Brumbach (personal communication) suggests that the advent of a viable horticultural adaptation could have caused a slow expansion of Iroquoians into favourable horticulture areas, ultimately resulting in the separation of northern and southern Iroquoian speakers.

In discussing the Iroquoian situation, Trigger (1970a) reminds us that language can diffuse independently of culture or physical type. Small numbers of Iroquoian-speaking newcomers could have spread their language to indigenous non-Iroquoian speakers (Trigger 1985:82). Similarly, Bateman, et al. caution that "the success of a language is primarily determined not by the genealogy of its advocates but by their social influence" (1990:12). Iroquoian language distribution may tell us more about the inclusive nature of Iroquoian ethnicity than it does about demographic rates or population replacement.

Summary

Most traits associated with historic Iroquoian culture developed over the last millennium. By and large, these traits are not exclusive to Iroquoian speakers. Given what we know about the precontact distribution of population, it seems unlikely that the ethnogenesis of historically known Iroquois groups in New York occurred much before the seventeenth century. Before then, it is unlikely that members of small communities identified themselves ethnically either with a historically known Iroquois group or as "Iroquoians".

High mortality rates stemming from the introduction of Old World pathogens as well as endemic warfare resulted in a dramatic alteration of the ethnic landscape in the Northeast in the seventeenth century. Both adoption and alliances were important mechanisms by which Iroquoians adapted to changing demographic and political environments. Both these mechanisms were probably used on a smaller scale by Iroquoians before European contact.

An ethnogenetic perspective on the origins of Iroquoian peoples can accommodate both population movements and local continuity, thereby avoiding a simplistic choice between migration or in situ development. "In a sense, Iroquoians did not originate, remain in situ, or migrate in the past; rather, they originate and are constantly being re-created in the present by both natives and non-natives" (von Gernet 1995:124).

To use a metaphor familiar to the Iroquois, the development of Iroquoian culture can be likened to the growth of a great tree which receives nourishment from roots spreading wide and deep. Some branches have died, but others continue to grow to this day.

Acknowledgements

Ron Williamson provided the initial impetus for this paper. I am especially grateful to Hetty Jo Brumbach who made extensive suggestions on an early draft. Tim Abel, Oscar Bartowchowski, Neal O'Donnell, and Martha Sempowski also made helpful comments. Michael Foster and Roy Wright provided feedback and references on Iroquoian linguistics after hearing an early version of this paper presented at the 1997 Annual Conference on Iroquoian Research. Blair Rudes provided information on current Iroquoian orthography.

THE COMPLEX FORMERLY KNOWN AS A CULTURE: THE TAXONOMIC PUZZLE OF "OLD COPPER"

6

Susan R. Martin
Department of Social Sciences, Michigan Technological University
Thomas C. Pleger
Department of Anthropology and Sociology, University of Wisconsin - Fox Valley

Uncertainties about the taxonomic status of the so-called Old Copper Culture plagued the archaeological literature following its initial description in the 1940s. Was it old, was it copper, and was it a culture? Was the presence of copper a useful criterion for a taxon? Could a whole culture be defined simply by the presence of a handful of specific artifact forms? Did dating uncertainties even allow one to call the manifestation "old"? In this paper, we examine these questions, review the use of the Old Copper Culture taxon in the region's archaeological history, and apply newly-obtained data to the issue of Old Copper taxonomy.

Background

During the late 1800s, much of northern and eastern Wisconsin was deforested as a result of lumbering and agricultural activities. When these areas were ploughed for the first time, farmers began to recover precontact copper artifacts in large quantities (Figure 6.1). Additionally, caches of copper implements were recovered during borrow pit quarrying associated with early road and city construction. Early archaeologists recognized the existence of precontact copper mining (Whittlesey 1863; Wilson 1856) and tool manufacturing in Wisconsin, Upper Michigan and Canada (Butler 1875-76; Reynolds 1856). James Butler was one of the first scholars to publish information on the heavy copper tool assemblages of the Western Great Lakes (Butler 1875-76). Like many other early scholars, Butler suggested that the hundreds of copper tools found in this region must have been manufactured by a pre-Indian culture, or race. His conclusions were certainly influenced by the then-popular "Mound Builder Myth" which also attributed the construction of mounds to a pre-Indian race or culture, popularized by Squier and Davis'(1848) writings concerning the origins of the mounds. By 1894, Cyrus Thomas dispelled this myth, and by the turn of the twentieth century, Great Lakes archaeologists recognized that copper fabrication technologies in the Great Lakes were indigenous to precontact aboriginal peoples (Brown 1904:52-53). However, there was no way of reliably assessing how old these tools were. During this time, a number of Wisconsin collectors specialized in the collection of precontact copper tools. Their efforts resulted in the gathering of massive collections, most notably the Hamilton collection, which is now housed at the State Historical Society of Wisconsin. Charles E. Brown published a detailed description of the classes of copper artifacts represented by the Wisconsin collections (Brown 1904).

Figure 6. 1: Sample of diagnostic tool forms of the Old Copper Complex, Great Lakes region. Collection from Menominee County, Michigan, USA, courtesy Menominee County Historical Society Museum. Scale in centimetres.

While in the process of developing a taxonomic system for Midwestern precontact history, William C. McKern recognized the existence of two distinct cultural patterns, Woodland and Mississippi. The Woodland Pattern was believed to be older than the Mississippi Pattern. McKern also recognized the existence of a pre-Woodland occupation within the Great Lakes region (1942). He proposed the term Old Copper Industry as a taxon for the heavy copper tools of Wisconsin. McKern conceptualized this industry as a pre-Woodland aspect, because Woodland mounds in general did not include heavy copper tools in the forms of projectile points and knives. When such tools were found, they were not associated with mounds or ceramics and therefore apparently preceded the Woodland pattern by an unknown span of time. George Quimby (1952) included McKern's Old Copper Industry in his summary of the archaeology of the Upper Great Lakes Area, stating that "the lack of association with cultures of later periods argues for an Early Woodland or Archaic context for the Old Copper industry" (1952:100).

Michigan Research

Though interest in Michigan's ancient copper mines had developed earlier (Holmes 1901; Whittlesey 1863; Wilson 1856), scholarly research on copper use developed in part from the University of Michigan's focus on precontact mining on Isle Royale and the Upper Peninsula only during the 1930s (Dustin 1957) and from 1953 to 1962 (Bastian 1963; Griffin [editor] 1961). This work complemented the analyses of likely related burial complexes in upper and lower Michigan (Binford 1962a, 1972; Papworth 1967). Griffin's 1961 work also summarized what was known of the geographical distribution of ancient copper implements in Ontario and Manitoba (Bell 1928; Griffin [editor] 1961:124-126; Popham and Emerson 1954; Reynolds 1856; Tanton 1931). Griffin also assessed the connection between Old Copper manifestations and Boreal Archaic/Laurentian cultures (1961:122).

The ecological framework within which Michigan archaeology developed in the 1950s to1970s (Fitting 1975) fashioned the use of taxa there, but they were used sparingly; comparing systems of adaptation was the basic operation. The data were exceedingly incomplete. As Fitting stated:

the best we can hope for is a series of sites within a fairly well-circumscribed region representing a single time horizon (broadly defined) which represent a single adaptive system. The archaeological "moment" may span thousands of years and the systemic variations which we can isolate may be very gross [1975:5].

The working definitions of Archaic taxa were explicitly material, temporal and related to adaptation. Identifying and isolating what processes caused change was all-important.

With little concern for consistency in the use of taxa in Michigan, many researchers skirted the problem by using what we call the "Archaic fill-in-the-blank" strategy. This allowed one to refer to "The Archaic" without a following descriptor; it was safe strategy for no one could call you wrong! But it is no surprise why this occurred; in print "The Archaic" was interchangeably referred to as a stage, tradition, or period (cf. Green et al. [editors] 1986 as well as Griffin [editor] 1961). So the Archaic had multiple definitions: a time period (Griffin [editor] 1961), an adaptive style (Griffin [editor] 1961), and a technological watershed (Fitting 1975), the latter based upon formal criteria. To Fitting, the hallmark of the Late Archaic stage was the establishment of essentially modern environments, a sentiment shared by Mason (1981). Formal variation within one period or stage was implicitly explained as seasonal variation rather than solely indicative of multiple cultures or of cultures that were inherently variable. Cultures by their nature were expected to be linked through time and space unless demonstrated otherwise (Fitting 1975). To account for the cultural integrative factors which he assumed were ever-present, Fitting used the Willey and Phillips (1958) concept of "widespread cultural horizon". In this way, the "Early Woodland Burial Cult" of Ritchie (1955) and the "Red Ochre Culture" of Ritzenthaler and Quimby (1962) were linked to Michigan phenomena.

The trouble with Archaic burial manifestations was that they did not inform much about environmental adaptations; cults and copper did not make a culture (Fitting 1975:81). Rather, Fitting referred to them as burial complexes, and interpreted them in a manner that was in keeping with Fogel (1963) by stressing their economic, environmental, and distributional correlates, with due attention paid to emerging social institutions and perhaps, social differentiation. Whether Old Copper was a "culture" or a "complex" was insignificant compared to posing questions about mechanisms of interaction (Fitting 1975:81-90).

Lewis Binford initiated research interests in social differentiation as well as contextual meaning in his seminal article, "Archaeology as Anthropology" (1962a) which argued that the uses of copper artifacts varied distinctively over time. Population growth ostensibly caused a shift in the functions and meanings of copper objects from technomic (purely functional) to sociotechnic and ideotechnic (i.e., representative of ideological categories). There were likely "increased selective pressures favoring material means of status communication once populations had increased to the point that personal recognition was no longer a workable basis for differential role behavior" (Binford 1972:20). Binford called forth the ghostly prime mover of population growth without demonstrable data to account for cultural diversity. This is hardly different from citing the classic favoured culture historical causalities such as migration and trade to account for similarities. Were these new taxa (technomic, sociotechnic, ideotechnic) any more useful, more empirically verifiable, more bounded, less problem-ridden than those they replaced? No, but they did free students from seeing copper materials simply as cultural traits, and underscored a new dimension—their social contexts— upon which to focus.

Wisconsin Research

McKern's Old Copper Industry became known as the Old Copper Culture in the archaeological literature shortly after the excavation of the Osceola, Oconto, and Reigh mortuary sites (Ritzenthaler 1957) during the 1940s and 1950s. The material culture recovered from these sites linked the thousands of surface finds of heavy copper implements to a specific population or populations of ancient people. Warren Wittry (1951) also identified a series of specific Old Copper Complex tool types and subtypes in Wisconsin museum collections, based upon analyses of morphological attributes. In mapping the distribution of his Old Copper artifact types, Wittry believed that the resulting distribution suggested a culture area or centre for the Old Copper Complex located along the western shore of Lake Michigan in Wisconsin.

The "Culture" and "Complex" taxa were subsequently applied interchangeably because Old Copper was thought to be linked by shared formal attributes represented by copper, bone, and stone artifacts such as those recovered from the Osceola, Oconto, and Reigh sites (Wittry and Ritzenthaler 1956; Ritzenthaler 1957). Radiocarbon dates from these sites indicated a temporal range of 7600 B.P.-3000 B.P. The earliest of these dates, the 7600 B.P. Oconto date, sparked a debate among a number of researchers concerning the true age of the Old Copper Complex. This early date, combined with the site's elevation, implied that the Oconto burials must have been subsequently inundated by the Nipissing High Water Stage of Lake Michigan (Mason and Mason 1961). However, as the Masons (1961) and later Lewis Binford, using a radiometric analyses of human bone (1962b), pointed out, no evidence indicated that the burials were ever inundated. As a result, most scholars accepted a more conservative 5000 B.P. origin for Old Copper.

Although no new major mortuary or habitation sites were discovered, interest in Old Copper continued into the 1970s. McHugh (1973) reexamined Binford's (1962a) systemic explanation for the disappearance of Old Copper tools in the archaeological record. McHugh concluded that although Binford's approach was intriguing, there were insufficient data to demonstrate a shift in the functional role of copper from utilitarian to status indicators during the transition from Archaic to Woodland. McHugh suggested that Binford's explanation failed to recognize that most copper objects were used as tools and that the majority of these tools were recovered outside of burial contexts. In an attempt to address the function of Old Copper tools, Penman (1977) analysed wear patterns on copper artifacts from the Hamilton Collection at the State Historical Society of Wisconsin. Penman concluded that some of the Hamilton projectile points exhibited wear patterns consistent with a multitude of uses including cutting, sawing and gouging and, therefore, appear to have been used primarily as tools. However, Penman indicated that his data and conclusions did not include burial context copper artifacts.

Both Michigan and Wisconsin were united by the recognition that even the well-excavated data were incomplete. Stoltman (1986:235) concluded his 1986 summary on the Archaic Tradition by stating: "It would seem that the overriding fact about the Archaic in Wisconsin is how much we still do not know", a statement which still generates cheers of agreement from those on the Michigan side of the border. Despite the excavated data from Archaic cemetery sites in Wisconsin, little had been learned in terms of social organization. Nor had there been a detailed study on the importance of copper technology and trade in precontact economies. By the 1980s, archaeologists were suggesting a true age for Old Copper materials as lying somewhere between 5000 B.P. and 3500 B.P., making it a Late Archaic Stage manifestation. The diagnostic artifacts of this manifestation consisted of socketed projectile points, socketed knives, socketed spuds, and crescent-shaped knives (Mason 1981). In 1986, Stoltman proposed that the term Old Copper Complex be revised and substituted for the Old Copper Culture taxon, due to the fact that there were insufficient data to conclude that this material represented a single culture. Stoltman suggested that the Old Copper Complex fell within his Middle Archaic Stage definition. This was based on the recognition that Late Archaic Stage cultures, including the Durst Phase and the Red Ochre Complex, postdated the Old Copper Complex but predated mound construction and the development of ceramics. Stoltman argued that formally, the Old Copper Complex was a Middle Archaic Stage manifestation. He suggested a temporal range of 5000-3200 B.P. (Stoltman 1986:217-226). His more recent work hypothesized that the classic cemetery sites of the Old Copper Complex (Osceola, Price III, Oconto and Reigh) could be construed as two phases (Osceola/Price III and Oconto/Reigh) representing both regional and temporal differences (Stoltman 1997:131).

Comparisons clearly suggest affiliations between Old Copper Complex related materials and Laurentian and Shield Archaic cultures to the north and east and later in time with Glacial Kame and Red Ochre Complexes/Cultures to the south (Figure 6.2).

For example, Old Copper tools were recovered in association with ground slate tools at the Laurentian and Shield Archaic Allumette Island-1 and Morrison's Island-6 sites in Québec (Kennedy 1966) both dating to the late fourth and early fifth millennium B.P. Interaction between later Old Copper Complex and southern Glacial Kame populations is documented by the presence of a marine shell sandal sole gorget (a Glacial Kame diagnostic artifact) recovered in direct association with an Old Copper Complex burial at the Reigh Site in Wisconsin (Baerreis et al. 1954). The spatial boundaries of Old Copper interaction should also include copper tools recovered from sites along the edges of the northeastern plains (Gibbon 1998; Steinbring 1975). The distribution of Old Copper artifacts and the commingling of regionally specific Archaic material culture suggest interaction between multiple Archaic populations over much of the upper Midwest. Equally impressive is the temporal range of Old Copper material culture. Radiocarbon dates from the Lake Superior Basin (Beukens et al. 1992) and from the Oconto Site (Pleger 1998) suggest a temporal origin of at least 6000 B.P. for the Old Copper Complex. Additionally, new dates from the Riverside site, 20ME1, in Menominee, Michigan, suggest a terminal age of about 3000 B.P. for diagnostic socketed tools associated with emergent Red Ocher Complex mortuary ceremonialism in the western Great Lakes (Pleger 1992, 1998).

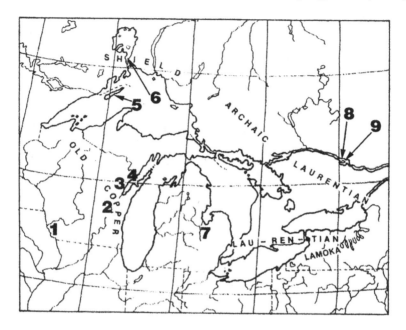

Figure 6.2: Old Copper Complex-related sites in the Great Lakes region.
1. Osceola; 2. Reigh; 3. Oconto; 4. Riverside; 5. Isle Royale; 6. McCollum;
7. Andrews; 8. Morrison's Island-6; and 9. Allumette-1.
From Mason 1981,Courtesy Academic Press.

Old Dilemmas and New Directions

New dates and re-examinations are helping to resolve some of the cultural-historical issues regarding the Old Copper materials, but they have also created new questions to resolve. For example, there is a question regarding the age and interpretation of objects thought to be part of the trait list of Old Copper diagnostic items. One example is a copper crescent, an artifact type which has been associated in burial contexts with socketed projectile points and other copper objects thought to have rather discrete distributions in time, around 3,000 years ago. However, this artifact type has also been recovered in the Lake Superior basin from an

Initial Woodland context at 20KE20, with an uncalibrated radiocarbon date on leather at 1570 ± 100 B.P. (Beta-24330) (Martin [editor] 1993). Other examples of socketed copper tools associated with Initial/Middle Woodland contexts come from the North Lakes region of Wisconsin (Salzer 1974). Are these heirlooms several millennia old? Are they long-lived artifact types from northern backwaters? Are our dates in error? This contradiction in our understanding of how old these core items really are forces us to pay attention to more complex questions, such as the social means by which artifact types survive for long-standing periods of time. What are the bases of their value? What social and ideological behaviours act to bestow value on material objects? Are they curated, or are some of the so-called classic forms perpetuated into later times? We think the answer to the last question is probably "both". There is no doubt at all that the technology which created socketed tools from copper was a long lived one in excess of 3,000 years in duration in this region, and that it was shared by many peoples over a broad region.

Recent research (Pleger 1998) comparing mortuary data between the Oconto (Ritzenthaler and Wittry 1952) and Riverside (Hruska 1967) sites confirms a decrease in the inclusion of utilitarian copper artifacts in mortuary programs by Red Ochre times (third millennium B.P.). Oconto's mortuary pattern suggests a relatively even distribution of primarily copper tools and several personal adornment items across age and gender lines suggesting an egalitarian or semi-egalitarian hunter-gatherer social organization. At Oconto, exotics and personal adornment items are rare. In sharp contrast, personal adornment copper artifacts in the form of beads dominate the Riverside Red Ochre mortuary feature assemblages. Additionally, status objects in the form of exotic cherts became increasingly important after the disappearance of socketed copper tools. Interestingly, the Riverside data suggest that these high status grave goods are predominantly associated with young adult females and children. This pattern is interpreted as representing the development of a complex inter-group interaction system that may have involved bridewealth exchange arrangements between Red Ochre populations.

There is no question that Red Ochre mortuary programs represent increased social complexity, trade, and exchange when compared to Old Copper mortuary patterns. The decline in socketed copper tool production during the third millennium B.P. may be related to the increased demand for copper personal adornment items used by Red Ochre individuals to enhance personal status (Pleger 1998).

Conclusions

There ought to be a taxon for cases where the long-standing presence of a unique material, technology and/or ideological behaviour is not the sole or critical, but perhaps the most visible, distinctive characteristic or factor linking a series of cultures. For us, the "complex" taxon fills the bill. We tend to conceptualize "complex" as a series of related cultures below the level of stage and, therefore, we understand Old Copper and Red Ochre as complexes, because it appears that each is made up of more than one culture, and because the core artifacts are endured long beyond the span of a phase. Whereas archaeological cultures are material remains of relatively stable ways and means of doing things which socially reproduce themselves and last through time, archaeological complexes are marked by an acknowledged incompleteness; we seem to know too much about some subsets of these manifestations and too little about other subsets. This conclusion is in agreement with virtually everyone who has written about copper recently (Fitting 1975; Martin [editor] 1993; Mason 1981; Pleger 1992, 1998; Stevenson et al. 1997; Stoltman 1986, 1997).

Current data suggest that the Old Copper Complex be viewed as a series of regional Middle and Late Archaic stage cultures that shared a basic copper fabrication technology. The view of a single culture should be abandoned in favor of the recognition that a series of cultures, over a 3,000 year span, existed within a large area that included much of the northern and western Great Lakes. We can justifiably call this manifestation old, and we can certainly call it copper, but we cannot call it a culture. Ironically, McKern's original Old Copper Industry taxon makes sense even now, because it can be conceptualized as time transgressive, spanning Middle and Late Archaic times.

EXOTIC CERAMICS AT MADISONVILLE: IMPLICATIONS FOR INTERACTION

7

Penelope Drooker
New York State Museum

S ites of the Fort Ancient archaeological tradition flourished in the central Ohio River valley, from southwestern Indiana through southern Ohio and northern Kentucky into western West Virginia, from about 950-250 B.P. (A.D. 1000-1700) (Figure 7.1). Madisonville, near Cincinnati, Ohio, is the westernmost protohistoric[1] Fort Ancient site (Figure 7.2). It is multi-component, with Late Woodland and Early-to-Middle Fort Ancient occupations in addition to a significant Late Fort Ancient occupation during the fifteenth to seventeenth centuries. European-related artifacts from Madisonville date to the late sixteenth and early seventeenth centuries, and show that residents there interacted with both the interior Southeast, as evidenced by a brass Clarksdale bell from a child burial at the site that was introduced by Spanish explorers, and the Iroquoian Northeast, where pieces from Basque iron-fitted copper kettles were obtained via the St. Lawrence estuary (Drooker 1996:Figures 2-6, 1998:Photos 42-44, 57, 58, 73-75, 89, 90, 97, 98, 109,114). Indigenous exotic artifacts such as redstone pipes and marine shell ornaments (Drooker 1997:Figures 6-19, 6-20, 7-6, 1998:Databases 7 and 8, Photos 355-359, 592-596, 665-753, 1006-1011) give evidence of Madisonville residents' participation in diverse and widespread interaction networks that include connections to Oneota groups in the upper Mississippi Valley as well as to Mississippian groups farther south.

Madisonville and nearby Late Fort Ancient sites also have produced a variety of non-local ceramics, which add another dimension to western Fort Ancient interaction patterns, in spite of the fact that no sophisticated analytical techniques have yet been applied to them. To date, this study has involved only very general considerations of style and context.

Because pottery was produced and used by different people and for different purposes than metal, glass, catlinite, and shell artifacts, the presence of non-local ceramics at Madisonville conveys additional information about the nature of long-distance interaction there.

Figure 7.1: Selected archaeological traditions of eastern North America.

For example, stone pipes are strongly associated with men at Madisonville. A large variety of pipe bowls was excavated at the site, quite a few of them non-local (Drooker 1997:Figures 6-20, 7-5, 7-6, 7-30, 8-25, 8-26, 8-27, cf. 1998:Database 8 and associated photos). Some of the largest and finest were buried with adult males who also had other significant grave goods. They, therefore, seem to have functioned as a symbol of male authority. Many non-local pipes, particularly disk pipes related to upper Mississippi Valley styles, probably were obtained in inter-group greeting rituals like the well-known calumet ceremony.

In contrast, pottery in this region is associated with women rather than men. Throughout eastern North America, ceramics are known historically to have been made and used almost entirely by women. For a long time, archaeologists were wont to attribute foreign sherds at an archaeological site to the presence of non-local women as wives or as captives—the so-called Captive Bride Syndrome—but this is by no means the only possible scenario (Latta 1981). For example, men or women can travel far from

home, bringing pots for their own cooking or to carry corn or other food
for gifts or exchange. Valued ceramics themselves might be given as gifts
or received during ceremonial rituals, as is hypothesized to have happened
with Ramey Incised ware from Cahokia (Pauketat and Emerson 1994).
Such gifts might be transported from the place of origin either by the giver
or by the recipient. Larger groups of people might migrate permanently or
periodically to another settlement, bringing some of their ceramics with
them.

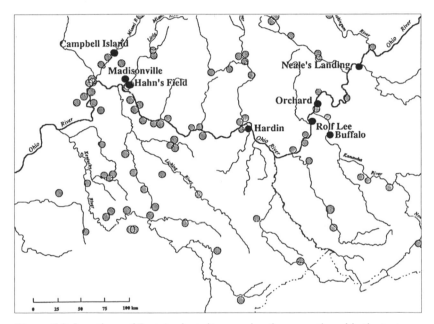

Figure 7.2: Locations of Fort Ancient sites, naming those mentioned in the text.

The *idea* of a vessel can travel, too, rather than the vessel itself. This
can result in copies of foreign ceramics being produced in local materials.
Such imitations might be made by local potters, copying foreign vessels
brought to their village or seen by themselves on visits outside their home
region or described to them by other travellers, or they might be produced
by non-local potters, working with their own familiar styles. The same
would be true for synthetic styles incorporating attributes from two or
more ceramic traditions but made using local clay and temper—either
local or non-local potters might be involved in their manufacture.

73

Contexts of disposition can be helpful in narrowing down possibilities. Vessels with highly valued associations might be found as grave goods. Utilitarian or less valued vessels are more likely to be recovered as sherds, from non-mortuary contexts. The presence of only a few sherds associated with a given foreign region would be interpreted very differently than the presence of many such sherds, reflecting the relative strength of a particular inter-regional relationship. Concentration of many non-local or synthetic sherds within a particular sector of a site might indicate a strong foreign presence there, as with a group of immigrants residing together. Non-local sherds scattered thoughout a site would warrant some other interpretation.

Indigenous sixteenth and seventeenth century Madisonville pottery is shell tempered. It consists of some bowls, but mainly jars with two to four handles, everted rims, and plain necks. Bodies can be plain, cordmarked, grooved-paddled, or net-impressed. Decoration in the form of notched lips or a line of notches or punctates around the shoulder sometimes is found. Such jars are known from all Late Fort Ancient sites (Figure 7.3), but they are particularly prevalent at the Madisonville site, where hundreds of whole vessels were excavated from burials (Drooker 1997:Figures 6-10, 6-11, 7-1, 7-2, 1998:Photos 156-330; Griffin 1943:Plates LX-LXX, Tables 2-5; Hooton and Willoughby 1920:Plate 3). The relative uniformity of this pottery type, which gives its name to the sixteenth-seventeenth century Madisonville Horizon, undoubtedly reflects significant levels of visiting and intermarriage among Fort Ancient settlements of this time period.

Exotic artifacts at Madisonville, including ceramics, come from the Northeast, the Midwest, and the Southeast (Drooker 1997). The Midwestern relationship, from northern Ohio to the upper Mississippi Valley, appears to have significant time depth. The Southeastern relationship was multi-faceted and important, but not as intense as the Midwest connection. The Northeastern relationship appears to have been short-term, coinciding with the early European Contact Period.

Madisonville's longest term and strongest ceramic relationship outside of Fort Ancient territory appears to have been with northern Ohio settlements belonging to the Indian Hills, Sandusky, and Whittlesey traditions (Figure 7.1). Both Middle Fort Ancient and Late Fort Ancient sherds have been reported from Sandusky and Whittlesey sites (Bowen 1994:2, Figures 11, 21; Brose [editor] 1976:32, 1994:55, Figure 5.2). Foreign sherds from northern Ohio do occur at Madisonville in some numbers, but the best evidence for a significant connection comes from mortuary vessels that probably were locally made.

At least five mortuary vessels have northern Ohio characteristics, the largest number of foreign-influenced mortuary vessels with any sort of common thread. One is a jar with formal attributes very similar to Tuttle Hill Notched (Drooker 1997:Figure 8-37b, 1998:Photos 261, 262), a Whittlesey type that incorporates a folded, notched collar (Brose 1994:Figure 5.13). Three others exhibit more-refined local adaptations of notched collars (Drooker 1997:Figure 6-60, 1998:Photos 179-181, 284). The fifth was decorated with a notched appliqué strip (Drooker 1997:Figure 8-37a, 1998:Photos 193, 194). These vessels were with three sub-adult and two adult burials, not clustered together, but all in the northern half of the site. They testify, I believe, to a resident northern Ohio influence at Madisonville, but not a foreign enclave.

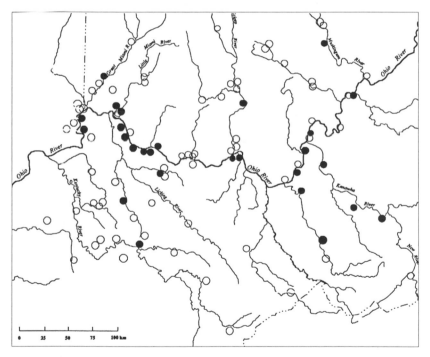

Figure 7.3: Fort Ancient sites known to have produced Madisonville style pottery.

David Stothers has proposed that some northwestern Ohio people might have sought refuge at Fort Ancient sites after Erie attacks during the early 1640s (Stothers 1994; Stothers and Abel 1991). This is highly probable, but it might not be relevant at the Madisonville site, for which there is no firm evidence of occupation after the first few decades of the seventeenth century. Before that, though, there certainly was an ongoing and significant relationship between the two regions, very likely including intermarriage (cf. Giesen 1992), that extended beyond Ohio to other areas farther west.

For example, two other mortuary vessels at Madisonville, buried with a teenager and a young adult female, have characteristics linking them to an Illinois ceramic series (Drooker 1997:Figure 6-61, 1998:Photos 197, 208, 209, cf. 1031). These jars had teat lugs combined with otherwise typical Late Fort Ancient forms. The lugs, along with other traits such as grooved paddling, probably were derived from the late precontact Riker-Wellsburg series in the upper Ohio River valley (Figure 7.1), reaching Madisonville through eastern Fort Ancient sites. Vessels very similar to the Madisonville examples have come from at least four other sixteenth-seventeenth century Fort Ancient sites, Buffalo, Neale's Landing, Orchard, and Rolf Lee (Figure 7.2; Hemmings 1977:Figure 42.g; Moxley 1988:4, Figure 7; Lora Lamarre, pers. comm. 1998; Ronald Moxley, pers. comm. 1994). All of them strongly resemble a four-lugged Keating cordmarked jar from Zimmerman, Illinois (Brown [editor] 1961:Figure 8D; cf. M. Brown 1975:50).

Evidence from non-mortuary ceramics at Madisonville corroborates and extends that from mortuary vessels. A few, definitely non-local, Indian Hills sherds were excavated at Madisonville from widely separated locations (Drooker 1997:Figures 6-59, 8-37c, 1998:Photos 1145, 1146, 1191-1193, 1223-1225). However, the most numerous indicators of northerly interaction are sherds with appliqued notched strips below the lip (Drooker 1997:Figure 8-37a, 1998:Photos 1045, 1046, 1067, 1075, 1085, 1086, 1097-1101, 1108, 1109, 1116, 1117, 1140, 1141, 1177, 1180, 1199, 1200, 1226-1230), which have come from most parts of the site. Many, based on visual characteristics of the paste, probably were local products, while others probably were imports.

This mode of decoration occurs in early sixteenth century Wellsburg ceramics of the upper Ohio River valley (Baker 1988:Figure 3) and across all of northern Ohio in ceramic types such as Reeve Filleted (Brose 1994:Figure 9) and Fort Meigs Notched Applique, as well as in southern Michigan and northern Indiana and Illinois in types such as Moccasin Bluff Notched Appliqué Strip, Danner Cordmarked, and LaSalle Filleted (Baker 1988:Figure 3; Bowen 1994:Figures 14, 16-20; Brose 1994:70-76;

Brown and Willis 1995; Cremin 1996; Mason 1986:215-217; Willis 1998). Danner ceramics with notched appliqué strips have been found as far west as the Haas-Hagerman site in eastern Missouri, which is thought to be the Illini village visited by Marquette in 1673 (Grantham 1993:2, 4, 5). Ronald Mason, who provided the best summary of these types in his Rock Island monograph, described them as similar enough and found in sufficiently corresponding chronological ranges to announce a common phenomenon, although he cautioned that in no case has the full range of variation been assayed, let alone compared with that of any of the others (1986:216). A fine-grained chronology is only now being worked out, primarily for the western variants (Brown and Willis 1995; but cf. Bowen 1994:3-4). Mason, Brown, Willis, and others associate these filleted ceramics with Central Algonquian peoples.

In spite of other evidence for significant ties between Madisonville and contemporaneous Oneota communities, ceramic data are not overwhelming. Examples include a massive handle similar to Huber ceramics from the Chicago area, abruptly-everted rimsherds with finely incised shoulder decoration, and a body sherd with deep, broad shoulder trailing (Drooker 1997:Figure 8-37d, 1998:Photos 1144, 1168-1172)—but no mortuary vessels. Additional examples were excavated at two late precontact sites not far from Madisonville, Campbell Island and Hahn's Field (Griffin 1943:Pls. LXXXVIII.9 and 10, XC.1). The relative scarcity of Oneota pottery at Madisonville (but the relative abundance of disk pipes and other male-associated artifacts) might indicate that contact involved men more than women and/or took place away from Madisonville rather than incorporating long-term Oneota residents at the site.

There is an important Middle Mississippi Valley ceramic presence at the Madisonville site, but, like Oneota, it is not as strong as that of less-distant regions. Recognizable styles include two Campbell Appliqué-like sherds and pieces from frog effigy and fish effigy bowls (Drooker 1997:Figures 8-37d, 8-38, 1998:Photos 212, 213, 1087-1089, 1149-1151, 1215, 1222). The famous and unique Madisonville human effigy vessel, which was interred with a young woman, bears an uncanny resemblance to Missouri styles (Drooker 1997:Figures 4-14, 8-39, 1998:Photos 288-290). The fact that the Madisonville jar was fashioned from local paste in a recognizably local jar form argues that it was made at Madisonville. The expertise of its maker argues that she was reproducing a style learned and perfected elsewhere.

The exotic sherds and foreign-influenced vessels at Madisonville from

Mississippian, Oneota, and proto-Algonquian groups all occur in combination with other indigenous artifacts such as pipes and marine shell ornaments that indicate long-term, multidimensional ties between Madisonville and these other groups. The situation seems to be different between Madisonville and Iroquoian groups.

When I analysed European goods excavated at Madisonville, I was startled to find a significant number of artifact types with ties to the late sixteenth century Iroquoian region. Several were the farthest west known examples of their types, including Basque kettle pieces and a brass spiral of the type that used to be called Basque earrings (Drooker 1996:Figures 5, 6, 10, 1997:Figure 8-5, 1998:Photos 67, 68). I was startled because there is no archaeological evidence at Madisonville or in the surrounding region for earlier interaction with Iroquoia. From the types of European artifacts, protohistoric interaction between Madisonville and the Northeast appears to have been relatively brief, from the last few decades of the sixteenth century to the beginning of the seventeenth.

Besides European goods, the little additional evidence of protohistoric interaction is mostly confined to unique ceramic artifacts. The definite connection is through a variety of Iroquoian ceramic pipes. Stemmed, pedestalled ceramic vessels provide a more ambiguous connection.

Iroquoian ceramic pipes constitute the second largest non-local group of pipes at the Madisonville site, after disk pipes. Unlike disk pipes, which were deposited as grave goods with a number of relatively high status men, all Iroquoian pipes excavated at Madisonville were broken and discarded as refuse. Although smoking was important in Iroquoian ritual and everyday life, pipe bowls were not typically exchanged in ceremonial greetings as was done in the upper Midwest. Thus, the presence of Iroquoian pipes implies the presence of Iroquoian people at Madisonville, rather than (say) long-distance, down-the-line exchange. The pipe fragments were diverse, and many had connections to sites or regions that produced some of the same types of European items as found at Madisonville.

Three out of four extant stem fragments had bulbous ends, which are typical of late sixteenth and early seventeenth century pipes from Niagara Frontier sites such as Green Lake, Christianson, and Hamilton, a number of which also produced Basque kettle parts (Fitzgerald 1982a:153-154; Lennox 1981:Figures 18, 42; White 1978:Figure 4; cf. Fitzgerald et al. 1993:Tables 1 and 4). Several different pastes and styles are represented at Madisonville, including trumpet, acorn, and humanoid and owl effigy forms (Drooker 1997:Figure 8-27, 1998:Photos 368, 374, 375, 382-384, 461, 462, 536, 537, 568-570). For most of these, I have not found exact matches, but both humanoid forms and large-eyed owl effigies are known from Ontario Iroquoian sites (Noble 1979:Figures1, 6). Owl effigies also have come from Susquehannock sites (Kent 1984:Figure 26). The most similar trumpet pipes with decorated rims that I have found were from New York sites (Drooker 1997:314; Parker 1922:Plate 95.6; Rutsch 1973:Figure 134). The variety of Iroquoian pipe styles and pastes, and their disposition in many parts of the Madisonville site, argue for multiple visits from different Iroquoian individuals. One other Fort Ancient site, Hardin, Kentucky, has produced a complete Iroquoian pipe—a bulbar ring style typical of Ontario Iroquoian forms (Henderson et al. 1986:Figure 33).

The only ceramic vessels at Madisonville with a possible connection to contemporaneous Iroquoian sites are the well-known pedestalled pots (Griffin 1945). Those from Madisonville often have been mentioned in the same breath as those from Ontario sites (Latta 1987, 1990:Figure 1; Orr 1914), but they may or may not be directly connected. The Madisonville examples include two with partial or restored pedestals, plus several fragments of pedestals (Drooker 1997:Figure 4-15, 1998:Photos 162, 1105, 1106, 1119-1121, 1155-59, 1233-1235; Griffin 1943:Plate LXVI.4). Stemmed, pedestalled vessels are represented at Huron and Neutral sites, but they also have come from Monongahela, Susquehannock, and Caddoan sites (Figure 7.4; Kent 1984:Figure 105; Johnson 1994:Tables 9 and 10; Perttula 1992:27, 103, 248; Turner 1978:98-103). The general consensus is that these were local copies of Catholic chalices or other European goblets that the potter either had seen or had heard about (Latta 1987; for a dissenting opinion, cf. Ramsden and Fitzgerald 1990). That hypothesis is borne out by the fact that wherever the top of the vessel has survived, it resembles local forms, as with examples from Texas that are thought to have been inspired by goblets carried by members of the de Soto entrada (Turner 1978:Figure 36), and a castellated Susquehannock example (Kent 1984:Figure 105), from a site that dates well after the founding of English Catholic Maryland in 1633.

The Madisonville pedestalled pots are completely typical of local forms and materials. It is extremely doubtful that any Catholic priest ever reached the settlement, but Madisonville residents could have seen or heard about goblets and chalices from French examples in Canada or from Spanish examples in the interior southeast. The local imitations were valued, since at least one was deposited as a mortuary vessel, with a child.

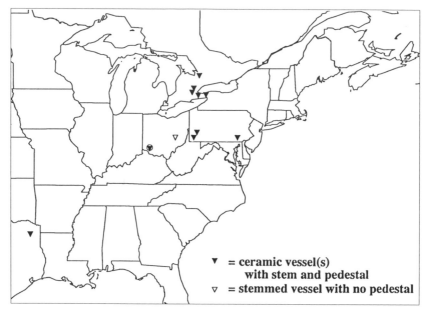

Figure 7.4: Geographical distribution of stemmed, pedestalled vessels.

From evidence at Madisonville, there is no reason to postulate an unfriendly or hostile relationship with Iroquoian peoples, but there is nothing to indicate a long-term or close one, either. At least until the early 1600s, Madisonville folk may well have been obtaining significant amounts of European metal via Iroquoian middlemen, but there is no obvious evidence that these trading relationships were cemented by domestic alliances.

Madisonville non-local ceramics are a rich source of information that has barely begun to be tapped. More detailed comparisons with foreign ceramic types and attributes, physical and chemical analyses of sherds, and chemical and radiocarbon analyses of the soot encrusting some of them could extend our knowledge significantly. So could the development of a more refined and comprehensive ceramic typology and chronology across a broad region south of the Great Lakes. Meanwhile, stylistic and contextual data from foreign and foreign-influenced ceramics at Madisonville, together with complementary information from other types of exotic artifacts, have significantly extended our understanding of the wide-ranging, heterogeneous, and heterarchical western Fort Ancient interaction networks.

Notes

1. Protohistoric refers to the time period between "the first appearance of European goods and the earliest substantial [written] historical records" (Trigger 1986:116).

A MIDDLE PHASE FOR THE EASTERN ST. LAWRENCE IROQUOIAN SEQUENCE: WESTERN INFLUENCES AND EASTERN PRACTICES

8

Roland Tremblay
Department of Anthropology, Université de Montréal

Systematic archaeological investigation of the late precontact period in the Lower St. Lawrence Valley began during the 1960s with Charles Martijn's pioneer work. This resulted in his 1969 paper on the Cache site on île aux Basque, an island near the south shore of the estuary between the towns of Rivière-du-Loup and Rimouski (Martijn 1969). Martijn took this opportunity to discuss the significance of the presence of Iroquoian-like pottery outside Iroquoian territory, the origin of the eastern St. Lawrence Iroquoians, and their disappearance. Unfortunately, his sample from the Cache site test pits was small. It included a few sherds of decorated pottery associated with an uncalibrated radiocarbon date of 780 ± 150 B.P. At the time, this collection was geographically remote from the Late Woodland manifestations that had been reported upon. When Martijn related this material to known archaeological cultures, the logical choice at the time was the Pickering branch of southeastern Ontario. Jim Wright had just published his hypothetical outline for an Ontario Iroquoian Tradition for the Late Woodland period (Wright 1966), and he suggested to Bruce Trigger that the then rare Late Woodland occupations of the eastern Valley were probably an eastern extension of Pickering (Trigger 1968b).[1] Prudently, Martijn suggested two other hypotheses to explain the Cache site occupation. First, the pottery could be Algonquian imitations of Iroquoian wares. Second, because he noticed some resemblances with New York Early to Middle Late Woodland pottery, he suggested a late Owasco/Oak Hill pottery association.

Since then, the discovery and study of numerous sites in the Valley have contributed to St. Lawrence Iroquoian archaeology. For instance, it has been illustrated that the Early Late Woodland period in the region east of Montreal can no longer be associated with Pickering occupations. The external, contemporaneous manifestation that this can now be related most reliably to is the New York Owasco (Chapdelaine 1980; Clermont and Chapdelaine 1982; Clermont et al. 1986). These local manifestations have come to be known as "Owasco-like" or "Owascoid", thus evoking resemblances but avoiding the creation of equivalencies (Chapdelaine 1995:84-85). Archaeologists increasingly agreed with an in situ origin for the St. Lawrence Iroquoians (Pendergast 1975; Chapdelaine 1980; 1989; Clermont and Chapdelaine 1982). At the same time, regional differences became apparent along the St. Lawrence River axis. This complicated the articulation of cultural continuity from earlier precontact times to the Late Iroquoian period. For instance, in the Montreal portion of the Valley, the Late Middle Woodland (referred to as the Melocheville Tradition) is dominated by dentate decorated pottery, the presence of collars, interior bossing and coil fabrication. This is attributed to the period prior to 950 B.P. Then suddenly, and for the next two to three centuries, the pottery is decorated with a fine cord-wrapped stick instrument, it has very few collars, very few bosses and is fabricated using a paddle and anvil technique.[2] All these innovations are characteristic of the southwestern Québec Owascoid, and since there is no indication of population movement, the passage from the Melocheville Tradition to the Owascoid is explained as a rapid and pervasive local acculturation (Clermont 1995a:70-75).

To the east, where Chapdelaine recently proposed a simple two-tradition Late Woodland sequence east of Lake Saint-Pierre (Chapdelaine 1995), the situation is different. For the first tradition, Chapdelaine has lumped together all the cord dominated wares that occur in the period from the eighth century to the thirteenth century into one big Late Middle to Early Late Woodland tradition. The latter portion of this ensemble, which dates from 950-650 B.P., is termed Owascoid in the Montreal region. In the region east of Lake Saint-Pierre, Chapdelaine joined to this Early Late Woodland time period the final centuries of the still poorly known Middle Woodland, because there seems to be no clear break in the evolution of Middle Woodland pottery to Early Late Woodland pottery.[3] This ceramic tradition includes attributes such as cord-wrapped stick decoration, cord malleated surfaces and flat horizontal lips. Other attributes seem to show chronological variability within the tradition, such as punctate bosses in earlier times, and low-collared rims, castellations, incised necks and check-stamped body treatment in later times (Chapdelaine 1995:84-85). The persistence of cord-wrapped stick decoration supports an argument in favour of Iroquoian cultural continuity in the region at least since the latter part of the Middle Woodland period

(Chapdelaine 1995:92-93). Ceramic attributes, including the late, classic, high-collared and castellated rims bearing complex incised and linear stamped motifs, constricted necks, and a rounded, often smoothed over body are associated with the St. Lawrence Iroquoians from the fourteenth to sixteenth century.

There is good reason to believe an in situ evolution existed in the Lower St. Lawrence Valley from the Late Middle Woodland populations to the Late Woodland Iroquoians, but this issue lies beyond the subject of this article. This discussion is limited to the middle of the Late Woodland period where we feel that the sequence needs chronological refinement. As a result, a taxonomical matrix focussed on Iroquoian cultural evolution is proposed on the basis of the ceramics. While this has the benefit of relating this manifestation in the Lower St. Lawrence Valley to some general cultural trends in the rest of Iroquoia, it also sets it apart from contemporary Algonquians in this region.

The chronological refinement presented here postulates the insertion of a phase between the Owascoid/corded period and the late classic Iroquoian period (Figure 8.1). This hypothesis is premised on material from two sites, both of which contain a chronologically isolated component dating to the middle of the Late Woodland period. Ten other sites of the St. Lawrence estuary which, though having chronologically mixed assemblages, had material from a contemporaneous component, contributed to the definition of the phase. Before describing the ceramic styles for which the proposed phase is defined, I will briefly describe the two major sites.

The Anse-à-la-Vache Site

The Anse-à-la-Vache site (DaEi-6) is a small sea mammal hunting site located on a sandy beach ridge six metres above sea level in a small cove on the northern end of île Verte, an island southwest of île aux Basque near the south shore of the estuary opposite the Saguenay River (Figure 8.2). A total of 67 m^2 of the site was excavated by the author, mostly in 1993 and 1994. Two vertically isolated occupation levels were uncovered in two major open areas (Tremblay 1994, 1998b; Tremblay and Vaillancourt 1994).

Level A, on which we limit this discussion, is an Iroquoian component dated to 700 B.P. It revealed 12 hearths, 20 post moulds and

	A.D.	
	1600	
	1550	
LATE	1500	HONGUEDO
ST-LAWRENCE	1450	PHASE
IROQUOIANS	1400	
	1350	
	1300	SAGUENAY
	1250	PHASE
	1200	
	1150	
EARLY	1100	
LATE	1050	
WOODLAND	1000	OWASCOID
	950	EPISODE
	900	
	850	
	800	
	750	
	700	
	650	
end of the	600	end of the
EARLY	550	EARLY
MIDDLE	500	MIDDLE
WOODLAND	450	WOODLAND

(Chapdelaine 1995)   (Tremblay, this paper)

Figure 8.1: Proposed sequences for the Eastern St. Lawrence Iroquoian Tradition.

five soft shell clam (*Mya arenaria*) concentrations. An analysis of a sample of nearly half of an impressive faunal assemblage (54,060 elements) showed that 90 percent of identifiable elements were seal. Of these, 78 percent were harp seal (*Phoca groenlandica*), the rest being harbor seal (*Phoca vitulina*) with a single occurrence of grey seal (*Halichoerus grypus*). A mid-spring to summer occupation of the site can be inferred by the presence of harp seal and newborn harbor seal (Rioux and Tremblay 1999). Other animals include, in decreasing order, beaver, moose, dog, muskrat, beluga, black bear, and sea sturgeon. Lithic artifacts comprise a total of 243 tools and 11,977 flaking by-products. The materials are mostly Ordovician cherts from the Appalachian range, with known sources situated in the Québec City region and in the hinterland of the Maritime Peninsula. There is also some evidence of local sourcing on the island as demonstrated by a cobble core industry. Bipitted anvils are present. Bone artifacts include two unilateral harpoons and a notched elongated point that may be a leister.[4]

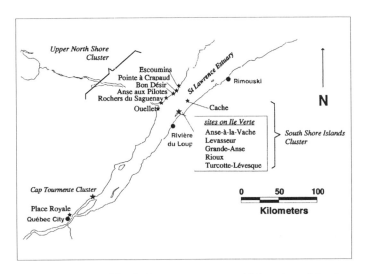

Figure 8.2 Map of the St. Lawrence estuary with location of the sites mentioned.

The ceramic collection is composed of a minimum of 20 poorly preserved vessels of which 13 retained sufficient intact attributes for analysis (Figure 8.3). Three undecorated fragments of pipe and a few lumps of clay complete the list of ceramic artifacts. Five radiocarbon dates are available from this component, of which two came from earlier excavations and their association with level A of the 1993 and 1994 excavations is uncertain (Table 8.1).

Table 8.1
[14]C dates for the Anse-à-la-Vache site (level A, all from wood charcoal)

Lab #	B.P.	2 Sigma calibration*	Sample association & depth
Beta 70234	660 ± 60	A.D. 1270 - 1412	Bottom of cooking pit (1993) - 49 cm
Beta 70233	740 ± 70	A.D. 1168 - 1398	Hearth with bones and ceramics (1993) - 29 cm
Beta 70232	860 ± 70	A.D. 1037 - 1280	Hearth with bones and shell (1993) - 35 cm
Beta 46999	1080 ± 100	A.D. 715 - 1186	From area 2, east of the road (1991) - 40 cm
Beta 39840	1140 ± 80	A.D. 700 - 1027	Test pit (1990) - At the base of the level, under a sand lens - 43 cm

* Calibration from CALIB 3.0.3 program (Stuiver and Reimer 1993)

87

The Ouellet Site

The Ouellet site (DaEk-6) is also a sea mammal hunting site 6 m above sea level, located on the north shore of the estuary, just west of the Saguenay River mouth, at Baie-Sainte-Catherine (Figure 8.2). The principal excavation, covering 300 m^2, was conducted by Michel Plourde in 1987 and 1988 when he uncovered an isolated archaeological layer of organic soil capped by a landslide clay layer at least 10 cm thick (Plourde 1990; 1993).

Figure 8.3 Rimsherds from the Anse-à-la-Vache site.

Features include 15 hearths and seven post moulds. The faunal remains total 4,793 elements, of which three species of seal (harbor, harp and grey seals) represent 95 percent of the identified elements. Beaver, fish and bird are also present. Lithic artifacts include 127 tools and 12,482 flaking byproducts. Materials are largely dominated by locally available quartz, followed by Appalachian cherts. The 70 ground stone tools include bipitted anvils and pestles. No cultigens were found, neither were bone tools present. The pottery consists of a minimum number of 50 vessels. A few lumps of unworked clay were also found, but no pipes. Five radiocarbon dates were obtained, two of which were rejected by Plourde as being too recent (Table 8.2).

Table 8.2
^{14}C dates for the Ouellet site (all from wood charcoal)

Lab #	B.P.	2 sigma calibration*	Remark
Beta 18130	890 ± 90	A.D. 989 - 1291	
Beta 18132	880 ± 70	A.D. 1016 - 1285	
Beta 22793	700 ± 70	A.D. 1221 - 1406	
Beta 22792	420 ± 60	A.D. 1419 - 1530	Rejected
Beta 18131	260 ± 80	A.D. 1466-1707, 1713 - 1821, 1836 - 1879, 1914 - 1955	Rejected
* Calibration from CALIB 3.0.3 program (Stuiver and Reimer 1993)			

Both these components (level A of Anse-à-la-Vache and the general level of Ouellet) are well defined chronologically. Essentially, they are contained in a single undisturbed stratigraphic unit and their ceramic assemblages are stylistically homogeneous. While these components may not represent single occupations, they most surely were produced in a relatively short period of time in which ceramic style evolution is barely detectable.

Ceramic Style

The pottery from the Anse-à-la-Vache and Ouellet sites is similar. Generally, it is characterized by the following attributes:

- a low, poorly defined, or incipient collar with a convex exterior
- thick, flat, horizontal decorated lips with no angle notching inside or out
- simple, poorly executed, motifs predominate, consisting largely of horizontals, obliques and criss-cross — some incipient complexities are present with rare horizontal secondary motifs under, or over, the principal motif
- linear stamp is the dominant decoration; incised and cord-wrapped stick decorations are second and third in frequency
- an absence of reed punctate circles, and an absence of earlier bossing
- corn ear and ladder plait motifs are absent
- a smoothed and incised decorated neck
- castellations are mostly rounded, never angled or overhanging
- a band of linear stamped decoration just under the collar base angle
- interior decoration immediately below the lip occurs in 50 percent of the cases

- exclusively paddle and anvil construction
- a variety of cord, checked and ribbed paddle body surface treatments, rarely smoothed over
- complete pots have an elongated sub-spherical shape

When compared with late St. Lawrence Iroquoian ceramics, all of these are early attributes. Their recurring combination on these two sites clearly suggests that they date to a time when the elaborate Late Iroquoian styles were being developed. Nevertheless, in light of an Owascoid/cord decorated horizon, many of these attributes are late, while others have not yet appeared. Consequently, a placement for this pottery between the Owascoid and the late St. Lawrence Iroquoian, generally mid-way in the Late Woodland period, is proposed. It appears to be more easily related to subsequent Iroquoian pottery traditions towards which it is clearly evolving. This would suggest that the Iroquoian tradition could be separated into two phases. On the other hand, there seems to be greater differences between the earlier Owascoid period and the middle phase which will be discussed later.

A Middle Late Woodland Phase in the Lower St. Lawrence Valley

The pottery styles mentioned above appear to represent a particular regional phase that I have designated the Saguenay Phase. The phase concept is used here in the Willey and Phillips (1958) sense, meaning it is a distinct and limited archaeological unit distinguishable in a temporal continuum, here designated the Eastern St. Lawrence Tradition. It is also distinguishable in a spatial continuum here defined as a horizon represented by the interaction sphere of the Iroquoian world. I have adopted this taxonomic approach, although the taboo of naming things lingers on in Québec, because we can now readily recognize and distinguish this pottery from the other Late Woodland manifestations. Consequently, this will avoid growing confusion in the terms archaeologists use to refer to this mid-Late Woodland period.[5] Indeed, identifying the problem is an essential step towards its resolution. The homogeneity of this style throughout the 70 vessels in the Anse-à-la-Vache and the Ouellet site samples is impressive. It is as if there was a strong compulsion guiding the potters within and between the communities that established their hunting camps in locations that were remote from one another. The use of the name—the Saguenay Phase—is derived from the region in which two clusters of sites contain the two principal sites representing the manifestation. While the concept has a geographical connotation, it should be clear that this phase applies to the eastern St. Lawrence Iroquoians as a whole, extending from the Portneuf region west of Québec City to the two clusters of sites in the Lower St. Lawrence Valley at the far eastern limit of Iroquoia (Figure 8.2).

This ceramic style is present on more than 10 other sites in the estuary but in more problematic multi-component contexts. On the north shore there are at least nine vessels from the Pointe-à-Crapaud site (Plourde 1995), seven from the Cap-Bon-Désir site (Taillon 1995), and examples are present on the Escoumins, the Anse-aux-Pilote and the Rochers du Saguenay sites (Plourde 1994). On the south shore, the Cache site on Île-aux-Basque has, apart from the vessel recovered by Martijn in the 1960s, four new examples from recent excavations which match the style (Turgeon et al. 1992, Fitzgerald 1993). On Île Verte, the small Levasseur site, which represents a unique occupation, has one large pot that has been restored (Figure 8.4).

Figure 8.4 Reconstructed vessel from the Levasseur site.

Figure 8.5:
Reconstructed vessel from the Grande Anse site.

Figure 8.6: Saguenay Phase rimsherd from the Rioux site.

It should be noted that this vessel contained the charred remains of butternut shells for which the furthest north distribution limits is one hundred kilometers upriver towards Québec City (Tremblay 1998a). The Grande-Anse site shows two vessels of the same style, one of which was restored to show the original shape(Figure 8.5). The Turcotte-Lévesque site as well as the Rioux site (Figure 8.6), located on the same island, revealed other similar examples (Tremblay 1995b; Tremblay and Vaillancourt 1994).

Chronological Position

Ceramic seriations from well known St. Lawrence Valley sites suggest that the Saguenay Phase might be placed in the 800-600 B.P. range, although, in an effort to respect the one sigma range of the dates from both major sites, the position of the phase might be moved back in time some 50 years. As a result, the core of the Saguenay Phase can tentatively be placed between 750 and 650 B.P. Nevertheless, before better chronological data are available to confirm this range, it might be prudent to extend it by plus or minus fifty years (Figure 8.7).

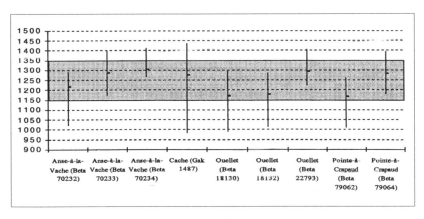

Figure 8.7: Calibrated dates for the Saguenay Phase with 2 sigma ranges.

In this configuration, the Saguenay Phase is squeezed into the Chapdelaine sequence *after* the early corded horizon, and as the *initial part of* the Early Iroquoian tradition. To differentiate these phases in the Iroquoian Tradition, the latter is named the Honguedo Phase. This term seems appropriate having been employed at the end of the Late Woodland by the Stadaconans to designate the Gaspesian region where they spent summers fishing and where Cartier met them in 1534 marking the first ever European contact with Iroquoians.[6] Because the Iroquoian presence on the lower St. Lawrence reflects a seasonal occupation by Stadaconans and other Québec City region villagers, the Saguenay Phase is also applied to the Québec City area, otherwise called the Canada Province by Cartier. In fact, this pottery style is present on Cap Tourmente sites and it is also in the Place Royale site in downtown Québec City.

Contemporary Manifestations

Farther up the St. Lawrence in the Lake Saint-Pierre/Trois-Rivières region which Chapdelaine named the Maisouna Province (Chapdelaine 1989), the latest occupation of the Bourassa site (dated at 675-650 B.P.) is clearly a manifestation of the same phase, with minor differences that may reveal regional variations (Clermont et al. 1986). These regional variations remain to be defined. Saguenay Phase traits have been found at sites excavated in the Montreal region where, for example, at Station 2 of the Pointe-du-Buisson fishing camp site which has been well-dated to 625 B.P. (Clermont 1995b) and at the recently uncovered McDonald village site (Gagné 1993), the pottery shows stylistic trends that match the earlier ware list.

In other words, it would seem that the middle and upper St. Lawrence Valley also present a distinguishable middle Late Woodland phase with diagnostic pottery that has minor regional variations. This is not a new hypothesis. It was already proposed by Pendergast (1975) as the "Early St. Lawrence Iroquoian" and again, with elaborations, by Chapdelaine (1989) as his "transitional period". What is new is the proposal that we also recognize this manifestation in the Lower St. Lawrence estuary region, in the easternmost part of Iroquoia.

Similar trends have been observed in the pottery attributed to the Ontario Iroquoian Tradition that evolved from Wright's early stage into the Uren and Middleport substages of Middle Ontario Iroquoian. Familiar pottery types, for instance, Ontario Horizontal, Middleport Criss-Cross and Ontario Oblique, to name a few, show striking similarities with Saguenay Phase pottery (Wright 1966). This differs from the ceramic patterns in eastern New York State, where the terminal Owasco and the Oak Hill phases demonstrate a higher degree of conservatism in their corded decorations.[7]

Thus, the eastern St. Lawrence Saguenay Phase shows a loosening of the ties of similarity that link these Iroquoians with those in New York—links that were clearly stronger in the earlier Owascoid period. There is also a stylistic connection with the Ontario Iroquoians. Collectively these data suggest that during the thirteenth century, the eastern St. Lawrence Iroquoians were participating in a realignment of the Iroquoian populations along the St. Lawrence axis, including those north of Lake Ontario. A north-south axis of influence was replaced by a shift to an east-west axis. This has been demonstrated by the ceramic stylistic trends examined here. Nevertheless, the pottery is but a reflection of the currents of cultural change flowing in the Iroquoian interaction zone. The introduction of corn agriculture is a singularly important element contributing to these cultural changes. The two earliest contexts for this cultigen in the Québec City region have been dated between 700 and 650 B.P. (Clermont and Chapdelaine 1992; Guimond 1994; Tremblay 1994). The fact that the eastern St. Lawrence Iroquoians always maintained a very mobile subsistence pattern makes them quite different from other Iroquoians. However, they also grew corn, beans and squash like their cousins upriver, as Cartier observed in 1535 (Bideaux 1986; Biggar 1924). Their adoption of an agricultural subsistence pattern started with the Saguenay Phase, probably, in part, as a result of their increased interactions with the Ontario Iroquoians who already had a long history of familiarity with maize (Crawford et al. 1997; Smith 1997) and who, at that time, were significantly increasing their commitment to food production (Chapdelaine 1993b), as well as expanding trading partnerships in a network of regionally based polities (Williamson and Robertson 1994a).

The Problem of Cord-wrapped Stick Decorated Pottery

If the eastern St. Lawrence tradition is divided into two distinct but clearly affiliated phases (Saguenay and Honguedo), how must we consider the preceding Owascoid tradition? Despite a rapid stylistic shift in the pottery, it is quite likely that the manifestations of earlier generations eventually became the St. Lawrence Iroquoians. While this hypothesis appears to work in the western part of the Valley, there are complications in the east.

Two explanations can be suggested to address this problem. First, because the chronological variations are not yet fully understood, 600 years of cord-decorated ware, encompassing Late Middle Woodland and Early Late Woodland pottery styles, have been lumped together by Chapdelaine (1995). Some elements are recognized as early, for instance, punctate bossing, while others, like the ridged rim, are late. Yet this development presents no rupture like the one between the cord-decorated pottery horizon and the subsequent Saguenay Phase.

Second, eastern margins of Iroquoia were influenced by Algonquian groups that were present. These may be divided in two categories: the northern Algonquians from the Subarctic, including the Montagnais bands, and the eastern Algonquians from the Maritime Peninsula including the Mi'kmaq, Malecite and eastern Abenaki (Figure 8.8).

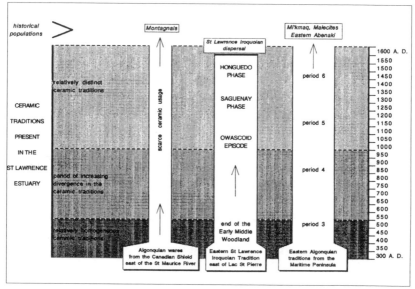

Figure 8.8: Ceramic sequences in the St. Lawrence estuary.

Unlike their western cousins of the Laurel, Blackduck and Selkirk traditions, the Montagnais bands and their immediate ancestors generally did not make use of pottery. Indeed, local ceramic traditions have yet to be identified in the Québec-Labrador peninsula east of the Saint-Maurice river. The few potsherds recovered in this region reflect exterior influences, from the St. Lawrence to the south, from the western Subarctic and from southern Ontario (cf. Moreau et al. 1991; Moreau 1995).

On the other hand, the eastern Maritime Algonquians have well established ceramic traditions as is demonstrated by Petersen and Sanger (1991) in their published synthetic ceramic sequence for Maine and the Maritime provinces. They separated their sequence into seven periods, of which their periods 5 and 6 are relevant to this discussion. This pottery is dominated by cord-wrapped stick decorations from 950 B.P. onwards into the period of European contact. Some of this pottery cannot be readily differentiated from the corded ware of the eastern St. Lawrence Valley, particularly that from the earlier late Middle Woodland assemblages. However, shell tempering, common in the C.P. 5 and 6 periods, may help indicate an Atlantic origin. This trait is definitely absent from the St.

Lawrence Iroquoian ceramic tradition and from any earlier St. Lawrence Valley ceramic wares. Shell tempered sherds were found, however, on at least three eastern St. Lawrence Iroquoian sites (Figure 8.9).

Figure 8.9 Examples of shell-tempered rimsherds from the Place Royale site. A: Vessel 26 – cord-wrapped stick with punctuates, everted rim; B: Vessel 45 – cord-wrapped stick, everted rim; C: Vessel 104 – dentate decoration, vertical rim; D: Vessel 111 – cord-wrapped stick, everted rim.

This situation resembles what Petersen has proposed to explain the presence of St. Lawrence Iroquoian ceramics in northern Maine and in the middle Kennebec River Valley; that is, evidence of a friendly relationship between eastern Abenakis and eastern St. Lawrence Iroquoians that can be traced to the fifteenth or fourteenth centuries (Petersen 1990, 1993; Tremblay 1997).[8] Nevertheless, the extent of this eastern Algonquian presence in the Lower St. Lawrence Valley will have to be defined if we are to understand the significance of corded ware in the region.

The identification of the corded pottery attributed to non-Iroquoians and regionally associated with similar corded pottery attributed to Owascoid people remains to be resolved. On the other hand, the cultural continuity from Owascoid to Iroquoian postulated in the Upper St. Lawrence Valley is also inferred in the Lower Valley. Some elements of the the Saguenay Phase material ease the transition of these two traditions.

For example, a vessel from the Ouellet site incorporates a ridged exterior rim with a linear impressed motif and incisions on the neck. Similar specimens combining typical early Owascoid traits and later Saguenay Phase traits have been found on other sites. These may offer opportunities to study this poorly understood Owascoid/Iroquoian continuity.

Conclusion

The Late Woodland in the eastern St. Lawrence Valley presents two ceramic traditions of different origins. The principal tradition stems from a still poorly understood Middle Woodland period and evolves into two final recognizable Iroquoian phases: the Saguenay Phase (800-600 B.P.) and the Honguedo Phase (600-370 B.P.) through an Early Late Woodland cord decorated ware that resembles New York Owasco. The second tradition consists of Eastern-Algonquian Late Woodland pottery that appears sporadically and which may reflect long-term social networks between the people on both sides of the Maritime Peninsula.

Eastern St. Lawrence Iroquoians during the Late Woodland also participated in the Iroquoian interaction sphere. This is demonstrated in their simultaneous sharing of stylistic pottery trends that characterize the evolution of ceramics up the St. Lawrence River and in southern Ontario. The Saguenay Phase is then but a regional variant of a wider "wind of change" observable throughout most of Iroquoia. But the eastern Iroquoians also retained subsistence preferences from earlier times that may have facilitated their ties with the Algonquian groups, particularly the Eastern Abenaki. The eastern St. Lawrence Iroquoians and the Eastern Abenaki both grew corn on its northeastern limits, with mobile settlement patterns that might be characterized as some sort of transhumance (Chapdelaine 1993a). Both the eastern Iroquoians and the Eastern Abenaki exploited marine resources to which they had direct access, and they also shared some lithic resources in the hinterland of the Maritime Peninsula (Tremblay 1995a, 1997). These associations may shed some light on the still poorly documented disappearance of the easternmost element of the St. Lawrence Iroquoians. Cartier's accounts suggests that the Stadaconans were hostile to the Mi'kmaq but this might not have been the case with the Eastern Abenaki. Leaving the causes of the disappearance of the St. Lawrence Iroquoians aside for the moment, it is suggested, as a final note, that some keys to our understanding of its consequences for the Québec City region Iroquoians may lie in the soils of Maine.

Notes

1. It was in this same article that Trigger offered refreshing hypotheses that led to the recognition of the St. Lawrence Iroquoian identity and also hinted at their in-situ development in the same fashion MacNeish had proposed for the rest of the Iroquoian world nearly 20 years before (MacNeish 1952).

2. This break in the pottery evolution is largely based upon Clermont and Chapdelaine's analysis of Station 4 of the Pointe-du-Buisson site (Clermont and Chapdelaine 1982). Recent studies suggest that the Montreal region pottery evolution from the Late Middle Woodland to the Early Late Woodland may, in fact, be more gradual than was earlier believed (Morin 1998; Gates Saint-Pierre 1999).

3. A similar phenomenon is observed in the Upper Hudson Valley, where the Saratoga Complex acts as a stylistic transition between the Middle Woodland and the Late Woodland Iroquoian styles. There, conversely, it is associated with Mahican Algonquians that are adopting traits linked to the spread of maize horticulture (Brumbach 1995:62-65). The Mahicans shared Mohawk ceramic styles in late precontact times (Brumbach 1975).

4. More than 30 leisters—mostly fragmented—were found on the Turcotte-Lévesque site a few hundred meters away from the Anse-à-la-Vache site, in an earlier Owascoid context (Tremblay 1993a, 1993b).

5. Apart from the "Owasco" and "Owascoid" terms that once were used (and in some cases still are) to lump together the first two thirds of the Late Woodland period, numerous devices have been used these past few years in the French literature to refer to this time unit. For instance, we find "Sylvicole supérieur médian" (Plourde 1995), "milieu du Sylvicole supérieur" (Tremblay et Vaillancourt 1994) and "Sylvicole supérieur moyen" (Tremblay 1995a, 1995b). Others have simply avoided the problem by speaking of the "période de transition" (Taillon 1995).

6. On the north shore of the St. Lawrence, a few sites with Iroquoian pottery are scattered along the coast all the way to the Strait of Belle Isle: Île du Havre in Mingan (Chapdelaine 1986); Kegaska (Wintemberg 1942; Chapdelaine et al. 1995); Red Bay in Labrador (Chapdelaine and Kennedy 1990) . Martijn suggests the Iroquoian presence this far east, which is documented historically, is a late and short-lived phenomenon, most probably linked to European presence in the Gulf (Martijn 1990:58). The same might be proposed for the Gaspé peninsula but at this time, no Iroquoian pottery, let alone an Iroquoian site, has been

found on the southern shore of the St. Lawrence, east of the Bic (Tremblay 1995a:272).

7. The situation is different in western New York where incised decorations rapidly replaces the corded decorations under the influence of Ontario Iroquoians (Niemczycki 1984:30-37, 1995).

8. Among other possible Algonquian presences in the region, there is the Mi'kmaq. After the St. Lawrence Iroquoian dispersion in the later part of the sixteenth century, the Mi'kmaq intensified their presence in the Lower St. Lawrence up to the Québec City region. Their knowledge of the Lower St. Lawrence certainly had roots in earlier times, as examplified by a conflict situation related to Cartier by the Stadaconans in 1535 and by Mi'kmaq legends (cf. Martijn 1986, 1991 for detailed discussions of the Mi'kmaq presence in the St. Lawrence Valley). The Malecite also were present in the region in early historic times. For example, Champlain met them in 1603 at Tadoussac where they celebrated, with their Algonquin and Montagnais allies, a victory over the Iroquois (Giguère 1973, vol. 1:70-84). Their ancestors also exploited resources in the Témiscouata area of the upper St. John's River drainage, only 70 kilometers to the interior from Rivière-du-Loup, on the Lower St. Lawrence south shore (Chalifoux et al. 1998).

Acknowledgements

I would like to express my gratitude to Ron Williamson, organizer of the symposium in North York, for giving me the opportunity to publish this paper. Some of the thoughts put forward here are part of my doctoral research which has benefited from a grant by the Social Sciences and Humanities Research Council of Canada. I wish to thank Jim Pendergast for his constructive comments and patient linguistic advice on a draft of this paper. I am also indebted to Norman Clermont, Pierre Dumais, Christian Gates Saint-Pierre, Laurence Johnson, Michel Plourde, and last but not least, my director Claude Chapdelaine, for comments on two French language articles that were synthesized here in English. Nevertheless, I remain solely responsible for the ideas herein. André Costopoulos and Mireille Laforge provided some help with my sometimes burlesque translations. James Petersen, Michel Plourde and Eugène Morin graciously shared unpublished information that has been useful. Photo credit goes to Michel Élie for Figures 4 and 5 and Pierre Fauteux for Figures 3 and 6. The Levasseur site vessel as well as the one from the Grande-Anse site were restored by André Bergeron of the Centre de Conservation du Québec.

CONTINUITY AND CHANGE WITHIN AN ARCHAEOLOGICAL SITES DATABASE

9

Robert von Bitter
Penny Young
Heritage Operations Unit
Ontario Ministry of Citizenship, Culture and Recreation
Rachel Perkins
Horniman Museum and Gardens, London, England

The Ontario Archaeological Sites Database (OASD) is the permanent, central computerized repository of attributes for approximately 13,000 registered archaeological sites in the province, which is maintained by the Ontario Ministry of Citizenship, Culture and Recreation (MCzCR). The OASD was managed on the Canadian Heritage Information Network (CHIN) until 1997, at which time it moved to an onsite system at the MCzCR. Site information includes registration numbers, location, investigation history, environmental data, cultural affinities, site type, researcher information, and references to published and unpublished reports and studies. Information continues to be contributed to the OASD by Archaeological Licence holders who are required to report on their investigations and submit Site Record Forms (Borden Forms) and Site Update Forms. Although the OASD is no longer managed on CHIN, the data entry rules and field descriptions have remained largely unchanged.

OASD information is used by numerous agencies and individuals in a wide variety of contexts. As part of standard background research for archaeological assessments (known in Ontario as "Stage 1"), consulting archaeologists use the presence or absence of registered sites in the vicinity of their study areas to help arrive at a detailed determination of archaeological potential and hence appropriate research methodology. Federal and provincial ministries and municipal governments require OASD information in the context of land use planning. Academics, students, and avocational archaeologists use this information for research purposes and federal, provincial and municipal museums request information from the OASD to document and maintain archaeological holdings in their institutions. First Nations also request data from the OASD as it relates to land use planning, land claims and the knowledge of heritage resources in their regions. On occasion, general members of the public also request information from this database. In short, the OASD serves a diverse clientele, all of whom deserve accurate and comprehensible information.

Given that hundreds of clients a year request information from the OASD, and that between 400 and 700 new archaeological sites are entered into the database annually, the OASD must be managed efficiently and effectively. There are, however, some specific issues surrounding the management of archaeological information, which can make this task exceedingly difficult. This paper examines a few of these issues, and comments on future directions for database management within the context of archaeological taxonomy.

Issues Surrounding Data Management

Some of the information provided by archaeologists, and contained within the OASD, is multi-faceted in nature. The definition for the "Cultural Affinities" field states that "this field identifies the culture(s) associated with activity on the archaeological site" (CHIN Archaeological Sites Working Group 1994:26-27). Archaeologists typically arrive at cultural affiliation using artifact typologies, settlement features, dating techniques, and historical and anthropological inference and this field similarly requests temporal, cultural, typological/material culture and spatial information. The results of a search on the field[1] are illustrated in Table 9.1. The terms reported in this table, are only those derived from *The Archaeology of Southern Ontario to A.D. 1650* (Ellis and Ferris 1990), since they are thought to reflect common usage within the Ontario archaeological community.

While the most frequently used terms obviously reflect the evolving popularity of taxonomic referents, the manner in which most researchers have responded is to offer a general temporal period for the site. It is, nevertheless, acknowledged that the terms that archaeologists use are a mix of temporal and cultural constructs within which are embedded further notions of period, type, phase, tradition, complex, and horizon. Indeed, many of those terms have multiple meanings. The term, "Clovis", for example, is a place in New Mexico, an archaeological site, a technological approach to flaking stone tools, a way of life (i.e., a population in the early post-Pleistocene Southwest), and a time period,

Table 9.1
Frequency of terms within the Cultural Affinities Field of the OASD

Paleo-Indian (220)	Early (12)		Gainey (1) Barnes (0) Crowfield (0)
	Late (52)		Holcolmbe (0) Hi-Lo (13)
Archaic (1986)	Early (234)		Kirk (6) Nettling (11) Bifurcate (1)
	Middle (169)		Laurentian (82) Brewerton (24)
	Late (525)		Narrow Point (1) Lamoka (16) Normanskill (10) Broad Point (11) Genesee (4) Adder Orchard (1) Perkiomen (1) Small Point (1) Crawford Knoll (6) Innes (1) Ace of Spades (0) Hind (0)
Woodland (2511)	Early (282)		Meadowood (60) Middlesex (0) Adena (10)
	Middle (518)		Saugeen (54) Couture (1) Point Peninsula (83) Sandbanks (3) Princess Point (76) Riviere au Vase (5)
	Late (931)	Early ^	Glen Meyer (103) Pickering (44) Younge (29)
		Middle ^	Uren (12) Middleport (102) Springwells (6)
		Late ^	Huron (159) Neutral (225) St. Lawrence (40) Wolf (2) Odawa (10) Petun (85)

^ — query not attempted

among others. Without a thorough study of the database, Site Record Form and/or archaeological report, it is not possible to determine whether an archaeologist has equated cultural affinity with temporal identification or has considered the site's location, artifact typology, or settlement patterns and offered an actual cultural referent.

Indeed, it is not always clear whether the archaeologist is aware of the differences between cultural and temporal constructs. For example, a site described as Middleport, often used as a cultural construct, might simultaneously be considered part of the Terminal Woodland, Late Woodland, Middle Late Woodland or Middle Iroquoian periods. Table 9.2 presents the various, sometimes confusing, combinations in which the term "Glen Meyer", another cultural construct, is expressed within the database.

Part of this confusion is due to the fact that, over time, archaeologists interpret the past in different ways and classificatory consensus has not always been reached. Often, new terms emerge which some practitioners believe better reflect past cultural realities. Some of these terms gain in popularity while others fall from use. Indeed, an archaeological site discovered 50 years ago might be described using a classification scheme popular at the time, but has been described differently by subsequent researchers conducting further investigations. Glen Meyer, for example, has generally fallen from favour for referring to regionally-based, autonomous Early Iroquoian communities (Williamson 1990:295; Ferris and Spence, 1995:106).

Like the construction of cultural-temporal identity, as reflected in the "Cultural Affinities" field, information recorded for the "Site Type" field is equally unruly and variable. For example, a surface collection of lithics may appear in this field in a number of ways including, but not limited to: a campsite, a workshop, a flake scatter, a chipping station or a lithic scatter (Table 9.3). In this example, the database contains many terms which convey the same meaning. In such cases, data management practices might be undertaken to enhance the clarity of the database. Guiding such an attempt, however, is the principle that data managers must standardize entries without changing their meaning.

The first and most obvious way to standardize and clarify the database is to eliminate variation that lacks meaning. This often occurs in the form of incorrectly spelled words or signifiers, and accounts for an estimated five percent of all variation within the OASD. Removal of this form of variation can be accomplished without fear that the meaning of these entries will change.

Table 9.2
Variation of how Glen Meyer is expressed within the OASD

Cultural Affinity	No	Cultural Affinity	No
Archaic, Glen Meyer	1	Woodland, Late, Glen Meyer	3
Glen Meyer	16	Woodland, Late, Glen Meyer Iroquoian, Early	1
Iroquoian, Glen Meyer (probable)	1	Woodland, Late, Glen Meyer, Early	1
Late Glen Meyer / Early Middleport	1	Woodland, Late, Iroquoian, Glen Meyer	2
Late Glen Meyer-Middleport	1	Woodland, Late, Iroquoian, Glen Meyer, Early	1
Probable Glen Meyer	1	Woodland, Late, Iroquoian, Glen Meyer, Levanna	1
Saugeen and Glen Meyer	1	Woodland, Middle, Glen Meyer	6
Woodland, Early Iroquoian, Glen Meyer	1	Woodland, Middle, Iroquoian, Glen Meyer	4
Woodland, Early, Glen Meyer	1	Glen Meyer ?	1
Woodland, Early, Iroquoian, Glen Meyer	1	Glen Meyer, Late	3
Woodland, Glen Meyer	6	Glen Meyer, Late or Uren, Early	1
Woodland, Iroquoian, Early, Glen Meyer	30	Glen Meyer, Late or Uren Early	1
Woodland, Iroquoian, Glen Meyer	6	Glen Meyer/Younge	1
Woodland, Iroquoian, Late, Glen Meyer	1	Glenn Meyer	1
Woodland, Iroquoian, Saugeen, Point Peninsula, Glen Meyer, Uren	1	Woodland, Late, Glen Meyer	4
Woodland, Iroquois, Glen Meyer	3		

Table 9.3
Terms With Similar Meaning Within the OASD

campsite	2623	station, chipping	211
campsite ?	204	station, flaking	5
campsite(s)	20	station, hunting	19
campsite,	12	station, lithic	11
campsite, seasonal	15	station, lithic processing	1
campsite, hunting	19	station, lithic manufacturing	1
campsite, fishing	14	station, processing	4
campsite, temporary	4	station, lithic ?	4
campsite(s), seasonal (5+)	4	station, extraction, processing	3
campsite (multi-component)	4	station, extraction	3
campsite, winter ?	2	station, chert	3
campsite, winter	2	Workshop	64
campsite, summer	2	Workshop?	11
campsite, processing	2	scatter, lithic	15
campsite, multicomponent	2	scatter	8
campsite, multi-component	2	scatter flake	4
campsite, gathering	2	chipping station	1
campsite(s), seasonal (5 +)	2		
campsite(?)	2		

Clarity can also be brought to the "Site Type" field through the use of standardized entries. In the lithic scatter/chipping station example, variation occurs when archaeologists use terms that denote both site function (i.e., a chipping station) and site form (i.e., a lithic scatter). While this relates to descriptive vs. functional categorizations, it may be possible in the future to standardize this field by using only one type of categorization.

Standardizing the "Cultural Affinities" field, however, is more difficult, given the lack of taxonomic consensus and the risk of changing the meaning of what was intended by the archaeologist when it was recorded. Previous examples illustrate how some terms are multifarious and, therefore, prove difficult for the data manager to ascertain their true or originally intended meaning. Likewise, if a data manager were to modify all aceramic sites to an "Archaic" signifier, this could be detrimental to the content and accuracy of the database; one could not be certain that the former signifier, for example, represented either a Paleo-Indian site or a Woodland site where ceramic materials were not recovered.

As illustrated above, the characteristics of archaeological data pose certain challenges with respect to effective management. How does one successfully store information on potentially multi-component sites that are visited over time by archaeologists who use different terms in different combinations? One approach is to use a database that encourages the researcher to choose multiple entries for each record, which both the old CHIN and the new OASD systems allow. The OASD is rich in information because the terminology within the database is an accumulation of various taxonomic schemes.

On the other hand, the OASD is dominated by unique entries. Sixty-nine percent of the entries in the "Cultural Affinities" field and 68 percent of the entries within the "Site Type" field are unique. This singularity is likely a by-product of the overlapping and subjective nature of archaeological data. As well, these statistics result from ambiguous rules regarding data entry. Although text string searches can successfully detect all variants of a form, it is absolutely necessary to ensure that users of OASD information understand what each term means.

It is, therefore, clear that databases such as the OASD should develop manuals which explicitly define each term and illustrate how terms relate to one another. Such a manual would provide information on existing terminology, and would also indicate preferred terms for any given archaeological observation. Such a manual might also reveal such information as who developed the term, and how terms might relate to one another in time and space. The ubiquity of older terms within the OASD makes this essential, and would also minimize future variation, although its revision must recognise the value of the uniqueness characteristic of many of the early entries.

The Future

It is likely that the OASD will continue to mirror current archaeological trends and practices within the Province. It may also be true that ongoing examination of the OASD in search of information gaps might direct researchers to sites which require further investigation. Indeed, missing or incomplete information, contained in fields such as "Site Type" or "Cultural Affinities", could become important points of departure; although it is acknowledged that most archaeological work is now undertaken in the context of cultural resource management and that most site forms now represent our only record of destroyed archaeological sites. In the future, it should also be possible to outline where, in Ontario, various terms have been used, and by which researchers, providing an important reflection on our own past, and perhaps even generating important data for future discussions on taxonomy.

As the database evolves, we may see changes in composition, the type of client using the system, and the ways in which the data are used. Virtual collections, or databases of archaeological information that can be accessed remotely, are a new media that offer many new benefits such as cost-effective access and wider public participation. Like the current debate, however, the accuracy of the data used within these virtual collections depends entirely on previous discussions of taxonomy.

Conclusions

The general principle of maintaining the meaning of information while furthering standardization is as relevant to the management of the OASD as to any other database. The management of archaeological information is, however, particularly challenging because of its fluid (and sometimes, fleeting) nature. The complexity of terms used by archaeologists to classify sites, however, need not obscure our understanding if clear definitions exist linking the past with the present.

Notes

1. The data presented reflects the composition of two fields within the Canadian Heritage Information Network on January 29, 1997. At that time, the number of occurrences of each entry was calculated. Within the Site Type Field there were a total of 13,072 entries captured and in the Cultural Affinities fields a total of 14,391 entries. The fact that there are

    1,319 less entries in Site Types than Cultural Affinities is attributed to the significant number of sites that are multi-component.

2. The results presented in this paper reflect queries made to these two fields. Wildcards were entered in conjunction with the minimum number of characters needed to identify a term, in an attempt to capture the maximum amount of relevant information from each query. The results of each term were checked to ensure that extraneous information had not been captured (i.e., to remove such things as Laurentian from queries made on the term "Uren"). Terms, including the larger cultural categories (Paleo-Indian, Archaic, and Woodland) and the unique or less common terms (i.e., Brewerton, Middleport etc.) were extracted from the whole data set. Counts of sites under the subdivisions of Early, Middle and Late within the larger categories of Paleo-Indian, Archaic, and Woodland, were narrowed down from only those three divisions, where relevant.

Acknowledgements

We were fortunate to have had the opportunity to discuss these ideas with Peter Carruthers, Martin Cooper, Gordon Dibb, Neal Ferris, Patricia Davis-Perkins, Stephen Perkins, Christopher Watts, Ronald Williamson and James V. Wright. While they contributed immeasurably to this paper, any errors in interpretation or omissions are the sole responsibility of the authors.

WHAT'S IN A NAME? THE IMPLICATIONS OF ARCHAEOLOGICAL TERMINOLOGY USED IN NONARCHAEOLOGICAL CONTEXTS

10

Neal Ferris
Heritage Operations Unit
Ontario Ministry of Citizenship, Culture and Recreation

The papers in this volume are about the taxonomy and language of archaeology. Indeed, jargon and technical language are necessary tools of any specialised group, serving as a sort of a technical shorthand or code (Lutz 1996), encapsulating the host of descriptive traits and theoretical concepts that is required when talking to other archaeologists about the resource and practice of archaeology. Since, as professional practitioners, we have all been trained within this specialized language, we understand the nuances of the special meanings our community has given to particular words. For example, the word castellation would bring to mind most often a bump on a ceramic rim sherd, rather than a distinctive architectural feature on turrets and other old buildings. Similarly, while some archaeologists use the term Glen Meyer to categorize sites of about 1,000 years in age located west of the Niagara Escarpment in Ontario, it is also the name of a small, rural town north of Lake Erie in the Region of Haldimand-Norfolk. Likewise, the word flake often refers to a small piece of rock, rather than a silly person.

Just like doctors in an emergency room, soldiers in a de-briefing room, or Star Trekkies on a convention floor, who all talk in what seems like an elaborate code, archaeologists use coded language. The words and phrases in this code act as very specialized signifiers infused with particular meaning only archaeologists can interpret. That we understand this meaning reinforces our membership within this community—we belong because we talk the talk.

While our specialized jargon is inclusive to members of the archaeological community, it is also exclusive to everyone else (Hodder 1984; Lutz 1996). I work as an archaeologist for the provincial government, at the juncture where the interests and concerns of the archaeological community intersect with all the other sectors of society who have an interest in the resource, either because it is their heritage or because they are required to comply with land use planning legislation. In this paper, I wish to explore some of the implications which arise when we, as archaeologists, must communicate with people outside of our own community. While I do not profess to have anything all that new or startling to offer on the subject, our ability to communicate with nonarchaeologists is something we need to think about, especially when, more and more, we are being asked to explain what it is we do, and why it should be considered important by society at large.

So how do archaeologists, with our jargon-laden and specialized language, talk to nonarchaeologists? Well, not surprisingly, the ability to understand the meaning behind the jargon, the context within which our technical shorthand is read, can be extremely limited for those who haven't invested years of their lives training to be archaeologists. Now, that is fine if archaeologists are not required or interested in communicating with anyone other than archaeologists. We live in a world, however, where over the last couple of decades, archaeology is increasingly likely to be addressed by government policy makers and planners, engineers, developers, politicians and the public. As well, in continued attempts to resolve issues and work with Aboriginal communities, archaeologists increasingly are bringing their concerns and their findings to, and soliciting input from, Aboriginal peoples.

We would not reasonably expect many people from these sectors to understand the distinction between concepts such as "early contact" and "precontact", "Paleo-Indian" and "Plano", or "Laurel", "Point Peninsula", "Princess Point", and so on. Frankly, I would suspect that many people from these sectors would not really care about those distinctions, which should not be taken to mean that these people lack perceptions, and often misperceptions, about archaeology (see, for example, Pokotylo and Guppy 1999; Stone 1989).

When we talk to people from these sectors about things like archaeological potential, site significance, or "good" and "bad" archaeology, such semantics assume more importance. Perhaps nowhere is this more of an issue than in the world of archaeological conservation within development contexts. Currently in Ontario, hundreds of archaeological sites are documented each year by privately employed contract archaeologists who perform a service for development proponents, both public and private, by addressing archaeological resource conservation requirements arising out of land use planning, environmental assessment, aggregate extraction and a host of other legislated development processes (Ferris 1998). In this way, the development sector is required to pay millions of dollars each year to have archaeological concerns addressed, regardless of what might be their personal views on the value of archaeology and heritage in our society. As few developers, if any, are also trained archaeologists, they are totally reliant on the archaeologists they hire to determine what costs are necessary, which of these newly documented sites are truly important, what minimally must be done for the province to clear the archaeological conditions imposed on their development, and so on.

Not surprisingly, a lack of personal familiarity with archaeology creates a basic uneasiness for many developers, not to mention planners, engineers, politicians, and others whose introduction to archaeology is through the conservation requirements in the land use planning processes. And this unease can be substantially heightened when the cost of addressing archaeology, as it can from time to time, extends into tens of thousands of dollars or more. In order to be reassured that what they are paying for is both necessary and of value, developers will seek reassurances from either their hired archaeologists, or provincial staff.

More often than we would probably prefer, however, developers do not get the kind of reassurance they are seeking. For example, on several occasions I have had meetings with very upset individuals who invariably have gone out to visit the site excavation, and were shocked to discover what it is that is being removed at their expense. Their complaint is often similar: they say that when they asked the archaeologist to show them what was being found, the archaeologist invariably reaches into a lunch bag and pulls out a bunch of rocks, what we recognise as flakes, fragments of bifaces, and maybe some fragmentary pottery sherds. At this point the developer will bluster, and all those anxieties will rise to the surface as they come to realize that they have just paid someone thousands of dollars to excavate what looks like little more than road gravel. They then usually ask the consultant why this "stuff" and the site is so important, only to find themselves listening to the consultant lecture at some length about what these broken bits of "stuff" mean to archaeologists, and what the archaeologist will do with them in the lab.

Usually, the anger that developers express arises directly from their frustration with not understanding what the archaeologist is really saying, of being held hostage to the obscurity of archaeology, reinforced by the jargon and technical language we tend to fall back on when asked to justify what it is we do. Unfortunately, this can tend to confirm in the developer's mind their suspicion that the only value to excavating the site was in the pay cheque that the archaeologist pocketed.

Figure 10.1: What archaeologists say to developers...

We know, of course, that this is not the case, but no one should expect developers to simply take our word that a pile of flakes was worth the ten or twenty thousand dollars it cost to extract them. While perhaps we might expect developers to accept our evaluations on the basis of our expertise, they are unlikely to do so if our language is inaccessible. We also should not be surprised if developers and others question the value of spending money, if their perception is that this is simply so a researcher can hide away and play with materials for no one's apparent benefit other than that researcher.

In effect, we need to reconcile economic value (dollars spent) with the social value of documenting our past, in language developers and others can understand. This message is an important one to deliver, if we want continued support in conserving archaeological sites, and we do need that support. As well, we need to keep in mind that developers are members of the "public". The demonstration to a developer as to why the expense of archaeological conservation has value, provides us with opportunities to demonstrate why archaeology is important to our society. Frankly, this should not be difficult. After all, archaeological sites are a much more exciting part of our heritage than a handful of flakes, and are all stories waiting to be read and passed on (Deetz 1998). Moreover, archaeology should be easy to promote, if we think through the message we want to deliver. In particular, we have to make a concerted effort not just to talk about sites and the past in terms that are of interest to us as specialists, but also to talk about what that place or those materials should offer to everyone—a rare and exciting glimpse into a part of our past that was unknown prior to its discovery.

A different set of problems can arise from the use of jargon and specialized language when archaeological investigations and findings are presented to, or sought out by, Aboriginal communities. At a basic level, people from Aboriginal communities often talk about the way the inclusive/exclusive nature of this language gives rise to the feeling that they are being talked down to by archaeologists (e.g. Downer1997; Nichols and Andrews 1997b). The unequal power relationship such exclusivity fosters means, therefore, that although the archaeological sites and materials being discussed are the heritage of these Aboriginal communities, there is a sense of the loss of ownership of this heritage to jargon-wielding archaeological specialists (Murray 1993). The unthinking use of our jargon can undermine the very attempts we make to communicate and forge partnerships with Aboriginal communities.

Furthermore, while many terms used by archaeologists may have perfectly legitimate internalized meanings, they are terms that, nonetheless, have different and potentially more negative connotations external to our community. For example, the term "prehistory" is a well-established label for that period of the Aboriginal archaeological record prior to the existence of written documents. In Ontario and much of the Northeast, this term is also synonymous with the term precontact, meaning that period of the archaeological record prior to contact with Europeans. While the term prehistory has been criticized for the arbitrary distinction that it implies (Lightfoot 1995), it also has been perceived as insulting or at least disrespectful. Not surprisingly, the use of the prefix "pre" can be misread by nonarchaeologists as implying "before history" or "lacking history". For some, this is seen as an intentional marginalization of Aboriginal heritage.

The thought of revising terminology to respond to the sensibilities of others, however, can sometimes be greeted with disdain. Such efforts might be perceived as another example of Political-Correctness, that rather clever catch-all label used in the 1990s by neo-conservatives as a convenient and derisive means of dismissing complex issues and remarginalizing those sectors of our society that have attempted to be included over the last few decades. More significantly, it has been argued that any debate over terminology serves as little more than a red herring, keeping us away from more important debates (Nichols and Andrews 1997a:xv).

While we know the term may not be intended in a pejorative sense, it can certainly read as such by nonarchaeologists. It is also worth keeping in mind that much of the jargon we use has a very judgement-laden history. It was not that many decades ago, for example, that the archaeological literature was filled with terms such as "primitive", "savage", "nomadic", "crude", and so on when describing Ontario's Aboriginal cultures and their archaeological remains. Many of these terms echo back to a Victorian sensibility (and earlier) that placed cultures and people in a Social Darwinism hierarchy, positioning colonial societies at the height of advancement, and others at some lesser point on the scale (e.g. Stocking 1987). These self-serving assumptions of racial, social, and moral superiority did much to reinforce the political, legal, economic, and social marginalization of indigenous peoples across the colonized world, and were thoroughly absorbed by and perpetuated in anthropological thinking (Gould 1981; MacKenzie 1984). In this way, the anthropological use of terms like "savage" was never seen as pejorative, simply "objective" measurements of the level of cultural "advancement". Today, no one would challenge the loaded meaning behind these words, and they are no longer used in the archaeological literature.

We should not, therefore, be surprised that other labels such as "prehistory" or "Archaic" are also read as pejoratives. The fact of the matter is that the world in which archaeology operates has changed, thanks in no small part to our own efforts. While it was not that long ago that archaeology was the domain of archaeologists alone, Aboriginal interests in Ontario's archaeological heritage are now welcomed by many archaeologists and most policy and law makers, and even the public itself. The Aboriginal community has a legitimate seat at the table in the shaping of future directions for archaeology. As such, we increasingly will be working with the Aboriginal community to achieve research and conservation ends. The continued use of terminology having negative connotations does little to strengthen relations or improve our ability to forge partnerships. Moreover, Aboriginal peoples are now *part* of the archaeological community, so as our values as a community change, our use of language will change to reflect both our collective experiences and attitudes.

Beyond establishing a false proprietorship and offending sensibilities, however, archaeological jargon also can have significant implications for shaping, and sometimes misinforming, contemporary Aboriginal issues in Ontario. This is particularly the case when we use specific ethnic or cultural labels (von Gernet 1994, 1995). As archaeologists, we like to borrow various cultural-linguistic terms and apply them to archaeological complexes, traditions and components that extend over broad geographic regions. As well, we sometimes engage in vitriolic debates over the cultural affiliations for people who have left behind only a small portion of their material culture and record of life. We toss around terms like Iroquoian and Algonquian on little more basis than the presence or absence of particular styles of marking pottery, differing subsistence practices, and so on. Such debates are important in framing interpretations of data, but we should not take as gospel these ascribed affiliations. After all, do we really feel the archaeological record is so profound and insightful, or that rules of group and self-identity were so fixed and simple in the past, that these labels can be anything other than convenient analogies for archaeologists?

Rather, at their most useful level, archaeological labels like Algonquian and Iroquoian, or Glen Meyer and Pickering, really only reflect broad geographic generalizations, basic categorizations of similarity and difference that can assist in sorting a large number of archaeological sites and the wide variety of material culture and settlement-subsistence data found on them. I emphasize archaeological sites, not people, because the data we read, describe and interpret only comes from, and are unique to, the formation of archaeological sites, not usually from overt acts of individual or group self-identity. No doubt, the broad cultural-geographic labels we develop will likely incorporate many actual past political, community, family and religious boundaries, while at the same time create arbitrary boundaries based on archaeological traits which may have little meaning except to an archaeologist.

When we lose sight of what these cultural labels are, and impose increasingly more specific meaning to them, far beyond that available from the archaeological record, we do so at our own peril. On one level this may be acceptable. These labels are the substance of theoretical debate, of interpretation, and then of re-thinking and re-interpretation of the observed data we work with every day of our lives. There are, however, real implications when we use these cultural labels unthinkingly outside the archaeological discipline. Obviously, nonarchaeologists will not be familiar with the long history and agreed assumptions lying behind these terms, and will little appreciate the subtle distinctions we imply when using labels like Iroquois and Iroquoian. When these terms are employed in the wider world, there is often little opportunity for us to explain their proper context, and their use may lead to inappropriate actions and decisions.

Some examples I have encountered demonstrate the implications these labels can have in the wider world. For instance, one example involving burials has recently arisen around Metropolitan Toronto, which has led to a rather intriguing practice. In this region, most archaeologists tend to assume that the archaeological remains of the last 1,000 years or more are likely the antecedents of the historic group of Iroquoian-speaking communities known as Huron, and label some or all sites predating contact with Europeans as precontact Huron. Whether or not the people who left behind those sites would agree that they are the great-great-great-great etc. grandparents of historically documented Huron communities, or whether these historically defined communities have such ancestry, are certainly topics for research and debate. For all intents and purposes, though, a term like precontact Huron can only ever be a convenient way of referring to archaeological sites dating roughly between 950 or 650 and 350 B.P., which exhibit broadly similar archaeological traits, and which are found between Georgian Bay and Lake Ontario, to the east of the Niagara Escarpment, and to the south and west of the Canadian Shield.

Among most archaeologists, this qualification of the term precontact Huron presents few problems. However, things get murky when dealing with modern rules for the discovery of human remains. Under current provisions of the Ontario Cemeteries Act, when burials are encountered, the Cemeteries Registrar is required to contact the nearest First Nation Council, as defined under the Indian Act (Canada), to act as representative for the deceased. This representative acts as de facto next of kin and, as such, is provided with the opportunity to have input in determining what the appropriate actions should be with regard to the burial. In the region containing sites commonly labelled precontact Huron, there are currently several First Nations communities who could act as representative for the deceased. As it happens, all of these communities are of Anishnawbe (Algonquian) people. However, some archaeologists have tended to feel that there was something not quite right about seeking direction from an Algonquian community for dealing with an Iroquoian burial. So they have tended to contact the Six Nations Iroquoian community on the Grand River, located about 150 km west of the core of precontact Huronia. Moreover, some of the members of the Six Nations community are actually the great, great descendants of the Five Nations Iroquois who, during the seventeenth century, warred with the great, great descendants of these buried individuals.

While the Six Nations community has repeatedly been willing to represent the burials of Iroquoian peoples, a couple of years ago they understandably began to express some discomfort in dealing with burials labelled as either precontact or contact Huron. They recommended that landowners and archaeologists contact a Huron community in Lorette, Québec, to see if they would act as representatives for the deceased. At the same time, the urban Native Canadian Centre of Toronto, representing a large community of First Nations people from across Canada, has also expressed a desire to be involved in the disposition decisions regarding burials found in a broadly defined Metropolitan Toronto region. While these intentions are perfectly understandable, and archaeologists genuinely are seeking to "do the right thing", a rather perplexing set of practices has evolved given that some archaeologists apply terms like precontact Huron and even Iroquoian more broadly than others. Specifically, depending on which archaeologist is involved, burials found from this region may be represented by Six Nations, if the archaeologist chose to declare the deceased as Iroquoian, by the Huron community of Lorette, if labelled precontact Huron by the archaeologist, by one of the nearby Anishnawbe reserves, if only identified as Aboriginal, or by a nondenominational burials committee of the Native Canadian Centre in Toronto. This is a direct result of our varying usage of cultural or ethnic labels for archaeological remains.

Another similar example concerns a single, bundled skeleton of an Aboriginal person discovered in 1996 during construction work on private property in Sauble Beach, on Lake Huron south of the Bruce Peninsula. The fact that the burial was in a bundle was seen as evidence of an age of at least several hundred years (i.e., precontact) by the investigating police and Ontario Coroner's representative. An assumption was made, somewhere between the Provincial Police media contact, the

Provincial Coroner's office and local media, that such an ancient burial must, therefore, mean the individual was Iroquoian. The conclusion probably arose from the fact that the burial was found just outside of the Saugeen First Nation reserve, an Ojibwa or Anishnawbe community whose reserve was established in the nineteenth century. Since the burial was thought to be much older, it was, therefore, assumed that it was not of Ojibwa ancestry, but of Iroquoian origin. Of course, short of DNA matching, no one can say what language this person spoke or identify the community to which she belonged. To the Saugeen community, however, who are in the midst of a lands claim for portions of Sauble Beach, labelling the burial Iroquoian was, at best, uninformed and insulting, or, at worst, an attempt to discredit their assertion of pre-existing claim to Sauble Beach. Therefore, when the landowner, the Saugeen First Nations, their lawyers and provincial staff all met to determine a course of action for the burial, as much concern was focussed on this label, as was what to do for the individual who was disinterred.

As seen in the Sauble Beach example, assertions of particular ethnic affiliation can have implications for Aboriginal land claims, an area where archaeological jargon can be debated by both sides of a litigation. During on-going research surrounding a land claims case between the federal government of Canada and the Six Nations, for example, Aboriginal assertions in the case included the usual statement concerning the community's long occupation of the region. Staff of the Litigation Support Directorate of Indian Affairs, as a background study, investigated the basis for the claims by Six Nations to cultural longevity in Ontario, and contacted the Ministry of Citizenship, Culture and Recreation, at which point they requested a list of all Iroquoian sites in southern Ontario dating after 1,050 B.P. The reasoning for the request was an assertion made in the claim that the Six Nations Iroquois are the true original possessors of southern Ontario, as evidenced by the archaeological documentation of a 1,000 year old Ontario Iroquoian Tradition. These data were needed to simply determine the extent of the archaeological occupation in anticipation of any possible future claims by Six Nations to some or all of this region.

Such a claim by Six Nations for southern Ontario simply because of the presence of archaeological sites labelled by archaeologists as Iroquoian certainly could be contested on many grounds. Indeed, it might lead to an intriguing series of debates regarding cultural ancestry, archaeological method and theory, the legitimacy of treaty possession (southern Ontario was occupied at the time of the Royal Proclamation of Ojibwa communities, not Iroquoian ones), among others. What was surprising, however, was that the Litigation Support Directorate made this request for data without also requesting some insight and background into the data they were about to receive. Indeed, they were prepared to accept those data having assumed the archaeological link between the Ontario Iroquoian Tradition and the Six Nations Iroquois. It had not occurred to them to check with archaeologists to determine if these terms were indeed linked.

More broadly, the thing about land and resource claims, of course, is that they operate within a litigious process. Where claims of ancestry are in dispute, both sides of that dispute will use archaeologists, and their ideas, as weapons to achieve success (von Gernet 1994). What this means, unfortunately, is that the heritage of Aboriginal peoples will again be used in opposition to those communities. Also, archaeological assertions of ethnic affiliation and cultural labels, though based on bits of obscure data, a lot of wild speculation, and frankly, personal preference, can end up being treated with a formal, legal legitimacy that they do not warrant and should never be given.

Archaeology is no different than any other specialized discipline. Our language and jargon serve a useful purpose in communicating with one other, hopefully effectively and clearly, to convey thought and description. By our own choosing, however, we are not an isolated group, left to pursue our interest in obscurity (Fagan 1984). We interact with other sectors of society, demand that the data with which we work be protected by society and demand monies from public and private development agencies to do archaeology. We also work with the heritage of a people who want to have real input in exploring and discovering who they are and from whence they came, but who must at present, obtain archaeological data largely at second hand. We also have to communicate effectively and clearly to a host of nonarchaeologists. This is hampered, however, when we rely on our coded language. This language can exclude, marginalize and divest the public and Aboriginal communities of any sense of ownership in our archaeological heritage (Ferris 1998). To address this issue we do not have to abandon our specialized language or "dumb down" archaeological discourse. Rather, effective communication may be achieved simply by recognizing and considering the audience being addressed.

Section II: Taming the Taxonomy

ARCHAEOLOGICAL IMPLICATIONS OF GREAT LAKES PALEOECOLOGY AT THE REGIONAL SCALE

11

William A. Lovis
Department of Anthropology, Michigan State University
Robert I. MacDonald
Archaeological Services Inc.

The formidable task with which we have been charged is to examine the changing environmental contexts of the Great Lakes region since deglaciation as a means of placing the other contributions in the plenary session into regional focus. At the same time, we are using this opportunity to act as *provocateurs* for a more ecologically based agenda for Great Lakes archaeology.

For our purposes, we have defined the region of interest as the Great Lakes drainage basin. Notably for us, this does not include the majority of the St. Lawrence River drainage, although we do occasionally stray beyond the borders of the drainage basin into both the St. Lawrence, as well as adjacent areas to the south and west of the Great Lakes. We also recognize that this convenient definition of the region of interest certainly does not remain stable over the millennia that we intend to consider in this presentation, and that this instability may have had considerable consequence for past human adaptation in the region.

Beyond this initial point, we perceive that our task in this paper is to fulfill three primary goals. First, we intend to fulfill the prescribed mandate of the plenary session by attempting to present an essentially nomenclature-free, discussion of changing Great Lakes paleoenvironments. The second major goal is to review both the program and the long-term agenda of an ecological/environmental archaeological approach in the Great Lakes region. Our final goal is to review the changing paleoecology of the Great Lakes region in terms of a suite of specific variables such as glacial activity, paleoclimate, changing lake basin evolution, and paleovegetation. Both singly and together we view this group of variables as most significant to subsequent discussion of human adaptation in the region.

Environmental Archaeology in the Great Lakes Region

Review and Prospectus

While insights concerning the relationships between humankind and the natural environment have been part of the academic tradition since at least the time of the ancient Greeks (Ellen 1982:1), the clearest early roots of ecological archaeology as a discipline are to be found in early nineteenth century Scandinavian archaeology. By mid-century, the Scandinavian interest in relative chronology, paleoenvironments, and precontact lifeways was also being pursued in Scotland and Switzerland, although a different agenda was underway in the pre-eminent European countries of England, France, and Germany (Trigger 1989:73-103). Scandinavian scholarship also took a leading role in the development of ecology as a discipline around the beginning of the twentieth century (Worster 1977:198 ff.). The Scandinavian work finally gained currency as Anglophone precontact historians turned their attention to human paleoecology in the second quarter of the twentieth century. In Britain, a functionalist approach to the study of human economies was being pursued by archaeologists such as V. Gordon Childe (1936, 1951, 1958), and this was put into practice most effectively in the pioneering ecological archaeology of Graham Clark (1952, 1954; Trigger 1989:250-270).

In North America, a similar theoretical ferment was taking place, to some extent catalysed by the "Ecology Group" at the University of Chicago, and by mid-century, Julian Steward had coined the term "cultural ecology" to describe his approach (Ellen 1982:52-65; Harris 1968:654-687; Steward 1955; Trigger 1989:279-282). Cultural ecology became a significant force in archaeology when Gordon Willey (1953, 1956) demonstrated its value in his seminal work on settlement archaeology, and it gained additional momentum during the 1970s and 1980s thanks to the so-called "New" or "Processual Archaeology", which emulated the natural sciences, embraced ecological methodology, and like ecology, adopted a systemic paradigm.

Ecological or environmental approaches in Great Lakes archaeology, with few exceptions, had their origins during the 1960s, synchronous with the arrival of the processualist paradigm in the subdiscipline, incorporating regionally based research designs, and an interdisciplinary perspective on human/environment relationships. In large part this was due to the formal coupling of Stewardian cultural ecological perspectives and a more concerted interest in the relationship between paleoeconomies and environmental change in small-scale societies. To a degree this was presaged in a cultural historical perspective by Joseph Caldwell in his 1958 discussion of Primary Forest Efficiency in the Eastern Woodlands. This model was intended as a vehicle toward understanding human/environment relationships, but was later extended by others into a formal integration of sister disciplines such as palynology, climatology, glacial geology, botany and zoology in a processual model. The broader perspective which evolved emphasized the cross training of students in both anthropological archaeology and various specialty areas, which in turn led to more ecologically focussed research questions reliant on more refined types of data recovery, noteworthy among which is the systematic application of flotation.

Within the Great Lakes region the programmatic impact of this new perspective was highly variable at an institutional, regional, and even a problem level, however. Several institutions and individuals asserted a concerted commitment to the paleoecological approach, among them the program directed by J.B. Griffin at the University of Michigan. This program was parallelled by that of David Barreis' at the University of Wisconsin-Madison, and Herbert Wright's collaborative Quaternary program at the University of Minnesota. Specialty programs also subsequently developed at the University of Toronto, where Howard Savage established a program in zooarchaeology and Gary Crawford and Jock McAndrews instituted paleobotanical studies. Finally, the magnitude of environmental change during the late Pleistocene and early Holocene required many individual researchers to become versed in paleoecology in order to improve their chances of locating sites and to properly understand the adaptations of the earliest inhabitants of North America. In so doing, many established interactive relationships with researchers in related fields and with multi-disciplinary organizations such as the Quaternary Sciences Institute at the University of Waterloo.

In recent years, the popularity of ecological archaeology has declined along with that of processual archaeology, yet it continues to have relevance because the material underpinnings of human society remain a fundamental concern of archaeological inquiry (cf. Legge and Rowley-Conwy 1988). This fact has been underscored by proponents such as Karl Butzer (1982) and Michael Jochim (1981, 1991, 1994), who have attempted to promote ecological archaeology as a discrete approach. Yet, in spite of the efforts of these and other advocates, it seems that the establishment of a paleoenvironmental perspective as a leading research agenda has met with only limited success. To what can this apparent lack of success be attributed? Several potential causes, both individually and collectively, can account for this phenomenon. First, time commitments may be the most significant factor. The returns of a paleoenvironmental approach are long term rather than short term. The reconstruction of paleoenvironments at the necessary scale and resolution, and concurrent investigation of the archaeological record at a regional level, is a daunting task. To be properly applied it requires considerable commitments, sometimes measured in decades, to properly marshal and associate data appropriate to an understanding of changing human/environment relationships at a refined scale.

Second, much of the necessary environmental data are scarce, unavailable, or are the purview of other specialty disciplines. This fact alone requires either effective inter- and multi-disciplinary research, which often is difficult to organize, manage and fund. Alternatively, one needs to train archaeologists as specialty producers, rather than consumers; a time-intensive task but one to which several institutions are committed. Even if appropriate data are available, and this is increasingly becoming the case, it may be at an inappropriate scale and resolution. This issue is addressed elsewhere in this presentation.

Finally, for want of another term, there is the "glitz" factor. Investigation of the post-glacial era is often not attractive to the sister disciplines with which we need to interact. It is easier to sell short-term payoff than long-term agendas to funding agencies. Site excavation and the display of artifacts has better public relations value than refining the scale of soils data, or redefining the evolution of a fluvial system, or taking multiple wetland cores to explore vegetation change.

To be sure, this synopsis omits significant contributions in ecological/environmental archaeology within the region. It is nonetheless true, however, that here as elsewhere such a perspective does not enjoy the same popularity as other research agendas. In fact, it is our opinion that paleoenvironmental approaches are most often applied *ex post facto;* to explain the distribution of sites discovered during survey on the landscape, to interpret individual site locations, or to address the context of economic or time specific assemblages. Primary goals still appear to be directed at the essentials of assemblage description, classification, and refinement of culture histories.

A noteworthy exception to this trend is the paleoenvironmental research involved in archaeological site potential modelling as undertaken for certain large-scale heritage planning initiatives (cf. MacDonald and Pihl 1994). Yet such studies are rare, and unless more archaeologists are willing to commit effort to *la longue durée*, ecological and environmental approaches will continue to take a back seat to more traditional archaeological enterprises.

Implications of a Paleoenvironmental Approach in Archaeology

For fear of being accused of beating a dead horse on this issue, since both of us have already railed on this subject in print (Lovis et al. 1994; MacDonald and Pihl 1994), we both believe that it remains appropriate to articulate the rhetoric in favour of environmentally based research in Great Lakes archaeology. Reconstruction of paleoenvironments at an appropriate scale and resolution allows us to investigate two issues which we believe are central to our archaeological endeavour. The first of these is largely prerequisite to the second; understanding the long-term regional processes responsible for the formation of the archaeological record as it currently remains for us to recover. The second relates to understanding the relationships between what we recover archaeologically, and the dynamic human behaviours of decision making and response strategies that allow us to understand the interactions between group adaptation and changing context.

We are certain most archaeologists will agree that the first issue is self-evident. The archaeological record as it remains for us to recover may not necessarily be representative of the population of sites present at any particular period of past time; we work with a sample that has been selected by regional taphonomic processes (Lovis and O'Shea 1994). Furthermore, even given this selective subset of remaining sites, many may not be either visible or recoverable due to post-depositional taphonomic events. We argue here that it is not possible to properly recover nor interpret the archaeological record on any scale without a clear understanding of regional processes responsible for modification of site populations (Lovis et al. 1994; Monaghan and Hayes 1997). A brief example might serve to clarify this issue.

Post-glacial events in the Great Lakes drainage basin during the period ca 9500 B.P. are familiar to the majority of Great Lakes archaeologists. This is a period of extreme water level recession across all of the lake basins, and collectively it is recognized that some component of the archaeological record is not present due to the fact that it lies beneath modern water planes. However, there are also additional consequences of this recession. These include, for example, those related to increased downcutting of drainages grading to lower elevations, which potentially impact on the preservation of floodplain-situated sites and may have differentially preserved sites in certain areas while destroying others. The alteration of the spatial locations of significant habitats such as wetlands, which may have been key to local economies is also a significant matter of concern. As the post-glacial lake level histories also reveal, this regressional stage was followed by water levels often above the modern one, posing additional questions central to interpretation and exploration of the record. Did transgression affect site preservation and if so how? If local drainages were grading to higher lake elevations, did this result in increased and perhaps differential alluviation resulting in the mantling of preserved sites with sediment, thereby making them either invisible, or visible only through certain exploratory techniques? In other words, how does the application of field method relate to regional formation processes and the exploration of the archaeological record?

With the rise of zooarchaeology and paleoethnobotany as established archaeological specialties, archaeologists are confronted with other interpretive issues. If human groups are in fact selecting a suite of resources from the environment, then the animal and plant assemblages recovered archaeologically cannot be assumed to be representative of environment. In fact, we all know this. However, what we do not know is often more important than what we know, and what we do not know may only be learned through study of data at a resolution to which we do not have access. If a large proportion of botanical remains are certain varieties of nuts, for example, is this a consequence of overall availability in the local environment, or is it due to the targeting of specific and restricted niches? Just as we want to know the position, availability, and abundance of flint or chert to understand extraction, interaction and exchange through time, we should want to know the position, availability and abundance of specific biotic resource items over time to assess changes in economic decision making and consequent social processes.

The recognition that certain kinds of data are either unavailable, or are not sufficiently refined to allow application to significant questions raises one of the more prevalent dilemmas in paleoecological applications to archaeology: the disparity in scales of interest between related disciplines and our requirements (cf. Karrow 1994:221). While not uniformly true, it can be reasonably argued that archaeologists have traditionally been consumers rather than producers of paleoenvironmental data. As consumers we complain about the refinement of the product we are acquiring from purveyors. When forced to produce our own commodities, we find out how difficult it is to produce a high quality product. Yet this is precisely the solution to our dilemma. We need to define our own scales of inquiry, and our own conceptions of appropriate data resolution as we address specific behavioural question(s), rather than remain largely reliant on other disciplines to fulfil our data requirements (Jochim 1994). This does not necessarily mean that archaeology should abandon an interdisciplinary approach, since by doing so we would risk reinventing the wheel. Rather, we should recognize when interdisciplinary endeavours are appropriate, and when they are not.

In fact, the very disciplines from which we often seek assistance contend with many of the same problems that we ourselves face. Paleoecology attempts to use physical evidence to construct meaningful models which describe past environments and their ecological processes. Two of the most fundamental problems in paleoecological research are the related issues of scale and resolution. Scale refers to the proportion that a model bears to the thing that it represents. On maps, which are a type of model frequently used in paleoecology, this proportion is often expressed as a ratio, for example the 1:50,000 scale of Canadian topographic maps. It is easy to forget that at this scale, a feature represented on the map will be 50,000 times smaller than it is in reality, notwithstanding conventional symbols which may not strictly conform to scale. For a large feature, for example Lake Huron, this may not pose many problems. However, for a small feature, say a kettle pond, it may literally disappear at this scale, due to the technical limitations of map production. Alternatively, small features may experience relatively greater spatial displacement from their true positions relative to other features due to the inherent distortion of maps. These are issues of resolution, or the ability to accurately render the significant components of that which is modelled. Considerations of scale and resolution in paleoecological research revolve around the questions of what are the significant components of the environment being modelled and, therefore, what is the appropriate analytical scale to employ in order to be able to resolve these components adequately?

Paleoenvironmental Framework for the Great Lakes Drainage Basin

Introduction

We now move to our assigned task, a review of changing Great Lakes paleoenvironments. In this attempt to provide the skeletal anatomy for subsequent discussions in the session we were forced to make significant decisions of inclusion and omission, and to grapple with issues of scale and resolution, as discussed above. Our approach was predicated on the fact that, of the suite of pertinent environmental variables affecting human adaptations in the region, we could not possibly perform a refined review of each across the entire drainage basin, particularly given the range of interpretive perspectives present for each. Rather, it was clear that we would need to distill our discussion down to a rather general level, presenting what we felt were the significant variations and the ones upon which most practitioners could agree. As such, what follows addresses macroscale issues, rather than those at the mesoscale or microscale. As indicated below, certain advantages accrue from such an approach.

Of the group of variables addressed here, a notable omission is that of reconstructed fauna, or paleozoology. Although made with some hesitancy, this decision involved the careful consideration of several issues which together conspire to make the reconstruction of past zoological communities one of the most difficult tasks facing paleoecologists. First are the related issues of faunal preservation, site formation, and taphonomy. In the case of paleontological samples, predator food preferences and differential digestion are among the factors which tend to skew the initial assemblage, while fluvial transport and other site formation processes may further alter the sample (Semken 1983:184). In the case of archaeological samples, cultural decisions ranging from prey preferences and butchering practices to cooking techniques and refuse disposal all contribute to the composition of the faunal assemblage. Taphonomic processes, which can differentially affect faunal remains of dissimilar size, density, and structure, affect both paleontological and archaeological faunal assemblages. Second there is the lack of any primary interest in Holocene studies, beyond that of the late glacial period, among vertebrate paleontologists, who view the Holocene as a period of essentially modern biotic-community structure, with an "impoverished residuum of late-Pleistocene fauna" and changes in climatic regimes that merely adjust existing ecotones (Semken 1983:202). As a result, Holocene faunal data have been derived primarily from archaeological sites (cf. Karrow 1994:232-233; Semken 1983:182). Accordingly, zooarchaeologists have had to set their own research agendas and have contributed substantially in this arena, with faunal analysis becoming a routine part of almost all site-level investigations. Most often these zooarchaeological data are used to infer seasonality, human predation patterns, and other cultural manifestations of faunal resource exploitation. Occasionally these data are also used to discuss the contemporaneous local biotic landscape as inferred from animal habitat preferences and, more rarely, to document local environmental change over time. While several recent graduate theses have demonstrated the potential to relate human economic strategies to macro-regional environments (cf. Molnar 1997; Needs-Howarth 1999; Smith 1996), a significant void remains in the synthesis of regional or macro-regional zooarchaeological and paleontological data. Among the significant issues to be broached by such syntheses are the twin conundra of being reliant on the flimsy extended logic of habitat reconstructions based on paleovegetation, geological, and climatic studies, and consequent species-level population inferences based on contemporary wildlife ecology. While a few pioneering syntheses have been undertaken (e.g., Cleland 1966; McAndrews and Jackson 1988; Semken 1983) and the development of broad-based data sets such as the FAUNMAP project (Graham et al. 1994) promise to facilitate regional synthesis, the current void precludes a meaningful summary at the scope of this paper.

Finally, this paper—particularly the associated figures—is cast against an essentially modern backdrop, and is devoid of specifics. For example, we have avoided trying to reconstruct specific temperature regimes, or to apply specifics of pro- and post-glacial lake elevations. In our opinion, this macroscale of information is best employed for purposes of understanding magnitude and rate of change at a general level, rather than quibbling over nuances of specific interpretation.

Deglaciation of the Great Lakes

The Wisconsinan glaciation of the Great Lakes advanced into the region from the north and northeast. As the Laurentide ice sheet advanced into the Great Lakes region, lobes of ice occupied existing topographical lows in the landscape, in particular the hypothesized preglacial drainageways that approximately correspond to the positions of the current five lakes. It is argued that ice thickness, as well as the rate of advance, produced greater erosional activity in these drainageways, thereby creating the modern lake basins. Eight major and minor lobes eventually expanded out of these basins (Leverett and Taylor 1915), merging and flowing southward to latitudes as far south as 39 degrees north across Ohio, Indiana, and Illinois, while leaving large areas of Wisconsin ice free (Figure 11.1a) (Barnett 1992:1029; Karrow 1989:340).

Deglaciation of the region progressed in approximately reverse order to its advance, on a lobate basis, and punctuated by frontal oscillations. Given that the glacial retreats were actually a pulsating phenomenon, traceable morainic features remain only where the ice margins stabilized for some time. Ice mass mobility likewise was variable on an east to west basis, making blanket statements about the deglaciation of the Great Lakes difficult at best.

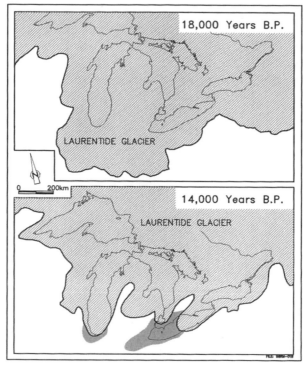

Figure 11.1: Great Lakes deglaciation at (a) 18000 B.P. and (b) 14000 B.P.

It appears that the primary recession with which we need to initially concern ourselves occurred ca 14000 B.P., primarily affecting the lobes in the Michigan, Saginaw and Erie basins (Figure 11.1b). This recessional event resulted in meltwater drainage primarily to the south, along multiple pathways, but ponded across the glacial fronts in varying configurations, at times separate and sometimes merged at elevations between 195 m and 245 m (Farrand et al. 1969; Hansel et al. 1985). Readvance of the ice to a maximum position ca 13000 B.P. likewise created ponded waterbodies frontal to the Michigan, Saginaw and Erie lobes (Figure 11.2a) (Hansel et al. 1985). Most of southern lower Michigan was free of ice and water at this time, as was most of southern and western Wisconsin; southern Ontario and the Ontario basin were still in the clutches of glacial ice.

While the ice mass continued to retreat northward, it was punctuated by short readvances. Among the more significant of these occurred ca 11800 B.P., when areas as far south as 44 degrees north latitude were re-occupied (Figure 11.2b).

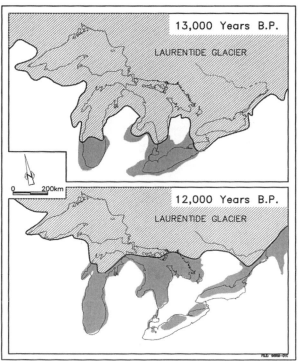

Figure 11.2: Great Lakes deglaciation at (a) 13000 B.P. and (b) 12000 B.P.

During the subsequent recessional period, however, much of southern Ontario became ice free, as did most of Michigan's lower peninsula. The early basins of Lake Erie, Lake Ontario, and Lake Michigan became recognizable, and parts of the northern Huron basin and Georgian Bay were filled with pro-glacial meltwater lakes. The western end of Lake Superior likewise became ice free by ca 11000 B.P., becoming a meltwater lake (Figure 11.3a) (Fenton et al. 1983). Minor readvances followed this period (Figure 11.3b), in particular one (ca 9900 B.P.) which actually re-occupied parts of Michigan's upper peninsula (Drexler et al. 1983; Clayton 1983).

Even as late as 9500 B.P., the effects of deglaciation were being felt in the basins of the Great Lakes (Drexler et al. 1983). Freeing of the northern outlets drained much of the Michigan and Huron basins (Figure 11.4), and the eastern outlets of glacial Lake Agassiz united the Agassiz and Superior basins.

It should be noted that much of this deglacial history is directly associated with the pro-glacial and post-glacial lake stages in the Great Lakes discussed in the following section. In addition, we have not even begun to address ongoing effects of post-glacial phenomenon such as isostatic rebound on these various processes.

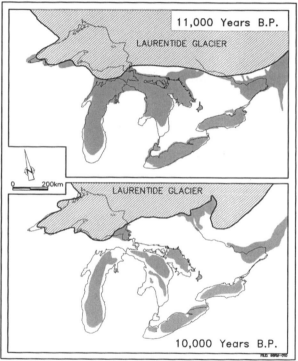

Figure 11.3: Great lakes deglaciation at (a) 11000 B.P. and (b) 10000 B.P.

Pro- and Post-Glacial Lake Levels of the Great Lakes

Among the more overt of the paleoecological changes evident in the Great Lakes region is the long-term formation of the five modern Great Lakes subsequent to the retreat of the Laurentide ice sheet and their stabilization at present elevations. Given the magnitude of these changes, and their coupling with other transformations of the ecosystem, there is no doubt that sequences of pro- and post-glacial lake-level change had substantial though varying impacts on the aboriginal populations of the Great Lakes. Likewise, it is not surprising that most Great Lakes archaeologists are attuned to at least the macro-scale events in their regions of specialization. The present discussion of these changes is directed at the specific topic of the relationships of past lake elevations to modern basin water planes as a means of assessing the relative impact of change on past systems. This in turn relates directly to issues of rate and duration of change. The intent here is not to address specific mechanisms responsible for the raising or lowering of lake elevations, nor to provide a compendium of lake stage names.

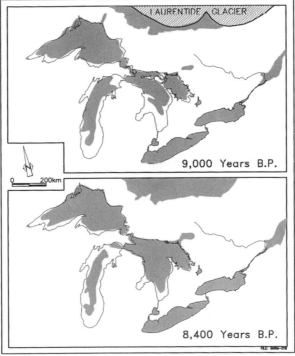

Figure 11.4: Great Lakes deglaciation at (a) 9000 B.P. and (b) 8400 B.P.

Starting with the most upstream of the Great Lakes, the Superior basin (Farrand and Drexler 1985) is both the deepest and the largest of the Great Lakes, and was the last of the basins to become free of glacial ice. Synchronous with deglaciation at about 12000 B.P. the Superior basin saw water ponded more than 100m above present levels along the glacial front (Figure 11.5). It then took about a millennium for outlet opening and erosion to drop basin water planes to about 45m below current levels. Isostatic rebound once again raised northern outlets more than 100m above present after this low stage, and subsequent outlet erosion largely accounts for substantial drops in elevation to about 50m below present altitude. Continuing rebound raised outlets with a commensurate slow and steady rise to elevations less than 15m above present by 5000 B.P. This post-glacial high water stand was relatively stable, undergoing slow regression for 3,000 years to a level below that at present, at which point rebound of the primary outlet accounts for rises to modern elevation.

The Huron (Eschman and Karrow 1985) and Michigan (Hansel et al. 1985; Larsen 1987) basins, apologetically combined here for the sake of brevity (Figure 11.5), experienced similar trends; early immediate deglacial highs at least 50m above present as a consequence of outflow ponding along glacial fronts, with at times abrupt changes in elevation as outlets shifted or eroded between 14500 and 11000 B.P. This was followed by a substantial drop in basin water planes to at least 100m below present, with short stabilizations periodically evident in the decline. As a consequence of changes in outlets, this extreme low was followed by a gradual rise to elevations less than five metres above present by 4500 B.P., with gradual drops to modern elevations over the next 2,000 years (Eschman and Karrow 1985; Hansel et al. 1985).

Lake Erie is the shallowest of the Great Lakes, and was deglaciated earliest (Coakley and Lewis 1985). While experiencing a similar series of early pro-glacial fluctuations and stabilizations, and an extreme low stage by ca 11500 B.P., Erie displays a relatively gradual rise to elevations slightly above modern by 5000 B.P. (Figure 11.5) (Barnett 1985; Calkin and Feenstra 1985; Coakley and Lewis 1985; Pengelly et al. 1997).

Deglaciation in the Ontario basin initially produced a series of localized, high-level, pro-glacial lakes along the ice front. By around 12500 B.P., continuing retreat of the ice had initiated the development of an extensive pro-glacial lake throughout the basin at elevations of between 45 and 145 m above modern levels. Drainage at this time was southeasterly through the Mohawk Valley. By around 11400 B.P., continuing ice recession had uncovered lower outlets in the upper St. Lawrence valley, initiating an extreme low-water phase up to 100m below modern levels. Isostatic rebound of these lower outlets subsequently raised water levels, although diversion of upper Great Lakes drainage to the Ottawa River at around 10500 B.P. significantly reduced water input into the Ontario basin. Between ca 5000 and 4000 B.P., the return of upper Great Lakes drainage through lakes Erie and Ontario overwhelmed the outlet channels, resulting in water elevations a few metres above modern levels. Within a few centuries, the outlets had adjusted to the new outflow, thereby lowering Lake Ontario to a few metres below modern levels. Continuing isostatic rebound of the outlets subsequently raised Lake Ontario to its present level (Anderson and Lewis 1985; Muller and Prest 1985).

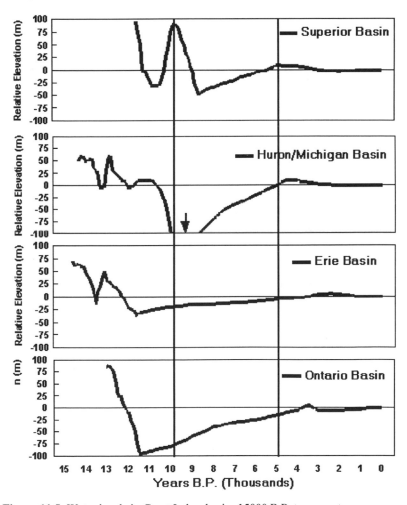

Figure 11.5: Water levels in Great Lakes basin: 15000 B.P. to present.

Of particular importance to this discussion is recognition that the events described are at the coarsest scale and resolution, what Butzer calls the macroscale. Recent research (e.g., Larsen 1985; Pengelly et al. 1997), has attempted to refine this to the so-called mesoscale of resolution, on the order of hundreds of years rather than thousands. These multiple levels of periodicity, and their interactions, have significance as the scale of resolution necessary to address specific problems changes.

Paleoclimate

Reconstruction of Great Lakes paleoclimate over the period since the glacial maximum about 18,000 years ago has largely been accomplished through the interpretation and comparison of pollen spectra and other fossil-plant assemblages recovered across the region. This approach is founded on the assumptions that climate is the primary ecological control agent at the sub-continental scale, that correlations between modern vegetation and climatic regimes can be used as analogues when drawing paleoclimatic inferences from fossil paleovegetation, and that inferred climatic changes tended to occur relatively quickly in response to the movement of major frontal zones or predominant air masses (Bryson and Wendland 1967; Delcourt and Delcourt 1987:100-101). In spite of a considerable body of literature which has employed and tested this approach, certain reservations persist regarding the reliability of its assumptions, partly because independent paleoclimatic data have been lacking (Delcourt and Delcourt 1987:100-101; cf. Bryson 1985). Gradually, however, the potential circularity of drawing inferences about paleovegetation, paleoclimate, and their inter-relationships from pollen data is being broken as new sources of information are brought to bear on this issue, including paleoclimatic records from marine foraminiferal assemblages (Delcourt and Delcourt 1984), paleoentomological data (Edwards et al. 1985), and isotopic records from a variety of materials (e.g., Edwards and Buhay 1994). Equally important are international interdisciplinary projects such as CLIMAP (CLIMAP 1981) and COHMAP (Webb 1985) which compile a broad range of data to formulate and test global paleoclimate simulation models.

Together, these various lines of evidence can be used to compile a consistent synoptic model of Great Lakes paleoclimate since deglaciation. As today, the paleoclimate of eastern North America is considered to have been determined by the interaction of three major air masses: cold, dry air which flows southward from the Arctic; warm, moist air which flows northward from the tropics; and mild, dry air from the Pacific which flows eastward between the other two airstreams. Interaction of these air masses occurs along frontal zones which tend to move latitudinally and change character according to season. The nature of the interaction, and hence the character of the frontal zone, is related to the predominant airflow. This may be either zonal, when moving west to east, or meridional, when looping northward and southward.

At the height of the last glaciation around 18000 B.P., the predominant climatic pattern is thought to have been a zonal flow of the prevailing westerlies across the mid-latitudes of North America. With the flow of Arctic air deflected by the Laurentide ice sheet, the Pacific and tropical air masses met along a frontal zone anchored between about 33 and 34 degrees north latitude. Between 17000 and 16000 B.P., this frontal zone began to widen as a result of a northward expansion of the tropical air mass, which increasingly began to affect the southern margin of the continental glacier. The tropical air mass continued to expand northward as the Great Lakes region underwent deglaciation, and by 10000 B.P., the Arctic air mass was again sweeping across the deglaciated area, between about 40 and 50 degrees north latitude, during the winter. With the tropical air mass pressing northward as far as 40 degrees north latitude in summer, the dominance of the Pacific air mass was restricted to the western portion of the continental interior. In addition, the frontal zone widened and moved northward to the edge of the Great Lakes basin, between 39 and 41 degrees north, as meridional atmospheric circulation replaced the predominantly zonal patterns of the preceding millennia. By around 6000 B.P., the remnants of the Laurentide ice sheet had ceased to affect the position of major air masses or frontal zones. The area north of 55 degrees north was dominated year-round by the Arctic air mass, while the frontal zone between the Arctic and tropical air masses spanned six degrees of latitude, encompassing the northern two-thirds of the Great Lakes region. Zonal flow strengthened at this time, and the wedge-shaped zone of Pacific air expanded northward and eastward across the mid-continent, reaching its maximum extent between about 7000 and 5000 B.P., when it encompassed the southern third of the Great Lakes region. Regional temperatures, which had been rising since the end of the glacial maximum, peaked at this time. Over the last 4000 years of the late Holocene, meridional flow has returned and intensified, such that the frontal zone now encompasses nearly all of the Great Lakes region. In addition, the tropical air mass has re-expanded northwestward, once again reducing the area influenced by the Pacific air mass. Nevertheless, the

Pacific air mass continues to play a dominant role in the southern and western portions of the Great Lakes region and the Midwest (Delcourt and Delcourt 1987:101-105; cf. Bryson and Wendland 1967; Bryson and Hare 1974; Bryson and Padoch 1981; Lamb 1982; Webb 1985).

Resolution of short-term climatic oscillations within the Holocene has proven to be more challenging than the interpretation of long-term trends when using vegetation analogues because short-term changes in pollen spectra are increasingly sensitive to regional and local conditions. While climate may still be an important agent of change, the sensitivity of various tree taxa to small-scale climatic change varies and may be expressed differently in the pollen record due to lags in range expansion or contraction. Indeed, short-term climatic events, which may have significant repercussions for human populations and their biotic resources, may not produce a signature in the pollen spectrum (Bryson 1985; Davis and Botkin 1985; Ritchie 1986). Nevertheless, other techniques for interpreting paleoclimate, such as isotope studies and tree-ring analysis, are offering promising results. To date, the best documented short-term climatic episode in the Great Lakes region is the Little Ice Age, a northern hemisphere cooling trend which occurred between about 400 and 100 B.P. (Bernabo 1981; Buhay and Edwards 1995; Campbell and McAndrews 1991, 1993; Edwards and Buhay 1994; Grove 1988; Swain 1978).

Paleovegetation

Under conditions of relative equilibrium, major vegetation communities assume a notably latitudinal orientation (e.g., McAndrews 1981), and paleovegetation reconstruction suggests that such a zonation existed at the height of the last glaciation around 18000 B.P. (Delcourt and Delcourt 1987:95). A discontinuous zone of tundra appears to have bordered the Laurentide Ice Sheet, particularly within re-entrants bordered by glacial ice. Tundra also extended down the crest of the Appalachian Mountains to at least 37 degrees north latitude. This narrow zone was intermittently broken by boreal forest which grew up to the ice margin. The boreal forest zone extended between 34 and 41 degrees north. The northern third of this zone, as well as the continental interior west of 95 degrees west longitude and the central Atlantic Coastal Plain, were relatively open, while the remainder was primarily closed-canopy forest. A narrow ecotone between 33 and 34 degrees north latitude marked the transition to northern hardwood forest, with temperate deciduous forest finding refuge on mesic sites among the xeric habitat preferred by the warm-temperate southeastern evergreen forest (Delcourt and Delcourt 1987:95-96).

A climatic warming trend, which began after about 17000 B.P., initiated a period of significant environmental change in regional biotic communities which lasted until at least 4000 B.P. During such periods, forest communities are in disequilibrium and their adaptive responses, as indicated by population shifts in location and relative dominance, are individualistic (Davis 1986; Delcourt and Delcourt 1987:293). Nevertheless, certain modal responses, or migration strategies, can be inferred from dominance data derived from pollen assemblages, and these are analogous to the roles of the various taxa in forest succession. At one end of the spectrum are short-lived, early successional taxa which are shade intolerant but which can germinate and grow in nutrient-poor soils. These taxa migrate in a wave-like fashion, thriving in one location for a few generations before giving way to competition from other species. At the other end of the spectrum are long-lived, late-successional taxa which are shade tolerant, prefer nutrient-rich soils, invest more energy in biomass, produce fewer but larger seeds with longer viability, and which slowly colonize and then maintain populations at or near a climax state. Other migration strategies include fugitive migration, whereby taxa survive in small, localized pockets over a large area by chancing into marginal habitats or temporary openings, and stress tactics, whereby taxa survive by exhibiting different growth behaviours in different parts of their ranges (Delcourt and Delcourt 1987:292-330; cf. Davis 1986; Webb 1986). The implication of these various successional and migrational strategies for paleoecology is that the shifts in the ranges of arboreal taxa which occurred after 17000 B.P. were not a step-wise northward progression of extant forest communities. Rather, they were a complex interplay of competing taxa colonizing newly opened landscapes to the north while local populations persisted in the face of climatic change and an influx of other taxa expanding their ranges from the south (Figures 11.6 & 11.7). This interaction was most evident in the ecotones between major forest communities, which tended to broaden through this period of change.

As deglaciation got underway, newly deglaciated terrain was colonized by tundra. By 14000 B.P., boreal forest dominated by spruce had expanded northward, especially into central Wisconsin, northwestern Iowa, eastern Ohio, and southwestern Pennsylvania. As this expansion progressed, other boreal and early successional taxa began to compete with spruce for local dominance, including pine, fir, hemlock, poplar, and ash (Figure 11.6). Retreat of the boreal forest zone along its southern margin was matched by northward expansion of the mixed conifer-northern hardwood forest ecotone. The temperate deciduous forest remained relatively stationary within its mosaic of refugia throughout the Gulf and southern Atlantic Coastal Plains (Delcourt and Delcourt 1987).

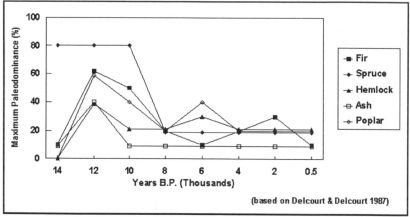

Figure 11.6: Maximum paleodominance of Great Lakes trees: Early successional taxa.

At 10000 B.P., deglaciation of the Great Lakes region was nearly complete. Discontinuous patches of tundra still trailed the retreating ice margin in northern Ontario, but boreal forest prevailed in the Great Lakes area. Spruce and pine continued to express high regional dominance, while the local dominance of early successional taxa declined. Oak established itself throughout the region, becoming locally dominant in the southern Great Lakes, while elm established local dominance in the southwestern area. With continued climatic warming, the boreal forest zone was squeezed between the Laurentide ice sheet to the north and the expanding zone of northern hardwood forest to the south, such that between 14000 and 10000 B.P., its southern margin shifted northward from about 35 degrees north latitude to the southern edge of the Great Lakes basin at about 40 degrees north. In contrast, the northern hardwood forest zone continued to broaden as it moved northward, and by 10000 B.P., it was a band two to three degrees of latitude in width located along the southern edge of the Great Lakes region. In the wake of the northward migrating northern hardwood forest zone, the deciduous taxa asserted dominance as forest succession developed, and by 10000 B.P., a broad zone of deciduous forest had become established between about 34 and 40 degrees north (Delcourt and Delcourt 1987:97-98).

By around 6000 B.P., with continued climatic warming, the boreal forest had expanded well north of the Great Lakes region, while retreating along its southern margin to a position slightly north of its current limit. The northern half of the Great Lakes region was occupied by the northern hardwood forest zone, which by this time had expanded in width to about six degrees of latitude. Spruce was replaced by pine as the principal dominant taxon in this area, while oak was the lead dominant in the south (Figure 11.7). Beech and especially maple also established their prominence at this time, and poplar and hemlock regained local dominance as the climatic warming peaked. The deciduous forest zone expanded northward into southern Minnesota, central Wisconsin, and Michigan, although it retreated to the southwest of the Great Lakes as prairie expanded along the main track of dry Pacific air. Savanna developed in the ecotone between the prairie and the closed deciduous forest (Delcourt and Delcourt 1987:98; Webb 1985).

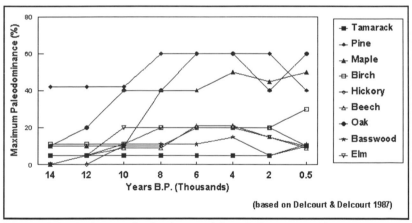

Figure 11.7: Maximum paleodominance of Great Lakes trees: Mid- to late-successional taxa.

After 4000 B.P., with slight climatic cooling, the southern margin of the boreal forest expanded southward in the Great Lakes region while the northern hardwood forest zone was displaced southward by approximately one degree of latitude. This, in turn, displaced the northern margin of the deciduous forest zone. Pine and oak continued to dominate the northern and southern halves of the region, respectively, although around 2000

B.P. oak declined somewhat in its area of highest dominance in the southwest, and pine has experienced similar minor declines since then. Maple continued to grow in prominence while beech waned slightly. The Midwestern prairie retreated somewhat as deciduous forest readvanced, although a significant prairie outlier remained across central Illinois. In Minnesota and Wisconsin, the southwesterly displacement of prairie was about 100km, while in the Prairie Peninsula of Iowa and Illinois, the westward shift was up to 400km (Delcourt and Delcourt 1987:98-99).

Conclusions and Implications for Great Lakes Research

In summary, we have attempted to present an argument favouring an ecological approach to archaeology and to demonstrate its relevance to Great Lakes research at a variety of different scales. We have also highlighted some of the more significant issues and logistical problems facing implementation of such an approach. Our preferred outcome is to promote a dialogue which catalyzes the development of regionally based paleoecological research agendas which address both the rethinking of established research problems, as well as the operational means of achieving these objectives. How then, does our previous discussion contribute to this goal?

The evolutionary ecology of the Great Lakes region since deglaciation, regardless of the specific point in time at which that occurs on a subregional basis, is a dynamic and complex interplay of several interrelated variables which have varying temporal, spatial, and scalar primacy in their potential effects on human adaptation. Clearly, at a macroscale perspective, deglaciation is a significant event for human adaptation, potentially allowing movement into newly opened biomes undergoing early succession (cf. Brown and Cleland 1968). This, of course, presupposes that such biomes were desirable to early human populations in the region (cf. Cleland et. al. 1998 on this issue). In fact, it is not simply deglaciation that opens new biomes, but also the dynamics of pro- and post-glacial lake events during the period from about 14000 to 10000 B.P, when ponded meltwater lakes at the glacial fronts undergo massive and relatively rapid elevational regression on the order of hundreds of metres. While there is a south to north time transgressive component to this process, the cumulative results for the southern Great Lakes is tremendous expansion of available land mass for occupation. Water level recessions result in significantly smaller waterbodies in the deepest parts of the lower Great Lakes, which undoubtedly reduced the moderating effect that such water bodies may have had on regional micro-climates. While the specifics of both climatic and vegetational change for this period have yet to be clearly resolved, the northern margin of the boreal forest moved northward on the order of five degrees latitude and the southern margin retreated on the order of 10 degrees of latitude, suggesting significant biotic change within this zone. Thus, there are two components to this issue. On one hand, the expansion of boreal forest habitat in the Great Lakes region was of potential significance to human populations at this time. At the same time, the overall contraction of this biome at a continental scale may also have had an impact on the spatial distribution of different hunter-gatherer adaptive strategies.

The period from ca 10000 to 4500 B.P. has attracted substantial attention from archaeologists because of the dynamics associated with the refilling of the Great Lakes basins, resulting in water levels higher than present, and therefore creating a visible archaeological record at the terminal stage of this long-term event. The refilling of the basins was not as rapid as their draining to extreme low water stages. In fact, the overall trend may only have been perceptible to human populations at a generational or multi-generational scale, and varied from basin to basin. The long-term responses to such change in the Erie basin, for example, were probably much less noticeable than similar responses in the Michigan/Huron basins. The long-term effect of such changes, however, could have dramatic consequences for human populations. The massive reduction in biome size resulting from rises of lake elevation may have resulted in reduced carrying capacity, although this effect may well have been offset by the introduction of more productive vegetation communities. Secondly, for many subregions of the Great Lakes, substantial reductions in land area would have resulted in increases in population densities and increased competition for resources. Some resources, for example certain chert sources, may have been reduced or rendered inaccessible by rising waters (e.g., MacDonald and Cooper 1997). In our opinion, questions about the social responses to such change should dominate the archaeological agenda.

Climatically, the general warming and drying trends dominate this interval. Synchronous with this trend is substantial alteration of the forest compositions of the region, including retreat of the boreal forest to the northernmost margins of the Great Lakes, the northward movement of mixed forest which eventually dominated the northern half of the Great Lakes region and finally, the establishment of deciduous forest as the dominant community in the southern half of the Great Lakes region.

These time-transgressive shifts in biome composition, in concert with the changes in land area and relative carrying capacity noted earlier, may well have resulted in substantial alterations in the social and mobility components of human adaptations in the region. Isolating the specifics of such adaptive transformation would appear to be an important arena for archaeological inquiry, despite the difficulties associated with an only partially recoverable archaeological record.

After about 4500 B.P., there is a decided settling down in the degree of environmental change at the macro level. Water planes in the Great Lakes basins undergo relatively small and gradual regressions toward modern levels, and a slight climatic cooling trend is reflected in proportionally slight southward migrations in the ecotones between the boreal, northern hardwood, and deciduous forest zones. At the macro level, the highlight in human ecology through this period is the development and adoption of food production through horticulture. Thus, more restricted patterns of mobility, i.e., greater "sedentism", coupled with the use of primary and immobile resources with a narrow range of environmental requirements, results in a shift of the scale necessary to understand the human/environment interaction. With this shift, the relevant ecological variables likewise shift focus, and ecological archaeology has tended to dwell more regularly on the meso- and micro-scales of investigation. Coincidentally, it is generally agreed that, for a variety of reasons, the current resolution of culture history and change is highest for this later period. Unfortunately, the current resolution of paleoecological developments is not on a par with the concerns of archaeologists, particularly with respect to pertinent variables. Greater resolution and more refined scale for variables such as microclimate and paleovegetation would greatly assist us in understanding strategies for food production. For example, small and short-term variations in temperature or precipitation do not result in major and short-term consequences in mature forest communities, whereas similar variations can have immediate and substantial effects on crop production. Thus, the scale at which one requires data for hunter/gatherer issues is quite different than that necessary for the study of horticulturalists or agriculturalists, and the relative adaptive risks associated with such changes may vary considerably.

Ecological archaeology has a continuing and important role to play in Great Lakes research. Refining problems, addressing issues of scale, and understanding the relationship of archaeology to other disciplines continue to provide significant direction for regional research. It now remains to be seen whether that within the context provided here, the taxonomy can indeed be tamed.

Acknowledgements

We wish to thank Ron Williamson for inviting us to contribute this paper to the symposium and for his insightful comments on earlier drafts. We also wish to thank the two anonymous reviewers who thoroughly critiqued our initial submission. Special thanks also go to Andrew Clish for his superb cartographic work, and to Christopher Watts and Caroline Thériault for their cheerful execution of various administrative and production chores on our behalf.

A FLEXIBLE MODEL FOR THE STUDY OF PRECONTACT SOCIAL AND POLITICAL COMPLEXITY IN THE MIDWEST AND GREAT LAKES REGIONS

12

Peter A. Timmins
Department of Anthropology, University of Western Ontario
John Paul Staeck
College of DuPage, Glen Ellyn

In this paper we confront two related problems dealing with the use of archaeological data to characterize past societies. First, we argue that the taxonomy that has been used to organize archaeological data in the Midwest and Great Lakes regions has been inappropriately applied to the task of understanding the social and political organization of precontact societies. Second, we argue that the traditional approach to understanding precontact social complexity inadequately accounts for the processes of cultural development and the variability in complexity observed among past societies.

Taxonomic units such as phases and branches have been commonly used to refer to past social and cultural groups (e.g., Bursey 1997), despite the fact that it has been acknowledged that these archaeological units have little social reality (Willey and Phillips 1958:50). Yet we recognize significant advantages to the formation of taxonomic units that correspond closely to past social and political entities in those cases where the archaeological database is sufficiently complete to allow such reconstruction (Mason 1997). In this regard, we follow Deetz (1967:12) in correlating archaeological assemblages from specific components with past groups of people, and recognize the need to contextualize archaeological interpretations through the use of ethnographic and ethnohistorical evidence (Clarke 1968:362).

We argue here for a reorientation of taxonomic efforts toward the definition of spatially and temporally clustered groups of archaeological sites that may represent local populations. We advocate recent archaeological approaches to the analysis of style and salient identity to assess the degree to which local populations formed distinct identities (Sackett 1990; Schortman 1989; Wiessner 1988, 1990), and comparative analyzes to assess the degree to which they shared such identities with adjacent archaeologically delimited populations. It is recognized that defining taxonomic units that are congruent with past socio-political entities is largely a problem for future research and we simply outline an approach to the problem.

Finally, following recent approaches to the study of complexity (Arnold [editor] 1996; O'Shea and Barker 1996) we develop a flexible model based on ranked social and economic variables to assess the cultural complexity of past populations. We apply this model to several local site groups (inferred populations) in southern Ontario and the upper Midwest and discuss the results. In sum, we argue that this approach better accounts for the localized character of most non-state indigenous groups and the continuous, multivariate nature of socio-political development.

Space and Time

Archaeological sites are not randomly dispersed across the land; they tend to cluster in areas of economic, socio-political or cultural significance. Accurately delineating settlement patterns, or the spatial distribution of sites on the land, is a basic analytical step in reconstructing past social and political entities (Renfrew and Bahn 1996:169). In areas where the archaeological record is poorly known, due to inadequate survey, there can be little hope for successful resolution of questions of past social and political organization.

The locality is recognized as a useful spatial concept. Following Willey and Phillips (1958:18), the locality may be defined as "the space that might be occupied by a single community or local group". Obviously, the size of a locality will vary with factors such as the mobility of the group and the nature of its seasonal round. With the massive increase in the number of known archaeological sites in both the Great Lakes and Midwest regions in recent decades, the localized structure of site distributions is more apparent than ever before. Rather than applying broad normative constructs to organize these data, we begin the analysis with the distribution of sites on the land, taking the locality defined by the site cluster as a basic analytical unit.

Controlling the temporal dimension is essential to this approach. Local sequences of components may be determined stratigraphically or by seriation of component assemblages within the same locality, however, each sequence should ideally be anchored with several chronometric dates. The goal of this analysis is not only to identify the sequence of sites in a locality, but also to identify sites that may have been occupied contemporaneously, and to thus identify groups of sites that may relate to local populations.

Once the spatial and temporal dimensions are adequately controlled, we proceed to the question of social identity through the analysis of style. Drawing on the increasing body of method and theory relating style and social identity, we must conduct analyzes to permit the identification of social identity at the community/locality level. Such analyzes also involve comparisons among communities/localities to determine the nature of their relationships.

Style and Salient Identity

Style and how it should be employed has been conceived of variably by different authors and, as a consequence, needs to be summarized in some detail here. In general and as a working definition for the following discussion, style can be conceived of as the expression of individual and/or group preferences in the production or modification of material culture. Stylistic elements exist below, within, and across typological boundaries (Davis 1990; Hodder [editor] 1982, 1990; Plog 1983, 1990; Sackett 1977, 1986a, 1986b, 1990; Wiessner 1983, 1984, 1988, 1990). By this we mean that stylistic variation can exist within a defined artifact type, may help to define an artifact type, or may be unrelated to the definition of a single artifact type and may occur on several different artifact forms.

Drawing on Plog (1983), Sackett (1990), and Wiessner's (1990) overviews, most stylistic analyzes have followed one of two paths, labelled passive and active respectively (Sackett 1990). These two views are not mutually exclusive and, indeed, few recently published stylistic analyzes have focussed exclusively on either one or the other position (e.g., Conkey and Hastorf [editors] 1990; Longacre 1991). These two positions can also be set off against the nature of the message signalled through stylistic expression. Wiessner (1983, 1984, 1988, 1990) has labelled these emblemic and assertive. Both pairs of concepts can be combined to form a fairly complete system through which we can view and interpret stylistic concepts (Staeck 1994).

Of particular importance to this scheme is the perception that the distances between the opposing ends of the axes should be conceived in terms of continua rather than as a series of definable discrete points. Upham (1990) has called this the analog view and opposes it with the digital view (that is, the definition of ideas and concepts as discrete points). Upham's purpose in this distinction is to argue that culture does not operate in terms of discrete points but instead functions according to a continuum that will be perceived differently by different members of the same culture. We find this position to be significant and have tried to incorporate it into our suggestions.

The various approaches to style can be summarized as follows:

1. *Passive*: Style is a natural byproduct of production among people who share common experiences and who interact with one another closely.

2. *Active*: Style is deliberately created by an artisan in order to transmit some sort of message regarding identity and/or belief.

3. *Emblemic*: Style that develops in direct reference to an extant range of discrete cultural symbols that an artisan can use in order to express ideas about identity and beliefs. In North American society the presence of a logo such as those used by BMW or Mercedes on automobiles might be viewed as an emblemic message, e.g., "I can afford to purchase a vehicle from one of these companies". Archaeologically this might be envisioned as the acquisition and display of an artifact form that associates its owner with a specific elite group. The recovery of a Ramey Incised vessel from a specific workshop in the American Bottom in southwestern Wisconsin (Late Woodland individual with a Mississippian vessel) may exemplify this.

4. *Assertive*: Style that develops in a general relation to extant cultural ideas that do not necessarily possess discrete emblems but rather refer to more vaguely defined but nonetheless functional ideas. In North American culture the presence of leather seats in an automobile might be viewed as an assertive message, e.g., "I am well-off and can afford this". The presence in southwestern Wisconsin of a variety of ceramic forms from the American Bottom (but not from any specific workshop) may exemplify this form of style.

A common thread unites each of these views of style. It is accepted that, to some degree at least, style can be perceived to reflect differentiation within and/or between past social groups (Staeck 1994; Schortman 1989). This acceptance is usually subsumed within the heading of "ethnic identity" but this term is frequently poorly defined and often does not follow the criteria established for it by Barth (1969). Further, ethnic differences are perceived to exist between discrete cultural groups when, in fact, considerable variation can exist across a variety of levels within a single socio-political unit (Nagata 1981; Steward 1955). Under the schemata proposed here, style can be seen to reflect salient identities, that is the various roles adopted by individuals within a society at a given moment given the social and natural environments in which they find themselves. Salient identity, then, more appropriately reflects the polythetic nature of identity signalling than do more static terminological sets (Schortman 1989; Wobst 1977; cf. Barth 1969). The overall acceptance of some form of link between style and identity is a key element in developing models designed to identify and explore precontact and early contact social structure.

Background to Complexity Theory

There are numerous models that seek to organize and describe human complexity. Perhaps the best known of these models, such as those by Service (1962, 1971, 1975), Sahlins (1968; with Service 1960), Boserup (1965), and Fried (1967), have sought to define stages of cultural complexity. These have ranged from systems emphasizing bands through states to others emphasizing kinship and social groupings. Despite the continuing popularity of these models in some circles, they have been subject to increasing levels of criticism over the past two decades. Flannery (1972), for example, has argued that while processes of increasing social complexity may be widespread and near universal, the specific causes that prompt these processes to operate vary widely through time and space. Consequently, archaeological manifestations of these processes will also vary widely through time and space.

This has had important ramifications for theoretical models that emphasize the importance of single mechanisms in the development and measurement of complexity, the so-called prime-movers (e.g., population pressure coupled with the control of some combination of vital resources, such as water, food, storage, and coercive force). A host of volumes and articles providing alternative models for dealing with complexity and subsequent critiques have been forthcoming, especially over the past decade (Arnold [editor] 1996; Brumfiel 1992; Drennan 1991; Drennan and Uribe [editors]; Earle [editor] 1991; 1987; Hayden 1995, 1996; Johnson 1982; Price and Feinman [editors] 1995; Upham [editor] 1990 among others). In general these more recent approaches and critiques have emphasized a number of similar concepts. These include, but are not limited to:

1. The recognition that broadly defined etic categories for defining thresholds of cultural integration cannot be used to adequately account for the intricacies of past social systems;

2. A call to account for regional, and hence cultural, variation in how complexity is created, including increased reliance on ethnographic research as the bases through which explanatory models are generated;

3. The abandonment of the concept of egalitarianism as it has been traditionally applied in the anthropological literature;

4. An increasing awareness that there are many *interrelated* paths through which social authority and cultural complexity may be generated;

5. The recognition that there is no universal correlation relating intensification to regional population growth, thus allowing for local developments to arise in seeming contradiction to broader-scale regional trends;

6. The realization that there is no single taxonomy or measure which can account for all possible variations on the theme of increased social complexity or, in short, an acceptance of polythetic set theory as it might be applied to human societies; and

7. The recognition that people may possess material culture typical of multiple archaeological taxonomic groups and use these different material cultures in dynamic social contexts, thus facilitating rapid shifts in salient identity in order to meet the perceived needs generated by the social and natural environments.

Despite such critiques, Earle (1987, 1991) has observed that it is virtually impossible to simply abandon most of the extant taxa within archaeology. At the very least he notes that such taxa, whether for measuring social complexity or labelling perceived groupings of archaeological components (e.g., phases, foci, and branches), provide heuristic mechanisms essential for the discussion of complex ideas (cf. Willey and Phillips 1958).

Given these themes we have opted to follow Upham (1990) and proceed with the task at hand by adopting the notion that societies cannot be codified according to a digital model. Hence, we will attempt to generate an analog organizational scheme that will allow us to compare specific archaeological manifestations without locking these manifestations into arbitrarily defined levels of perceived complexity. It is essential that the reader understand that this model is a tool which is researcher- or research team-specific. Since the system is analog and deals with perceptions of identity and ranking, the system is meant primarily as a tool to organize the analysis of archaeological manifestations. Secondarily, should researchers wish to compare notes, the system does afford them the means through which to discuss what we feel are key factors in addressing issues of socio-political complexity. Researchers should also note that the methodology proposed here allows them to modify the specific variables examined on a project by project basis.

Developing a Model of Cultural Complexity

The need to identify and decouple the variables that contribute to social complexity is recognized in some recent literature (Feinman and Neitzel 1984; Arnold 1996; O'Shea and Barker 1996), although there have been few comprehensive attempts to develop models that allow the independent assessment of a range of variables. O'Shea and Barker, among others, argue for the use of continuous rather than dichotomous (presence/absence) variables, pointing out that the presence or absence of a particular variable can often be ambiguous or distorting (1996:14, 20). For example, it is more informative to ask "to what degree" a variable like subsistence intensification is present, rather than "if" subsistence intensification is present at all (O'Shea and Barker 1996:14). The use of continuous variables to measure indices of complexity thus contributes to the analog nature of the complexity model.

Examination of the literature reveals several social and economic variables that may serve as indices of complexity (Drennan 1996; Hayden 1981, 1995; Price 1981; Price and Brown 1985). They include mode of production, population (or population density), the organization of labour, economic specialization, subsistence intensification and protection from subsistence risk, exchange, conflict, identity signalling, and mortuary differentiation. These variables were selected because their archaeological correlates are relatively robust and can be fairly consistently observed. Many other variables or indices of complexity are possible and may be incorporated into the model as necessary. Different variables may be relevant in different cultural contexts and one of the advantages of the proposed model is its flexibility which allows one to tailor the analytical framework to different situations.

Although viewed as continuous variables, these social and economic dimensions can be treated as ordinal measures in the construction of the complexity model. We devised a method of ranking the evidence for each variable on an ordinal scale between 1 and 5 (where 1 = low complexity and 5 = high complexity). A site data worksheet was developed that listed the complexity variables, the evidence relating to each variable and the values assigned. An average site complexity index was then calculated for each site. Once all sites in a local group are scored in this manner, it is possible to derive an average group complexity index as well. If the average group complexity index is used, it is essential that the groups are comparable and not biased towards any specific site type. Alternatively, it is possible to apply the model to local site groups as a whole (rather than individual sites) depending on the scale of the analysis and the nature of the groups involved (Arnold 1996; Chapman 1996; Price and Brown 1985).

As with most models, the system described here will be most effective when applied to relatively complete archaeological databases where all site types are represented and no single type is grossly over-represented. The nature of archaeological investigation and funding, however, only infrequently affords researchers the opportunity to generate such complete data sets. Nonetheless, contributions may be made with less complete data sets and these contributions may, ultimately, allow archaeologists to better contextualize their findings as their research progresses.

There are obvious issues of consistency of inference and judgement in assigning complexity values. To address these concerns a ranking guideline was developed that indicated values assigned for typical types of archaeological evidence (Table 12.1). Although this guideline helped to make ranking decisions more objective, there were still slight differences between the co-authors in the way that they assigned values, even when using the same data. These differences did not significantly affect the overall site complexity rankings. Nonetheless, we caution that the methodology outlined here is simply a tool for case study analysis and comparison. The average group complexity indices are only general indications of complexity with respect to the variables considered and relative to other sites or groups of sites analyzed as part of the same study. Moreover, it is important to keep in mind that the indices are also researcher, or research team, specific. Hence, they are designed as a tool to facilitate interpretation on a specific rather than discipline-wide scale. The reader will note, however, it is possible for researchers to make comparisons across projects by either working back to the original variables or by agreeing upon a scaling system among themselves.

It is expected that the most important information will lie in the pattern of variation among the economic and social dimensions considered. It is through the detailed examination and comparison of these dimensional data that the unique historical trajectories of different groups may be traced. In this way it is hoped that the model will reveal what

Hayden has termed different "pathways to power" and thus will provide a more accurate view of the development of past societies (Hayden 1995; Feinman 1995).

Application of the Complexity Model

Examples from Southwestern Ontario

Application of this approach to southwestern Ontario is facilitated by the fact that regional archaeological studies have become common over the past three decades, even if our overlying archaeological taxonomies have failed to reflect this change. Intensive archaeological survey, in both academic and CRM contexts, has resulted in the definition of clusters of related sites within well defined localities. Such clusters may be defined as early as the Paleo-Indian period (Ellis and Deller 1990), largely as a result of concentrated research on early sites. Spatial clustering among related sites is less obvious in Archaic times, but this probably reflects limited problem oriented research. By Middle Woodland times distinct regional developments become apparent, and evidence is accumulating for the definition of localized complexes in most major river drainages throughout southwestern Ontario (Spence et al. 1990:148).

Temporal control is another matter. An attempt to apply the complexity model to spatially distinct Middle Woodland site clusters was stymied by a lack of chronological control on some sites, especially multi-component ones where it is not possible to assign parts of assemblages to discrete time periods. Radiocarbon dating is under-utilized in some cases. Given that documentation of regional variability is a prime objective, inter-regional comparisons lacking good temporal control are of limited value as they do not allow us to distinguish temporal from regional (and presumably social) change.

By Late Woodland times regional site clusters are clearly defined across southern Ontario and chronology is somewhat better controlled. Accordingly, one of the authors (Timmins) compiled comparative data from two early Late Woodland site clusters (Caradoc and Dorchester) dating between 850 and 650 B.P., and three contact period Neutral site clusters (Spencer-Bronte, Fairchild-Big and Eastern Niagara) dating to between 335 and 350 B.P. The site clusters were specifically chosen to examine regional variability among groups that are traditionally subsumed under broad taxonomic categories (Wright 1966).

The Caradoc Cluster (850-650 B.P.) is a series of 25 related sites located on the Caradoc Sand Plain just west of London, Ontario (Figure 12.1) (Williamson 1985,1986,1990:314-320). Analysis focussed on a group of five excavated sites including one village (Roeland), three hamlets (Kelly, Yaworski and Berkmortel), and an enclosure associated with a deer drive (Little). While these sites were probably not all contemporaneously occupied, they define the settlement system of a local population within a restricted temporal span.

The Dorchester Cluster (850 to 650 B.P.) is a series of six related sites located on a small sandy area surrounding the Dorchester Swamp just east of London, Ontario (Figure 12.1). Analysis focussed on the extensively excavated Calvert site, a small village with well preserved community pattern data (Timmins 1997). The remaining sites in the cluster have not been excavated.

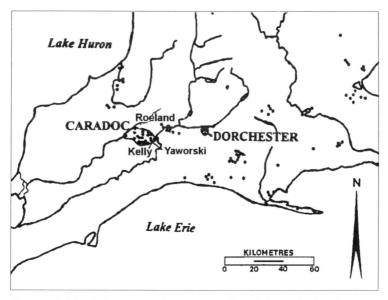

Figure 12.1: Early Iroquoian Site Clusters (850 to 650 B.P.) in Southwestern Ontario.

The chronology of contact period Neutral sites has been refined by William Fitzgerald (1990) and others through seriation of glass trade beads. To achieve temporal control, the Neutral sites considered here all date to Fitzgerald's Glass Bead Period 3, (GBP3 - 320-300 B.P.), with the exception of the Thorold site which appears to overlap the end of Glass Bead Period 2 (350-320 B.P.) and the beginning of Glass Bead Period 3 (320-300 B.P.). It is recognized that minor differences of opinion exist regarding the beginning date of Glass Bead Period 3, with Ian Kenyon placing it between 335 and 325 B.P. (Kenyon 1984; cf. Ferris 1998).

The Spencer-Bronte cluster is a group of contact period Neutral villages and related sites located just west of Hamilton, Ontario (Figure 12.2). These sites represent two or three distinct sequences of village movements beginning in the sixteenth century and lasting until the dispersal of the Neutral in A.D. 1651 (Fitzgerald 1990:278). Although at least six villages, associated cemeteries, and several hamlet sites are known for the 320-300 B.P. period in this cluster, the analysis focussed on excavated villages, Hood and Hamilton, associated hamlets, Bogle I and Bogle II (Lennox 1981; 1984a, 1984b), and the Dwyer cemetery (Fitzgerald 1990:286; Lennox and Fitzgerald 1990:455). Dwyer is the only GBP3 cemetery in the cluster for which reliable excavation data have been preserved (Ridley 1961:28-30).

The Fairchild-Big cluster (Figure 12.2) is located 10-15 km southwest of the Spencer Bronte cluster and consists of three sequences of village movements (Fitzgerald 1990:300). While three villages and associated cemeteries and hamlets fall into the GBP3 period, the analysis focussed primarily on the only well excavated and reported village—the Walker site and its associated cemetery (Wright 1981).

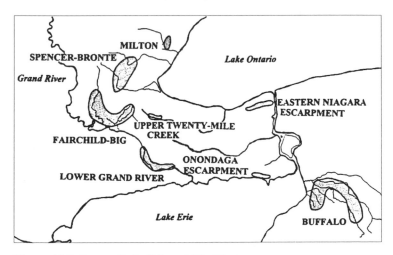

Figure 12.2:Contact Period Neutral Site Clusters.

Table 12.1

Guideline for Assigning Complexity Values

RANKING	1	2	3	4	5
MODE OF PRODUCTION	Nuclear Family	Extended Family/ Lineage	Multiple Lineages or Clan Segment	Village/ Community	Multi-village
POPULATION OF SETTLEMENTS	<50	50-500	500-2000	2000-5000	>5000
ORGANIZATION OF LABOUR	Small houses, base camps...	Large houses, small villages, communal resource extraction	Larger villages, communal works: palisades, mound building...	Large complex villages and towns, communal defensive constructions...	Ceremonial centres, public works, ceremonial structures...
SPECIALIZATION	None		Increasing number of specialized areas of technology... (Ceramics, lithics, metal, bone, shell...)		Many
SUBSISTENCE INTENSIFICATION	Generalized hunting and gathering	Communal hunting and gathering, developing agriculture	Full scale agriculture, some hunting and gathering	Minor agriculture intensification (minor irrigation)	Major agricultural intensification (irrigation, terracing...)
EXCHANGE	Little		Increasing exchange indicated by greater numbers of trade items		Much
IDENTITY SIGNALLING AND CONFLICT	Little	Belonging to a general pattern within a small region	Distinct from other contemporary sites in region OR reflecting a distinct regional or multi-regional iconography	Distinct from other sites in region AND reflecting a distinct regional or multi-regional iconography	Distinct/unique within a multi-regional iconographic system (i.e, Spiro, Oklahoma with shell engraving or Moundville, Alabama with ceramics)
MORTUARY DIFFERENTIATION	Little		Increasing evidence of mortuary ceremonialism and status differentiation		Much

The sites of the Eastern Niagara cluster (Figure 12.2) are more dispersed than the other clusters and are strung out along the Niagara escarpment at the eastern end of the Niagara peninsula. At least six sites are known, in what appears to be a single sequence of village relocations. Two villages from this cluster (Thorold and Steele) can be assigned to the 1630-50 period, but only Thorold has been excavated (Noble 1980). As noted, the Thorold occupation actually overlaps GBP2 and GBP3 (Fitzgerald 1990:330), so its initial occupation date may be slightly earlier than the other sites considered in this analysis.

Table 12.2 presents the results of the complexity analysis, applying the ranking system as described in the previous section. With respect to the first two site clusters, Caradoc and Dorchester, the sites considered show relatively similar low values for most behavioural variables. As expected, the hamlets have lower complexity index values than the villages. The Little site deer surround yielded evidence for a mode of production involving groups larger than the lineage or household. The nearly contemporaneous Calvert and Roeland sites have distinct ceramic assemblages, with the Calvert ceramics showing much higher incidences of cord-wrapped stick decoration, more exterior punctates and less linear stamping (Timmins 1997:220-222). In traditional taxonomies these attributes are considered to be temporally sensitive; this analysis reveals that they have a significant spatial/identity component and suggests that inter-regional seriation may be quite misleading. As Table 12.2 shows, Roeland and Calvert have very similar complexity index values, but examination of specific behavioural variables reveals that they are complex in different ways. Roeland is a relatively large site (Williamson 1985) with a large inferred population; Calvert housed a much smaller group but shows systematic village planning and reorganization through three rebuilding episodes (Timmins 1997). Average, or overall group comparisons are not possible with these groups because the datasets are not comparable given the presence of hamlets in the Caradoc sample and the lack of excavated hamlets in the Dorchester sample.

Turning to the contact period Neutral site clusters, the analysis reveals some interesting differences in behavioural variables among the groups examined. When major villages are compared, the Spencer-Bronte villages, Hamilton and Hood, yielded higher complexity indices than the Walker village of the Fairchild Big group and the Thorold village of the Eastern Niagara group. The Hamilton and Hood sites were ranked highly for Mode of Production and Exchange because of strong evidence that the

Table 12.2
Data Summary from Southwestern Ontario Sites

Site	Mode of Production	Population	Organization of Labor	Specialization	Subsistence	Exchange	Identity Signalling and Conflict	Mortuary Differentiation	Other*	Summary	Index
Roeland, Caradoc, Ont.	2	3	2.5	1	2	1	2.5	-	1.5	15.5/8	1.94
Kelly, Caradoc, Ont.	2	1	1.5	1	2	1	2	-	-	10.5/7	1.50
Little, Caradoc, Ont.	3	-	2	1.5	2	-	2	-	-	10.5/5	2.10
Berkmortel, Caradoc, Ont.	2	2	1.5	1	2	1	2	-	-	11.5/7	1.64
Yaworski, Caradoc, Ont.	2	2	1.5	1	2	1.5	2	-	-	12/7	1.71
Calvert, Dorchester, Ont.	2	2	2.5	1	2	1.5	2.5	-	2	15.5/8	1.94
Hamilton, Spencer-Bronte	3.5	3	3	1.5	3	4	4	-	-	22/7	3.14
Bogle II, Spencer-Bronte	2	2	2	1	3	2	3	-	-	15/7	2.14
Hood, Spencer-Bronte	3.5	3	3	1	3	4	3.5	-	-	21/7	3.00
Bogle I, Spencer-Bronte	2	2	1.5	1	3	2	2.5	-	-	14/7	2.00
Dwyer, Spencer-Bronte	-	-	-	-	-	-	-	3	-	3/1	3.00
Walker, Fairchild-Big	2.5	3	2.5	1.5	3	4	2.5	3	-	20/8	2.75
Thorold, East Niagara	2	3	2.5	1.5	3	-	4.0	-	-	16/6	2.67

"_" denotes insufficient data to assess this variable   * village organization was used as a variable in comparing Roeland and Calvert

Caradoc Group: (Roeland, Kelly, Little, Berkmortel, Yaworski) Developing agriculture, limited village organization, locally distinct ceramics.

Dorchester Group: (Calvert and associated sites) Developing agriculture, intensive hunting, planned village organization, regionally distinct ceramics.

Spencer-Bronte Group: (Hamilton, Hood, Bogle I and II, and associated villages, cemeteries and hamlets) Full-fledged agriculture, intensive hunting, village-hamlet relationships, intensive European and southern trade, defensive concerns, independent foreign policy, influx of foreign population reflected in ceramics.

Fairchild-Big Groups: (Walker, Sealey, Burke and associated cemeteries, hamlets and camps) Full-fledged agriculture, intensive hunting, village-hamlet relationships, less European and southern trade, less defensive concern, less evidence for warfare and influx of foreign population.

Eastern Niagara Escarpment Group: (Thorold, Steele, and associated cemeteries) Full-fledged agriculture, distinctive village locations, no evidence of hamlets, interaction with NY Iroquois evident in ceramics, distinctive architectural patterns.

large villages controlled external trade while their associated hamlets were only involved in domestic production at the household level. This is demonstrated by the fact that the villages have consistently yielded four to six times as many European goods and imported shell artifacts than the hamlets (Lennox 1984b:268). Moreover, the Spencer-Bronte villages, seem to have pursued an independent foreign policy whereby they were involved in a longstanding war with the Fire Nation of Michigan and Ohio (Lennox 1981; Fitzgerald 1990). This is most clearly seen in the relatively high frequency of shell-tempered pottery on Spencer-Bronte villages which is interpreted as evidence that Fire Nation captives were living in Spencer-Bronte group villages. In fact, Fitzgerald suggests that the Spencer-Bronte group took large numbers of Fire Nation captives for the express purpose of re-populating their villages after the devastating losses of epidemics and famines between 1634 and 1640 (Fitzgerald 1990:293-298). In this analysis, these activities lead to high rankings in the variable related to Identity Signalling and Conflict while showing the fluidity of the concept of social identity in the turbulent contact era.

The Dwyer cemetery was looted at an early date and various accounts indicate that large numbers of individuals were buried in several pits (Fitzgerald 1990:286). It was likely in use during the epidemic period (1634-1640) and it may have been similar to the better documented Grimsby cemetery. The Grimsby cemetery yielded evidence of social ranking based on age and sex, as older men tended to be buried together (Jackes 1988:135). While we lack similar osteological evidence from Dwyer, both Rutherford Smith and Ridley reported the presence of a sub-floor in one of the Dwyer ossuary pits (Ridley 1961:30). It is possible that such a structural feature may have separated individuals of different social rank (Noble 1985:141), although we have no evidence that such positions were inherited. Moreover, it is also possible that the segregation could reflect other divisions in Neutral society, or extended use of an ossuary over a long time (Lennox and Fitzgerald 1990:455). Therefore, we have assigned a moderate value (3) for Mortuary Differentiation at Dwyer.

The Fairchild-Big group, represented by the Walker site, shows slightly lower values with respect to Organization of Labour and Identity Signalling/Conflict when compared to the Spencer-Bronte group. The Walker site was not palisaded and there is little archaeological evidence that the Walker people engaged in significant warfare (cf. Noble 1985). The Walker ceramic assemblage is relatively plain and undifferentiated, reflecting what Milton Wright called "cultural conservatism" (Wright

1981:72). It is possible that Walker had a dominant relationship over an associated hamlet, as was the case with villages of the Spencer-Bronte group, but such a relationship has not been demonstrated. However, there is significant evidence of European and aboriginal trade at Walker (Wright 1981:135-141). The Walker cemetery, which is reported to include two vertically stratified ossuaries (Jamieson 1996) may also reflect some differences in social rank, therefore, a moderate value was assigned for the Mortuary Differentiation variable.

Considering the Eastern Niagara group and the Thorold site, a rather different picture emerges. Thorold is comparable to Walker across most variables, however, it was assigned a significantly higher score on several counts related to identity signalling and conflict. The site is located atop the Niagara Escarpment in a naturally defensive location. Confusingly, its southern approach is reported to have been both heavily fortified (Noble 1980:52-53) and minimally fortified (Noble 1984:13). Longhouses at Thorold had tapered ends unlike those in the Spencer-Bronte and Fairchild-Big clusters (Noble 1980:50). Moreover, they lacked "slash pits" (the functional equivalents of bunkline support posts) which are common structural features on post-350 B.P. Neutral sites in the Spencer-Bronte and Fairchild-Big groups, (Lennox and Fitzgerald 1990:443). Noble (1980:52) reports that the ceramic assemblage from Thorold differs substantially from the Walker and Hamilton site collections in having a higher incidence of collared vessels, and a lower occurrence of plain rims. The Thorold collection also contains a significant amount of Genoa Frilled pottery indicative of interaction with Cayuga and Seneca populations in New York (Noble 1980). Finally, it has been argued that the lithic assemblage from Thorold is different from other Neutral sites, with high frequencies of serrated scrapers and flakes, and shorter projectile points (Noble 1980). These observations are confirmed in data presented by Jamieson (1984:158, 186-235). These attributes point to the development of a distinct identity for the Eastern Niagara Neutral population, and possibly, an independent policy with respect to interaction with nearby Five Nations Iroquois groups.

It is possible that many of the differences observed in the Thorold lithics relate to their slightly earlier temporal position. Jamieson (1984) identifies several trends in Neutral lithic technology that she believes spread from east to west through time. She argues that artifact shapes and sizes, flake scar forms, scar orientations, scar patterns and scar dimensions became much more uniform among sites through time, reflecting "the development of the chiefdom and the suppression of tribal autonomy" (Jamieson 1984:385).

Our data suggest that the populations of the three contact period Neutral groups considered here must have varied significantly. This is apparent from the inference that the Eastern Niagara cluster involved a single village moving through time, while the Spencer-Bronte and Fairchild-Big clusters involved at least three contemporaneous villages. Noble estimated the Thorold site population at between 1200 and 1500 individuals (1980:53). The Fairchild-Big and Spencer-Bronte populations would have been considerably larger, especially when the hamlets are considered.

In sum, application of the complexity model highlights many important differences as well as some similarities among the historic Neutral site clusters. The differences observed may indicate the expression of distinct identities and independent foreign policies at the group level. These results support the proposition that the Neutral site clusters represent distinct and autonomous political entities (Lennox and Fitzgerald 1990; Fitzgerald 1990), rather than a chiefdom unified under an absolute, supreme chief (cf. Noble 1984, 1985; Jamieson 1984:5, 74, 367). This does not preclude the possibility that the Neutral were a group of relatively complex tribal polities (Jamieson 1996). It is possible that the trends toward uniformity in lithic technology identified by Jamieson (1984) relate to increased interaction as a result of the formation or strengthening of a tribal confederacy among the Neutral.

It is recognized that societies may have cultural constraints that operate against the development of hierarchical systems (Trigger 1990a). It is anticipated that operation of such mechanisms will be reflected archaeologically by differential development of behavioural variables related to complexity. For example, in cases where certain variables like population growth or population density indicate conditions for increased complexity, but such complexity is not reflected in other behavioural variables (e.g., mortuary differentiation), cultural constraints against complexity may be operative. This appears to be the case among some Iroquoian groups such as the Huron (Trigger 1990a, 1990b).

Examples from the Upper Midwest

Turning now to the Upper Midwest we find a different set of challenges. First and foremost we are faced with a shortage of excavated village and habitation sites, especially for the Woodland and Archaic eras.

Second, we are faced with adherence to type-series ceramic analyzes that have yet to consistently move toward stylistic comparison between and within components. That is to say we spend a great deal of time fitting ceramics into extant categories while spending a notably smaller amount of time looking at the variability between ceramic assemblages. Ultimately this makes it difficult to identify any groupings of sites beneath the level of a phase or focus.

With these limitations in mind one of the authors (Staeck) has compiled comparative data from a variety of sites in three different time periods. These are summarized here for purposes of illustrating the sorts of analyzes that the authors have proposed and the range of results that we might expect. It is important to note, however, that the data presented here are not necessarily directly comparable in terms of placing the various manifestations on a unilineal sequence of socio-political complexity (e.g., Service 1962). Rather, the process of generating these data compels researchers to address a wide range of indices that can be associated with multiple trajectories of socio-political complexity. As discussed previously, these indices will vary across regions and temporal spans. The identification of specific trends, though, will help researchers to identify specific behaviours that were locally significant to the formation of complexity in the past and then to compare these formations on the nominal and ordinal levels.

The sites considered here are divided into four groups as follows:

1. The Hartley Fort, Lane Enclosure, and Flatiron Terrace complex (collections of Luther College Archaeological Research Center; Betts 1997), northeastern Iowa, and the Tremaine Complex (O'Gorman 1995), southwestern Wisconsin, dating to between about 550 and 350 B.P. (Figure 12.3). These names represent a relatively small geographic area within which there are listings for multiple sites; in most cases these multiple listings represent subsequent site registrations that did not take into account previous listings. In essence, this complex represents a relatively large site or site complex that sprawled across the terrace and which was used repeatedly over several generations. Significant variation in pottery form and decoration, as well as some unique stylistic blends of pottery, exists at the Hartley Fort and Flatiron Terrace complexes, potentially reflecting:(a) group metamorphosis from Late Woodland to Upper Mississippian lifeways (e.g., Gibbon 1972), (b) interweaving occupations by discrete peoples bearing differing material cultures, or (c) a location where segments of a diversified population possessing multiple forms of material culture met and interacted (e.g., Staeck 1994).

2. The Sanders and Bigelow sites (Hurley 1975) from southern Wisconsin, both dating to between approximately1250 and 1050 B.P. (Figure 12.3).

3. The Holdener Site (Wittry et. al. 1994) from the American Bottom Uplands of Illinois, dating to between1250 and 1050 B.P. (Figure 12.3).

4. The Lohman (Esarey and Pauketat 1992) and Willoughby (Jackson 1990) sites from the American Bottom region of Illinois, dating to between 950 and 850 B.P. (Figure 12.3).

As presented in Table 12.3, the data from these groupings cluster around different sets of variables. For example, group 1 sites do not emphasize any particular behavioural variable but instead suggest increased complexity along a number of fronts. Substantial population levels at these sites along with concomitant levels of organization of labour, identity signalling, and mode of production seem to be at the core of behaviours relating to socio-political complexity here. Not surprisingly these sites represent villages which possess longhouses for extended families and evidence for group (perhaps extended family) acquisition and storage of resources.

The group 2 sites present a different pattern of behaviours related to socio-political complexity. These sites show increased levels of identity signalling in the form of the construction and display of mounds. Significantly, these mounds seem to correlate to ethnographically known clans (Hall 1993) which, in turn, suggests that clan segments cooperated in the construction of these features. Further, many of these constructions are deliberately and consistently located on steep bluffs and high ground overlooking rivers (major arteries for transportation) and this likely reflects additional identity signalling (cf. Charles and Buikstra 1983). Importantly, however, these sites do not cluster around large villages which were occupied year-round. Instead, they appear to have been focussed on smaller seasonally occupied villages. The avenues toward socio-political complexity here seem to vary notably from the sites summarized in group 1.

Group 3 consists of a single site from the American Bottom Uplands. The site dates to between approximately 1250 and 1050 B.P. and has been included here for comparative purposes only. We need not discuss the implications of this site beyond noting that it provides background to the later Lohman and Willoughby sites in this region as well as an interregional check for the Sanders and Bigelow sites.

Group 4 sites present yet another distinctive pattern of behaviours related to socio-political complexity. These sites represent different settlement forms within a contemporary hierarchically-organized social

Table 12.3
Data Summary from Upper Midwest Sites

Site	Mode of Production	Population	Organization of Labor	Specialization	Subsistence	Exchange	Identity Signalling and Conflict	Mortuary Differentiation	Other	Summary	Index
Hartley/Flatiron Terrace, IA.	2	2	2	1	2	2	2.5	2	-	15.5/8	1.94
Tremaine, WI.	2	2.5	2	1	2	2	2	2.5	-	16/8	2.00
Sanders, WI.	3	2	2.5	1.5	-	2.5	2.5	-	-	14/6	2.33
Bigelow, WI.	3	-	2.5	-	-	2	2.5	2	-	12/5	2.40
Holdener, IL.	1	-	1	-	1	-	1.5	-	-	4.5/4	1.13
Lohman, IL	4	2	3.5	3	3	3.5	4	3.5	3.7	30.2/9	3.36
Willoughby, IL	1	1	1	1	3	2	2	-	-	11/	1.57

Group 1: (Hartley / Flatiron Terrace and Tremaine) Generalized activities, broad range of equivalent behaviors.

Group 2: (Sanders and Bigelow) Generalized subsistence and economy inferred, increased emphasis on clans and identity signalling.

Group 3: (Holdener) Broad spectrum subsistence and economy, limited identity signalling.

Group 4: (Lohman and Willoughby) Contemporaries within a hierarchical system; Lohman is a central place with increased complexity in all levels of behavior; Willoughby represents an isolated farm/homestead involved in agricultural production for the larger hierarchical system.

system. The Lohman site is a central place that possesses platform mound construction and evidence for interaction with parallel levels of settlements from elsewhere in the American Bottom. This site evinces relatively high rates of socio-political complexity through all indices measured in this review and generally seems to represent a place where identity marking and power were concentrated.

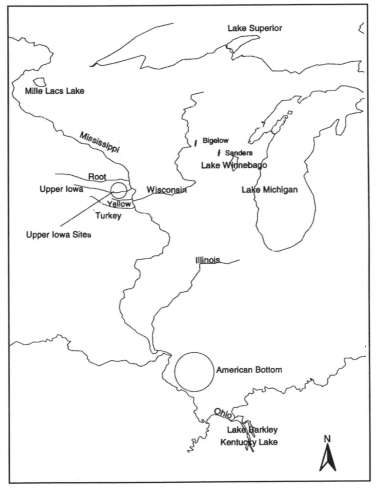

Figure 12.3: The Upper Midwest with sites and site areas identified.

The Willoughby site, however, represents a small farming homestead that lies on the social and economic periphery of the socio-political system at hand. This site displays low measures of complexity except in those areas that tie it to larger centres such as Lohman. In dealing with socio-political complexity in these two sites we might reasonably expect people at Lohman to be intimately concerned with demonstrations of identity and power while we would be surprised to see such behaviours regularly expressed at Willoughby or similar sites. We might also expect that there are corresponding levels of individual and family autonomy within this system as well as, perhaps, commensurate levels of individual concerns about participating in the different levels of social interaction. In essence we might postulate an urban and rural dichotomy that existed on political, economic, social, and ideological levels.

It is important to consider this latter set of comparisons in the broader context of Mississippian expansion. It has been the stock and trade of many archaeologists to discuss the nature of inter-site complexity within the Cahokia socio-political sphere and many of these discussions have proven insightful. Yet, analysis and interpretation of intra-site stylistic variation often suffers in this scheme since the emphasis of interpretation is placed squarely on considering how the different sites fit together rather than how a relatively small community such as Willoughby is structured. If we consider Wobst's (1977) discussion of identity signalling, for example, we might be surprised to note little intra-community identity signalling taking place. Residents of smaller communities were likely to have been intimately familiar with their fellow residents and there was no need for displays of prestige and rank within such settlements. Hence, if we are to identify and reconstruct the nature of the day-to-day lives of people within a large and complex socio-political system, such as is represented by eleventh and twelfth century developments in the American Bottom, then we must focus on the day-to-day context of life rather than on the higher levels of community articulation within the system. The data presented here identify precisely the sort of differences that should receive our attention in this matter.

To conclude this Upper Midwestern comparison we should note two significant trends. First, there is considerably more complexity inherent in Late Woodland Effigy Mound sites than is often perceived. This complexity is comparable to that found within Orr Phase Oneota sites in adjacent and overlapping regions. This implies that the Late Woodland era encompasses behaviours other than those that are generally presupposed to be present, that is small family groups living in generalized egalitarian bands and engaged in undifferentiated broad-spectrum foraging activities. Second, the tendency to view Mississippian culture in terms of models for elite interaction at mound sites belies the presence of less stratified segments of society for which extensive identity signalling was the exception rather than the rule. This range of behaviour is consistent with the polythetic nature of social systems as well as with the variable needs of individuals to express differentiated salient identities within the context of flexible social milieux.

Conclusions

In summary, we stress that this paper represents an initial attempt to develop a flexible approach to the analysis of socio-political complexity. Our objective was to model the true multivariate nature of social and political change to permit the comparison of sites and groups of sites in a systematic way. We believe the examples discussed demonstrate the potential of such an approach to reveal the richness and variability of Aboriginal history.

At the same time, this approach highlights the inadequacies of our archaeological databases. In particular, a lack of well excavated habitation sites within some site clusters makes it difficult to proceed to comparisons beyond the site level. This is especially true of the Upper Midwest where studies of household organization and socio-political complexity have focussed principally on Mississippian and related sites. We require more regional studies involving extensive excavation and continued refinement of the chronology of individual site clusters. Without firm temporal control, detailed comparative analyzes are of limited value.

On a methodological note, we need to reconsider our analysis of artifact assemblages and comparisons among them. Rather than focussing on technological traits or artifact types that may be shared across many regions as the basis of broad normative taxonomic units, we must deconstruct artifact types on an attribute by attribute basis and explore attribute combinations to determine if it is possible to define locally distinctive styles. Detailed comparisons among site clusters analyzed in a similar manner would permit an assessment of the degree to which distinct styles and perhaps social identities are shared among contemporaneous groups. While advances have been made in this area (e.g., Jamieson 1984; Smith 1987), detailed comparative studies are still rare.

Implementing such a program of research will obviously require a common collective effort involving changes in the way that we organize our data. The benefits will accrue over the long term as we systematically build a socially and culturally congruent archaeological taxonomy from the ground up. In this manner, archaeologists may eventually be able to address complex questions relating to issues of identity signalling that are relevant to Native history and current political issues involving group identities, territories, and even land claims. The alternative, to maintain an archaeological taxonomy with no correspondence to social reality, simply means that archaeology will become largely irrelevant in the real world.

Acknowledgements

The authors would like to thank Susan Jamieson and an anonymous reviewer for their thoughtful comments on the paper. Timmins would also like to thank Paul Lennox and Michael Spence for their assistance in providing source material. Finally, we thank Ron Williamson and Chris Watts of Archaeological Services Inc., Toronto, for their patience and persistence, and for pulling it all together.

A BRIEF HISTORY OF ABORIGINAL SOCIAL INTERACTIONS IN SOUTHERN ONTARIO AND THEIR TAXONOMIC IMPLICATIONS

13

Susan M. Jamieson
Department of Anthropology, Trent University

As defined here, southern Ontario is that region north of Lakes Ontario and Erie and the St. Lawrence River, and east of the St. Clair and Detroit Rivers and Lake Huron, south of the Canadian Shield, eastward to the Ottawa River. In this paper, I briefly summarize and discuss archaeological evidence from southern Ontario for interaction among populations through the past 11,000 or so years.

What is evident in this summary is the pervasiveness of local or short distance alliances and exchanges of goods and concepts. This pattern is punctuated by cyclical episodes of long distance interaction. Cross-cultural anthropological data suggest that local/short distances often fall within three days' travel time, or less, and that within kin-based societies, such as those typical of Ontario's past, sustained local interactions initiated and maintained through ethnic or kin-group (including intermarriage) linkages are the norm rather than the exception (Bettinger 1991; Headland and Reid 1989; Moore 1983; Root 1983; Spielmann 1986; Wobst 1976, 1978:304). Periods during which peoples travelled long distances (i.e., more than about three days' travel) to forge social relationships are in addition to local interactions and would have increased local social diversity and variability (Piddington 1965:xii).

It is important that we understand that, in the past, each person simultaneously would have been a member of a spatially dispersed social unit (whether it be one day's travel or five days' travel) and at least one crosscutting spatially integrated unit. In theory, the strengths of social links would have varied positively with the amount of intergroup mobility (Bettinger 1991:194-200; Davis 1983:66,72; Hulin 1989). The larger the integrating unit, the greater the potential for increased variability and diversity. The resultant archaeological model for any given time period, then, may be envisioned as a "diversified network of geographically disparate, albeit overlapping [i.e., integrated], socially and/or ethnically

Susan M. Jamieson

related foci", "each of which predominantly exploited its own local region" (Jamieson 1992:71, 81).

Two of the many dynamic social agencies which underlie the above discussion are mobility and diffusion. Mobility "includes all kinds of territorial movements, both temporary and permanent, over various distances" (Lewis 1982:8). This is the meaning of the term "migration" as I have previously used and referenced it (Jamieson 1992:73), but I now prefer the term "mobility" as it better indicates the processes whereby spatially dispersed social units were integrated. Studies of human mobility within the past few centuries indicate that large-scale, invasive, and unidirectional population movements as historical events are extremely rare: more common are sustained small-scale temporary movements combined with "backflow" to the place of origin (Anthony 1990:897-898; Lewis 1982:10,18).[1] The latter varieties typically involve circumscribed ethnic or kin groups which have specific objectives targeted on destinations and travel routes known from first hand experience or from kin-based or interethnic communications (Anthony 1990:896, 899-900; Lewis 1982:51; Schortman and Urban 1987:64-68). Essentially, social scientists have concluded that cultures do not migrate (Anthony 1990:897, 908; Gadacz 1978:151; Kershaw 1978). Mobility and diffusion are not necessarily dichotomous but are part of the same temporal and spatial processual continuum (e.g., Davis 1983:62-70; Kershaw 1978:6-7). This is because intergroup mobility, no matter what its scale, also entails the diffusion of objects and information about social institutions and ideology (Schortman and Urban 1987:68) through gift-giving, warfare, marital exchange, funerary rites, and tokens of apology and alliance.

Osteologists have observed that it is often difficult to demonstrate unidirectional and invasive population movements using only osteometric or epigenetic traits (Heathcote 1978:47-51; Lasker and Mascie-Taylor 1988:4; Majumder 1991:97-117): this has proven to be the case in southern Ontario (Molto 1983:252-259). Furthermore, the biological data that we have from this area, with the exception of all but the most recent few centuries, is limited by serious sampling problems. The result is that any claim for migration as an historical event is not supported and osteological data seem to point to intergroup mobility as a long-term process.

Consistent with current models of interregional interaction and cultural transmission (e.g., Bettinger 1991; Schortman 1989; Schortman and Urban 1992, 1987), I conclude that the effects of contacts were

176

substantial. Indeed, because they were not a unitary phenomenon and, because they expanded differentially, they may have resulted in varied ideological and sociopolitical outcomes among the Northern Iroquoians (e.g., Jamieson 1981, 1989, 1996). I further argue that the combination of dispersive and integrative processes led to regional and local clinal distributions of material culture and promoted socio-political coevolution over large areas. As the extent and intensity of relationships varied through space and time, their archaeologically visible effects are not evenly distributed. I infer on the basis of cross-cultural anthropological data that the channel of interaction was of equal or greater value to that which was being exchanged, as it marked important social relationships. Because such channels are to be found along major routes of interaction, archaeologically visible effects, again, are not likely to be evenly distributed. Clearly, one cannot reasonably interpret local developments without due consideration of appropriate regional context and vice versa, given reflexivity between the two (e.g., Wright 1990:493). Our current taxonomy is based on linear, bounded, and centralized constructs into which archaeological data are fitted, but it is an inadequate base from which to address the web-like social relations of the past and their effects on the archaeological record, as it cannot readily accommodate time-transgressive processes, such as mobility and diffusion, which occur at a pan-regional scale and result in a matrix of interconnections.

Regional interaction was facilitated by the fact that native belief systems were (and continue to be) ideologically conservative (e.g., Brown 1997; Feest 1986; Hamell 1987; Vastokas 1987). Indeed, there are conceptual and stylistic contiguities and similarities in the Northeast, which originate in the Midwest and Southeast, can be traced back several thousand years, and inform later developments in southern Ontario (Penney 1987). This is not to be construed as a denial of "symbolic and informational meaning" (Williamson and Robertson 1994b:47) or to be interpreted that local groups were "passive receptors of external fashions" (Ferris and Spence 1995:111). Rather, it is an acknowledgement that certain material objects, if viewed as iconographic symbols which transcended linguistic boundaries, were capable of communicating a wide variety of messages and were one means by which interregional communication was fostered. It is an acknowledgement that there was a broad ideological basis which served to integrate social units over large areas, thereby promoting receptivity to, and acceptance (albeit often qualified) of, the exogenous, even though specific details may have independently developed in any given context (e.g., Jamieson 1992:70,74-76; also cf. Brown 1997:473-476; Ellis 1994). It is an acknowledgement that, locally, "People's symbols, and their behavior, do change...[and] these changes are very much linked to external events" (Kertzer 1988:175), and that individuals could manipulate objects and their messages to create or alter relationships within and between groups. The most robust evidence for interaction is invariably expressed in the ritual sphere. Ritual is used to symbolize, simplify, and enhance political messages (specifically, to build political organizations, to create political legitimacy, and both to create solidarity and to incite political conflict) (Kertzer 1988). It can increase or reduce local social diversity and variability.

Chronology of Interaction

As is almost invariably the case in any overview such as this, I must enter the caveat that knowledge of southern Ontario's archaeological record, hence any interpretation of it, is incomplete, even for the best-known and most fully researched period, which encompasses roughly the last 1,200 years. Evidence for interaction is addressed in chronologically arranged blocks, from early to late. Owing to limitations of space, neither physical nor cosmological landscapes are discussed. Nonetheless, their importance is acknowledged.

11000-10500 B.P.

The primary social unit of the earliest human populations in the Northeast—makers of fluted, bifacial projectile points—is generally assumed to have been a small exogamous group. Group territories are inferred from the stylistic uniformity and distribution of lithic assemblages relative to frequency of represented toolstone types and their locations in conjunction with other site and environmental data. Generally, groups are believed to have ranged over large territories and to have exchanged finished goods and raw materials, ceremonies, etc. over vast distances, principally for social reasons (e.g., Anderson 1995:13-19; Deller 1989; Ellis 1989, 1994; Ellis and Deller 1990:53-54; Meltzer 1989; Petersen 1995), although as Storck and Speiss (1994:136) note:

The range of possible human adaptations is considerable, extending from a logistical strategy related to long-distance movements of large herds to, on the other extreme, an opportunistic strategy related to the local availability of faunal resources. Alternately, some mix of the two strategies may have been employed on a seasonal basis" [cf. Timmins, 1994].

Deller's (1989) analysis of toolstone type variation from southwestern Ontario sites of the 11000-10500 B.P. period concludes that ca 11,000 years ago, interactions were with southerly areas, as evidenced by small amounts of Upper Mercer (Ohio) chert on sites not only in southwestern Ontario, but also on those from adjacent areas of southern Michigan. By 10,700 years ago, Bayport chert (Michigan) is the low frequency exotic, indicating that interactions were with more northerly populations (also cf. Deller and Ellis 1992:135). The direction of long distance interaction is further confirmed by the ceremonial cremation found at the ca 10500 B.P. Crowfield site, which has been linked to slightly later ceremonial activity at the Renier site in Wisconsin (Ellis and Deller 1990:52). Both patterns are consistent with small-scale movements into Ontario combined with return movements.

Using a combination of site and toolstone distributions, Kapches (1994) has reconstructed the initial major transportation routes. These principally trended southwest, southeast, and north-south (also cf. Anderson 1995:Fig. 1.3). Numerous other more localized routes likely were in less intensive use as well (Jackson 1978:192; Kapches 1994).

10500-5000 B.P.

Archaeologists believe that earlier trends continued, specifically, large territories and low population densities are indicated, as is the use of predominantly local lithic resources. Nonetheless, increased projectile point stylistic variability, decreased distances to lithic sources, and increased numbers of sites and findspots suggest that group territories were decreasing in size as population densities increased (Ellis and Deller 1990:61-63). Intergroup interaction, most likely in the form of connections between certain individuals, is inferred. One example of this may be seen in a distinctively flaked, narrow laceolate point form that is restricted to easternmost southern Ontario, westernmost southern Québec, and northern Vermont (J.V. Wright, personal communication, 1988; Ritchie 1969:18-19), although this form (in broader stylistic expression) itself has a wider eastern distribution (Ellis and Deller 1990:59). Another example of intergroup interaction may be found in Onondaga chert (Ontario and New York) artifacts recovered from sites in northwestern Ohio (Stothers 1996:187).

Approximately 10,000 years ago, notched points appear in southern Ontario (Ellis et al. 1990:71; Wright 1978). Owing to a paucity of excavated relatively undisturbed sites, the degree of cultural continuity is unclear. Indeed, we know very little of the period between 10,000 and 5,500 years ago other than that there was change throughout much of the eastern half of the continent and that point forms and tool kits are very similar over vast areas (e.g., Petersen 1995:216-217).

Ellis et al. (1990:123) infer that during this long time span:

peoples in southern Ontario lived in hunter-gatherer bands whose social and economic organization was probably characterized by openness and flexibility. The consequence of this flexibility may be that both biologically and culturally, "ethnic" boundaries are weakly defined...

We do know that group territories decreased in size throughout this period and that "by around 5500 B.P., there are indications of increasing populations" (Ellis et al. 1990:93).

Stothers (1996:194, 197) observes that for southwestern Ontario, "the... distribution of...projectile points fashioned of non-local chert resources suggests population movement between lithic source areas and distant site locations", citing the large assemblage of artifacts made of Pipe Creek chert (Ohio) recovered from the Nettling site (southwestern Ontario) as supporting evidence (cf. Ellis et al. 1991). Following his analysis of ground stone artifacts, Lackowicz (1996:146-175) concluded that there was an unmistakable connection between the eastern part of southern Ontario and the Atlantic region, likely along the St. Lawrence drainage. These connections persisted throughout much of this long period.

5000-3000 B.P.

By ca 5,000 years ago, there appears to be an increase in stylistic diversity in southern Ontario. Adzes with bevelled side margins have been reported from the Niagara Peninsula (Ritchie 1969; MacDonald et al.1997:373), supporting Ritchie's (1944, 1969) contention that populations there were interacting with those in central and western New York and northern Pennsylvania. A small, narrow, stemmed or side-notched point having a thick, unfinished base is associated with these adzes, but has a wider distribution in the Northeast, including throughout much of southern Ontario (Ellis et al. 1990:98; Roberts 1985).

Around 3,800 years ago, broad points appear in southern Ontario, consistent with the wide distribution of this type, now generally regarded as representing a shift in lithic reduction strategies in association with intra-and inter-regional trade in lithic materials (e.g., Petersen 1995:221). Stylistic similarities of some southern Ontario broad point and associated tool forms in the Niagara Peninsula (including at least one steatite vessel) indicate continuing ties with New York and northern Pennsylvania (Ellis et al. 1990:100-101, 103; Mason 1981:208), while others indicate ties between southwestern Ontario and southeastern Michigan and northeastern Ohio (Kenyon 1980, 1983). Also, the broad point burials found at the Peace Bridge site resemble, in overall form and character, the cremation burials of the mid-Atlantic coastal region (Robertson et al. 1997:499).

In southern Ontario, Burgar (1985) has convincingly delimited broad point group territories associated with the distribution of white-tailed deer. He additionally confirms the stylistic separation in the Toronto area first noted by Wright (1960) and established by Roberts (1985) as occurring along the Humber River, which appears to have marked a significant social boundary.

Broad points are supplanted by a series of small, interrelated point types ca 3500 B.P. (Kenyon 1989). Small points from southwestern Ontario show strong similarities to counterparts from eastern Illinois, Michigan, Ohio, and Wisconsin (Ellis et al. 1990:107-109). Associated bannerstones further indicate that these populations were evidently interacting with those located to the southwest of Lake Erie (Wright 1960). According to Kapches (1994), this interaction was in "a distinct southern direction [towards the mid-continent]".

Hedican and McGlade's (1993) identification of taxometrically similar copper projectile point clusters imply that at this time there was extensive trade or other forms of social contact between the north and eastern Ontario, a pattern earlier observed by Ridley (1954, 1966). Copper artifacts in eastern Ontario are clustered along the Trent-Severn system, the Rideau system, and the Ottawa River, on which basis Kapches (1994) concludes that the Trent-Severn route extended "to the Upper Great Lakes" and that this

> seem[s] to mark an early appearance of a well-established northwest to southeast route which continues in use in later periods.... One direction of transportation to the southeast was apparently through the Oswego and Seneca rivers, then to the Oneida/Mohawk/Hudson river valley routes.

The distribution of ground slate projectile points further indicates that eastern links extended along the St. Lawrence and into New England. Populations living in extreme southwestern Ontario did not participate in this eastern interaction network to any great extent (Lackowicz 1996:98, 160). Kapches (1994) summarizes these trends as indicating "expanded routes to the north and east, as well as a continuation of routes to the southwest and southeast".

3000-1200 B.P.

By ca 3,000 years ago, the first of a series of widespread mortuary complexes using a variety of exotic items (including galena, copper and marine shell) as grave goods and common concepts (e.g., clay balls, paired objects, iconography, modified animal bone, smoking ritual, colour and material categorization, interment in an elevated feature) can be identified in southern Ontario (Donaldson and Wortner 1995). This implies that peoples intensified and expanded upon the older pattern of exchanging finished goods and raw materials, ceremonies, etc. over vast distances (in this case, from Indiana, Ohio, Michigan, northern Vermont, and southern Ontario) principally for social reasons. This is an expansion of the "Red-Ochre" theme (Hall 1983) first evinced a few hundred years earlier on the north shore of Lake Erie (Spence et al. 1978; Spence and Fox 1986:8). The distribution of Ramah quartzite (northern Labrador) in Ontario during this period (Mima Kapches, personal communication, 1994) suggests that there also were linkages to the northeast.

Some 2,800 years ago, ceramics were introduced into southern Ontario, but there is no discontinuity with earlier cultural manifestations (Spence and Fox 1986:8-12). Sassaman (1993) concludes that where pottery was adopted quickly and widely, as in southern Ontario, groups were involved in alliances that put demands on individual labour.

Although the evidence is equivocal, it is generally inferred that during the early part of this period peoples continued to live in small hunter-gatherer groups characterized by openness and flexibility; however, there is increasing evidence for localized heterogeneity (Ferris and Spence 1995:95-97). At this time, large numbers of Onondaga chert biface preforms were exchanged from southern Ontario into Québec, northern Vermont, northwestern Ohio and adjacent portions of Michigan (Beld 1991; Clermont and Chapdelaine 1982; Loring 1985; Stothers and Abel 1993). As Ferris and Spence (1995:93) point out, this exchange may have been largely social in nature and also encompassed pop-eyed birdstones and trapezoidal gorgets. These same authors (1995:95-96) note that, curiously, marine shell and galena are absent in southern Ontario at this time even though ties with "New York should have allowed access [to these goods]. Thus the wide trade networks of the preceding period seem not to have been lost so much as refocussed." If Lackowicz (1996:157-186) is correct in his assessment that many of the widely distributed Northeastern ground stone tools types usually assigned to earlier times may actually date from this period, Ferris and Spence's conclusion is given additional support.

Certainly, by 2300 B.P. there is sound evidence for exotic mortuary goods (e.g., copper, silver, cut sheet mica, marine shell, shark's teeth, Ohio fireclay pipes, toolstones from Ohio, Michigan, and Québec) and participation in a widespread belief system (e.g., iconography, modified animal bone, panpipes, smoking ritual, colour and material categorization, interment in an artificially elevated feature). These are localized manifestations (i.e., selectively integrated) of a complex that originated in the midcontent and extended through much of the Northeast (Fox and Molto 1994a; Funk 1983:335; Ritchie 1969:218, 234, 238; Spence et al. 1990:157-158). Nonetheless, eastern Ontario manifestations have their closest parallels in northeastern New York State (cf. Wallbridge [1860] and Beauchamp's [1905] descriptions of the Perch Lake Mounds). Many of the more prosaic[2] artifacts are shared over a large area (Ritchie 1969; Spence et al. 1990:159), including a variety of stamped, incised and cord-stamped, ceramic types (Ferris and Spence 1995:98; Funk 1983:338). In the Niagara Peninsula, ceramic and projectile point types are closely aligned with those from adjacent areas of New York State (Ritchie 1969). In the former region, too, corn was introduced as this period came to a close (Crawford and Smith 1996:785, 787).

Researchers basically infer that there was increased sedentism owing to intensified use of local resources. Generally, egalitarian social organization is surmised although the Rice Lake area may be an exception given that there is limited osteological evidence for ascribed rank (Ferris and Spence 1995:101). However, these same data have been used to argue for egalitarianism: essentially, a hierarchical rather than a ranked structure is indicated (Spence 1986:91). This confusion may stem from the use of Fried's (1967) typology, which is an abstraction without existence in reality (Upham 1990:89). As Fiedel (1994:9) observes, "the 'egalitarian' label probably obscures significant leadership roles". His reconstructed Proto-Algonquian (PA) vocabulary implies that "PA sociopolitical organization encompassed large seasonal villages, totemic clans, ranked lineages, and hereditary chiefs", archaeological traces of which should be found during this time period "in the presumed Proto-Algonquian homeland [southern Ontario]" (Fiedel 1994:1). The Trent-Severn trade route and its New York linkages are clearly emphasized (Kapches 1994), but we must consider that Niagara Peninsular, extreme southwestern, and northern connections also played a significant role in southern Ontario developments during this period (Spence et al.1990:155-156, 164, 166).

1200-250 B.P.

For the first three hundred or so years of this period, the trade networks of the preceding period appear to have been refocussed insofar as the Trent-Severn trade route and its New York linkages were maintained (Kapches 1994) and Niagara Peninsular, extreme southwestern, and northern connections continued to be significant (Jamieson 1992:73; Ridley 1954, 1966), but there is no sound evidence for "exotica" in southern Ontario. It may be that groups became more dependent upon close-range ties, possibly because exotics were imbued with notions of authority and status that no longer existed. On the one hand, we have little evidence for ritual contexts, so this refocussing may be more apparent than real. On the other hand, the inference of a refocussing at this time is in accord with the contrast between those archaeological assemblages which immediately precede and follow. As in the previous period, however, prosaic artifacts were shared over a substantial area (Fox 1990a; Murphy and Ferris 1990; Ritchie 1969; Stothers 1977), including small, triangular projectile points and cord malleated, cord-wrapped stick, dentate stamped, and punctated ceramic types (Fox 1990a) having parallels throughout the larger Northeast (Funk 1983:343, 348-349, 361). In the Niagara Peninsula, ceramic and projectile point types continued to be closely aligned with those from adjacent areas of New York State (Ritchie 1969; Stothers 1977).

After 850 years ago there was a general progression from hamlets to villages, agriculture definitely became part of the subsistence economy and populations became more sedentary. Significantly, and in accord with poorly understood processes which occurred throughout the Eastern Woodlands, the core areas of population were not the same as those of the previous period. Groups remained open; however, there is increasing evidence for localized socio-political integration (including population movement and coalescence) coupled with internecine warfare, which implies factionalism, a struggle of competing groups to improve their position or to overthrow leaders. Status distinctions developed and, for at least one southern Ontario polity, arguments have been advanced that there is evidence for vertical social segmentation (e.g., Jamieson 1996; cf. Ferris and Spence's [1995:115] argument for communal and egalitarian lifeways).

During this period, the more prosaic artifacts continued to be shared and to undergo a similar pattern of change over a large area. The configurations behind this distribution are discussed in detail by Jamieson (1991, 1992, 1996) and Williamson and Robertson (1994a). There is evidence for increasing heterogeneity in southern Ontario as exogenous stylistic and conceptual elements (with their ultimate genesis in the Southeast, mid-continent, and north) were integrated. Elements arrived piecemeal, in attenuated, disconnected, and modified form, having been filtered through channels of interaction (Jamieson 1992:70-71, 77-78, 80-81). Temporally and spatially variable interactions among southern Ontario populations, and between them and populations in the Upper Great Lakes, western New York, the mid-Atlantic region and the Upper and Middle Ohio, Upper Delaware, Susquehanna, and St. Lawrence drainages have been documented for this period (Jamieson 1991, 1992). Some of these contacts may be inferred to have been direct, given coeval and reciprocal distributions of material culture.

Northern populations also are known to have participated in a far-ranging trade network that linked southern Ontario groups to those in Wisconsin and ultimately (Jamieson 1992:76) to the middle Mississippi and lower Ohio valleys. In turn, lower Ohio valley polities interacted with those located along the middle Mississippi, in central and eastern

Tennessee, and along the middle Ohio (Griffin 1983:282, 289-294). The last-noted ultimately interacted with southern Ontario groups. There are tantalizing clues that while earlier contacts during this period may have involved Wabash River or other Middle Mississippian groups, later involvement was directed toward Mississippian or Mississippian influenced polities in the Tennessee Valley. Southern Ontario populations, thus, were well positioned to participate in these far-ranging relationships, and the ancient north-south route through the Niagara Peninsula and up the Humber River became an increasingly important link (Kapches 1994) which effectively completed this "circle of interaction". While Williamson and Robertson (1994a, 1994b) and von Gernet (1994:4) have misapplied Jamieson's (1992:70) definition of the term "Mississippification", it is true that peoples in southern Ontario did not participate to any great extent in the Southeastern socio-ideological system, that they did not have "large scale or highly developed relations...[with] peoples in the southeast or midwest", or that integrated components invariably originated among the most powerful elite of the Mississippi River Valley.

This notwithstanding, increasing numbers of exotic materials and concepts (notably marine shell and ceramics, followed by chunky stones and European goods) entered southern Ontario. While exotics (or local copies thereof) are not unknown from sites dating to the early and middle parts of this period (e.g., Pergentile, Zamboni, Middleport, Murphy-Goulding), the major influx of exogenous items and concepts occurred during the late sixteenth and early seventeenth centuries (Jamieson 1991, 1992; McGarry 1997; Robert 1996). Given its substantial time depth in the Northeast, it was likely earlier, rather than later, that the widespread Southeastern maize complex, consisting of material and nonmaterial traits (including the Green Corn Ceremony), gained a foothold in southern Ontario[3] (Witthoft 1949). Fenton (1940:191-194) has commented upon the exogenous origins (both north and south) of other adopted and adapted ceremonies. During the latter part of this period, at least some southern Ontario peoples were participating in ritualistic behaviour involving, among other things, exotic mortuary goods (e.g., copper cut-outs and spirals; marine shell objects) and a widespread belief system (e.g., iconography [including weeping eye, rattlesnake, curvilinear and other Ramey Incised motif elements, and Underwater Serpent design elements], modified animal bone, secondary interment in communal and stratified repositories) which had its main focus in the Tennessee Valley and its tributaries.

In the mid-seventeenth century, populations in southern Ontario were dispersed as political entities. It is not insignificant, in light of the interactions outlined above, that remnant southern Ontario populations dispersed to the Green Bay area or into Pennsylvania (Heidenreich 1990; Pendergast 1991). Southern Ontario was briefly "outposted" by small groups of League Iroquois who were accessing the Upper Great Lakes but, by the late seventeenth century were forced to withdraw by southward moving Ojibwa, Nippising, and Mississauga (Hammond 1904; Jennings 1984:207; Konrad 1981; Orr 1915, 1917). To this day, the latter peoples maintain their northern social links.

Discussion

In broad outline, what is represented throughout southern Ontario's past are expanding, decentralized relationships that depended on constant intergroup linkages to ensure equal opportunity of access to critical resources, both physical and conceptual. Sustained access was gained by practising varying degrees of mobility in the course of inter-marrying and forging alliances so that memberships were maintained both in spatially dispersed social units and in spatially integrated units that crosscut and balanced one another. This "contradiction" is visible as differing patterning in material remains. There are suggestions that during the past 3,000 or so years, local effects of spatially integrated units were playing a more important, if discontinuous, role than they had previously, promoting hierarchical or even ranked structures within social units located along major channels of interaction. During these periods, mortuary ritual was emphasized, including enhanced integration of concrete and conceptual exotics. There is, therefore, a general trend from simple to more complex socio-political development at the local scale. This is often modelled as linear and directional change. However, as participants in, and contributors to, a much larger system, southern Ontario populations were affected by its transformations, so the trajectory is not one of simple growth and development at this larger scale. Rather, here development is nonlinear, even cyclical in its promotion of hierarchy.

Various ethnographic and archaeological examples have highlighted the importance of the exogenous to the development of hierarchy. This lends support to the suggestions of Schortman and Urban (1992) and Edens (1992) that we really need to consider the channel of interaction and its correlation to particular groups within interacting communities before we can fully determine the effect of exchange on local development. Revisionist ethnographies additionally teach us that societies are continuously created, maintained, and transformed through exogenous interactions. These are processes which occur at multiple temporal and spatial scales.

By way of explanation as to how hierarchical and ranked societies could have developed, consider the following. Complex kin-based societies are typically segmental and composed of structurally equivalent groupings (e.g., Dole 1968:95). When there is inter-group cooperation or competition promoted by social obligations (including leadership roles), then kin-ordered hierarchies may arise as one group outdoes another in amassing critical resources (Chagnon 1990:90-91, 97-98, 103-104; Creamer and Haas 1985:739; Feinman and Neitzel 1984:61-62; Haas 1990:172-174). The exotic, either physical or ideological, is used to mark status and materialize political relationships insofar as "control of the distribution of foreign objects can be used to draw in a local population and reward its participation" (Earle 1989:85). At this point, leadership tends to be ephemeral (Spencer 1987:370). If cooperation continues within kin groups and competition continues between them, eventually some develop characteristics and properties that are independent of lower levels, and ranked hierarchies emerge (Shryock 1987:246-247) in which "positions of valued status are somehow limited so that not all those of sufficient talent to occupy such statuses actually achieve them" (Fried 1967:109). Ranked hierarchies are governmental insofar as actions at one level stimulate or limit those at other levels, but there is no validation of office (Creamer and Haas 1985:739; Shyrock 1987:246). Big-man societies are of this type (Feinman and Neitzel 1984:48).

Societies postulated for the Rice Lake area ca 2,000 years ago may very well have been characterized by ranked hierarchies. Despite claims that societies living in southern Ontario at the time of European contact had structurally equivalent kin-ordered groupings (i.e., were "egalitarian") (e.g., Ferris and Spence 1995:115), the historical literature points to the fact that diversity and variability were increasing and that ranked hierarchies were emerging (e.g., Sagard 1866:3:802; Thwaites 1896-1901:10:205, 231-233, 253, 13:11-17; Trigger 1990a:81-90, 99-101; Wrong 1939:157). That these societies had strong communal characteristics is a reflection of their kin-ordering: each individual had socially defined obligations to others. Elsewhere, I have argued that one southern Ontario group had become a nascent chiefdom by the early seventeenth century (e.g., Jamieson 1996). This is not a very large departure from the big-man society. The major difference is that the leader has gained socially validated control over the hierarchy (Creamer and Haas 1985:740; Dole 1968:95; Earle 1978:2-4; Fried 1967). Chiefs, like headmen, can function administratively on a part-time basis (Steponaitis 1978:420), and emergent chiefdoms need not be particularly unified or hierarchical in their structure (Earle 1989:87). Indeed, component groups of nascent chiefdoms are often self-sufficient owing to the fact that there is little central coordination (Spencer 1990:7). As noted in my introduction, ritual is used to symbolize, simplify, and enhance political messages and can be used to build, maintain, or destroy political power (Kertzer 1988). McGarry's (1997) analysis of exogenous artifacts from late sixteenth and early seventeenth century southern Ontario clearly supports this argument, as she concludes that it was social and economic stress that spurred increased spatial integration at that time.

The peer polity interaction concept developed by Renfrew and Cherry (1986) has been invoked to address intergroup relations in southern Ontario (Williamson and Robertson 1994a). However, as defined by Renfrew (1986:1), the model stresses horizontal political relationships, at the expense of other social relations. Furthermore, examination shows that the approach focusses on sites of equivalent rank and size in adjacent hierarchies, hence, not only pairs equality among polities with a hierarchical structure within each polity, but also assumes regional organizational homogeneity and ignores potentially important interactions within pan-regional entities. The result is that many of the assumptions prevalent in the neo-Adam-Smithian variety of world systems theory (and in the core-periphery model) are implicit in this perspective.

Crumley's (1987:158) concept of "heterarchy" is likely to prove a more profitable way of understanding the spatial integration of social units than either the core-periphery or peer polity model as it avoids any assumption of hierarchical relations. Crumley (1987:158) defines structures as "heterarchical when each element is either unranked relative to other elements or possess the potential for being ranked in a number of ways". Thus, heterarchy subsumes hierarchy and accepts fluid intergroup relations and resulting heterogeneity.

Because our existing taxonomy derives from the cultural-historical paradigm, it is built upon assumptions which model culture either as normative or adaptionist, hence as homogeneous, bounded, and passive. Thus, there is no room for material variation to be interpreted from the perspective of human action. Indeed, the taxonomy effectively precludes analyzes of societal interaction at any scale and constrains our thinking about this.

It should be evident from the above discussion of archaeological evidence for interaction that effective analyzes require multiscalar approaches: what appears to be a homogenous pattern at one scale may appear heterogeneous at another both through time and over space. Researchers critical of my earlier work do not appear to have fully grasped this fact. For example, I argue that after 1,200 years ago, some southern Ontario polities exhibit characteristics implying similarities in social relations at a regional scale and document that the directions of interaction change through time. Yet, analysis of many artifact assemblages at the local scale, as pointed out by Williamson and Robertson (1994a), reveals heterogenous "style zones". These are "part of a long-term process of continued interaction between communities sharing similar decorative practices" (Cobb and Nassaney 1995:211). These are local scalar patterns influenced by socio-historical structures and past material culture constructs. That is why I argue that spatial variation cannot be understood apart from historical context. Thus, the integration of social groups over the landscape is predicated not only upon ongoing manipulation of intergroup relations but also upon the previous states of the groups in question. The contrastive patterns of group development in southern Ontario were influenced by both local and regional processes of articulation (Jamieson 1992:81).

Hence, both the local and the regional must be investigated in tandem if we are to reach a broader understanding of past social dynamics. This can be achieved not only by examining the distributions and sources of exogenous settlement data and artifact styles that have high public visibility or prominent repetition (i.e., material culture that has enhanced communication potential), but also by studying the distributions of prosaic artifacts and settlement information. Ultimately it should be possible to construct taxonomies of local and interregional contact webs.

In conclusion, archaeological taxonomic conventions that presuppose linearity, boundedness, homogeneity, and stasis may only be applicable in very restricted contexts (e.g., to develop initial, local cultural-historical outlines). Beyond this low level of application they are too simplistic and limiting in their scope to adequately classify and summarize the diversity and variability evident in the archaeological record or to permit historical contextual data to be appropriately investigated. Furthermore, we need to clarify linkages between social groups and technology, ritual, and other aspects of life if we ever hope to address more fully the extent to which these groups may have shaped the societies of which they were a part. To be successful in these endeavours, we need a better integrated research base and a greater degree of coordination among researchers.

Notes

1. A contrast exists between the view of migration as an historical event and the view of migration as sustained movement over time. When related societies are observed geographically distant from each other, proponents of the former view invoke hypothetical migrations to have gotten them there. This kind of thinking is prominent in most of the older linguistic, archaeological, and biological anthropological literature, and largely has been refuted by more recent scholarship. Nonetheless, modern researchers continue to speculate about specific times and places of hypothetical migrations which have implications for southern Ontario's past (e.g., Chapdelaine 1992; Snow 1992a, b, 1994, 1995a, b, 1996). The alternative approach to migration, as exemplified here, may be characterized as gradual rather than historical or transformational, insofar as intergroup mobility, diffusion, and assimilation are regarded as long-term, sustained processes. The latter view conforms with current interpretations of the spread of languages (e.g., Nichols 1997:372,380) and human DNA (e.g., Lasker and Mascie-Taylor 1988). I conclude that the gradual model best accommodates the Iroquoian biological and archaeological data from southern Ontario and accounts for the invisibility of the hypothetical migration in these records. It additionally accounts for the widely divergent conclusions reached by linguists on this topic.

2. This term is preferred to "utilitarian", which carries with it strong positivist connotations I wish to avoid.

3. The ca 750 B.P. Pergentile site produced a nearly intact locally made vessel representing a gourd or squash. This vessel, which lacks carbon encrustations, was recovered from a pit containing sherds from vessels which had been used for cooking (Robert 1997:91-92, 130). Kelly (1991:86) observes that gourd or squash effigy vessels "may be related to fertility ceremonies that were pan-Mississippi valley in distribution. They may represent gifts presented to or obtained by local elites during such ceremonies.... In many respects these ceremonies may have served as an integrative mechanism not only for social and religious reasons, but also as a means of reaffirming exchange relationships with trade

partners." Emerson (1997a) establishes Kelly's argument in greater detail, noting various contexts in which lobed (squash/pumpkin effigy) vessels have been found in "world renewal" pits associated with broken ceramics. He builds a case that these are part of a rural fertility cult correlated with Green Corn ritual, among other things.

Acknowledgements

I gratefully acknowledge Mima Kapches for providing me with copies of unpublished manuscripts on trade, one of which informed part of this paper. Comments by Bill Engelbrecht, Dean Snow, Mike Spence, David Stothers, Bruce Trigger, and an anonymous reviewer helped me sharpen my thinking. I consequently trust that this paper is more readable than my 1992 publication on interaction, hence may be better understood and more accurately cited. However, like Bill Engelbrecht, I hold no illusion that it will necessarily "promote a more integrative or holistic understanding of Great Lakes archaeology". Portions of the introduction, discussion, and footnotes derive from a paper which I presented in February, 1992, at the Annual McMaster Anthropology Society Symposium, Hamilton, Ontario.

ALGONQUIANS AND IROQUOIANS: TAXONOMY, CHRONOLOGY AND ARCHAEOLOGICAL IMPLICATIONS

14

Stuart J. Fiedel
John Milner Associates

This paper begins with a discussion of some basic principles of linguistic classification, and applies them to the aboriginal languages of the Great Lakes region. I then explore the demographic, chronological, and archaeological implications of linguistic taxonomy.

The Dendritic Model in Historical Linguistics

In historical linguistics, languages are explicitly assigned to "genetic" taxa as members of descent lineages. This classification reflects an underlying model of human expansion and differentiation, which is ultimately derived from the Biblical account of Noah's descendants. This genetic model was central to early nineteenth century ethnological and linguistic research. Although cultural anthropology has moved away from a concern with origins and shared descent, the powerful metaphor of a tree of descent, branching out ever wider with each successive generation, is still important in linguistic taxonomy, as it is in biology.

Critics of the dendritic model observe that languages are not really transmitted like genes. Language, like culture more generally, can be shared by people of diverse genetic origins; vocabulary and even grammatical structure can be borrowed. But these truisms should not obscure certain other basic facts. In a preliterate society, language can be transmitted only by face to face interaction. People who do not interact frequently will inevitably develop mutually idiosyncratic speech variants that, accumulating through time, may impede their conversation. As in biological speciation, separation by geographic barriers is the most obvious cause of such divergence. As small populations grow more numerous and expand over greater territorial ranges, diversity will increase. This leads first to accent differences, then, as sounds and words change, to local dialects. Ultimately, dialects become so differentiated that they are mutually unintelligible, and at this point one can speak of the emergence of separate languages.

Languages that demonstrably developed by divergence from a common ancestor are classified as members of a single *family*, such as Indo-European, Finno-Ugric, Semitic, or Algonquian. In fact, linguists use the term "family" rather haphazardly for all orders of relationship. If Indo-European is a family, what entity is represented by Romance, or Germanic, or Celtic? The nineteenth century linguist and exponent of the tree-model, August Schleicher, called these lesser-order branches "fundamentals"; perhaps we could call them sub-families. Moving down toward the metaphorical tree-trunk, if we could show that Indo-European, Finno-Ugric, and Semitic are derived from a single ancestral entity (what Russian linguists have called Nostratic) what would we call them collectively? In classifying American languages, linguists such as Edward Sapir and Joseph Greenberg have used taxa such as "stock" or "superfamily", and "phylum", for comparable larger lineages. Greenberg (1987) has hypothesized an ancestral entity, from which all American languages except Na-Dene and Inuit-Aleut are derived; all Amerind languages thus would belong to a single phylum or macrophylum.

Lexicostatistics and Glottochronology

Some linguists, following Morris Swadesh (1955), have tried to recognize different taxonomic levels on the basis of lexicostatistical comparison. Relationships between two languages can thus be quantified in terms of percentages of shared cognates in core vocabulary: dialects of one language, more than 81 percent; languages of a family, 36-81 percent; families of a stock, 12-36 percent; stocks of a microphylum, 4-12 percent; microphyla of a mesophylum, 1-4 percent; mesophyla of a macrophylum, 0-1 percent. In practice, it would be very difficult to prove a genetic relationship beyond the stock level, since chance lexical resemblances may be as high as six percent.

Glottochronology attempts to translate these percentages into time depths; that is, centuries elapsed since divergence from an ancestral proto-language are inferred from cognate percentages, on the admittedly dubious assumption that the core vocabularies of all languages change at the same rate. Swadesh suggested up to five centuries for dialects; 500 to 2,500 years for languages of a family (36 to 81 percent cognate sharing); 2,500 to 5,000 years for a stock, 5,000 to 7,500 years for a microphylum, 7,500 to 10,000 years for a mesophylum, and more than 10,000 years for a macrophylum. It should be emphasized that no obvious lexical traces of relationship will remain after 10,000 years of separation. If one assumes

Clovis ancestry for all Native Americans, and takes a calibrated date of 13500 B.P. for Clovis expansion (Taylor et al. 1996; Fiedel 1999), it is obvious why Greenberg has had such a hard time demonstrating the reality of his Amerind macrophylum to the satisfaction of other linguists. Since both Algonquian and Iroquoian languages are recognized as families with cognate sharing in the 36 to 81 percent range (and with internal differences roughly comparable to those of the Romance languages), in each case, a proto-language can be postulated within the last 2,500 years. In both cases, break-up of the proto-language during the Woodland period is implied.

Language Expansion and Replacement

A proto-language in its initial state—prior to expansion and diversification—is just like any other functioning, internally coherent language (in fact, it probably begins as a mature regional dialect of some other widespread language). To maintain this coherence, its speakers cannot be very numerous, and they must occupy a relatively small territory. As the original linguistic community expands, dialects begin to form, which are the seeds of the descendant languages of the family.

Archaeological and historic evidence shows that languages sometimes undergo rapid, explosive expansion through migration of their speakers. If such expansion and linguistic replacement did not occur periodically, every linguistic landscape probably would look like aboriginal California or New Guinea, with their mosaics of tiny unrelated languages. Examples include the Numic expansion from southern California into the Great Basin, the Athapaskan migration from the Yukon to Arizona, and the Inuit migration from Alaska to Greenland. In the Inuit case, a migrating population, represented archaeologically by the Thule culture, traversed and occupied a 3,200 km expanse in about 150 years (1050-900 B.P.), replacing the long-resident indigenous Dorset culture in the process. It is important to note that by the nineteenth century, the Inuit formed a chain of dialects across the Arctic; neighbouring groups could communicate, but the dialects at opposite ends of the chain had become mutually unintelligible. The point here is that soon after dispersion, dialect fragmentation begins all over again.

Historic evidence indicates that the distributions of the Cree and Ojibwa in the eighteenth century represent similar explosive expansions (Bishop 1981), although it is uncertain whether they began to move west in the Late Woodland (as perhaps manifested by distributions of Selkirk and Blackduck pottery [Wright 1981]) or in the late seventeenth century. I have argued (Fiedel 1987, 1990, 1991) that Proto-Algonquian underwent a phase of similar rapid territorial expansion, as its speakers fanned out from a small homeland.

The Proto-Algonquian Homeland

The location of that homeland was first specified in a now-classic article published in 1967 by Frank Siebert. He defined a suite of trees, fish, birds, and mammals that must have been familiar to the Proto-Algonquians, based on surviving cognate words that refer to particular species. The homeland is located in the area where the native habitat ranges of these species (including seal, caribou, bison, and lake trout) overlap. Siebert (1967) determined that this area lies in southern Ontario, between Lake Ontario and Georgian Bay. In the late sixteenth century, much of this area was occupied by the Iroquoian-speaking Huron, a fact that emphasizes the intrusive character of the Northern Iroquoians.

Speculative Models of Proto-Algonquian Demography

The area delineated by Siebert represents only the minimal size of the original Proto-Algonquian territory. This area can be estimated as only about 8,000 square miles (20,718 square km). The hypothesized size of the original community will vary based on our assumptions about population density. Unfortunately, there is a huge range of plausible density figures. The Huron, who actually lived in this area at contact, numbered some 20,000 people within a 340 square mile (880 square km) area (Heidenreich 1978), for a density of 60 per square mile (or 23 per square km). Of course, this population was sustained by maize agriculture, which probably was not practised by Proto-Algonquians if they had emigrated before 1300 B.P., as seems likely. A plausible estimate of contact-period Ojibwa population, with a non-horticultural hunting-fishing adaptation, is about 100,000, living in a territory of roughly 50,000 square miles (129,490 square km) (Ritzenthaler 1978). This yields a density of two per square mile (less than 1 per square km). At the other extreme, Rogers and Leacock (1981) tentatively estimated that 4,000 Montagnais-Naskapi occupied 300,000 square miles (776,940 square km) before contact (one person per 75 square mile [194 square km]). Even at this very low density, they risked episodes of starvation. Actual historic Northern Athapaskan language territories averaged about 55,000 square miles, or 140,000 square km; Northern Ojibwa dialect territories averaged about the same, but Cree dialect territories seem to have been somewhat greater, such as ca 120,000 square miles (310,000 square km) for East Cree, but about 45,000 (72,000 square km) for East Swamp Cree.

We can entertain two equally plausible models for the original Proto-Algonquian territory and community. Taking the two person per square mile density figure from the Ojibwa, we could postulate some 16,000 Proto-Algonquians in a minimal territory of 8,000 square miles (20, 718 square km). They would be speaking a single language, like the historic Menominee or Potawatomi. Assuming Cree-like density, however, this small area could support only about 100 people—barely a single macroband. Joseph Birdsell (1968), drawing mainly upon Australian data, articulated the concept of the dialect tribe, a fundamental viable social and linguistic unit of about 500 people. This is roughly equivalent to the number that Martin Wobst (1976) derived for the minimum biologically sustainable human population. The hypothetical population of the minimal Proto-Algonquian homeland would fall significantly below the 500 number. If we assume a Subarctic density of one person per 80 square miles (207 square km), a hypothetical Archaic dialect tribe of 500 might occupy a territory of about 40,000 square miles or 103,000 square km, roughly equivalent to actual Cree and Athapaskan dialect territories.

Excluding uninhabitable water surface, the Great Lakes region contains some 250,000 square miles (647,000 square km). This is not a huge area, in comparison to the historic ranges of Cree and Ojibwa. Cree encompassed nine dialects, spanning a distance of about 2,400 miles (3800 km) (ca 500,000 square miles [1,294,900 square km]). Ojibwa was comprised of eight dialects, spoken in an area of about 550,000 square miles (1,424,390 square km). It is, therefore, entirely plausible to suppose that Proto-Algonquian was a single language occupying this entire area of 250,000 square miles (647,450 square kilometes).

Let us assume that each of the 11 historically attested descendant branches of Algonquian (Menominee, Ojibwa, Potawatomi, Cree, Sauk-Fox-Kickapoo, Miami-Illinois, Shawnee, Arapaho, Cheyenne, Blackfoot, and Eastern) began as a dialect of one extended proto-language. If anything, this is a minimal figure, since other languages may have disappeared before recording (like the Precontact languages of Ohio). Packed in, more or less equally around the lakes, each dialect would have occupied some 23,000 square miles (59,500 square km). Based on differing density assumptions, the population of each dialect group could have ranged from 46,000 to as few as 307 people. The latter figure falls well below the 500-person limit for viability. By assuming a minimum of

500 speakers per dialect, we get 5,500 as the minimum total Proto-Algonquian population of the entire region, at a density of one person per 46 square miles (119 square kilometers). On the other hand, applying the Ojibwa-based density of two persons per square mile, we would get a total population of over 500,000. But the Ojibwa density seems aberrant, compared to estimates of contact-period population for other Central Algonquians (e.g., ca 9,000 for Potawatomi [Clifton 1978], 9,000 for Sauk-Fox-Kickapoo [Callender 1978a, 1978b; Callender at al. 1978; Goddard 1978a], 10,000 for Miami-Illinois [Callender 1978c and 1978d], and only 2,500 for Shawnee [Callender 1978e] and also for Menominee [Spindler 1978]). If we assume instead a figure of 10,000 per original dialect tribe, we get 110,000 as the population of the Great Lakes region at the time of Algonquian dispersal. If the population was in that range, it had to double over the course of about 1,500 years to get to the approximate 200,000 or 250,000 figure that I would estimate as the minimum total population of Eastern and Central Algonquians at Contact.

Dating Algonquian Expansion

When did the proposed Algonquian expansion occur? Siebert and other linguists have advanced fairly consistent intuitive estimates for the divergence of Central and Eastern Algonquian languages: 3150-2850 B.P. (Siebert 1967); 2450 B.P. (Goddard 1978b); 2950 to 1950 B.P. (Haas 1966). Charles Hockett (1964) dated the break-up of proto-Central Algonquian at around 1450 B.P. Glottochronological estimates range from 2950 to 1050 B.P. When I compared vocabulary lists for 11 languages, cognate percentages ranged between 59 and 78 percent in comparisons of Eastern and Central languages (except Micmac, with a range of 42 to 54 percent) (Fiedel 1990). These numbers imply divergence between 1780 and 960 B.P., although the Micmac percentages could support an earlier date of about 2400 B.P.. My analysis of glottochrological dates for Northern versus Southern Athapaskan languages indicates that separation times should be regarded with an inherent error factor of ± about 400 years. The average of 21 Eastern versus Western comparisons is 68 percent, indicating separation at ca 1450 B.P.; an acceptable range is 1850 to 1050 B.P., and the date could even be pushed back to 2450 B.P. to accommodate the Micmac percentages.

Linguistic and Archaeological Precontact History of the Algonquian and Iroquoian Families

My interpretation of Algonquian and Iroquoian linguistic precontact history (Fiedel 1991) can be summarized as follows (Figure 14.1).

Proto-Algonquian developed initially as a regional dialect variant of a still earlier ancestral entity called Proto-Algic. The only other surviving descendants of Proto-Algic are two neighbouring languages of northern California, Wiyot and Yurok. Based on the small number of shared cognates between these languages and Algonquian languages, the common ancestor probably broke apart before 6950 B.P. The limited archaeological evidence from northern California suggests that the Wiyot and Yurok immigrated, perhaps from the Columbia Plateau, after 1050 B.P. (Moratto 1984). Certain grammatical resemblances to Northwest Coast languages imply that Proto-Algic may have been located in the northern Plateau region. The eastward spread of Plano assemblages across the Shield about 8950 B.P. perhaps represents Proto-Algic expansion; there is no later archaeological entity that encompasses both the northern Plateau and the Shield. Presumably, the Shield Archaic cultures developed in situ from late Plano roots. Proto-Algonquian began to develop around the Great Lakes during the Late Archaic as a dialect of Proto-Algic (or some temporally intermediate entity that left no other descendant languages).

Any archaeological complex that would be a plausible candidate for identification as the material remains of Proto-Algonquians must satisfy these criteria:

1. initial appearance and development in or near southern Ontario;
2. expansion between 2450 and 1050 B.P.;
3. evidence of intrusion on the Atlantic coast in the same period, and probable retention of contact with related groups in the eastern Great Lakes.

The most convincing candidate for Proto-Algonquian is the Point Peninsula complex. Around 2250 B.P., there was an apparent population explosion in southern Ontario. Middle Woodland occupations occur at many sites where there is no previous Early Woodland presence. Saugeen pottery, initially produced as early as 2550 B.P., quickly gave rise to two related ceramic traditions—Laurel, which spread north and west around 2150 B.P., and Point Peninsula, which spread east into New York, New

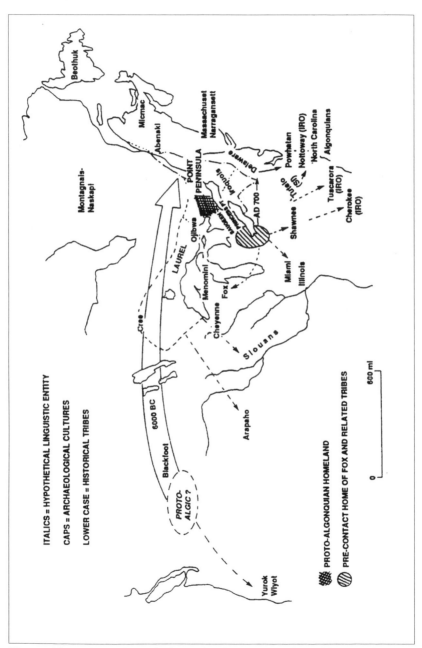

Figure 14.1: Distribution of Algonquian languages and neighbouring language groups, ca A.D. 1600 in relation to archaeological cultures and hypothetical linguistic entities.

England, and the Maritime Provinces between 2150 and 1750 B.P. Ritchie (1965:207) observed that sherds of this tradition from Minnesota and New Hampshire were nearly identical. These pots were not trade items; they must have been made by women who travelled across huge distances. Fitting (1965a) recognized the stylistic and adaptational unity of this vast culture area, referring to it as "Lake Forest Middle Woodland".

Several centuries later, ca 1200-1000 B.P., we find evidence of a post-Hopewellian mortuary-focussed exchange network that linked late Point Peninsula complexes on the Atlantic coast to contemporary populations living east and south of the Great Lakes. Items circulated within this network included: steatite platform pipes, carved in Rhode Island quarries and traded as far as Ontario, Ohio, and Indiana (Seeman 1981); Jack's Reef pentagonal and corner-notched points (many made of Pennsylvania jasper) pentagonal cache blades, moose-antler combs, and barbed bone harpoon-heads. During this period, there are evident relationships among assemblages from Michigan (the Wayne mortuary complex), Ohio (Intrusive Mound culture), Ontario (late Point Peninsula), Delaware (Island Field), New York (Kipp Island) and Vermont (Winooski). The extension of this network into the Mid-Atlantic region may be an archeological correlate of a secondary migration or a wave of linguistic diffusion, represented by the phonologically distinctive Unami, Munsee, and Mahican languages.

It must be emphasized that the Iroquoian languages are totally unlike Algonquian in vocabulary, phonology, and grammar. If these families are genetically related at all, they must have split apart many thousands of years ago, perhaps at a time depth equivalent to the Paleo-Indian horizon. Greenberg (1987) has suggested that both families belong to a single phylum, but most linguists regard this as an unsubstantiated hypothesis. It should be noted, too, that very few loanwords appear to have passed between these families. This may reflect not only their very different phonologies and grammatical structures, but perhaps also indicates that their geographic propinquity is a recent phenomenon.

At the time of initial European contact in the sixteenth and seventeenth centuries, a belt of Iroquoian speakers stretched from the mouth of the St. Lawrence River through southern Ontario and central New York State, and into central Pennsylvania. Speakers of closely related Northern Iroquoian languages—Nottoway, Meherrin, and Tuscarora—occupied the fall line in Virginia and North Carolina. The Cherokee, who spoke a more distantly related Southern Iroquoian language, occupied the Appalachian Summit region, centred in western

North Carolina. The Cherokee may have an analogous role in Iroquoian to that of Wiyot and Yurok in Algonquian reconstruction. Their location tends to pull the centre of Proto-Iroquoian development southward (although it must be recognized that Cherokee origins remain obscure, and it is very unlikely that their historic location is near the Iroquoian homeland). Furthermore, linguists such as Wallace Chafe (1973) have noted a distant lexical relationship of Iroquoian to Caddoan and to Siouan, which are families of the South and Midwest; a Proto-Macro-Siouan entity has even been proposed. In view of this evidence, it would be very difficult to argue that the Huron represent an indigenous population present since Archaic times in Ontario.

When Floyd Lounsbury (1961,1978) applied the glottochronological technique to Iroquoian, he estimated that the divergence of the Five Nations' languages occurred between ca 1450 and 950 B.P. Is the similarity of these Iroquoian and Central versus Eastern Algonquian separation estimates coincidental? I think not. It seems obvious that a northward Iroquoian migration, pushing to the mouth of the St. Lawrence River, cut off the ancestral Eastern Algonquians from their congeners around the Great Lakes.

By linguistic reconstruction, it can be shown that the Proto-Algonquians probably possessed the bow and arrow, smoking pipes, and pots. There are also some hints in Proto-Algonquian, such as a reconstructed word meaning "seed saved for sowing" (Siebert 1975) that imply the practice of some sort of horticulture in the ancestral homeland. Reconstructed Proto-Northern Iroquoian (ancestral to all the historic languages except Cherokee) contains several words referring to the bow and arrow, and also words for "corn", "bread", "bottle or jar", and "town" (Mithun 1984). Thus, the break-up of Proto-Algonquian must have occurred after the diffusion of the bow and arrow into the Eastern Woodlands; this is generally dated to ca 1350 B.P. Proto-Northern-Iroquoian languages apparently diverged after the introduction of maize, also ca 1350 B.P.

It has been noted recently (Crawford and Smith 1996) that the presence of maize in Princess Point contexts in Ontario poses a major problem for Dean Snow's hypothesis that interprets Owasco as an intrusive Proto-Iroquoian agricultural complex. Snow has responded that this only means that the intrusion should be pushed back from ca 1050 B.P. to 1350 B.P., and that Princess Point and Clemson Island may represent the Proto-Northern Iroquoians. I previously suggested this identification (Fiedel 1987), based on David Stothers' 1977 view of

Princess Point. Subsequently, Stothers sharply revised his interpretation, stressing continuity of Princess Point with the earlier Point Peninsula complex, rather than its similarity to Late Hopewellian assemblages. He now regards Princess Point as ancestral to the Iroquoian Neutrals. Stothers would also derive the Algonquian Mascouten from an Upper Mississippian tradition of northwestern Ohio (i.e., Sandusky) with ultimate roots in the regional Late Archaic Feeheley phase (Stothers and Graves 1992). The Kickapoo and Fox would descend from the same source as the Mascouten, but their cultural lineage diverged around 1050 B.P.

Several aspects of Stothers' model appear dubious. For one thing, if we identify the Ohio or southeast Michigan Late Archaic as specifically proto-Mascouten/Kickapoo, we must push the break-up of the larger Proto-Algonquian entity even earlier, before 3950 B.P., and this seems implausible to me. My Canadian colleagues' interpretation of Point Peninsula as an ancestral Iroquoian tradition is equally problematic. What does that imply about the very closely related Laurel complex? Can anyone point to a descendant Iroquoian population in Manitoba, or for that matter in the Maritimes, or in northern New England, where Point Peninsula ceramics are common? In any case, there now seems to be some consensus on a discontinuity in the ceramic sequence in Ontario: "differences between Princess Point and Point Peninsula in both ceramic manufacture and style are, in fact, rather striking" (Crawford and Smith 1996:788); "The discontinuity is now clearly at the boundary between Princess Point and Point Peninsula, around 1350 B.P. or earlier" (Snow 1996:792). Princess Point leads to Glen Meyer, which in turn is ancestral to the Ontario Iroquoians.

Recognition of Linguistic/Ethnic Entities in the Archaeological Record: Problems and Prospects

I conclude with the following observations on the potential congruence of archaeological and linguistic/ethnic entities: (1) The absence of distinctive diagnostic material culture traits in the archeological record does not preclude the incursion of a new population and/or language. There are several good examples from California, such as the virtually identical material cultures of the Algic Yurok, Hokan Karok, and Athapaskan Hupa; (2) Conversely, people of a single linguistic stock can adopt radically different adaptations and material cultures—consider the Athapaskans of the Yukon and the Navajo, or the

Shoshoni, Hopi, and Aztec, all members of the Uto-Aztekan family; (3) Sharp social and political boundaries can develop between people of the same language family and material culture—consider the Neutral, Petun and Huron and the Five Nations; (4) Intrusive groups typically incorporate members of the precursor population—we should therefore expect substantial evidence of biological continuity in skeletal and genetic evidence, even where a migration can be inferred from linguistic or archeological data; 5) Continuity in settlement location primarily reflects the constancy of the landscape and water sources, rather than ethnic continuity; and (6) Significant population replacement may be most evident in surviving elements of material culture at the level of the most basic motor behaviour—Snow has suggested that coiling versus modelling of pottery is such a distinction, and James Adovasio has argued (Adovasio and Pedler 1994) that different basic techniques of twining and coiling can be used to distinguish basketry of Numic immigrants from that of their precursors in the Great Basin. Bill Johnson has been studying percentages of Z-twist versus S-twist in cordage applied to cordmarked ceramics in the Mid-Atlantic. He observed a radical change from S- to Z-twist predominance in ceramics of the Virginia Coastal Plain at the Middle to Late Woodland transition, ca 1150 B.P., which is best explained as an indication of population replacement (Johnson and Speedy 1992:99), perhaps by intrusive Eastern Algonquians. Similar analysis may clarify the issue of Point Peninsula-Princess Point relationships.

CONTRIBUTIONS OF SKELETAL BIOLOGY TO GREAT LAKES PRECONTACT HISTORY

15

George R. Milner
Department of Anthropology, Pennsylvania State University
M. Anne Katzenberg
Department of Archaeology, University of Calgary

When invited to participate in the Plenary Session entitled Taming the Taxonomy we were faced with a difficult problem: what could possibly be said about how human skeletons can be used to sort ancient materials into temporal and spatial units that contribute to understandings of the past? That is, how can old bones be used to construct culturally meaningful categories that are useful to archaeologists? These categories, of course, are mostly based on bits of stone and pottery along with the remnants of buildings and the like. Upon some reflection, we decided that the only way to tackle this problem was by focussing on topics where human remains represent the primary, if not the only, way to determine how people lived in precontact times. After all, the classification of ancient societies according to ways of life has had a long, although checkered, history in archaeology.

We focus on several theoretical, methodological, and data-related issues that pertain to four questions that have long been the subject of archaeological study. First, what can skeletons tell us about the degree of morphological similarity, hence biological relatedness, among different human groups? Second, how can bones be used to determine what precontact people ate? Third, how healthy were these people? Fourth, did they get along with one another or did they fight at every opportunity? In keeping with this volume's geographical focus, we emphasize skeletal remains from Ontario and the states bordering the Great Lakes.

Biological Relatedness

There once was a time when biological relationships were an indispensable part of classifications of archaeological complexes. Perhaps the words "implicit" or even "explicit" capture the sense of this relationship better than "indispensable". Even in the absence of skeletal data, it was commonly assumed that discontinuities in regional cultural sequences indicated wholesale replacements of one group of people by another, with separate populations often identified by the shapes of their heads. Quite simply, different peoples were carriers of distinctive cultural baggage. An emphasis was placed on identifying ideal cranial types (e.g., Iswanid and Lenapid [Neumann 1952; for an opposing view cf. Wilkinson 1971]) that supposedly could be used to detect the ebb and flow of discrete populations across broad geographical regions. Archaeologists are now several decades beyond simplistic linkages between people and particular kinds of pots, tools, houses, and the like. It has even been argued that the pendulum has swung too far in the other direction. With the emphasis on in situ developments of new ways of life, archaeologists have tended to overlook the fact that people do move and some changes in regional sequences are certainly attributable to shifts in population distributions (Anthony 1990; Snow 1994, 1995a, 1995b).

Our purpose is not to go into a prolonged discussion of the relative merits of arguments over shifts in population distributions in any part of the upper Midwest and Northeast. It is sufficient to say that population movements in precontact history, including how they can be identified in the first place, continue to be of great interest to archaeologists. For example, Dean Snow (1995a, b) recently proposed that the emergence about a millennium ago of the Iroquois cultural tradition in upstate New York was a consequence of the arrival of people who had moved northward from Pennsylvania. Considering the emphasis on in situ cultural development over the past few decades, it is not surprising that Snow's (1995) migration scenario is hotly debated by regional specialists (Chapdelaine [editor] 1992; Clermont 1996; Crawford and Smith 1996).

Population movements among small-scale, kin-based societies are now viewed differently than they were several decades ago. It is not much of an exaggeration to say that migrations in precontact history were once treated by archaeologists as if culturally and biologically uniform peoples swept across vast areas on a wide front, pushing along and replacing their predecessors as they went. Such movements now tend to be treated as a jostling of ever-changing constellations of communities for advantageous positions in heterogeneous social and natural landscapes. The composition of these groups, and the alliances among them, changed over time as circumstances dictated, as did their geographical disposition, sometimes with a tendency to move farther in one direction than another.

The question that naturally arises is whether it can be determined from skeletons if the archaeological picture of change over time is related to population replacement or to shifts in how people lived. Both scenarios might produce changes in artifact inventories and styles, architectural details, community configurations, and diets, all of which are used in classifications of ancient societies. Osteologists have traditionally relied on multivariate analyzes of either skeletal dimensions or discrete (nonmetric) traits—that is, measurements of bones or frequencies of minor but variable skeletal features such as bony spicules in certain foramina— to determine the extent of morphological similarity among different groups of skeletons. While the genetic contribution to overall bone shape and minor skeletal (and dental) traits requires further study, seemingly explicable geographical and temporal patterning in skeletal (and dental) characteristics have been identified repeatedly in studies of both human and nonhuman samples. Furthermore, osteologists typically eliminate from their analyzes the skeletal characteristics that were clearly affected by the environment, such as skull dimensions modified by artificial cranial deformation.

The use of nonmetric traits for this purpose was pioneered by James Anderson (1968), and it has been applied widely to precontact Ontario skeletal collections. Of particular relevance was J. E. Molto's (1983) study of cranial nonmetric traits. His results were consistent with an in situ development of Ontario Iroquoians and, hence, they were in agreement with long-accepted archaeological thinking about Iroquoian origins (MacNeish 1952; Wright 1966). Snow's (1994, 1995a) recent critique of this conclusion, at least for the New York Iroquois, serves as an impetus for further studies of human remains using newer methods and incorporating a temporally and spatially wider range of samples.

Turning to the Midwest, Dawnie Steadman's (1997) recent study of cranial dimensions addressed the sudden appearance at about 700 B.P., of Oneota sites in west-central Illinois. These sites have been interpreted by archaeologists as a penetration southward of people who pushed into an area previously occupied by culturally dissimilar folk (Santure et al.[editors] 1990). This analysis indicates that the Oneota are indeed outliers relative to nearly contemporaneous skeletons, as well as those predating them by several centuries. The Oneota thus appear to be newcomers to the Illinois River valley, an interpretation that fits comfortably with the artifactual evidence. Populations, therefore, were clearly moving from one place to another. The possibility of such movements should never have been questioned considering what is known from historical and ethnographic sources about the disposition and relations among the communities that make up small, kin-based societies.

The problem archaeologists face, of course, is identifying when and why such movements took place. It would also be valuable to know if there were particular times and places in precontact history when movements of people were particularly common. The Oneota movement, for example, coincides with an increase in intergroup aggression from the northern Plains eastward through the northern Eastern Woodlands, as indicated by skeletons with conflict-related trauma and settlements surrounded by walls (Milner 1999; Milner et al. 1991; Willey 1990).

Steadman's (1997) study also indicated that there was considerable continuity among most of the peoples who inhabited west-central Illinois throughout much of the late precontact period. These findings are consistent with earlier studies of metric and nonmetric skeletal characteristics where major changes in ways of life were shown not to have been associated with the arrival of large numbers of outsiders (Buikstra 1977; Droessler 1981). Biological continuity across broad areas and over great periods of time in southern Ontario and Ohio also appear to be indicated by skeletal morphology (Molto 1983; Sciulli et al. 1984). Such results are consistent with Russell Nelson's (1997) findings that collections of late precontact skeletons from widely distributed sites tend to cluster together into regional groupings. A separation of west-central Illinois from Great Lakes skeletons makes perfect sense from an archaeological perspective considering the marked differences in cultural traditions between those areas. In addition, Stephen Langdon's (1995) recent analysis of anthropometric measurements taken a century ago has shown that several northeastern Iroquoian and Algonquian groups were more similar to one another than they were to the geographically more distant Cherokee and Shawnee. Any such patterns, however, are clouded by complex histories of movement and amalgamation among large and small groups from the seventeenth century onward. Thus across much of the upper Midwest and the Great Lakes, there was considerable population continuity over long periods of time. It is emphasized that we are referring to the occupation of broadly defined geographical regions, and are fully aware of both variation among contemporaneous archaeological complexes within them and change over time in the spatial distribution of population aggregates.

There have also been recent and rapid advances in the study of ancient DNA. Ancient DNA—here we are speaking for the most part about mitochondrial DNA—holds great promise for some areas of archaeological research. One such example is the genetic significance of the different ways the dead were treated within cemeteries. Knowing which individuals might have been related—maternally related in the case of mtDNA—could provide some insight into how past societies were organized. In fact, the most extensive mtDNA study, to date, of a single precontact site anywhere in the Americas focussed on a 700 year old cemetery from west-central Illinois (Stone 1996). But despite rapid advances in ancient DNA research, it is not practicable with existing methods and using ancient bones to sort out the degree of genetic relatedness among separate precontact communities distributed across the upper Midwest and Northeast. For example, the study of skeletons from the late precontact cemetery in Illinois found the four principal mtDNA lineage clusters that have been identified to date in contemporary Aboriginal Americans (Stone 1996; Stone and Stoneking 1993, 1998). Differences among precontact Great Lakes region peoples in the proportions of the principal mtDNA lineages would be exceedingly difficult to interpret. These reasonably fluid populations consisted of social groups that divided and combined with one another in highly structured ways while they expanded, moved, and contracted over time (cf. discussions in Merriwether et al. [1997] and Parr et al. [1996]). Simply knowing the relative proportions of a limited number of mtDNA haplogroups in samples widely scattered in time and space would not be sufficient to sort out complex histories of movement, amalgamation, and fragmentation of small communities.

Diet

Subsistence practices are integrally related to many aspects of people's lives—from the tools they used to where they settled and their social organization—so it is no surprise they have been used for classification purposes. In fact, a heavy reliance on maize is one of the defining characteristics of many late precontact Eastern Woodland societies, along with distinctive kinds of pottery, architecture, and the like. Yet identifying the range of plants and animals that were consumed is not the same as estimating the contribution of these foods to the diet. The latter is a much more difficult endeavour. Bone composition—particularly its stable carbon and nitrogen isotopic signatures—represents the most direct means currently available for measuring the dietary contribution of several kinds of food. Of greatest interest to archaeologists working in the northern Eastern Woodlands is the ability to investigate the consumption of maize (Buikstra 1992; Katzenberg et al. 1995). It has also been shown using stable isotopes that people at one site along Lake Erie ate more fish than their nearby contemporaries in the interior of Ontario (Katzenberg et al. 1995). Generally speaking, the use of maize across much of the Midwest and Great Lakes area parallelled patterns found in many, but not all, parts of the Eastern Woodlands (Buikstra 1992; Katzenberg et al. 1995; Smith 1989). Maize consumption increased late in the first millennium A.D., and only after about 1000 years ago did people in many places come to rely on it heavily. Figure 15.1, derived from data by Katzenberg et al. (1995), shows the stable isotope composition of "collagen" samples from sites distributed across the midcontinent and into the Great Lakes.

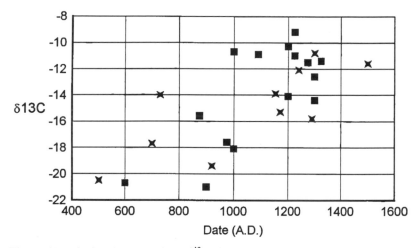

Figure 15.1: Carbon isotope values ($\delta^{13}C$) from sites in the midcontinent (squares) and Great Lakes region (stars); data from Katzenberg et al. (1995).

The overall pattern throughout much of the Eastern Woodlands is surprisingly consistent: little or no maize was consumed and then, within a matter of a few centuries, it became a major component of diets. Relative to the length of time people occupied the Eastern Woodlands, this shift occurred rapidly. There were regional differences, however, in the degree to which maize was a dietary staple and when large quantities of it began to be consumed. It also appears that the degree to which people relied on several indigenous plants prior to the adoption of maize varied greatly throughout the Eastern Woodlands. Judging from botanical remains, pre-maize horticultural systems based on several indigenous plants were more developed in the midcontinent than in the Northeast and

Deep South. The reasons for such variability are at present unknown. As far as the adoption of maize is concerned, differences in the extent of its use would have been related to the length of the growing season, the likelihood of crop failure, and the need for an efficiently harvested and readily stored food (Katzenberg et al. 1995). Overall, reliance on maize, or on a combination of maize plus animals that consumed C_4 plants, was slightly greater in many midwestern populations than in those of Ontario.

The relatively sudden and widespread adoption of maize by culturally diverse groups of people who lived in different environmental settings raises an important issue. It is as if some threshold had been reached, beyond which people in many places at roughly the same time (i.e., within a few centuries) found it advantageous to shift to maize as a major component of their diet. This shift occurred during a period of accelerated population growth across eastern North America, assuming there is some rough relationship between the numbers of sites and overall population size. It is during this period when steps were taken to enhance resource productivity and reliability by growing several indigenous cultigens and, later, maize and beans.

Health

It is now commonly claimed that the health of precontact peoples varied in a regular fashion according to broadly defined ways of life (Cohen 1989, 1994, 1997; Cohen and Armelagos 1984). With regard to diseases of infectious and nutritional origins, conditions are believed to have worsened with the shift to agriculture, and they deteriorated still further with the development of civilizations. This claim is based in part on anecdotal accounts of people living in traditional settings and, more importantly, on medical and osteological findings.

Skeletons from the Midwest and Ontario have contributed greatly to a rapidly growing body of literature on the pathological conditions experienced by precontact peoples (for recent reviews, see Larsen [1995, 1997]). In fact, studies of the Dickson Mounds skeletons from west-central Illinois by several researchers, most notably George Armelagos and Alan Goodman, were quite influential in the development of the now commonly accepted view that agriculture and sedentary ways of life had deleterious effects on the well-being of past populations (for summaries of this work, see Buikstra and Milner [1989]; Goodman et al. [1984]). Problems stemming from a heavy reliance on just a few dietary staples have received considerable attention, but like other osteologists we emphasize that diets are only part of the story. How people distributed themselves across precontact landscapes and how they interacted with one another—including regional population density, intergroup relations, and settlement size, longevity, and compactness—appear to have had as much, and probably more, of an effect on health as diet alone (Katzenberg 1992; Milner and Smith 1990).

The kinds of infectious diseases from which people were likely to suffer also changed over time. Differences in exposure to potential pathogens must have been related to variation in ways of life, particularly those behaviours that affected the likelihood of pathogen transmission among human hosts. For example, bony lesions bearing a striking resemblance to the primarily destructive forms of skeletal involvement associated with tuberculosis have been identified in a number of Eastern Woodland skeletal collections, including those from the Great Lakes area, that date to late precontact times (Buikstra and Cook 1981; Buikstra and Williams 1991; Milner and Smith 1990; Pfeiffer 1984; Powell 1991). This disease appears to have been absent or extremely rare earlier in time, at least in a form that produced distinctive bony lesions.

In the past few years, however, it has become clear that the interpretation of skeletal lesion frequencies is not as simple as it once seemed (cf. Ortner [1991], Wood and Milner [1994], and Wood et al. [1992]; for an opposing point of view see Cohen [1994, 1997] and Goodman [1993]). There are a number of problems with drawing inferences about living populations from mortality samples. The principal difficulty stems from heterogeneous frailty and selective mortality (for a discussion pertaining to paleodemography, see Wood et al. [1992]). Quite simply, those who died at a given age cannot be considered a random sample of all people who were ever alive at that age. Thus saying something about a living population from the characteristics of those who died is not at all straightforward. These issues, often labelled the osteological paradox after the title of a recent article (Wood et al. 1992), have stirred considerable controversy and have prompted some thoughtful analyzes (for a brief review of this ongoing debate cf. Buikstra [1997]).

Here we raise a related concern that is more in line with this volume's purpose: to what extent is it even appropriate to think of the populations that make up archaeological categories, which invariably have considerable temporal depth and geographical breadth, as being more or less healthy than others? Yet it is precisely this sort of simplistic thinking that underlies most research oriented toward understanding the effects on health of changes in ways of life. Keep in mind that according to conventional wisdom, conditions deteriorated for human populations in a stepwise fashion as people started to grow crops and herd animals, and they then worsened as people began to live in the politically centralized and economically differentiated societies often called states (for the longest and most coherent statement of this position see Cohen [1989]). This descent to distress in a few discrete steps is reminiscent of the so-called Neolithic and Urban Revolutions, with all that these terms might imply about the convulsive suddenness of such transitions and a stage-like view of cultural change. Abundant evidence from around the world, however, indicates that the shift from fully hunter-gatherer to agricultural economies spanned very long periods of time, as did the transition to the socio-political systems labelled states. It should be immediately apparent to eastern North American archaeologists that considerable cultural variation is subsumed by subsistence-based categories such as hunter-gatherer and agriculturalist. In the Eastern Woodlands, the road to agricultural ways of life was long, and even the groups that relied heavily on crops continued to fish, hunt game, and gather wild plants (Smith 1989).

The numerous studies of the Dickson Mounds skeletons from west-central Illinois are widely regarded as strong support for the great costs to human health of the transition to agriculture (Goodman et al. 1984; see summaries of many publications in Buikstra and Milner [1989]). Yet all of the Dickson Mounds skeletons were derived from populations that were a long way from practising either fully hunter-gatherer or agriculturalist subsistence strategies. The varied picture of health—regardless of how the lesions are interpreted (Cohen 1994, 1997; Goodman 1983; Goodman et al. 1984; Wood and Milner 1994; Wood et al. 1992)—underscores the diversity expected within any broadly defined subsistence category, in this instance one where people relied heavily on both wild and cultivated foods.

Our point is a simple one. There is no reason to expect uniform effects in terms of health from the diverse ways of life encompassed by the kinds of gross categories typically used in the osteological literature. Neither should we expect consistency in the health of populations subsumed within archaeological units more narrowly defined in time and space. That is, it would be unlikely that peoples classified as agriculturalists in a particular region were uniformly worse, or better, off than their hunter-gatherer predecessors. These categories encompass considerable cultural and environmental variability, which would affect the likelihood of experiencing malnutrition or exposure to particular kinds of pathogens.

The morbidity and mortality characteristics of closely related communities, even those of the tribal-scale societies scattered across the northern Eastern Woodlands during late precontact times, would have varied depending on local circumstances. For example, it is likely that the food-procurement options of an Oneota community in west-central Illinois were reduced by the dangers posed by their enemies (Styles and King 1990). Many of these hard-pressed villagers had suffered from chronic illnesses by the time of their deaths (Milner and Smith 1990). Infectious diseases could only have been aggravated by hunger, perhaps sometimes outright starvation, stemming from disruptions in subsistence activities. For these people, long subsistence-related trips far from the protection of the village would have been curtailed by the threat of attacks. The danger was very real—many of the victims of violence were represented by skeletons that were partially disarticulated and damaged by scavenging animals, characteristics consistent with death occurring where bodies were difficult to find, probably some distance from the village. Susan Pfeiffer (1984) earlier made a similar argument concerning a late precontact Ontario Iroquoian community.

James Wood (1998) has recently proposed an alternative model to the conventional view of a stepwise deterioration in the human condition; that is, ever greater toil, hunger, and sickness. Simplifying his argument greatly, the well-being of past populations varied depending on whether they possessed the capacity to produce enough to eat. Innovations that increased production, resulting in times of relative plenty, permitted population growth. By innovations, we are referring to changes in technologies, foods, and the organization of labour—anything that improved productive output. Inevitably, however, populations found themselves at the point where further increases pushed them into Malthusian misery. These people found themselves back where they started, although there were more of them and their ways of life had changed.

Wood's (1998) considerably more complex model is mentioned because we should expect to find populations that varied to some extent in their disease experience, even those from the same region with similar subsistence practices. His model encourages us to examine specific periods of innovation, demographic expansion, and stagnation, many of which occurred within the context of broadly defined stages such as hunting-and-gathering or agriculture. This approach is markedly different than the conventional comparison of a few samples supposedly representative of discrete subsistence types that are internally uniform in terms of disease experience. The effects on health of changes in subsistence strategies were simply more complex than conventional wisdom, which is based on a stage-like view of the past, would have us believe.

Warfare

We now turn to the final topic: warfare in ancient times. Human skeletons, plus the walls that sometimes surrounded settlements, provide our best evidence of conflicts among the small-scale societies that were once scattered across the northern Eastern Woodlands. To be sure, there are those scholars who cling to images of a pacific precontact history, but signs of violence are so overwhelming it is increasingly difficult to deny the importance of studying the role of conflicts in precontact history (for summaries of Eastern Woodlands data see Milner [1995, 1999]; for a general treatment of this subject see Keeley [1996]).

The skeletal evidence from the Eastern Woodlands indicates there were two broadly defined periods of time when people often fought one another (Milner 1995, 1999). The earliest such time occurred during the mid-Holocene, the late Middle to Late Archaic periods. Conflict-related deaths are best known from the shell and debris heaps in the Midsouth, but they are not restricted to such places. In contrast, there is scant evidence anywhere in the Eastern Woodlands of intergroup conflicts about 2,000 years ago during Middle Woodland times when large mounds and earthworks were built in the Midwest and elsewhere. Conflicts increased late in the first millennium A.D. The skeletal evidence for intergroup fighting is much greater than it was in samples from somewhat earlier times. In addition, palisades surrounding villages began to be erected, and they became much more common in the eleventh and subsequent centuries (Milner 1999).

The pattern for the combined Midwest and Great Lakes area generally parallels trends elsewhere in the Eastern Woodlands. The initial increase in intergroup conflict, however, appears somewhat later than it does in the Midsouth where people created great piles of debris when they camped alongside major streams. While this discrepancy in the regular appearance of victims of violence may reflect a temporal lag in conflicts that resulted in the loss of life, we can not exclude the possibility that this finding is largely a result of uneven sampling. The shell mounds of the Midsouth yielded large numbers of well-preserved skeletons, many of which have been examined systematically by osteologists.

Because of sampling problems, it is difficult to detect more fine-grained temporal and geographical patterns through the study of skeletons alone. Nevertheless, it is likely that the chance of lethal conflicts breaking out varied greatly from one place to another. There is no doubt that some communities on the leading fringes of movements of people suffered heavy losses from encounters with their enemies. Not surprisingly, fighting was likely to occur when groups expanded at the expense of their neighbours. One such example is the earliest known Oneota community in the central Illinois River valley dating to about 700 B.P. (Figure 15.2; Santure et al. 1990).

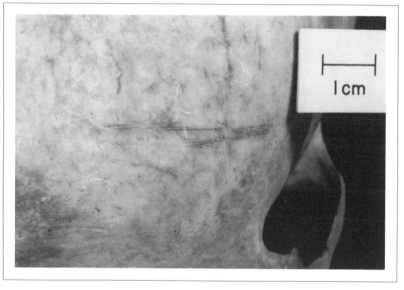

Figure 15.2: A cranium from Norris Farms #36 in Illinois with incisions on the left frontal bone from scalping (Courtesy Illinois State Museum collection).

These people experienced high warfare-related mortality; at least one-third of the adults, both males and females, died as a result of their injuries (Milner et al. 1991). They were killed in separate attacks—probably ambushes of situationally vulnerable people, considering the presence of wounds consistent with being struck while fleeing from danger—each of which resulted in only a few casualties. Despite the fact that in the precontact Eastern Woodlands most attacks resulted in few casualties, there were occasions when they cumulatively produced warfare-related mortality as great as that recorded for conflict-prone tribal societies from the recent past (Keeley 1996).

There is no reason to believe that all communities subsumed within a particular archaeological category would have experienced the same level of warfare-related casualties. The hard-pressed central Illinois River Oneota found themselves in a difficult position. For some reason they moved into a land that was a dangerous place to live and they stayed there, presumably because they had no other better choice. No large skeletal sample from anywhere else in the northern Eastern Woodlands contains enough victims of violence to indicate that casualties from warfare were as high as those experienced by this particular community.

Summary

Returning to the purpose of the original Plenary Session, we might once again ask whether human skeletons can help us straighten out the classification of archaeological cultures in the northern Eastern Woodlands. While examinations of bony structures to evaluate the degree of relatedness among different groups of skeletons can make a contribution to such endeavours, at present morphological data can do little more than provide a coarse picture of population affinities, largely because of the spotty temporal and geographical distribution of large, well-preserved skeletal samples. It seems that in many places populations remained essentially in place for many generations. Nevertheless, groups certainly moved, although it is only possible to say that such movements occurred, not provide a detailed picture of the ever-changing distribution of populations across broad geographical areas. The other aspects of human skeletons that tell us a lot about how people lived—diet, health, and conflict-related trauma—provide a varied picture within the kinds of categories that archaeologists have constructed to sort out temporal and geographical variability in artifacts and architecture. Yet without such data our knowledge of life in the past and models of cultural evolution are greatly impoverished. One might say that without the information that only skeletons can provide, it is not worth doing archaeology at all.

CONTINUITY AND CHANGE IN THE LITHIC TECHNOLOGY OF THE PRECONTACT GREAT LAKES REGION

16

Toby A. Morrow
Office of the State Archaeologist, University of Iowa

The following discussion highlights some of the major trends in stone tool technology that characterize the sequence of precontact occupation of the Great Lakes region. This synoptic overview is written from the perspective of a Midwesterner. I am most familiar with lithic assemblages from the Upper Mississippi Valley and the westernmost part of the Great Lakes area. This slanted view may emphasize things that are peculiar to the region in which I have worked the most, however, broadly similar trends appear to characterize the remainder of the Great Lakes region as well. From the outset, I think it is important to point out that, while our focus here is on a particular circumscribed area, we cannot fully understand Great Lakes precontact history apart from what was occurring in adjacent regions, indeed from what was happening across the whole of eastern and midcontinental North America in general. The precontact inhabitants of the Great Lakes region did not live in isolation from the rest of the New World. Judging from the styles of artifacts and the foreign raw materials present in the area, interregional contact was not uncommon, though the scale and intensity of this varied somewhat through time.

In summarizing any aspect of the precontact occupation of the Great Lakes region it becomes immediately clear that we know considerably more about some periods than we do about others (Fitting 1975; Mason 1981; Ritchie 1980). In particular, the earlier periods of precontact history are very poorly documented. Radiocarbon dates securely associated with archaeological contexts earlier than about 5000 B.P. are very scarce in the region and they are almost non-existent for any time before 10000 B.P. Floral and faunal data are generally lacking from early sites. Most of what we know about the earlier periods of the occupation of the region comes from stone tools, the raw materials from which they were made, their distribution across the landscape, and their spatial association within sites. This underscores the critical role of artifact typology and classification in developing our understanding of the first several millennia of the occupation of the Great Lakes area. The ages attributed to these early sites and their associated complexes are based largely upon cross-referencing with similar or identical artifact styles that have been radiometrically dated in other regions.

Projectile Point Morphology and Typology

Though certain other artifacts in stone toolkits are reasonably good time markers (e.g., Ellis et al. 1990), projectile points have become the "index fossils" of North American precontact history. Indeed, projectile point type names are ingrained in American archaeology. They serve as important communicative tools in that they summarize a great deal of technological, morphological, and chronological data into a single and generally recognized term. At the same time, artifact type names can carry unintended and perhaps inappropriate connotations. Type name designations are such a part of our thinking that they become more than simply designations for a particular form of stone tool. Especially in the case of the long era of eastern North American precontact history that preceded the widespread use of ceramics, the names given to specific projectile point forms have come to symbolize entire cultures.

There is no denying that certain artifact forms vary considerably in time and space. The concept of a type is intended to partition this variation into convenient and meaningful subunits that correspond to time, space, and/or function. However, artifacts like projectile points do not always present themselves in neat tidy groupings. They exhibit a considerable range—and sometimes a seemingly continuous stream—of variation.

Artifact designs changed as a result of innovations as well as in gradual and less dramatic ways. Innovations in projectile point design sometimes appear suddenly in the archaeological record and spread rapidly across a region. Deeply notched projectile points and knives seem to appear abruptly in a fully developed form in the Lower Illinois River Valley around 9500 B.P. without any intermediate or developmental precedents. While there are such examples of seemingly abrupt morphological changes in projectile point shape through time, there are just as many, and probably many more, cases where different types grade rather smoothly into each other (cf. Shott 1996 for discussion). The morphological evolution of one type into another is readily apparent in several projectile point sequences that have been developed. The "intermediate" or "hybrid" forms do not fit well into the rigid pigeonholes we have constructed for our classification. This kind of incremental variation appears to occur both through time and across geographic space. The question of just where to draw the line between one type and another type is an important one that has not received the serious attention it deserves.

Another important consideration in assessing stylistic and morphological relationships is the overall intricacy of artifact design. Artifacts with complex outlines characterized by stems, notches, incurvate or excurvate blade or basal edges, or particular distinctive traits of manufacture are much more readily divided and subdivided in typological schemes, although it is acknowledged that some unique attributes such as seriation transcend temporal periods and may be misleading typologically. Artifacts with simple forms (e.g., triangular and lanceolate projectile points) are not so easily separated into distinct groups. The variable simplicity, or alternatively the complexity, of artifact shapes can and does affect our acuity in artifact typology.

There are also problems resulting from provincialism in typology, that is, those cases where very similar—sometimes practically identical—artifact forms are referred to by different local or regional names (e.g., Clovis-Gainey, Kirk-Nettling). Though perhaps not a severe problem in lithic typology, provincial type designations can mask underlying interregional continuities and lead us into thinking of past cultural boundaries that never really existed.

We should always keep in mind that artifacts like projectile points and knives were often extensively maintained tools with long use lives. As a result, they may have been considerably altered in appearance from their original pristine shape by the time they were discarded. What appear impressionistically and even statistically to be quite distinct projectile point/knife types might simply be the same general form in different states of sharpening and repair. Hoffman (1985) has convincingly argued that many so-called "types" of stemmed southeastern points are in fact variations resulting from the reworking of the same basic form. The degree to which projectile points and knives were sharpened, repaired, and otherwise maintained before discard is influenced by several factors including the overall original size of the artifact and its capacity for reworking, tool use patterns, the reparability of damage and breakage, and the immediate availability of stone (and time?) for making a replacement tool. Generally, larger individual tools could be expected to be more considerably reduced prior to being abandoned than smaller tools. In regions where raw material sources are of less desirable quality and character, or where raw materials are scarce in general, we might also expect to see a more intensive degree of tool maintenance.

It can be overly tempting to ascribe functional significance to variation in artifact design. Environmental correlates to observed changes in projectile point shape are often implied but seldom specified or demonstrated. The mere fact that, through time, a great diversity of projectile point sizes and shapes was used in eastern North America and the fact that the principle prey species did not change appreciably through the same interval makes a simple correlation between point morphology and intended target very doubtful (alternatively, see Ellis and Deller 1997). Point size is almost certainly partly related to weaponry systems (e.g., spears, atlatl darts, bow and arrow). Point size and proportions, particularly width and thickness, must have influenced penetration and killing power. However, it is quite important that we keep in mind that the projectile points we find on archaeological sites were a very small part of the total composite projectile assembly. The weight and velocity of the complete shaft, foreshaft and point assembly may have been able to compensate for much of the potential performance variation in projectile point design. Differences in outline shape and, in particular in haft element design, probably had a negligible affect on actual projectile performance. At the same time, variation in size, shape, and perhaps in hafting design, could have had important implications for function and uselife in cases where these artifacts were used for additional tasks as multi-purpose hafted tools.

Just what similarities and differences between projectile points mean is not always clear. Though we often fall into thinking of these things as representing precontact cultures or ethnic identities, this may be reading more into the artifacts than is warranted. Variation in projectile point styles might just as well reflect degrees of social distance rather than being signatures of ethnic affiliation. This variation may reflect patterns of social integration and interaction at a much higher level than that of the local ethnic group. Though it would be fantastic if we could discern distinct social entities from these lithic artifacts, the higher order magnitudes of social connectedness are, nonetheless, quite intriguing and worthy of further exploration.

Variation in Lithic Technology

All stone artifacts begin as a rock in some type of geologic context. The characteristics of stone sources that were available in a given region can have profound impacts on local lithic assemblages. The size, shape, and overall flaking quality of pieces of flakable stone influence reduction strategies, tool size, and to some degree, tool morphology. Some cherts occur in large nodules or in thick nodular beds while others are available only in much smaller packages. Pieces of knappable stone in secondarily transported gravels tend to be smaller than pieces available at the parent bedrock source. Because of this, the same kind of artifact made from different chert varieties or from pieces acquired from different kinds of sources can vary considerably in size. Large, relatively unflawed masses of stone place few constraints on tool manufacture, however, smaller pieces of stone or stone occurring in a particular piece shape can limit choices in reduction. The common presence of bipolar core reduction in many areas of the Great Lakes region is a predictable response to local lithic sources characterized by small piece size (cf. Shott 1989 for discussion). Generally, bipolar reduction is rare in areas of the Midwest and Great Lakes where good quality pieces of knappable stone are available in large masses. Before going too far in the interpretation of variation in lithic assemblages, I think it is important that we understand the nature of the raw materials employed and their respective limitations with regard to stone tool production.

Access to lithic raw materials would have been affected by territory and range size, among other things. Local groups whose subsistence rounds brought them within range of good quality localized stone deposits would have had the opportunity to discard worn down equipment and gear up with the fresh cores, blanks, and/or finished tools they would take with them when they left. Less mobile populations residing in areas with abundant local stone would also have had regular and predictable access to these raw materials. People who were not so fortunate would have had to make special efforts to procure good quality stone through direct acquisition by making special trips to quarry areas or by relying on exchange networks, or they simply would have had to make do with the stone that was locally available. Lithic raw material supplies are by no means unlimited, even in areas where they are abundant. Increased pressure on localized lithic raw material sources or changing environmental conditions could have resulted in periodic or even chronic shortages of good quality stone. When we consider the impact that a few modern flintknappers can have on chert sources, the precontact depletion of raw material sources becomes an increasingly real possibility. Quarrying into deposits of good quality stone by excavating pits and trenches into them is one potential response to the continuing demand for raw material in the face of short supplies accessible at the surface.

Various options in the structure and organization of lithic reduction systems have differential advantages and disadvantages (Morrow 1997). Large bifacial core and blade core reduction strategies are efficient in terms of minimizing waste by-products and thus are well-adapted to conditions of extensive mobility. Random core and bipolar core reduction are considerably more wasteful of raw material. Parry and Kelly (1988) have argued that the shift to simple flake tools and less refined reduction strategies is related to increasing sedentism.

The concepts of residential versus logistical mobility (after Binford 1980) have played a major role in structuring hunter-gatherer studies in the Midwest and eastern North America. Though technological correlates of these two mobility strategies have been proposed (Binford 1979, 1980), they are still imperfectly developed. From Binford's argument, heavily curated tools should be characteristic of logistical collectors while more expedient tools should be found in the assemblages of residential foragers. Aside from differences in tool curation and expediency that have been shown to correlate with respect to access to, and distance from, raw material sources (Bamforth 1986), the whole concept of tool curation is undergoing a critical re-evaluation (e.g., Odell [editor] 1996). Quite simply, curation and expediency have various meanings and in part, form a continuum of artifact use lives rather than two dichotomous states. Even within a single assemblage there can occur tools that would be considered expedient (e.g., unretouched utilized flakes) and others curated (e.g., hafted bifaces). Thus these concepts cannot simply be used to pigeonhole precontact tools, let alone entire lithic assemblages.

Lithic Technology in the Great Lakes Region

The earliest known and uncontested occupation of the Great Lakes region took place sometime between about 11000 and 10000 B.P. The lithic technology practised by these early inhabitants was both refined and highly distinctive. Fluted lanceolate projectile points are the archaeologically recognized hallmark of this period. In the characteristic fluting of their bases, these early projectile points represent a feature that was spread across most inhabitable regions of North America as well as into parts of Central and South America near the close of the Pleistocene. This degree of stylistic and technological uniformity over such a large geographic area is not represented at any later time in New World precontact history. Though the makers of fluted points may not have been the initial inhabitants of all areas of the New World, a strong case has been made that these were the first people to live in the then freshly deglaciated areas of the Great Lakes region (e.g., Mason 1958; Stoltman and Workman 1969).

Fluted projectile points were made through a complex reduction sequence. The specific steps and procedures followed in their manufacture provide important clues regarding the relationships and inter-relationships among fluted point complexes in the Great Lakes region and beyond (e.g., Roosa 1965). There are some indications that the reduction of large bifaces was an integral part of the structure of the lithic technology, particularly in the earlier part of this period. These large bifaces served the dual function of blank for the eventual manufacture of refined bifacial tools and the role of core for the production of flake blanks for use as various retouched and unretouched flake tools. The integrated role of bifaces as cores and blanks made for a readily transportable tool kit adapted to conditions of extensive group mobility (Morrow 1996). While true blades and blade cores are associated with early fluted points in parts of western, midwestern, and southeastern North America, this technology appears to be absent from most of the Great Lakes region. However, trianguloid end scrapers, large side scrapers, and gravers, like those commonly associated with fluted point complexes elsewhere in North America, are well-represented in the region.

Lithic technology at this time appears to have been essentially limited to chipped stone artifacts. Intentionally shaped pecked and ground stone tools are not associated with these early fluted point assemblages. Notably absent are any sort of specialized heavy woodworking tools, such as adzes, gouges, axes, and celts. Plant processing equipment like manos and metates and mortars and pestles are also unknown from these early contexts. While plants were probably consumed by these early people, the utilization of plant foods was likely limited to those that required little in the way of special processing. Presently, there is little justification to suggest that the use of plant resources between 11000 and 10000 B. P. was as intensive as it became in the following periods.

Larger and partly fluted points are believed to be the earliest fluted point forms in the region (Ellis and Deller 1990). These are similar to fluted points found throughout most of eastern North American and the Midwest and morphologically they are closest to the earliest fluted points dated at 11400 to 10800 B.P. in western North America. Presumed later fluted point forms in the Great Lakes region are characterized by generally smaller size and more pronounced flutes, often running close to the full length of the point (Ellis and Deller 1990). These later fluted points appear to be more geographically restricted, some styles being largely limited in occurrence to the Great Lakes area. Lithic assemblages of this era commonly reflect the long distance transport of high-quality lithic raw materials. The particular prevalence of certain non-local raw material varieties in several sites suggests that groups geared up at localized quarry areas (e.g., Seeman 1994). Generally, there also appears to be a decrease in the distances that raw materials were moved through this period (e.g., Seeman et al. 1994). Together, the changing point styles and lithic raw material utilization patterns suggest a gradual decline in territory or range size during the course of this period.

Beginning around 10000 B.P. is a period characterized by a suite of distinctive projectile point/knife forms that reflect the complexity of regional and interregional developments under conditions of increased technological and stylistic differentiation between areas. Some of these artifacts appear to represent local developments out of the preceding fluted point forms while others are related to two broad regional sequences that characterize the adjacent northern Great Plains and the Southeastern United States.

Lanceolate points lacking basal fluting are widespread in the Great Lakes region. Most are yet to be securely dated. Some of these points are reminiscent of the earlier fluted forms but are generally smaller in size. These may have developed into somewhat thicker and less carefully made points that take on a very weakly side-notched to stemmed appearance. It has been hypothesized that an early side-notched point form developed out of this trend (cf. Ellis et al.1990; see also Shoshani et al. 1989, 1990).

Many of the later lanceolate and stemmed lanceolate points in the western part of the Great Lakes in Minnesota and Wisconsin are direct analogues to point styles characteristic of the northern Great Plains dating between 10500 and 8000 B.P. In fact, examples of these points made of raw materials from sources in the Plains region, such as Knife River Flint, are not uncommon in the western Great Lakes. All of the point styles in the sequence developed from the Hell Gap site in Wyoming (Irwin-

Williams et al. 1973) are represented to varying degrees in the western Great Lakes area (Mason 1963; Salzer 1974). The Wyoming sequence begins with unfluted and unstemmed lanceolates followed by long-stemmed and weakly shouldered lanceolates, to shorter-stemmed, markedly shouldered lanceolates and ends with unstemmed lanceolates exhibiting parallel-oblique to random pressure flaking. Like their counterparts on the Great Plains, these unstemmed and stemmed lanceolate points are characterized by generally above average size, fine workmanship, and haft element grinding.

Notched and stemmed projectile point forms related to contemporary developments in the southeastern United States occur over much of the Great Lakes region as well (e.g., Stothers and Abel 1991; Wright 1978). Southeastern point styles form a coherent progression of technology and morphology between about 10000 and 7000 B.P. The regional sequences represented at the St. Albans site in West Virginia (Broyles 1971) and at sites in the Tellico Reservoir in Tennessee (Chapman 1976) begin with early side- and corner-notched point forms that gradually evolve into smaller stemmed points with indented or bifurcated bases that then gave way to similar stemmed points lacking the pronounced basal concavities. Blade edge serration is a common feature and some points were resharpened by alternate bevelling. Grinding to dull the edges of the haft elements is common. Certain forms appear to have been used mostly as hafted cutting tools while others served a dual role of cutting tool and projectile point.

Aside from the diagnostic points and knives themselves, little has been documented about this period in the Great Lakes region. End scrapers, side scrapers, and gravers are distinct tool forms that carry over from the preceding fluted point period. The heat treatment of certain chert varieties was practised in the adjacent Midwest at this time, but heat treatment was not done on the scale or regularity that it was in later periods. Drills, often made from reworked projectile points and knives, became a common tool form. Chipped stone adze blades are common on sites of this period in the adjacent Mississippi Valley. Ground stone "celts" (perhaps used as adze blades) have been documented from ca 9000 B.P. contexts in the Tellico Reservoir in Tennessee (Kimball 1992) and at the Nettling site in Ontario (Ellis et al. 1991). Manos and metates and mortars and pestles are represented at some southeastern and midwestern sites of this period.

Overall, patterns of lithic raw material use and transport during this time reflect diverse, but generally declining, territory or range sizes.

Continuity in the selection of certain non-local high quality cherts occurred for a time (Stothers and Abel 1991). However, in contrast to the preceding era, lithic raw material acquisition was somewhat more local and not as heavily focussed on single, high quality raw materials from sometimes distant sources (Ellis et al. 1995:77). The beginnings of this trend were noted in the preceding period and this pattern certainly continued to intensify in the times that followed.

In contrast to the preceding period, chipped stone tools from the period following 8000 B.P. exhibit a noticeable decline in refinement and morphological sophistication. In many areas, side-notched, comer-notched, and stemmed projectile points are generally thicker, more irregular, and less carefully made than the earlier forms. Medium-sized, side-notched projectile points are a particularly widespread diagnostic artifact of this era. By this time, random blocky cores of medium size become the predominant source of flakes for tool blanks. Formal flake tool categories, like those associated with the previous periods discussed here, are generally absent. In their place, informal unretouched and retouched flake tools appear to have been used. In terms of the chipped stone category, the lithic assemblages of this era offer little that is distinctive or striking. In fact, archaeological components of the period between 8000 and 5000 B.P. went largely unnoticed in parts of the Great Lakes region for a long time. This prompted early theories regarding an apparent hiatus in the archaeological record of the region (cf. Ellis et al. 1990; Fitting 1975; Stoltman 1986). Today, we know that sites of this time are not uncommon, though much work remains to be done regarding the chronology of the period and in isolating time-diagnostic markers.

While the care lavished in the manufacture of chipped stone tools of the preceding periods was largely abandoned, a great diversity of pecked and ground stone artifacts emerged. By sometime between 8000 to 6000 B.P., grooved axes became a common woodchopping implement. Ground stone celts and gouges are common in some areas, particularly in the eastern Great Lakes. Ground slate projectile points (bayonets) and lunate knives also occur in this area. Bannerstones were often made from carefully selected and visually striking stone like banded slate or porphyry. Similar raw materials were used to make later ground stone gorgets and birdstones. Though sometimes thought of only as "ceremonial" or "wealth" items, bannerstones, birdstones and stone gorgets possibly also functioned as weights or counter-balances on atlatls. The fact that these unusual ground stone artifacts are only rarely found outside of mortuary contexts probably reflects their relatively long uselives (and hence, their infrequent discard on habitation sites) and their inclusion in graves, perhaps·as personal property of the deccased.

A succession of notched, stemmed, and lanceolate points characterizes the Great Lakes region between 5000 B.P. and the appearance of ceramic vessels by about 3000 B.P. In general, projectile point styles analogous to those from other neighbouring regions are found across the Great Lakes, but the overall ranges of these styles appear somewhat reduced over previous forms. Broad bladed stemmed points dating to about 3500 B.P. exhibit a distinctly eastern orientation in their distribution. Medium-sized to small stemmed and corner-notched points dating slightly later are similar to forms found in the Mississippi River drainage. Roughly flaked lanceolate and stemmed lanceolate points once thought to date much earlier (Fitting 1975) are now known to belong to this interval of time (Kenyon 1980). Similarly, roughly contemporary lanceolate points in the Midwest were also once thought to be considerably older. The later temporal placement of these leaf-shaped points should warn us against being too bold and simplistic in our assumptions regarding artifact types and their correlative ages. While these later points are similar in outline shape to older lanceolate forms, they are technologically quite different. Ground stone celts appear to have replaced the earlier grooved axe forms shortly before the introduction of ceramic technology into the region.

Generally, through this period there appears to have been a marked decline in the distances that lithic raw materials were transported. Assemblages are typically dominated by local raw materials or by local stone and that obtained from adjacent regions. Home ranges or territories were likely considerably more reduced than in previous times. The same pattern characterizes the adjacent Mississippi River valley. The intentional heat treatment of chert became a common practice in the Mississippi Valley around 8000 to 7000 B.P. Heat treatment allowed for greater ease in manufacture of stone tools, particularly when applied to lower quality cherts. However, there were also definite costs associated with heat treatment including the additional labour investment in heating blanks or preforms, the potential loss of some stone to thermal fracture, generally lower tool durability, and correspondingly more frequent tool replacement. Thus, heat treatment was not simply technological innovation that resulted in higher quality of stone for flaking. Rather, the greater reliance upon heat treatment may have been a response to declining range size, more limited access to various regional lithic raw materials, and growing pressure on local stone sources being exploited by a less mobile resident population. It should be kept in mind that the overall frequency of the heat treatment of chert through precontact history can vary tremendously from one region to another and in particular from one chert variety to another. Some cherts (generally those of lesser flaking quality that contain a larger proportion of non-silica impurities) are dramatically transformed by heat treatment. Other, better quality, cherts are not so markedly altered by the process and may even be more susceptible to thermal stress and breakage during heating.

Over the next millennium, range sizes and overall mobility levels declined and populations appear to have become more settled across the region, resulting in the development of interregional exchange networks. The transference of exotic raw materials in these later times was notably different from the long distance transport of lithic raw materials seen in the earlier periods. Non-local materials in these later sites are represented by a select group of items, sometimes derived from far distant sources. Often, these exotic goods occur in the form of particular artifact styles that are sometimes quite different from the range of artifacts made of more local raw materials and used in day-to-day activities. Some of these exotic items are decorative and certain others do not appear to have been directly functional. Whether we choose to think of these artifacts as items representing "prestige", "wealth", or "risk-pooling", it is clear that many of them were not directly necessary in the daily lives of the people acquiring them. Some of the exchange materials made their way into the daily economy, but much of this material was destined to become mortuary offerings or was otherwise discarded. In some regional manifestations dating between 3000 and 2000 B.P., the exotic goods recovered from mortuary contexts are so different from the locally made artifacts found on habitation sites that archaeologists have had difficulty in relating burial complexes to contemporary living sites.

One of the more noticeable features of certain trade goods made of exotic chipped stone is their overall refinement and quality of manufacture. Thin and well-made triangular, ovate, or bi-pointed bifaces appear to have been an important medium of exchange between about 3000 and 2000 B.P. (Fitting 1975; Mason 1981; Ritchie 1980; Spence et al. 1990; Stoltman 1986). Certain forms are associated with specific kinds of raw materials and with circumscribed parts of the region (e.g., Didier 1967). Thin, side-notched ovate points of this era appear to have directly descended from a corner-notched local form. Bifaces appear to have been made at or near particular chert sources and then were taken or traded to outlying areas (Robertson et al.1997:500-501). Unused caches of these artifacts have been found in several sites across the Great Lakes (Granger 1978,1981). Batches of artifacts appear to have been made expressly for exchange to other areas. This apparent mass-production along with the common excellence expressed in the manufacture of these artifacts suggests that a limited number of artisans was responsible for producing their production. This is perhaps the first time in Great Lakes precontact history where we can safely infer some level of part-time craft specialization.

The apparent zenith of interregional exchange in eastern North America took place between about 2200 and 1800 B.P. A wide range of exotic goods derived from many different regions was circulated through the Great Lakes and Midwest during this time. Obsidian from Rocky Mountain sources, Knife River flint from North Dakota, Burlington chert from the Upper Mississippi River Valley, Cobden chert from southern Illinois, Wyandotte chert from southern Indiana, Vanport (Flint Ridge) chert from Ohio, Great Lakes copper, mica sheets from the Appalachians, and Gulf Coast marine shell were among the roster of trade goods distributed across the area. Many of these non-local materials made their way into the daily economy thereby littering many habitation sites of the period. Even so, enormous caches of exotic goods and artifacts have been found in mortuary contexts, indicating their sacred function. As was the case before, many of these exotic raw materials were manufactured into finely crafted and non-utilitarian artifacts. The size and refinement of large notched and stemmed bifaces recovered as grave goods is highly suggestive of the work of craft specialists.

Along with the finely crafted grave goods, other aspects of lithic technology were widely adopted at this same time. Ovate projectile points with bold corner notches are a particular diagnostic form that is found from southern Ontario to Mississippi and from Ohio to Iowa. True blade and blade core technologies are particular hallmarks of chipped stone assemblages that correlate with this era of far-flung exchange. Blades and blade cores are abundant on habitation sites of this period from Ohio to the Mississippi River Valley. Blades become rare on the fringes of this regional fluorescence. They are relatively scarce in southern Ontario (Spence et al. 1990) and likewise are rare in parts of the Upper Mississippi Valley and western Great Lakes. Heat-treatment was commonly practised, at least on those raw materials that were amenable to the process. The colours and colour combinations seen in many artifacts made of Burlington chert at this time suggests an intentional selection for pieces of this raw material that would exhibit the most striking enhancement of colour through heat treatment. Aesthetic concerns seem to have been important in raw materials. Of the myriad of cherts and other knappable stones that could have been acquired, the exchange system appears to have focussed on those that were the most lustrous and colourful.

Sometime between 1800 and 1500 B.P., the far-flung exchange network faded (or collapsed, depending on one's position and point of reference). A marked change in projectile points and subsequent changes in the overall structure of chipped stone technologies followed shortly thereafter. Small, light, and thin side- and corner-notched projectile points appear to have abruptly replaced earlier, heavier bodied forms across the area (Fox 1990a; Ritchie 1980). The appearance of these light, thin points appears to follow a north to south progression, beginning about 1600 B.P. in western Canada, reaching the Great Lakes region by 1500 to 1400 B.P., and the adjacent Midwest by 1300 B.P. The implication of this is the introduction and spread of a whole new hunting technology—the bow and arrow. While some choose to believe that the bow and arrow is much more ancient in the New World, the earlier appearances and subsequent disappearances of small projectile points in the archaeological record of North America makes this position difficult to reconcile (cf. also Nassany and Pyle 1999).

The small, thin projectile points used to tip arrows were commonly made on selected flakes that were not much thicker than the finished form. Though some points are completely flaked, many were made simply by marginal retouch to shape the outline of the point. Thus, the manufacturing trajectory followed in producing these small points was fairly simple. Along with the change in the manufacturing trajectory and sizes of projectile points was an apparently related trend in overall patterns of chipped stone technology. The common reliance on small flake blanks for the production of projectile points appears to have resulted in an overall down-scaling of the entire chipped stone industry. Cores, often relatively small to begin with, were reduced to a considerably smaller size than was typical of earlier periods when larger projectile points were being made. Flake tools derived from these cores are likewise generally smaller than the flakes that were selected for use in preceding periods. Thus, not only were projectile points smaller in these later periods, but other tools such as drills and end scrapers were also comparatively diminutive. Certain raw material varieties that occurred in smaller pieces as well as small secondary chert cobbles became much more practical as a raw material base for chipped stone production. Some raw materials that had been little used in the past took on a new importance. Grand Meadow chert from southwestern Minnesota, a high quality chert that tends to occur in fist-sized nodules, was used throughout precontact history, but became a particularly widely used lithic resource after the introduction of the bow and arrow. The progressive trend toward restricted regional access to lithic raw materials noted earlier in this overview appears to have become particularly attenuated at this time, at least in many parts of the region (e.g., Lennox and Fitzgerald 1990). In some areas of the Great Lakes where knappable stone of any kind is scarce, chipped stone tools in general are also rare (e.g., Jamieson 1990). While overland access to certain lithic raw materials may have been restricted, groups living on the Bruce Peninsula took particular advantage of multiple chert sources near the coast of Lake Huron that were accessible by water transport (Fox 1990b).

Early arrowpoints in the Great Lakes area were side- or corner-notched. By about 1200 to 1100 years ago these were replaced over much of the region by unnotched triangular points. These range from squat, stubby equilateral forms to narrower, elongated triangular shapes. Basal configurations range from convex to straight to concave and there are suggestions that these characteristics vary through time and across the region (e.g., Dodd et al. 1990; Lennox and Fitzgerald 1990). Even so, there is relatively little pronounced stylistic variation in these late unnotched points. There are, after all, only a limited number of ways to elaborate upon a basic triangular shape. Faintly side-notched points co-occur with triangular forms on some sites. Serrated, elongated triangular points are found in the Ohio drainage. Tri-notched and multiple-notched triangular points are found on the western fringes of the Great Lakes region, but these forms are much more common in the Mississippi Valley and in the eastern plains. While these contemporary varieties of late arrowpoints do correspond generally to broad regional patterns in the archaeological record, they would appear to fall quite short of providing the fine-grained resolution necessary to isolate linguistic groupings and ethnic affiliations.

Conclusions

There are pronounced changes in lithic technology through the precontact sequence of the Great Lakes region. At the same time, there appear to be relatively few instances of sharp breaks in their development. Instead, long term trends and gradual changes through time are evident, both in the forms of artifacts and in the overall reduction strategies and organization of the technology. From initially complex chipped stone technologies that emphasized good quality lithic raw materials and highly refined tools we can see a long and gradual decline in the sophistication of chipped stone tools. This trend has been noted in eastern North America before and various explanations for its occurrence have been proposed. Torrence (1989) compared both North American and Old World chipped stone industries, noting the same general decline in sophistication through time. She proposed that with the advent of agriculture, hunting technology became less critical and more time was needed for other tasks. Parry and Kelly (1988) note the correlation between sedentism and amorphous flake core technologies across North America. They suggest that sedentary groups were able to stockpile raw material, thus eliminating the need to conserve stone by making refined and long-lived tools. While both of these arguments are compelling, a much more basic reason can be proposed.

Throughout the sequence of Great Lakes precontact history there is, in general, a progressive trend toward decreasing territory or range size and lessened group mobility (cf. also Ellis and Spence 1997). This is evident not only in the distribution patterns of specific artifact forms, but also in the ranges to which non-local raw materials were transported at different times. Regional population levels almost certainly increased through the sequence as well, though we can not be sure if this was gradual or was characterized by periods of punctuated growth. The end result was that there were more people living and travelling in smaller geographic areas. The potential for increasing pressure on plant and animal food resources should be evident. Unlike plants and animals, lithic resources are finite in quantity and nonrenewable and the pressure on local stone sources could have been even more pronounced. With decreasing accessibility of good quality knappable stone, groups may have been forced to adjust their technologies to accommodate smaller pieces and less desirable raw materials. Heat treatment was one way to make poor quality stone easier to flake. The increased application of heat treatment noted in some areas may be related to the declining accessibility of better grades of stone. An increased reliance on alternative technologies, such as pecked and ground stone tools and bone tools might also be expected. The fluorescence of ground stone technology between 8000 and 3000 B.P. could be just such a response.

The trend toward decreasing chipped stone tool size and sophistication is a relatively pervasive one. The only exceptions appear to correlate with intervals of extensive interregional exchange, particularly the interval between 2500 and 1800 B.P. In these cases, stone was acquired from a limited number of localized sources where exchange products were made, perhaps by part-time craft specialists. Good quality cherts and other knappable stones appear to have been highly valued as trade commodities. The emphasis on unfinished blanks and preforms would suggest that it was the raw materials themselves, and not just the time and skill invested in manufacture, that were important.

Though this overview has pertained to the Great Lakes region, similar trends would appear to be equally prevalent in other parts of midwestern and eastern North America. The timing of certain developments may vary somewhat from region to region, for example, the same patterns appear to emerge somewhat earlier in the lithic technologies of the southeast. Nonetheless, the similarities are more striking than the differences. Despite variations in environment, subsistence, and levels of socio-political complexity, human societies across a vast area left behind a record of changing lithic technology that is remarkably ubiquitous.

Following are some suggestions for future research in the lithic technology of the Great Lakes area: (1) Obviously, the whole story is not yet known and there continues to be a desperate need for sites with secure, datable contexts representing the earlier periods. The ages of many early complexes are merely assumed and others are based only by cross dating time-diagnostic artifacts across large areas. The recovery of additional floral and faunal material from these early sites would go a long way toward furthering our knowledge. (2) There needs to be continued study of lithic raw material sources and methods for their identification. We need to know not only where raw materials were available but also the relevant characteristics of those raw materials for chipped stone technology, such as overall flaking quality, piece size, form, and relative abundance. (3) While the lithic assemblages from several early sites have been exhaustively analyzed, the more mundane stone tools of certain later periods have received much less attention. In preparing this overview, it became quite apparent that in the face of abundant floral, faunal, feature, and ceramic data, stone tools on many later sites have all but been ignored. We need to know about assemblages of all periods before we can refine our understanding of technology and technological change through time. Stone artifacts could also hold important clues to questions of interregional contacts and relationships that have so far been addressed largely through inferences based on ceramics. (4) We can not and should not have to abandon type names. However, we may need to restructure how we conceptualize them. The continuous variation apparent in certain artifacts through time and across regions makes it very likely that our present typological divisions are somewhat arbitrary. We need to recognize this. A nested hierarchical scheme (clusters, types, varieties) (cf. Justice 1987) might be a conceptually adaptable means of structuring a typology that is more in keeping with the real artifacts we study without dismantling the existing scheme we have come to know. (5) Our artifact classifications must allow for variance due to raw material constraints, sharpening, and repair. We cannot afford to ignore these factors if we are striving to discover the cultural significance of lithic artifacts. (6) Artifact typologies need to be based on more than impressions. If you can see it, it can be quantified. Quantification could become an important tool for assessing relative degrees of similarity and difference through time and across the region. This could open new doors to research that are now closed by rigid typological pigeonholes and provincial type names.

THEMES AND VARIATIONS: IDEOLOGICAL SYSTEMS IN THE GREAT LAKES

17

William A. Fox
Parks Canada
Robert J. Salzer
Department of Anthropology, Beloit College

Some elders say medicine power is a loan from the Creator to help us live and that we don't need it now. We have grocery stores to feed us, clothing stores to clothe us and welfare cheques if we can't earn enough money to live. Medicine power was available when the survival of people was in question, when it meant the difference between life and death. In the modern world, we hardly ever have life-and-death survival situations, so the Creator took the powers back. We have churches for religion, the law protects us from criminals and we have our health-care system to look after us when we get sick.

George Blondin, Dene Elder, quoted in
News/North, Monday, November 17, 1997

In his eloquent synthesis of anthropological, archaeological and psychological perspectives relating to Amerindian belief systems, von Gernet (1992) argues for the accessibility of Hawke's highest level of inference, based on the prudent use of analogy and supported by the well documented and widespread regularities in Amerindian ideology. He quotes Peter Furst's proposal that the fundamental features of Native religion arrived in the Americas with the first Paleo-Indians, participants in a circumpolar belief system, and notes evidence for the ideological conservatism of Amerindian groups. One of the most widespread expressions of this system among hunting and gathering groups is the institution of shamanism. Eliade's (1974:51) comparison of Aboriginal Australian, Siberian and South American religious motifs tends to support Furst's (1974:52) suggestion of antiquity for this belief system. Shamanic activities have been postulated on the Agate Basin Jones-Miller site in Colorado by Dennis Stanford (Frison 1978:168) and may be expressed among purported Paleo-Indian petroglyphs documented in the Black Hills

(Tratebas 1992). To suggest that the earliest immigrants to the New World arrived without such ideologies is untenable, since it would be to deny their humanity.

Shamanism is an individualistic religious practice born of the uncertainties of a hunting and gathering subsistence tradition situated in some of the least hospitable environments on the planet. Shamanism is characterized by a spiritual partnership or contract with those game species and natural resources most critical to a society's survival. Among Great Lakes groups, there exist various levels of reality, literally, with the universal religious paradigm of upper and lower realms relative to the everyday plane of human existence. Mediators between "The Real People" (each group's name for themselves) and the powerful spirit forces which control subsistence success and influence the state of individual human health are the shamans; male or female individuals of varying degrees of ambivalent power. This power could save the corporate group from starvation, but could also inflict pain or death upon any individual who angered the shaman. A shaman, assisted by spiritual partners, can travel as a spirit or "fly" (Eliade 1974:477) to obtain information or inflict pain from a distance. Such information could involve subsistence issues, such as the whereabouts of game or social information, such as the location of hunting parties late on their return (Brown and Brightman 1990:83).

The individual and corporate desire for reassurance and a secure future remains basic and pervasive world-wide. Religious history is replete with spiritually powerful group leaders, and it also affirms a universal correlation between the development of social stratification and the codification of religious ritual by the power elite. The latter reality, in providing some constraints to individual expression, creates a higher level of symbolic uniformity which increases the potential for both the identification and understanding of archaeological evidence related to past ritual activities. Repeated associations of artifacts and ecofacts strengthen evidence for traditional activities such as specific types of ceremonies.

Having asserted the universality of shamanism and its underlying ideological bases in North America does not mean that we subscribe to the proposition that it is fruitful or even possible to trace those ideologies from their earliest presumed appearance in Paleolithic times in Europe to their expression in more recent times in the New World as Grieder (1982) has proposed. Rather, it seems to us that the wisest and most defensible strategy is to employ the recent ethnographic and ethnohistoric record to develop models as far back in time as those data permit.

Turning to the archaeological record in the Great Lakes region, we must consider how those spiritual beliefs which structure the Aboriginal world might be expressed tangibly. There are many variables to consider, based on the scale of expression. For instance, the ethnographic and historic records document numerous natural landscape features of spiritual significance. We resource managers are now familiar with the concept of cultural landscapes, but some of these were and are more sacred than secular. The falls of Niagara, the Scenic Caves of Collingwood, Ontario and certain white quartzite hills along the north shore of Georgian Bay/Lake Huron come to mind. Certainly, the rock art sites of the Canadian Shield (Rajnovich 1994) and Midwestern United States (Carver 1956:63; Martin 1965:81ff, 104ff; Salzer 1987, n.d.), when viewed as a geographic complex, can be considered to constitute a sacred landscape. The ethnographic records for the Menomini (Skinner and Satterlee 1915:341ff) and for the Hochungara (Winnebago) as documented by Radin (1954:96f) refer to the sacred nature of rock art sites in the oral traditions of both groups. Indeed, armed with such data, the idea that settlement patterns (and "catchment areas") reflect subsistence strategies alone needs to be reconsidered. Historical records also reference trees carved and painted with totemic symbols which are now invisible landscape components, as opposed to many rock art sites. Recently, Gartner (1996) has made a preliminary attempt to unravel the complexities of regional patterning of contemporaneous sacred constructs such as mounds and also villages containing ritual structures.

Obviously, the degree to which we, as archaeologists, can "see" these cultural landscapes depends upon both the amount of the picture remaining and the presence of the appropriate paradigm in "the eye of the beholder". The degree of organic preservation will be a major factor in sacred site visibility and readability, and CRM archaeologists are those most acutely aware of the amount of the picture lost forever on a regional basis due to modern economic development activities. At a more restricted spatial scale, mortuary sites express the sacred so powerfully that anyone can see, even if they do not understand. Such is not necessarily the case on apparently secular sites. Modelling the expected archaeological expressions of ethnographically documented ritual, such as specific religious ceremonies, points to the potentially ephemeral nature of such evidence on camps or villages (Fox 1997). Obviously, this is particularly problematic on sites which are only partially excavated or have been

239

destroyed in part. Taken to an artifact-specific level, many of the relatively few material culture items preserved in the average Great Lakes archaeological record, can only be seen to have sacred significance in their feature context associations with other items. It is the rare artifact, other than a smoking pipe or symbolically engraved item, that speaks clearly on its own (von Gernet and Timmins 1987).

One avenue to the ideological interpretation of archaeological data which has been explored to a limited extent, on the part of the senior author, is the concept of a "faunal lexicon". That is, if there is a culturally widespread similarity in those character attributes ascribed by Aboriginals to particular animal species, then these perceived characteristics may be projected with greater comfort backward in time. The general idea was that the sum total of animal qualities represented in, for instance, a faunal assemblage interred with an individual, might speak to past symbolic intent. An ethnographic literature review was undertaken, during which time it was noted that species depictions in folklore often reversed expected characteristics for humour and moral emphasis. This was followed by a week of sporadic interviews with an Algonquin Elder in Québec. Much research remains to be accomplished in order to assess the feasibility of this approach.

Subsequently, several attempts were made to apply this concept using ethnographic data in the context of two precontact mortuary sites in Ontario; one an adult male, who may have been a bear shaman (Fox and Molto 1994b) and the other being the remains of a child buried some 1,500 years ago with what seemed to be a medicine bundle (Fox and Molto 1994a). Grace Rajnovich (1994) has explored the meaning of animal symbols at rock art sites through reference to Algonquian picture writing as represented on Ojibwa bark song records. A very similar concept has been applied recently to the interpretation of Paleo-Eskimo Dorset art. McGhee (1996:158) alludes to a "grammar of animals" and notes that:

> just as a society shares a set of language rules, they also share a set of meanings that they associate with the various elements of their art. If we treat an artistic tradition as analogous to a language, we may be able to reconstruct some of the meanings behind the various depictions that are central to the tradition being studied.

Certainly, art/iconography and language are comparable symbolic communication mechanisms. This led Greber (1983:92) to speak of "looking for elements (of ethnographically documented religious beliefs) which are basic parts of an Eastern Woodlands culture and which have stability through time; that is, we are looking for a proto-culture as a linguist seeks a proto-language."

Nevertheless, ethnographic data cannot be used uncritically. Certainly, each of the ethnographers brought their own cultural and intellectual biases to their efforts. While the time has long passed in many regions when we could gather data to confirm their observations and findings, modern Aboriginals can provide current interpretations and translations of documents and words that were either written by their ancestors or are found in the field notes of the ethnographers. This emphasizes the importance of communication with Aboriginal peoples in the iterative process of hypothesis development and testing through archaeological evidence. As in the case of archaeological reports, it seems reasonable to assume the greatest reliability for the lower levels of descriptive detail found in the ethnographic reports and to ascribe less credibility to the inferences and interpretations of their authors.

To illustrate, even a casual overview of the ethnographic data from North America reveals the fundamental and widespread importance of feasting as ritual behaviour that is at the same time symbolic and deeply rooted in ideology. Blitz (1993) has developed a model of feasting that was applied to the ceramic and faunal remains found at the Lubbub Creek site in Alabama, where it was employed to identify status differentials between elites and commoners. It is remarkable that research in North America has been able to identify so very few feasting examples of any kind (Fox 1988; Ritchie 1947). It seems likely that the lumping of faunal remains from a site in an effort to accomplish our over-riding objective of defining subsistence strategies has led us to minimize and, therefore, overlook evidence of such discrete ritual events.

Recently, Hollinger (1995) has resorted to ethnographic analyzes to test hypotheses generated by Overstreet and Richards (1992) and Collins (1989) who postulated dramatic shifts in residence patterns among some groups in the upper Midwest in late pre-contact times. Specifically, it is suggested that sometime around 550 B.P., some groups of peoples shifted from patrilocal to matrilocal residence, and that by contact times, shifted back to patrilocal residence. If this was so, there must have been ideological changes that accompanied such a shift in residence behaviour.

Hollinger's research has resulted in powerful arguments that these changes did, in fact, take place, based on statistically significant ethnographic correlations between ideology and the size of domestic structures. He also notes similar trends in other areas, including Iroquoia. In a somewhat similar fashion, Renfrew (1994) has employed both ethnographic and archaeological data to develop a model which can be used to identify ritual behaviour in the past. Although Renfrew's analyzes focussed on European data, his model aptly applies to, for example, Mound 72 at Cahokia in the New World (Fowler 1991).

It seems likely that archaeology has been relying on the symbolic and ideological context and expression of precontact ceramics for some time. The fact that our seriations of potsherds and our culture-historical typologies have had some success as the basis of our social and chronological constructs implies that the decoration on pots is not merely doodling. The alternative conclusion is, of course, that such motifs have meaning(s) that were shared and understood by the ancient artisans. Changes in ceramic attributes, and stone tool forms for that matter, would be more enlightening indicators of past lifeways if we could understand at least some of the deeper levels of meaning(s) that are represented. It is inescapable that such efforts will be predicated in part on ethnographic information, as evidenced in a number of recent attempts (Emerson 1989; Sampson 1988). Hall (1977), for example, has called attention to the widespread use of both synecdoche and metaphor by Aboriginals. Phillips (1989) has used a different kind of ethnographic data, in this case museum specimens, to make compelling arguments supporting the idea that a wavy line or zigzag is a metaphor for the underworld and that vertically oriented nested diamonds and "hourglass" motifs represent the world above. The fact that the first of these motifs is a common and widespread design element on pots—usually placed beneath an upper rim decorative band—should elicit our interest.

Hall (1979) has also noted that excavators have encountered unusual "dirts" in burial pits or mounds. It is unfortunate that physical and chemical analyzes of such distinctive sediments and deposits in mortuary and non-mortuary contexts have not been attempted generally, since such research might provide an empirical data set that can, as Gartner (1993) has observed, alert us to alternative sources of information on symbolism and ideology in the past.

The rich iconography of the late precontact peoples in the Midwestern and Southeastern United States has recently come under intense scrutiny.

Phillips and Brown (1978, 1984) analyzed more than 1,000 engraved shell cups from the Spiro site in Oklahoma and were able to define two major "schools" of such art. More recently, Brown and Kelly (1995) have done some remarkable detective work using archaeological data alone to develop arguments that one such school was employed, if not developed by, the people responsible for the emergence of the Cahokian ritual centre. It may be of more than passing interest that this vigorous art style developed along with the intensification of maize agriculture and the evident emergence of elites in what must have been a stratified society at that site. Such use of increasingly complex iconography and its accompanying elaborated ideology to reflect increasingly complex social conditions and as a mechanism to sanctify and legitimize such a political structure is not without precedent. It should be clear from these and other examples in the literature that symbolism and meaning in the archaeological record are indeed accessible. However, such efforts are limited at present by the absence of the sort of research strategies which have been developed over the last several decades by archaeologists interested in matters such as subsistence patterns and technology.

It was over 35 years ago that William Sears (1961:223) noted that "Most of the time, thought, and attention of persons working in this field [archaeology] is still given to description, basic artifact typology, definition of cultural units of varying dimensions, and arrangement of these units in time and space". Evidently, not a great deal has changed as we struggle to erase the intellectual walls created by modern political boundaries in an effort to refine our "cultural unit" constructs. Our modern materialist society encourages us to quantify artifact attributes, to "see the trees" of culture, but rarely do we stand back to consider the spiritual "forest". Given what has been documented throughout the Americas and the belief systems maintained to this day by Aboriginal traditionalists, it is hard to imagine any aspect of the archaeological record which does not reflect on ideology. Ramsden's (1990) insightful application of post-processual perspectives to the Southern Ontario Woodland era archaeological record speaks to this reality and the potential for its interpretation. It is an exceptional article in the current literature on Ontario.

Sears (1961:229) suggests that:

it is to be expected that inferences made on the basis of ceremonialism and religion will refer back directly to social data and inferences. Study should begin with conceptually discrete segments of the overall religious and political systems. But, since these were real cultures, full comprehension, reconstruction, and interpretation will develop from and into an interlocking web.

While Ramsden (1990:179) has referred to the testing of ideology-based explanations as a "red herring" and the use of ethnographic analogy propounded by Sears "has long been an object of uneasy mistrust among archaeologists" (Wylie 1985:63), there are methods for evaluating its application to the archaeological record (De Montmollin 1989:34-35; Wylie 1985:69-73, 97-100). It need not be "over extended", to quote Wylie (1985:68). Using temporal, spatial and cultural criteria for selection, we may choose ethnographically documented ceremonies, construct models of predicted archaeological expression and test archaeological evidence against them for congruity, much as William Ritchie (1947) did intuitively half a century ago regarding Owasco evidence for bear ceremonialism.

Wylie (1989a:26) argues for an iterative or "recursive" (Wylie 1985:104) approach to "source- and subject-side research" data as a "strategy of exploiting as many different sources of constraint on knowledge claims about the cultural past as possible". The use of ethnographic data is likewise advocated by De Montmollin (1989:36) in order "to set some limits on models and interpretations". We agree with Wylie (1985:107) that "there are criteria and associated methodological strategies for strengthening and evaluating analogical inferences, if not for 'proving' them, that clearly provide a basis for weeding out and decisively rejecting those cases of false analogy".

It may be instructive to review research at specific archaeological sites in order to illustrate the concepts presented above, and to explore ways in which precontact ideologies can be extracted from the ground. In these examples, ethnographic data and "hard science" are employed in combination to achieve that objective.

The Elliott Villages

In the fall of 1982, roughly a third of the Early Ontario Iroquoian Elliott site was excavated (Fox 1986a). Two complete villages and a portion of a third earlier village were exposed and mapped. Thirteen thousand postholes delineated three former palisade alignments and 24 house structures (Figure 17.1). One hundred and eighty-eight of 484 hearth and pit features were excavated in a little over one month. Radiocarbon dates indicate an eleventh century date for Village II (the more easterly, with north-south trending houses) and a thirteenth century date for Village III.

Elliott is but one of many "Glen Meyer" sites situated on the Norfolk sand plain north of Long Point Bay on Lake Erie; however, even as evidence came from the ground it became obvious that the village was singular. A V-shaped antler comb, as well as red ochre paint palettes of ceramic sherds and turtle shell fragments recovered from a limited number of houses, promised to provide new insights into Early Ontario Iroquoian ritual activities.

Excavation of a large, 1.4 metre diameter pit (Feature 283) in the vicinity of several palisade lines exposed scattered human remains (Figure 17.1). Work ceased and Dr. Michael Spence of the University of Western Ontario agreed to examine the deposit (Spence 1988). Except for a single human molar from a small ash pit in House 14 (Fox 1986b:29), Feature 283 produced the only human remains encountered during the excavation of over two hundred features. This large pit was unusual in a number of other attributes, including its placement. Only one other "Type 1" (storage) pit was located outside a house and it too was situated adjacent to a palisade (Fox 1986a:Figure 4).

Figure 17.2 illustrates the north-south profile of Feature 283. It is characterized by complex layering typical of many such flat-bottomed pits on Early Iroquoian villages, which appear to have been progressively infilled by periods of natural erosion and human deposition of refuse following their abandonment for food storage. The west half was removed to expose the profile and then the east was excavated in 5 layers, defined by the cultural strata (Figure 17.2). Human bone was found scattered over the surface of Layer 4 and within Layer 3. In addition to having been mapped, the profile and horizontal distribution of human bone were documented with colour slide and black and white photographs, which assisted in refining the feature history reconstruction presented below. Stratigraphic excavation of fills from the east half of the pit provided both artifacts and ecofacts critical to feature interpretation (Tables 1-3, at end of chapter). A total of 119 litres of fill from the west half of the pit, as well as the remaining east half portions of Layers 4 and 5 were retained and processed through flotation. Carbonized wood from the west half sample was submitted for radiocarbon dating, resulting in a calibrated date of 670

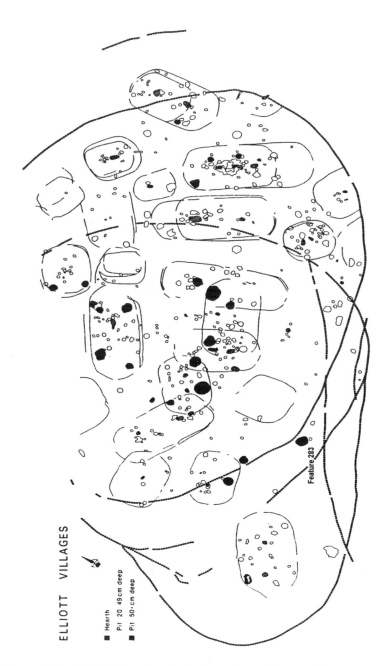

Figure 17.1: Elliott village site plan. Note location of Feature 283.

± 80 B.P. (Fox 1986b:3). This is the latest of four dates derived from the site, providing some support for its Village III affiliation (Fox 1986a:Figure 3). The Village III palisade was expanded to incorporate House 24, so that Feature 283 is located just inside a gap in the pre-expansion south palisade line (Figure 17.1).

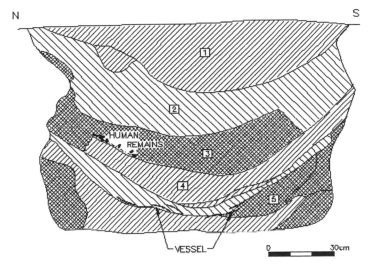

Figure 17.2: The north-south profile of Feature 283.

Figure 17.3 utilizes all the artifact and ecofact data, combined with profile information to present a hypothetical history of events involving Feature 283. Data relating to probable season of procurement for fauna (particularly fish and migratory fowl) have played a major role, as have carbonized berry seeds and evidence of periodic pit wall collapse.

Most of a shattered vessel along with a massive deposit of fish bone in Layer 5 have been interpreted as refuse relating to a feast. It is significant that this layer produced 6,769 of the total 8,536 bone elements recovered from Feature 283. Further, this pit total represents an amazing 29 percent of the faunal remains obtained from 188 features across the entire site area salvaged. The vessel itself is unique in several respects (Figure 17.4). Standing over 40 cm in height, with an orifice diameter of just over 33 cm, it is one of the largest vessels from the site. Moreover, it displays a double row of interior punctates producing exterior bosses—a

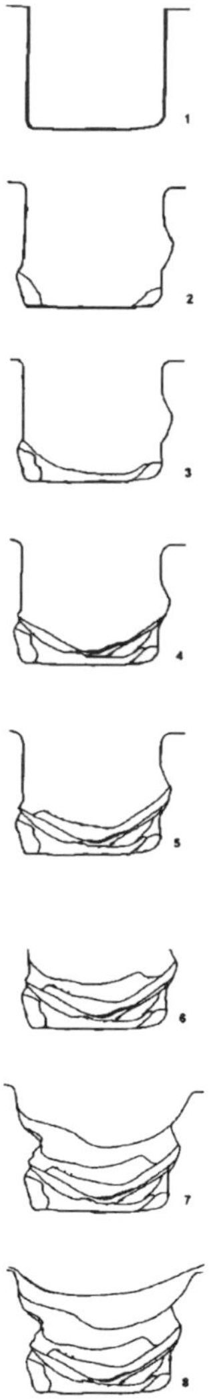

	Annual Cycle	Events
Year I (1 & 2)	Winter	Storage
	Spring	Abandonment/
	Summer	Erosion
	Fall	
Year II (3 & 4)	Winter	Refuse Deposited
	Spring	Erosion
	Summer	Feast Refuse Deposited
	Fall	
Year III (5)	Winter	
	Spring	Erosion
	Summer	Refuse Deposited
	Fall	
Year IV (6)	Winter	
	Spring	Deposit Human Remains, Erosion/Refuse Deposited
	Summer	
	Fall	
Year V (7)	Winter	
	Spring	Erosion
	Summer	
	Fall	
Year VI or VII (8)	Winter	
	Spring	
	Summer	Deposit Refuse in a Sheet Midden
	Fall	

Figure 17.3: Feature 283-hypothetical history by season.

248

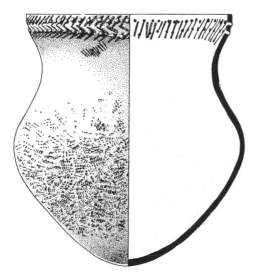

Figure 17.4: Artist's reconstruction of feature 283, layer 5 vessel.

decoration motif found on no other Elliott vessel. Finally, there are 11 short lines in a row, which were incised in an oblique pattern into the wet clay of the vessel neck (Figure 17.4). This idiosyncratic expression has never been observed by the writer on any other Ontario Iroquoian vessel. What these eleven strokes represent remains an enigma.

The next event represented within the fills of Feature 283 is unequivocally ceremonial. Human remains were exposed on the surface of Layer 4, closely associated with three small marine shells *(Marginella sp.)* and a golden(?) eagle wing digit. These were the only eagle or marine shell remains identified among the 29,000 elements recovered from the site (Prevec 1987). Could the eagle digit represent the last vestiges of an eagle wing fan? Were the shell beads deposited as condolence offerings?

Following a period of substantial (primarily natural?) infilling represented by a light coloured, artifact poor deposit (Layer 2), an artifact rich, ashy midden blanketed the pit feature (Layer 1). It is this uppermost and last deposit which produced all the ceramics with layer provenience which cross-mend to other Village III features (Fox 1986b). The mends connect Feature 283 to Houses 18, 19 and 20, with two separate vessels cross-mending to House 18. The latter connection is further strengthened by the recovery of two red ochre stained palette fragments (one ceramic, one turtle shell) from Layer 1. Three storage pits in House 18 also produced ochre stained turtle shell palettes, while only one other feature on the entire site contained such an item. What is more, the Layer 1 faunal assemblage - probably a spring deposit considering the quantity of sucker and pike bone, plus the presence of burbot and passenger pigeon (Table 2), is very similar to the assemblage characterizing the pit layer producing turtle shell palettes in House 18.

Returning to the ceramic cross-mends, it should be noted in defense of the postulated lengthy period of Feature 283 infilling that there are no evident inter-layer/intra-pit cross-mends. There are only mends within layers or between layers and the general west half provenience. Sherds from the west half also cross-mend with other Elliott site features, creating a certain frustration with this necessarily general provenience unit. This is exacerbated by the recovery of two unique faunal specimens from the west half of the pit—a moose incisor and a fisher foot bone. The latter could indicate the former existence of a fisher pelt, and both articles could represent artifacts associated with ritual events evidenced in the pit.

To summarize, Feature 283 seems to contain evidence of three separate ritual events. The first was a feast (possibly village wide), featuring panfish which were probably acquired through net fishing in Long Point Bay to the south during the early summer months when these fish spawn in the shallows of the bay. These small fish were returned to the village whole (dried?), and thus the period of consumption may considerably post-date procurement (i.e. fall or winter). A lack of ceramic cross-mends to village houses, plus a major portion (made up of large sherds) of a large vessel, suggest that the ceremony may have taken place nearby Feature 283.

The second event was a mortuary ceremony which may have occurred during late winter or spring (Figure 17.3). Part of the program involved the selection of bone elements for reburial elsewhere (Spence 1988). The presence of tiny phalanges from a one-and-a-half to two year old child suggests that the individual was wrapped (in bark?), that the container did not disintegrate (in or above ground), and that the bone selection was done in the container and/or adjacent to the pit. It is possible that some of the large post holes near Feature 283 and the palisade supported burial scaffolds. It is also possible that the anomalous structure—virtually featureless and square (House 21) just north of Feature 283, functioned as a meeting place in Village III, housing events such as the feast and mortuary ceremony. Perhaps it even served as a charnel-house.

Evidence presented above relating to the third event suggests that it occurred across Village III in House 18, the longest house in that village phase (Figure 17.1). It also seems to have been held in the spring. Red ochre palettes from Houses 5 and 6 of Village II indicate that similar ceremonies may have been practised two centuries earlier on the Elliott site.

Any attempt to further understand this limited archaeological evidence must, of necessity, turn to ethnohistoric and ethnographic information which post-dates the Elliott villages by over four centuries. Assuming that our current culture historical constructs are correct, the descendants of the Elliott populations were among the Neutral Confederacy in the Hamilton vicinity during French contact in the early seventeenth century. We have some French observations concerning Ontario Iroquoian rituals prior to their mid-seventeenth century dispersal; however, extremely little pertains to the Neutral, whose mortuary traditions were different obviously from those of their better documented Huron neighbours. The most detailed accounts of Iroquoian ritual derive from nineteenth and early twentieth century ethnographic observations concerning the Six Nations Iroquois. Much relates to the Seneca tribe who are reported to have destroyed the Neutral nation. It is based on this tenuous seven century thread of continuity that the following "historical upstreaming" (Voget 1984) is offered.

If we turn to the most evident ceremony, involving mortuary ritual, we find two associated elements—the eagle bone and three marine shell beads. The use of shell beads is amply attested as part of the Iroquois condolence ceremonies attending the death of a chief (Hale 1895). A.C. Parker (Converse 1974) provides a number of observations regarding eagles. Of the formerly secret Eagle Society, he states that "the sign of membership...is a round spot of red paint on either cheek" (Converse 1974:69). Parker notes that Oh-swe-da (Spirit of the Spruce) wears the wings of an owl and an eagle on his head. This spirit is related to the origin of the Oh-gi-we Society ("Talkers with the Dead"), who present the Death Dance (Converse 1974:83). Finally, in connection with the killing or releasing of a bird above the grave of the newly dead, he observes that "the eagle is the only bird that looks straight into the eyes of the sun" (Converse 1974:96).

Of the 'Ohgi'we (Feast of the Dead of the Nations), Fenton and Kurath (1951:145) report that this semi-annual feast was held either in the late fall (late October - December) or early spring (April), and was referred to as the great kettle by the Huron and Six Nations Iroquois. The large vessel from Feature 283 (Figure 17.4) would have constituted a "great kettle" on the Elliott site, but need not relate to the feast of the dead. Among the modern Seneca, there are seven "festivals of thanksgiving", primarily associated with plant foods (Fenton 1941:145). If the Layer 5 fish were consumed shortly after they were taken, then the

Feature 283 feast may have been analogous in timing to the Green Corn Festival. Indeed, it may represent one of an ancient series of thanksgiving festivals relating to fish and game. Could this have increased the annual calendar of feast events to eleven—the number of strokes on the vessel?

Turning finally to the springtime ritual involving the use of red ochre paint, we have relatively few references among the Iroquois to the use of red paint outside of war. Fenton and Kurath (1953:102) have suggested that the Eagle Dance ritual presently connected with the Eagle medicine society derived from ancient war and peace rites. Parker (Converse 1974:142) states that if a purple wampum belt was adorned with red paint or a red feather it signified war. As noted above, Parker (1909:174) states that "every member participating in the (Eagle Dance) ceremony paints on each cheek a round red spot" and that the "signal pole and the striking stick are spirally striped with red paint" (Parker 1909:176). Nevertheless, this very sacred ceremony does have a healing aspect in that it revives dying or old people.

We have seen that the eagle is also closely associated with death ritual. The life/death dichotomy is also expressed through the use of red body paint in the legend entitled "The Dream Fast, Jis-go-ga, the Robin" (Converse 1974:109), where the narrator states "I was willing, and painted my body red when I felt my spirit departing" and later exclaims, "Jis-go-ga, the Robin, the bird which brings us the spring!" (Converse 1974:110) Could it be that the Elliott site 'Ohgi'we Death Chanters spoke to the dead in the spring of rebirth? Could it be that the bi-annual ritual events evidenced in Feature 283 all reflect different aspects of ancient Iroquoian mortuary ceremony?

The Gottschall Site

The Gottschall site (47Ia80) is a medium sized sandstone rockshelter located in the unglaciated southwestern area of Wisconsin. More than 40 individual painted figures were discovered there by a local farm boy in 1974. Excavations begun in 1984 by Beloit College have revealed more than 5.6 metres of clearly stratified and essentially undisturbed sediments that have accumulated on the floor over at least the past 3,500 years (Salzer 1987) (see Figure 17.5).

Nearly all of the paintings were done in a blue-black pigment and most are badly eroded and faded. Photographic recording of the artwork was accomplished immediately and every effort was made to enhance the

Figure 17.5: Profile of south wall of S18W10. (Scale at bottom is 30 cm long, right to left is approximately 2 m.)

definition of the surviving images. Research has focussed on a group of five human and animal figures that were painted on a prepared (sanded) surface, thereby indicating that the artist's intent was to create a composition (see Figure 17.6).

Robert Hall has identified this group as representing the main characters of a HoChunk (Winnebago) oral tradition—the Legend of Red Horn—which had been written down around 1900 by Elders and translated into English (Radin [editor] 1948). A similar legend was recorded for the closely related Ioway by Skinner (1925). The lengthy story is a saga that details some of the exploits of the main character. At one point, the hero is joined by his friends, Turtle and Storms-As-He-Walks (a thunderbird) in a contest with the champions of a race of giants who had been raiding the villages of Red Horn's people. The two large figures on the left are presumed to represent the giants, the smaller human on the right, Red Horn. The crested falcon-like bird is the thunderbird—the HoChunk note that such creatures tie cedar boughs to their heads, which may explain the "crest". The legend goes on to say that one of the giants, a chieftainess, has red hair, and one of the giant figures has red paint behind (her) head.

William A. Fox and Robert J. Salzer

Figure 17.6: The Red Horn composition A.D. 850-950. A. "Giant"; B. Red-haired giantess; C. Turtle; D. Thunderbird; E. Red Horn.

Excavation of each stratum is occurring in two centimetre levels and the artifacts are mapped in place. Post-settlement alluvium has capped and protected the precontact deposits. Excavations directly underneath the Red Horn group have revealed a paint spill, a portion of an exceptionally thin cord impressed (Effigy Mound) vessel, and debris resulting from the sanding of the wall. Immediately above this stratum is a series of small, irregular, burned areas. The light from these fires would have illuminated the Red Horn composition. Since substantial details of the paintings relate to early Mississippian art styles (Phillips and Brown 1978; Brown and Kelly 1995) it must be that the Gottschall artists were sharing many of the symbols, and the motivating ideology, with Emergent Mississippian peoples (i.e. Lohman and early Stirling Phases at Cahokia, 950-850 B.P.). Three radiocarbon assays, from tightly controlled contexts, indicate that the composition was painted around 1050-950 B.P., supporting the preceding conclusion. The implications of these dates are significant and profoundly important to archaeology because they indicate that at least some oral traditions can maintain their integrity for at least a thousand years (Salzer 1993).

A total of sixteen AMS and eight standard radiocarbon assays document a long sequence of occupations beginning in Late Archaic times (3450- 2450 B.P.), followed by Middle Woodland (1700 to 1250 B.P.), early Effigy Mound (1150 to 950 B.P.), early Oneota (950 to 850 B.P.), Late Woodland (950 to 650 B.P.) and Developmental Oneota (850 to 550 B.P.). Clearly, the artists must have been the ancestors of the HoChunk and Ioway peoples, but stratigraphically, they must have been the Eastman Phase (early Effigy Mound) occupants. This is at variance with the widely held consensus that it is Oneota, not Effigy Mound, that is the precontact expression of the HoChunk and Ioway (Mason 1993; Overstreet 1993). This view is based in part on the fact that it is Oneota, not Effigy Mound material culture, which persists after 650 B.P. and into the contact period. However, the HoChunk have claimed that their ancestors built the effigy mounds (Radin 1923), and they continue to do so—now with some archaeological support. It remains for archaeology to find some answer to this apparent contradiction in realities. That this dissonance is a function of archaeologically constructed material culture taxonomy is also apparent.

Gartner (1993) has analyzed the sediments at the site and most of the strata provide important information on the source and mechanisms of deposition in the shelter, relating to local and regional paleoenvironmental changes. However, more than twenty cubic metres of sediments were identified as being fabricated—they are man-made dirts. Standard and micromorphological analyzes (Courty et al. 1989) indicate that these dirts were manufactured and periodically laid down in shallow increments beginning around 1600 B.P. and ceasing around 950 B.P., although small quantities were laid down sporadically earlier and later than these dates. The dirts comprise ashes from coniferous trees and grasses; burned and powdered limestone, the closest outcrop of which is more than four km from the site; and crushed clamshells, the closest source being fifteen km from the site. Excavations have revealed an earth oven where the limestone was cooked, and the firm radiocarbon assays for this feature range from 2500 to 2650 B.P., implying a considerable antiquity for the fabrication of these dirts at the site. The sanding debris and paint spill associated with the Red Horn composition were located within the uppermost of these dirts, indicating that the artists were also making and laying it down. The clear conclusion is that the artists were only one of the later peoples who shared the formulae and ideological concepts of these dirts. Equally clear is the recognition that our cultural-historical taxonomy tends to obscure the ideological, if not ethnic, continuities of the precontact past.

In 1992, a carved and painted sandstone head was found in the stratum immediately above the man-made dirts (950 to 900 B.P.), associated with a pile of sherds from a large vessel and a heap of animal bones (see Figure 17.7). The head is manufactured from local rock, is about 26 cm high and 9 cm in diameter, is roughly cylindrical, and is delicately sculpted with

eyes and nostrils indicated (Pringle 1993; Weintraub 1993). It is painted with a blue-black pigment in parallel vertical lines on the face. There is a small dotted circle on the chin, and a case has been made for this motif to be associated with creatures that inhabit the underworld (Salzer n.d.). Orange-red pigment was painted inside the open mouth. Radin (1923) notes that sometimes the HoChunk put red paint in the mouth of a deceased person to let Earthmaker know that the person is happy to enter the afterlife. Striations

Figure 17.7: "Mr. Head". Note vertical blue-grey painted lines; circle with central dot on chin. Late effigy mound (A.D. 1000-1050). 25 cm in height.
Photograph by Chuck Savage.

on the unfinished neck suggest that the head was inserted into a hole of some sort, perhaps at the end of a log support.

The associated vessel is decorated with complex cord impressions and is clearly related to Effigy Mound ceramics (see Figure 17.8). Beneath the main field is a horizontal meander motif that Phillips (1989) identified as a metaphor for the underworld (waterspirit, underwater panther). In 1997, a HoChunk visitor to the site remarked that the Bear clan sometimes paints a dotted circle on the chin of a deceased member. The Bear clan is the most important representative of "those below" among these people (Radin 1923). The animal bones have been identified by Prof. James Theler, University of Wisconsin-La Crosse (personal communication 1993). He notes that a minimum of five deer and one canid (probably domestic dog) are present, and that the deer were fawns that had been killed in November or December. Also, the elements are marrow-rich—they are the "best cuts".

According to Radin (1923) the most important ceremony of the HoChunk was the War-bundle Feast, which was held in the winter. At that

Figure 17.8: Cord-impressed vessel found with "Mr. Head" (A.D. 1000-1050).

feast, the person who represents an important war spirit, Disease-Giver, receives the "best cuts" of the meat and he, alone, is allowed to eat the dog that has been ritually strangled. The association of Disease-Giver with death (and life) is certain (Radin 1923). The head, then, is best interpreted as a mortuary figure, quite possibly a portrait of a specific individual. The entire complex, including the head, the pot, the season of the year, and the details of the feast, argues convincingly that the (Effigy Mound) ancestors of the HoChunk and probably the Ioway engaged in a ritual that has remarkable parallels to what they performed some 900 years later.

A "saturation" survey of the small valley where the site is located was completed by David Lowe in 1990. A large village was found at the point where the creek enters the floodplain of the Wisconsin River. Surface materials indicate that this village was occupied during the same periods that are represented at Gottschall. This is likely to be the summer settlement for the artists and others who used the shelter in the winter. Across the river and slightly downstream is a very large Effigy Mound group and associated village. One of the bird mounds in this group has a wingspan of almost 400 metres. A radiocarbon date from a hearth at this site indicates that it is contemporary with the period of the painting of the Red Horn composition (Robert Birmingham, personal communication).

The Gottschall site meets nearly all of the criteria that Renfrew (1994) used to identify a cult shrine, and archaeological data indicate that it was used repeatedly over a period of at least 700 years (1600 to 900 B.P.). More importantly, ethnographic data provide a solid basis for identifying the participants in the rituals as being part of the ideological ancestors of the modern HoChunk and Ioway, and these peoples certainly included the artists who painted the Red Horn group of figures. Those peoples were, during the period of use, members of an archaeological construct called the "Effigy Mound culture"; but at contact times, at least, the Ioway and probably the HoChunk can be identified with the "Oneota culture". The information from this site strongly argues for ideological continuity between additional archaeological "cultures"; materially discrete manifestations which do not readily appear to express such an ideological (ethnic?) continuum. Further, the regional context of Gottschall strongly suggests the presence of a cultural landscape revolving primarily around ritual, as opposed to subsistence activities. Research at the Gottschall site is on-going, but even at this point, it demonstrates that archaeological access to symbolic expression is not beyond our grasp. It also demonstrates the value of using ethnographic data and a variety of kinds of "proof" to amplify the meaning(s) of the data that we recover.

The case studies presented have provided the "subject side" archaeological data in detail, and the "source side" ethnographic data against which all may compare the relative fit. Does the interpretation stretch the empirical "limits" (Wylie 1989b) of the archaeological "fact" any more than reconstructions of seasonal subsistence activities and movements based on recovered faunal remains or utilized toolstones? Wylie (1989a:26) suggests that archaeologists "should develop Nunamiut-style wisdom about when to amend methodological and theoretical rules in the light of the exigencies of experience and practice". More than half a century ago, Taylor (1948:110-111) pointed out that:

> Culture, consisting as it does of mental constructs, is not directly observable. It cannot, therefore, constitute the empirical data of any discipline. Culture can be studied only through the instrumentality of observable phenomena, through what have been called the objectifications of culture: cultural behavior and the material and non-material results of such behavior...[the identification of a mental construct] remains always in the realm of plausible inference. If the inference explains other phenomena satisfactorily and if it serves as a practical and trustworthy premise for logical reasoning and the explanation of observable fact, then it may be accepted as an approximation of a cultural idea.

Put in plain terms by Ramsden (1990:179), "if an explanation is consistent with our prior experience, does not contradict anything we believe to be true, is consistent with more than one line of evidence, and appears to 'make sense' within the particular context, then it is good enough to be getting on with"—that is, it is a viable hypothesis or model.

Taken as a whole, the available archaeological evidence as applied against ethnohistoric and ethnographic data for the Great Lakes region suggests that the basic themes of religious beliefs and their contextual ideological world view were ubiquitous over a great period of time. That individuals and specific corporate groups expressed variations is clear; however, detailed spatial and temporal mapping of these iconographic and ceremonial expressions is at present so incomplete as to render their use as precontact ethnic markers highly tentative. This does not mean that progress is impossible, only that more effort must be committed by researchers to the reading of this, the most definitive human narrative in the archaeological record before us.

Table 17.1

Feature 283 Artifact Recoveries by Pit Layer

West Half of Feature		
Ceramics	411	25 rim sherds
Lithics	888	15 tool fragments, primarily Onondaga chert
Layer 1		
Ceramics	336	5 rim sherds, 1 pipe bowl fragment, 1 palette
Lithics	346	2 tools/fragments, primarily Onondaga chert
Layer 2		
Ceramics	25	
Lithics	44	Onondaga chert debitage
Layer 3		
Ceramics	17	
Lithics	70	1 biface tip
Bone	1	awl
Layer 4		
Ceramics	106	1 rim sherd
Lithics	170	5 tools/fragments
Shell	3	3 Marginella beads
Layer 5		
Ceramics	400	c. 80% belongs to single large vessel
Lithics	78	1 biface
Bone	1	awl (?)

Table 17.2
Feature 283—Faunal Material

| Class and Species | East | | | | | | West | TOTAL |
	L1	L2	L3	L3*	L4	L5	all	
MAMMALS								
Deer	13		1	8	20	152	82	276
Grey Squirrel			3	2	16	1	5	27
Raccoon					2	5	8	15
Beaver	3					2	2	7
Bear						1	4	5
Meadow Vole						4		4
Chipmunk					3		1	4
Woodchuck	1						2	3
Moose							1	1
Marten							1	1
Fisher							1	1
Unidentified	85	5	17	4	75	680	485	1351
BIRDS								
Greater Scaup						14		14
Duck sp.			1		5		1	7
Turkey					1	2		3
Blue Jay							2	2
Passenger Pigeon	1							1
Grouse sp.					1			1
Golden Eagle				1				1
Unidentified	4		1		5	2	5	17
FISH								
Rock Bass					63	698		761
Pumkinseed					21	317		338
Perciformes sp.	3				33	286		322
Bass sp.	2				38	228	22	290

Class and Species	East						West	
	L1	L2	L3	L3*	L4	L5	all	TOTAL
Perch						152		152
Burbot	1			1	22	3	18	45
Brown Bullhead					4	5	10	19
Sucker sp.	6						11	17
Bluegill	2						13	15
Smallmouth Bass					1	11		12
Catfish	8			1	2			11
Walleye					10			10
Whitefish					5		4	9
Sturgeon	1	1			2	1	3	8
Pike	6							6
Largemouth Bass						6		6
White Bass					4			4
Bowfin	1				2			3
American Eel							2	2
Trout					1			1
Lepomis sp.					1			1
Unidentified	33	3	7		374	4195	80	4692
REPTILES								
Painted Turtle					12	1	10	23
Blading's Turtle					1			1
Unidentified Turtle	2		5			2	2	11
AMPHIBIANS								
Toad							7	7
MOLLUSCS								
Marginella					3			3
Clam (elliptio sp.)				1		1		2
CLASS UNCERTAIN		4					20	24
TOTALS	172	13	35	18	727	6769	802	8536

Table 17.3
Botanical Recoveries from Feature 283 Floatation Residues

West Half		
Heavy Fractions		
Corn	12	7 kernel fragments, 2 cob fragments, 3 cupules
Squash	1	1 seed
Butternut	105	105 shell fragments
Layer 4		
Heavy Fraction		
Corn	39	14 kernel fragments,25 cupules
Wild Plum	1	1 pit
Light Fraction		
Corn	210	3 kernels, 68 kernel fragments, 139 cob fragments
Raspberry	60	60 seeds
Strawberry	7	7 seeds
Tobacco	6	6 seeds
Sumac	5	5 seeds
Goosefoot	4	4 seeds
Purselane	2	2 seeds
Nightshade	2	2 seeds
Spikenard	1	1 seed

Section III: Taming the Tamers

COMMENTS: TOWARD A NEW UNDERSTANDING OF GREAT LAKES ARCHAEOLOGY

18

Dean R. Snow
Department of Anthropology, Pennsylvania State University

It is difficult to offer brief comments without seeming to reduce the arguments of my colleagues to simple cartoons. I think I can avoid going the next step, which would be to render their views as caricatures, but I feel compelled to apologize in advance for any oversimplification my attempts to summarize might impose on their words.

It is important to understand the profound differences in the points of view represented by the papers presented by Fiedel and Jamieson. These differences might not be entirely apparent at first hearing. Not (I hope) to put too fine a point on it, Fiedel sees the events of precontact history at large scale as a series of population expansions. The most apt analogy might be the expansions of biological populations at large spatial and temporal scales. Of course he allows for the effects of mixture and absorption as well as displacement and extermination, for no experienced researcher denies that human societies interact in ways very different from biological species. Nevertheless, it is fair to say that his model of paleodemography at large scale is one that allows for the expansion of dominant populations at the expense of subordinate ones, and that the long-term consequences of that complex process was part of what led to the crazy-quilt distribution of North American Indian language families familiar to modern historical linguists.

Jamieson's view is much more one of human population as medium. In her discussion, key artifact types often move as particles through that medium, often along well-travelled routes. At other times, change seems to move as waves in that medium. Thus we read that around 11,000 years ago southwestern Ontario was interacting with southerly areas, as indicated by the occurrence of Upper Mercer (Ohio) chert on sites there. Later we read that by 10,700 years ago interactions had shifted northward, as indicated by the appearance of Bayport chert from Michigan and the cessation of imports from Ohio. I suspect that Fiedel would put a very different spin on this evidence. He might even suggest a population expansion into southwestern Ontario out of Michigan at the expense of an earlier population that was alternatively absorbed, displaced, extinguished, or more likely some combination of those, by the expanding population.

Is there any common ground between the views expressed by Fiedel and Jamieson? Would a more realistic assessment of the ways in which human beings behave at large scale yield an understanding of processes that would incorporate or at least satisfy both points of view? Do we have the means to detect those processes archaeologically? These are questions that have occupied me for the last few years and explain why I have published the articles I have on Iroquoian paleodemography.

Unfairly represented as cartoons, the views of both Fiedel and Jamieson can be made to look simplistic. This is a debating technique that is both familiar and offensive; I will make no use of it here. Instead, consider the animated weather maps that we now see every night on the evening news. Air masses are not clearly bounded, yet meteorologists find it possible to draw moving fronts, the edges of which are often quite well defined. My point is that the atmosphere moves, but that it is at the same time a medium. Particles can pass through it, but they can also be carried by it for great distances. It seems likely to me that both Stuart Fiedel and Susan Jamieson are quite comfortable with the animated representation of our weather on the evening news. It also seems to me that they would also be quite comfortable with a clearer shared understanding of the way in which human societies operate at the same scale. Of course artifacts move through the medium of linked human societies, and of course those societies sometimes move. All the while individuals and social subsets are also moving, sometimes regularly, sometimes cyclically, sometimes sporadically, and at a variety of scales. That said, it seems unlikely to me that we will ever be able to understand these complexities by empirical archaeological means alone. Our understanding is predicated on the development of realistic theoretical models, work that still lies mostly, but not entirely, ahead of us.

For example, Jamieson observes that after 10500 B.P. territories were decreasing in size as population densities increased. This is at once a simple and profound observation. It is consistent with what we can observe in nineteenth century Aboriginal Australia. As human hunter-gatherer population densities grew, the minimum number of face-to-face interactions necessary to keep a breeding population viable could be realized across smaller and smaller regions. Fiedel mentions the magic number of 500 that Birdsell proposed many years ago and that has recently been revived by Hunn (1994). This precise number has been convincingly disputed (Kelly 1994), but the basic idea seems indisputable. More dense populations need less space to maintain the same number of internal face-to-face interactions. Moreover, observed archaeological signatures are quite consistent with this theoretical model. It seems clear that this process led to the emergence of social boundaries as time went on. Still later, mechanisms were developed to transcend those boundaries. Among those mechanisms were intersocietal trade, exchange, and fictive kinship. But there were undoubtedly also mechanisms that led to the displacement or erasure of those boundaries, and in these cases we must regard the societies involved as more than just media for the transmission of ideas.

Finding the archaeological signatures of these processes is not easy, which I judge is why processual archaeologists long ago told us we need not bother. I spent a month in the British Isles in 1997 trying to isolate the signatures of a well-known and generally-accepted population replacement during the Early Christian period, and I can vouch for the difficulty of the task. But surely we gain nothing by ignoring such problems because we find them inconveniently difficult. Jamieson notes that both before and after 1200 B.P., utilitarian artifact types were shared over a very large portion of the lower Great Lakes region. She does not offer a mechanism for how this came about beyond the implicit one involving the spread of traits through an essentially immobile human population. Fiedel does suggest an explicit mechanism for the same phenomenon, but it is one that emphasizes the mobility of human populations.

Once again, I do not intend to set up a false dichotomy here. There is much that Fiedel and Jamieson can agree on I am sure. But there are fundamental issues here that I think are very exciting anthropological problems, the solution of which should be a high research priority. To that end I think that it is high time that we stop burying these issues in discourse that is cleverly vague. For example, it is no longer sufficient to say, as does Jamieson, that the "Southeastern maize complex...gained its foothold in southern Ontario." Sooner or later we must explicitly address the range of reasonable mechanisms by which maize might have come to Ontario, reduce those to a finite set of concise hypotheses, and set about finding clever ways to test them. Trade, along with peer polity interaction, are components of one hypothesis. The range of demographic processes that we lump under the term "migration" can be used to generate two or three more hypotheses. I have already put my oar in the water regarding how I think it all sorts out when one considers the evidence in light of William of Occam's axiom, and I won't repeat it here (Snow 1995a, 1996).

Colin Renfrew has recently argued that archaeology simply cannot go it alone (Renfrew 1997). If we are to solve anthropological problems we must, he says, integrate archaeology, historical linguistics, and biological anthropology. I have argued much the same thing in an article that is still on an editor's desk, although I would add ethnological theory to the mix. Archaeology cannot succeed alone. However, if we are to succeed in using these lines of evidence in concert, we will have to be very careful about our units and contexts. A biological species is not a very good analogue of a human society, and neither is it a very good analogue of a language. Fiedel provides us with a careful discussion of dialects, languages, and the growth of language family trees over time, but he could take it further. Languages often map onto societies quite well, but it is still the case that societies are very unstable in terms of the individual humans that are their units of transformation. People join or leave societies individually or in groups. Individual biological organisms or groups of them do not join and leave species. More to the point, people join or leave social groups much more easily than they acquire or abandon languages. Moreover, much more than societies, languages are complete logical packages that are only very rarely blended or hybridized. Many languages, for structural reasons, even resist taking on loanwords. English is a great consumer of loanwords, while any Iroquoian language virtually prohibits such borrowing. It should be no surprise that few loanwords have been exchanged between Algonquian and Iroquoian languages but that many have been borrowed from both by English.

My larger point is that while we must consider linguistic, social, and biological lines of evidence in an integrated way, we must nevertheless treat each of them in terms of their own distinctive mechanisms of change over time. If we do this carefully, then it is quite understandable that Fiedel should be bewildered that anyone could assert that Point Peninsula was an ancestral Iroquoian tradition. Given the existence of the Laurel complex and many other entailed anomalies, such an assertion simply does not make sense to either Fiedel or me. I would add that to simply dismiss the issue as meaningless because we all know that language, biology, and society (or culture) operate independently is to beg what I regard as the primary questions challenging anthropologists today. Like Renfrew, I believe that the primary questions are anthropological, that archaeology all by itself cannot do much to answer them, but that with biology, historical linguistics, and adequate theory added to the mix we have a chance to do so.

Other papers in this set focus on the contributions of particular lines of archaeological inquiry. Toby Morrow looks at lithic technology and makes some very interesting points. Like many others he notes that as population density increased societal territories decreased. I have already said that I regard this as an important fundamental, even elegant, process. I must confess, however, that I am puzzled by Morrow's characterization of its effects on lithic assemblages as being the consequence of "pressure on finite lithic resources." It seems to me that this is an almost but not quite accurate characterization. Sources of high quality cherts are scattered to be sure, and with the contraction of societal territories a few societies found themselves possessed of rich local chert sources while many others found themselves cut off from the best quarries and had to settle for inferior local cherts. Thus high quality cherts were scarce from the point of view of those societies not having local access to them, but they were hardly finite, especially from the point of view of the smaller number of societies that did have access to them. In this case the notion of resource pressure seems to me to be misplaced. A small point perhaps, but I do not think so. It is not that the resource is scarce but that access to it is restricted by social and political constraints, something that introduces social factors to the equation.

Elsewhere Morrow speaks with refreshing candour and perception about the use and misuse of point types. We should all relish his lucid discussion of the projectile point sequence, which is deliberately free of unnecessary and even confusing type names. And we should thank the editor who asked for this approach. One of the observations that emerges as a result of it is that light, thick points progressed southwestward out of western Canada starting around 1600 B.P. and reached the Midwest by about three centuries later. Morrow infers that this is the signature of the spread of the bow and arrow, a view that seems to be achieving general acceptance. Fiedel would take inference a step further and associate the phenomenon with the expansion of a dominant Algonquian-speaking population of people equipped with bows and arrows. I judge that this is probably a correct inference. Whether it is or not, I am convinced that this is the scale at which some of the most interesting hypotheses can be examined by archaeologists in the next century. I am pleased to see us getting such a good start here. We are not about to abandon type names, but Morrow is quite right to urge us to restructure how we conceptualize them.

George Milner and Anne Katzenberg point out that osteological studies can be used to assess relatedness, diet, health, and conflict. Of all of these I find the recent work in genetics and its implications for relatedness to be most interesting. The authors and their students are in the vanguard in this kind of work, even while keeping the other three lines of research moving ahead. The archaeology of the future will not amount to much if we do not use it in concert with genetics, historical linguistics, and ethnological theory. It saddens me to say that much of what has passed for ethnological theory in recent years is worthless, but a fraction of it is quite useful.

In this volume and his other recent publications, Milner also has presented data to support the conclusion that there were two broadly defined periods of widespread conflict prior to 450 B.P. in North America. One of these occurred in the Middle to Late Archaic. The second began around 1150 B.P. and became quite common in the last centuries before contact. Something very important was going on in both of those periods. To put it another way, why is there so little evidence of conflict around 2,000 years ago? This is the same period that produces an unexpectedly small number of sites in some parts of the Eastern Woodlands. What was going on here? Surely it must be something profound that can be studied in demographic terms. But once again it is likely that we can come to grips with it only by examining it at very large temporal and spatial scales.

The papers by Lovis and MacDonald on the one hand, and by Salzer and Fox on the other, offer another striking study in contrasts. Lovis and MacDonald take the long view of paleoecology, in terms of both time and space. Like Morrow they have taken to heart the session mandate to avoid jargon. They wonder near the beginning why ecological archaeology remains so underdeveloped. It seems to me that the rest of their paper makes the answer to this question quite clear. Two of the most fundamental problems in paleoecological research are indeed related to scale and resolution. Perceptible patterns are most apparent over large regions and long periods. It also takes a long time to develop research programs. In other words, it makes no sense to take on a paleoecological research program until after one has tenure someplace, and it is unwise to say anything really controversial until one has been promoted to full professor and one's hair has either fallen out or turned white. Paleoecological research remains underdeveloped because it requires such a large investment.

Lovis and MacDonald go on for ten manuscript pages before getting to paleoecological generalizations about the millennia that are the focus of most other papers in this set. And in the remaining pages they often return to discussions of paleoecological phenomena that largely predate human occupation in the region. At the opposite extreme, Salzer and Fox attempt to deal responsibly with ideological systems. Their subject forces them to focus on the recent and the particular. There must be reference to ethnography, and the rock art sites they need are both scarce and very difficult to interpret. But as they say at the end, there is no shame in the effort. The Gottschal site is an extraordinary one where astonishingly good fortune and admirable archaeological cleverness have been combined to produce results that one might have previously thought to be impossible.

Yet there seems to be a gulf between these last two papers, as Lovis and MacDonald put it, a disparity in scales of interest. Can we hope to bridge that gulf? I think that we can, but it will not be easy. It will take all of our capabilities and some that we have not invented yet. It will take integrated consideration of the separate lines of inquiry that I have already mentioned twice, as well as constant reminders that we are ultimately engaged in anthropological inquiry that must be founded on adequate theory.

An example of the last requirement emerges from Salzer and Fox's discussion of the hypothesis of Overstreet and Richards (Overstreet and Richards [editors] 1992) and Collins (1989). It is that sometime around 550 B.P., some groups of peoples shifted from patrilocal to matrilocal residence, and that by contact times, shifted back to patrilocal residence. I have not yet read Hollinger's (1995) test of this hypothesis using ethnological arguments, but everything I know from the ethnological literature, from Murdock's classic *Social Structure* (Murdock 1960) to Divale's more recent cross-cultural work (Divale 1984), indicates that such a sequence of changes is so unlikely as to be practically impossible.

The papers in this volume tell us much about the archaeology of our region, both actual and potential. As impressive as that is, it should be clear to all that archaeology, by itself, cannot accomplish much. The array of techniques drawn from many sources is impressive and necessary. So to are the larger contributions of biological anthropology, historical linguistics, and ethnology. The enterprise is still anthropology and the paradigm is still science.

COMMENTS: THE SOCIAL FOUNDATIONS OF ARCHAEOLOGICAL TAXONOMY

19

Michael W. Spence
Department of Anthropology, The University of Western Ontario

The objective of these papers has been to explore the validity and utility of the taxonomies on which we base our accounts of Great Lakes and Midwestern precontact history. The durability of some of these concepts, even under sustained attack (e.g., Ferris and Spence 1995:110; Williamson 1990:311-312; Wright 1992), is perhaps an indication not so much of their reality as of the necessity for some sort of framework within which we can organize data. They are often more convenient fictions, devices for intelligible communication, than real categories (Williamson and Robertson 1994a:33). In evaluating them, and the stories we create from them, we must keep in mind Williamson's (this volume) advice: always ask how they work out "on the ground" (see also MacEachern 1994). With any taxonomic category, relevant questions would include:

How was it formulated, that is, what processes and interactions created this apparently uniform (at one level of observation) unit?

How was it maintained over time?

How real was it to the people subsumed in it, in what ways did it touch their lives?

Most taxonomies start at the palisade and work outward, ordering components in time and space. The archaeological sites (communities) become basic, and often indivisible, building blocks in the development of larger taxonomic categories. Surprisingly often there is no real attempt to determine how these larger units came to be. The unifying traits that characterize them are duly identified, but not explained—a heritage, perhaps, of the relatively static Midwest Taxonomic System.

When explanations are attempted, they may invoke a variety of mechanisms: trade (Jamieson 1991), warfare (Finlayson 1998:408-410; Keener 1995; Wright 1992), migration (Snow 1995a, 1996; cf.

Chapdelaine 1992), ideology (Ritchie 1955), environmental adaptation (Braun and Plog 1982; Lovis and MacDonald, this volume), etc. Marriage is only occasionally suggested, and usually then as subordinate to one of the other mechanisms. Very few of the papers in this volume assign it an explicit and major role (Jamieson, this volume). Yet I suspect that it is the mechanism by which the most concrete of our taxonomic units came into being. Our most real and important categories, then, may also be identified as connubia (Williams 1974).

Trade can certainly lead to some cultural convergence between interacting groups, particularly if complexes of belief and behaviour surrounding the traded items are also adopted (Jamieson, this volume). Nevertheless, the impact of trade is usually restricted to particular spheres of culture, rarely resulting in the transformation of the participating groups. Although core-periphery theory raises the possibility of more fundamental change (Dincauze and Hasenstab 1989), its applicability to Great Lakes and Midwestern interactions has been challenged (Williamson and Robertson 1994a: Jamieson, this volume). Exchanged goods were largely items involved in ritual and social display: panpipes, marine shell, etc. They created a patina of exotic goods that cannot mask the underlying distinctiveness of the participating cultures.

One possible exception to this may be the Meadowood complex of New York, Ontario and Quebec, characterized by widespread similarities in material culture, particularly ceramics and chipped stone tools (Spence and Fox 1986; Morrow, this volume). This homogeneity was largely a product of the wide circulation of chipped stone preforms, with some attendant stylistic concepts (Granger 1978). The subsequent modification and recycling of tools from these preforms further constrained the variability of tool assemblages. Nevertheless, there is still localized variation in Meadowood (Spence and Fox 1986). It is probably wiser to identify Meadowood as an exchange network that touched on a variety of distinct cultures (e.g., Chrétien 1995).

Warfare might lead to the creation of new sociocultural units, as groups develop alliances or modify their own internal structure in the face of external threat. Again, however, the pervasiveness of these changes is questionable. Some aspects of culture may be altered while most remain essentially unchanged. More profound changes will occur if one group conquers the other, and then maintains its control rather than withdrawing. This, Wright (1992) argues, was the case with the Early Ontario Iroquoians (but see Spence 1994; Williamson 1990:311-312).

On the other hand, if the relationships and alliances created by trade or warfare are reinforced by intermarriage, deeper changes can occur. Here, though, intermarriage is the proximate cause, and it can occur without the encouragement of the pressure of military threat or economic advantage. In fact, given the relatively small size of many precontact communities, some degree of intermarriage with neighbouring groups would have been inescapable.

The inclusion of outsiders in the community through marriage can be expected to lead to significant changes. Such intruders are, in effect, cultural seeds, bringing with them a different set of knowledge, skills, beliefs and practices, perhaps even a new language. Also, their impact on the community would not be superficial or ephemeral, like that of a visiting trader. They will be members of the community for life, and they will play a role in the enculturation of the next generation. They will thus have a profound and enduring effect on the local culture.

This leads us back inside the palisade, to a consideration of the internal structure of the community and of the concerns and customs guiding marriage and post-marital residential choices. Difficult though it may be, we must try to determine what proportion of the community enters it at marriage, and from how far afield these people are likely to be drawn. Of particular interest is any gender imbalance in exogamy or post-marital residence. Which gender is more likely to leave the community at marriage? In other words, which set of gender-related knowledge and skills is circulating more widely in and beyond the society?

Archaeologists and physical anthropologists have developed a variety of techniques for investigating these questions, though regrettably these attempts have, for the most part, been sporadic and inconclusive. Kapches (1990) has measured the degree of organization of Ontario longhouse interiors and suggests that, as matrilocally-structured households developed, a greater degree of order was imposed on the interior structure and functions of the residence. She sees this shift occurring sometime after the tenth century. Although not conclusive in itself, this approach can then be compared with others. It will require the convergence of several different lines of evidence to confidently trace the development of Iroquoian matrilineality and matrilocality.

One of these other lines of evidence is osteology. Osteological data can contribute to two relevant questions. One of these is the identification and definition of biological units, regional populations, and even of intrusive groups within them (DeLaurier and Spence 1998; Milner and

Michael W. Spence

Katzenberg, this volume). Molto's (1983) analysis of Mean Measure of Divergence among a number of skeletal series to define a single biological population in south central Ontario is a case in point. Also, Lennox and Molto (1995) have tentatively identified a distinct "Algonquian" Western Basin biological population in the southwestern corner of Ontario, and Spence et al. (1984) have discussed the biological and cultural parameters of a Middle Woodland complex in the Rice Lake area. However, the most sophisticated method for defining the boundaries of a biological population is the "wombling" method applied by Konigsberg and Buikstra (1995) to several skeletal series in west central Illinois. Of interest is their observation of a lack of congruence between biologically and culturally defined units there, a finding that might raise some questions about my suggestion above that "real" cultural units and connubia should be largely isomorphic.

The other topic that can be investigated with biological evidence is post-marital residence. Lane and Sublett (1972) approached this question by using non-metric traits to compare male and female inter-group distances among the Seneca. Buikstra (1980) did a similar study of the Middle Woodland Klunk mounds in Illinois. My own work with several Terminal Archaic to Middle Woodland series in Ontario followed a slightly different approach, testing the degree of homogeneity within each sex through similarity coefficients (Spence 1986). Recently Konigsberg (1988; Konigsberg and Buikstra 1995:194-200) has proposed a more refined method, migration matrix determinant analysis, for determining epigenetic homogeneity.

All of these approaches have been applied to the recently excavated Moatfield series, an early Middle Iroquoian (620 B.P.) ossuary of some 90 individuals from the Toronto area (DeLaurier and Spence 1998). Unfortunately, no clear definition of the Moatfield post-marital residence practices was possible because our Mean Measure of Divergence comparisons between Moatfield and other regional series indicated that a subset of the Moatfield women was from a distinct population, probably one in the Niagara area. Although these could have married into the Moatfield community over some time, following a patrilocal residence pattern, a careful consideration of the data suggested that they may instead represent a unique event, perhaps the incorporation of captive women after a successful military venture against a distant community. The "normal" practice at Moatfield may actually have been matrilocality (DeLaurier and Spence 1998).

278

More recently, the development of procedures for extracting DNA from bone has opened up new possibilities. Stone and Stoneking (1993) have demonstrated the potential of this approach for the reconstruction of past post-marital residential practices by identifying a group of maternally related males in the Norris Farms #36 site in Illinois. However, DNA analysis may be less useful in the identification of large taxonomic units like populations (Milner and Katzenberg, this volume).

The most widely known methods of identifying post-marital residence are based on ceramics. Deetz (1965), Whallon (1968) and Horvath (1973) have all used measures of ceramic stylistic homogeneity to assess residence practices (see also Williamson 1990:317-319). These early analyzes have attracted criticism, and their basic premises have not always been borne out by ethnoarchaeological studies (Longacre 1991; Plog 1978; Stanislawski 1969; but note DeBoer 1990 and Roe 1980). It is possible that too many factors impinge on ceramic decoration to allow us to tease out the evidence of early enculturation.

These methods share a passive view of style, the assumption that style faithfully reproduces the ideas and habits absorbed in enculturation when, as a child, the individual learns how to make pottery from kin or other community members. This view may be contrasted with a more active perspective of style, in which it is seen as a vehicle for social expression and even manipulation (Braun 1991; Timmins and Staeck, this volume). These two perspectives are not necessarily mutually exclusive. However, if we are to grant the active potential of style, then we cannot expect it to also present a clear and durable expression of enculturation. The post-enculturation encroachment of social and even personal considerations on the potter would surely muddy that earlier water.

As a medium for social expression, style may lead us to the "emic" units, taxonomic categories which may have been recognizable on some level to the people subsumed in them (e.g., Graves 1991:116-119). Two major vehicles for the expression of such groups are style (considered in its active voice) and ritual, particularly integrative ritual. Yet it is clear that both can be very flexible, capable of reflecting a wide range of relationships and concerns. Identifying these can be a daunting task. Consider, for example, the varying "readings" of Ramey vessels (Galloway 1997:60; Timmins and Staeck, this volume).

Here again we must heed Williamson's admonition to consider how our reified concepts work out on the ground. In the case of style, we must identify the *audience* for the message; in the case of ritual, the *participants* are of concern. The identification of the audience is rarely a straightforward matter. In one West African society, the only audience for some forms of ceramic decoration are the ancestors and spirits (Sterner 1989). Among the Kalinga, the messages of person and group encoded in ceramic form and decoration are invisible to males, who simply have no interest in them (Longacre 1991:102-105). Braun (1991) has noted that the location of use, visibility, and function of a vessel must be determined if its role in social interaction is to be understood.

The scale of participation in ritual can also be difficult to judge. Two forms of integrative ritual in the Great Lakes and Midwest can be examined through their correlated and archaeologically accessible features, burials (e.g., Spence 1994) and sweat lodges (MacDonald 1988, 1992). It has been suggested, for example, that the Early Ontario Iroquoian Pickering complex was an "emic" unit, its communities cooperating in a military campaign against the Glen Meyer communities of southwestern Ontario (Finlayson 1998:259-260, 408-410; Wright 1966, 1992). An analysis of their mortuary patterns, however, suggests that each localized cluster of Pickering and Glen Meyer communities developed its own set of burial practices, and that integration beyond that level, if it occurred at all, was not expressed in burial (Spence 1994).

We must also keep in mind the fact that the scale of integration expressed in a ritual can change as a community's circumstances and needs evolve. The presence of sweat lodges in many longhouses in Middle and Late Ontario Iroquoian communities suggests that the participants may have been the men of the house, and that a ritual sweat acted to integrate and reduce tensions among the males of matrilocally organized households (Kapches 1995:90). However, at an earlier point in time the social focus of the ritual may have been somewhat broader. Howie-Langs (1998) has analyzed the structure of the Praying Mantis site, an Early Ontario Iroquoian village in southwestern Ontario. One of the three longhouses in the village appears to have had community-wide functions, visible in a sweat lodge and a multiple secondary burial of eight individuals associated with the house (Howie-Langs 1998; Spence 1994). Also present, and very near the human burial, was a ritual deposit of several mammals (Muir 1997). These features, and the ceramics associated with the house, suggest that it was the locus for integrative rituals that involved the community as a whole, rather than just the occupants of that particular house (Howie-Langs 1998).

In sum, archaeological taxonomy is becoming an increasingly

complex topic. In the past it has been dominated by relatively straightforward questions of chronology and adaptation, but now it must also accommodate concerns raised by evolving concepts of style, the postprocessual critique, and gender. These certainly complicate our task, but at the same time they make it much more interesting, and make the results of our work potentially better approximations of the past societies and processes that we wish to investigate. Consider, for example, the implications of recent concepts of style which assign priority to a presumably female medium (ceramics) in the expression of group boundaries and membership, despite the fact that interactions and communications between communities have traditionally been viewed as part of the male domain (Conkey and Spector 1984:12; Longacre 1991:105). It may be that women, if they were not actually making decisions on inter-group relations, at least had a major role in creating the conceptual framework within which these affairs were deliberated. If we are to keep our taxonomies "on the ground", in future we will have to consider more than just chronology and seriation. We will have to explicitly include questions of gender, factionalism and agency. We may then achieve a clearer understanding of the processes involved in the creation of our taxonomic categories, and by extension of the "reality" of those categories.

COMMENTS: TAXONOMIC CLASSIFICATION AND RELATED PREREQUISITES OF SCIENTIFIC RESEARCH

20

David M. Stothers
Department of Anthropology, University of Toledo

The call for papers for the OAS-MAC symposium stated that:

> currently an imponderable number of traditions, co-traditions, horizons, phases and 'cultures' are in use in the archaeological literature of the Great Lakes region. The goal is to identify new directions for a taxonomy that would enhance communication among researchers in neighbouring regions.

With this directive in mind, several researchers delivered papers at the meeting held in Toronto that attempted to address this issue. I thank Ron Williamson as program convenor and the OAS for the opportunity to critically review and comment on those proceedings.

It is my position that taxonomy (classification) lies at the very foundation of scientific pursuit. There is a need in any discipline of science to classify and compare entities in order to discern similarities and differences, thereby arriving at interpretive inferences. As such, increased information and knowledge must inevitably lead to taxonomic proliferation. This is not an "avoidable problem", but rather it is a requisite consequence and should be expected.

As early as 1946 John Brew argued for the need for more extensive classification, not less, in archaeological research for these very reasons (Brew 1946). More recently Robert Dunnell has reiterated this admonition when he stated that "Classifications are logical constructs whose justification lies in their utility. They are not inherent, nor do they explain. They are imposed constructs that function to order data so that explanation is possible"(Dunnell 1971b:118).

To preface my comments, I must first state that I believe that the authors of this symposium were given a task which was quite impossible. Once again, the age-old problem of taxonomic classification has reared its "ugly head". Although many of the authors made a valiant attempt to follow the guidelines given them, most regressed into traditional taxonomic classification or replaced these taxonomies with others just as subjective and problematic as the originals. Under these circumstances, most of the papers "dissolve" into generalized, non-specific, and "possibilist" stories. One should be immediately skeptical of generalization and "possibilist" arguments which lack substantive foundation.

I would first like to make brief comments on papers from the symposium and conclude with my perceptions concerning the critical necessity for taxonomic classification in archaeology, as well as comment briefly upon related problems of great concern to the discipline of "scientific" archaeology.

The papers presented in this symposium can, in my opinion, be divided into two categories: those which choose to deconstruct taxonomic classification and those which endeavour to develop a new system of classification to replace the existing taxonomy. Of the papers which attempt to deconstruct classification, Susan Jamieson's paper perhaps best achieved this, but like any approach which deconstructs taxonomy, one is left with generalizations which do little to build upon our existing knowledge. Rather, scientific advancement is built upon specific and ever-more refined information which will facilitate the process of comparison and contrast. Similarly, William Lovis and Robert MacDonald have accomplished the same in the context of paleoenvironmental data which relates to archaeological cultures, although in an earlier publication (Lovis et al. 1994) the same topical issue has greater significance for research advancement because the extensive use of a scientific lexicon allows for greater and more refined interpretive inference. Toby Morrow in his effort to adhere to the guidelines of the conference presents a good overview summary of continuity and change in lithic technology within the region of the Great Lakes. Many of the other papers offered at the conference, however, avoided taxonomic deconstruction (e.g., William Green, Penelope Drooker, and Stuart Fiedel).

Other papers instead chose to construct new systems of classification to replace traditional classification. Because these new systems are based on subjective evaluation, they perpetuate the same problems. Simply changing the lexicon does nothing to eliminate the problems! In this vein, Peter Timmins and John Staeck attempt to replace traditional categories of "Band", "Tribe", "Chiefdom", and "State" with a new system of ranking which they claim is objective. It might be stated that there is much assumption, let alone subjectivity, in their complexity ratings. Essentially, their approach needs to be much more explicit and objective in defining categories of social and political ranking, a situation which may be difficult if not impossible!

As the paper by Christopher Watts indicates, the debate concerning taxonomy/classification is nowhere more apparent than in the field of precontact ceramic research. Many have debated the validity of "types" as opposed to "attributes"(see Smith 1990 for a summary overview for Iroquoian research in the Great Lakes region). Despite this debate, both are valid categories of analysis and each category has its place in Northeastern and Midwestern Archaeology (see Engelbrecht 1980 for a similar view).

That the perspective of historical linguistics concerning the cultural affiliation of precontact and early contact populations is of major interest to archaeology is demonstrated in the paper by Stuart Fiedel. Citing Snow (1996), Fiedel believes that linguistic data supports Snow's hypothesized Iroquoian intrusion which is further hypothesized to have separated the Central and Eastern language groups of Algonquian speakers during the 1350 to 1050 B.P. time period. Contrary to Dean Snow's unfounded assertions, there exists considerable evidence (both published and unpublished) to support an interpretive model of continuity, not discontinuity, from Middle into Late Woodland times throughout southern Ontario, the Upper St. Lawrence Valley and the 'Owasco' areas of Northern New York and Pennsylvania (see among many others Chapdelaine 1995; D'Annibale and Ross 1994; Fox 1990a; Moreau 1995; Smith 1997). Such "possibilist" hypotheses are questionable, suggesting that this migration theory can not be supported. Thus, the use of linguistic hypotheses must be secondary to archaeological data, which must take priority.

The paper on native ideological systems by William Fox and Robert Salzer, which utilizes as a case example the Gottschall rockshelter site, is indeed interesting, but highly speculative, while interpretations are based upon "oral literature" and "mythic history". Ronald Mason (1993) has commented upon this site and the problems and dangers associated with use of these types of unfounded information. The use of this kind of information leads to the construction of unfounded "possibilist" interpretive models which are not directly testable.

Aside from the theme of the symposium, there are a few other aspects within some papers which deserve specific attention. For instance, Ron Williamson and Neal Ferris both presented papers dealing with Cultural Resource Management work. In Ron Williamson's paper, he mentions that CRM reports are open and available to all. However, based upon personal experience, not only are academic researchers not made aware that these reports exist, but they are often not made readily available. Obtaining permission to see reports is often difficult and in the end, permission is denied in many cases. This is a serious problem in both Canada and the United States. Although Ron Williamson and others suggest that CRM work is accomplishing significant results, no one knows what lies in this "great, vast, gray unknown" literature! The "great contribution" of CRM work is thus highly questionable.

There is much good that has come from David Smith's and Gary Crawford's labours over the past several years. They have helped to revitalize an interest in the Princess Point Complex and the advent of agriculture in the Northeast. However, I have some concerns relating to recent published articles. I have observed the debate and discussion relating to Princess Point with great interest, reserving my comments for the appropriate time. Essentially, I see little new information since the 1977 monograph on the Princess Point Complex (Stothers 1977). I would like to see work on Princess Point continued, modified and critically analyzed, because such is the nature of science. I look forward to advancements in the areas of ceramic studies, chronology, settlement, and subsistence. Based upon my familiarity with the region, I would suggest that sites and data, which will clarify the debated issue of population continuity versus migration replacement as proposed by Dean Snow (1995a, 1996), exist in that region. A concerted effort to investigate sites which bear upon this critical issue would be beneficial, especially now with the rapidly increasing rate of urban and commercial development of the lower Grand River Valley.

I would also like to reiterate a point which Lovis and MacDonald make in their paper, and which should be heeded by everyone. Long-term commitment (*la longue durée*) needs to be made by all researchers to their respective local and regional areas. This long term commitment leads to a sufficient data base from which the individual researcher can make testable inferences, and avoid unfounded speculation. This local and regional focus, although important, should be tempered by greater cooperative efforts between researchers. This cooperation needs to take place across all provincial, state and international boundaries. If native populations did not stop at the border then neither should researchers! Priority should also be placed on the development of cultural-historical frameworks and settlement distributions, despite recent "neo-revisionist" trends which are critical of such.

I also see major problems relating to the selective use of literature with the intent of promoting one theoretical model over another. Such a selective distortion of information, certainly does not bode well for the advancement of any scientific discipline. Scholarship goes beyond listening to "party-line" dogma and citing only those publications that are part of a single network. Over the decades, I have become increasingly disenchanted with what is alleged to be "scientific" research. The denial of opposing viewpoints is no more obvious than in a recent article (Ferris and Spence 1995) where published documentation is ignored. Scientists must acknowledge alternate models of interpretation. To ignore and avoid alternate viewpoints simply because they do not concur with a favoured position is scientifically inappropriate (Goldstein 1998). In addition to the need for greater awareness and familiarity with the published literature (on a broad geographic base) relative to any issue of investigation, there is a need for scholars to attribute ideas and information to the proper original sources, rather than to more recent contributions which lay claim for what has already been established and documented by others. I am further disenchanted by "networking" in academic circles in order to block publication of submitted information and interpretations which do not agree with "party-line" dogma. Such is not appropriate and will not lead to any "real" advancements in knowledge!

In addition, established scientific priority in taxonomic classification dictates that a scientific label not be used in more than one context. However, since the original definition for the taxonomic construct "Western Basin Tradition" (Stothers 1978), the same taxonomic label has been assigned to a more recent but different taxonomic construct (Murphy and Ferris 1990; cf. also Stothers et al. 1994). Such is inappropriate and violates a fundamental scientific rule, that of priority. Additionally, such situations confuse and obfuscate proper understanding of scientific issues.

Taxonomy is fundamental to science! In his summary commentary which concluded the symposium, Bruce Trigger outlined the historical development of taxonomic classification and the importance of taxonomy to scientific pursuit. Taxonomy and classification are the foundation upon which models are constructed and research is conducted. By definition, science is a process that builds structure, organization and, as a result, understanding. Science utilizes paradigms or models to structure and organize information. Models are frameworks which explain the interrelationship of the taxonomic categories which are subsumed into their structure. Thomas Kuhn (1970) has outlined the theoretical importance of models or paradigms to science in general, while Bruce Trigger (1968a:4-5, 1969, 1978a) has outlined the importance of structural and taxonomic models to the discipline of archaeology. Colin Renfrew (1968:132) has stated that theoretical constructs or models are of major importance to archaeology in that "factual information only has relevance within some more general frame of reference." An absence of taxonomy and models results only in random fact gathering!

As in other scientific disciplines (Kuhn 1970:43-52) structural models must take priority. As such in archaeology, cultural-historical models must first be established. Until such models are established (based upon current and accepted taxonomy) little or nothing will ensue to further our understanding of the past!

In retrospect and to conclude, I would like to state my position outright. Research advancement is dependent upon taxonomy. Taxonomy can and must be continually revised and modified to accommodate an ever increasing data base. If Northeastern and Midwestern archaeologists think that there is a problem with the existing taxonomy, let them try to communicate without one!

COMMENTS: ARCHAEOLOGICAL CULTURAL CONSTRUCTS AND SYSTEMATICS: A PROPOSED CLASSIFICATION SYSTEM FOR CANADA

21

James V. Wright
Curator Emeritus, Archaeological Survey of Canada
Canadian Museum of Civilization

In the preamble to a Symposium on *Turning the Taxonomy: Towards a New Understanding of Great Lakes Archaeology*, held during the 1997 joint meeting of the Ontario Archaeological Society and the Midwest Archaeological Conference, it was stated that

> It has become clear that we can no longer investigate complex cultural developments using simplistic taxonomic tools or superficial models. We need to not only question the usefulness of current archaeological constructs but rethink our archaeological lexicon entirely!

While I certainly have no argument with the need to continuously reevaluate our archaeological constructs, I have the uneasy feeling that this expresses the desire for a complete purge which, in my opinion, would be tantamount to "throwing the baby out with the bath water". Rather than totally abandoning earlier classifications, I would suggest that the increasingly sophisticated nature of archaeological research can be readily accommodated within many of the current classificatory structures. Archaeological cultural construct classification should be viewed as a multi-layered structure wherein the different levels of cultural abstraction can be differentiated from one another. Such a hierarchy of descending particularism, extending from the very general to the very specific, is necessary if archaeologists are to communicate effectively with one another, much less with the growing community of interested nonarchaeologists. Before proceeding to the mechanics of how this can be accomplished, however, it may be useful to first consider the general nature and purpose of classification systems.

Disciplines, like biology and archaeology, that must control large bodies of data in a systematic fashion, need to establish objective classification systems whose principles of organization are agreed upon by all. Without such classifications there would be a lack of consistency in communication leading to the unacceptable situation of people talking about the same phenomenon using different terms or, conversely, applying the same nomenclature to different phenomenon. In biology, all animals and plants are assigned to different categories that are serially ranked depending upon the level of biological relationship being considered. Ultimately, taxonomy and systematics are essential to control what would otherwise be a situation of descriptive chaos relative to the enormous numbers of different animals and plants in the world. Archaeological classification shares a number of important features with biological classification. First, archaeological cultural classification is hierarchical, with differing levels of abstracted relationships. Such a ranking of degree of relationship is, in a very general sense, equivalent to the twelve levels of descending relationships in biology extending from Kingdom through to Species or Subspecies. As in biology, where the genus *Canis* subsumes a number of different species like grey wolf (*Canis lupus*), coyote (*Canis latrans*), and domesticated dog (*Canis familiaris*), in Arctic archaeology, as an example, Pre-Dorset is treated as a lower level unit of Early Palaeo-Eskimo culture which, in turn, falls under the blanket classification of the Arctic Small Tool tradition. Pre-Dorset is then further subdivided into a number of regional expressions to which a series of specific components can be assigned. Second, biological and archaeological classification systems are essentially based upon external appearances. And third, both systems possess evolutionary and ecological dimensions. In both archaeological and biological classification, however, there are unavoidable subjective elements, as well as areas requiring periodic adjustments to the classifications in order to accommodate advancements in knowledge.

Where biological and archaeological classifications clearly part company is in the area of the phenomenon being classified. The key determinant in biological classification is genetics, albeit subject to evolutionary processes and mutations. In contrast, archaeological classification is based upon culturally determined phenomena. Further, in the absence of any currently known controlling natural laws, such as genetic heredity, archaeological classification will always be considerably more amorphous in structure than its biological counterpart. This condition imposes a need for continuous modification and refinement of any archaeological cultural classification. As classification in archaeology is dependant upon data which is inherently fragmented and incomplete, any scheme to objectively maintain control over said data must be both vertically and horizontally flexible and capable of adjusting to frequent modifications. In a very real sense, archaeological classification will always precede all of the pertinent evidence as such evidence will *never* be available in total. Thus, archaeological cultural classification is inherently premature and in a state of constant flux, and is dependant upon the whims of archaeological discoveries and cultural construct building. Another area where biological and archaeological classification differs is the degree of disinterest in broadly based and holistic classification systems on the part of many archaeologists. Most archaeological classification functions at a different level, being directed to specific aspects of technology such as pottery or stone tool analyzes, for example, in order to gain insights into local and narrow archaeological problems. Even here, there has often been a lack of classificatory rigour and consistency in the usage of terms by different archaeologists and in different languages (see Marois 1975, 1984). In most areas of the world, including North America, there has been relatively little effort to classify archaeological cultural phenomena in an all-inclusive fashion, incorporating all levels of archaeological classificatory abstraction extending from the general to the specific. A biologist can discuss issues relative to a descending level of relationship such as Phylum, Class, Order, Family, down to Species and, in so doing, communicate clearly to the audience. An archaeologist, in a majority of instances, can only discuss a site or a cluster of related sites grouped into a general cultural construct with any hope of achieving a similar level of communication. Such a fragmented and often subjective classification of archaeological phenomena was understandable during the early years of the discipline when chronology and cultural construct formation were in a rudimentary state. The discipline is past the stage, however, where such idiosyncratic and usually parochial procedures are acceptable. The audience concerned with archaeological knowledge is no longer a few regional archaeologists but includes the general public, native people, lawyers, and the national and international scholarly community. For these reasons, Canadian archaeology requires a national archaeological classification system within which progressively regional archaeological phenomena can be incorporated in as objective and systematic a manner as possible.

As a person concerned with the mechanics and underlying principles of archaeological classification, I was naturally delighted to be able to act as a discussant of some of the papers to be presented in the 1997 Joint Symposium of the Ontario Archaeological Society and the Midwest Archaeological Conference. I was not happy with the title of the major Symposium, *Taming the Taxonomy: Toward a New Understanding of Great Lakes Archaeology*, as it is impossible to tame an inanimate taxonomy and, further, if there was any taming to be done it should have been directed towards the archaeologists. To be candid, I was disappointed with the drift the Symposium took; not with the specific content of the papers presented *per se* but with the fact that rarely was the issue of archaeological classification addressed. Even Bruce Trigger's summary presentation assiduously avoided what I had, apparently naively, believed to be the focus of the Symposium. Martha A. Latta of the University of Toronto, came closest to considering classification in the abstract, rather than the specific, sense. Her observation that taxonomy is an essential tool that must build upon earlier classification systems while recognizing that earlier taxonomies acquire a certain immutability with time and use and are, thus, difficult to change, was certainly pertinent as was her concluding observation that "...the way we order is the way we think". Subsequent papers, however, tended to concentrate their efforts on specific or regional topics and, in particular, upon the analytical procedures required to address relatively narrow archaeological problems, rather than having anything to do with the systematic organization of cultural constructs. While most of the papers touched upon aspects of the complex dimensions of the phenomena to be classified, as well as weaknesses in current classification systems, few offered any suggestions for a classification system that could be applied to the Great Lakes area much less large areas of North America. While ultimately pertinent in the structuring of any broad cultural classification system, such details represent incorporated elements rather than having any bearing on the fundamental organizing principles. An exception was the paper by William A. Lovis and Robert I. MacDonald which stressed the importance of considering the environment and environmental change in any broad archaeological classification system. The paper by George R. Milner and M. Anne Katzenberg focussed on the role of human biology in furthering our understanding of certain aspects of the archaeological record. Jamieson emphasized the importance of human relationships as detectable in exchange networks and other lines of evidence. This, of course, includes the relationship between different cultures and not just the different societies of any single archaeological culture. William A. Fox and Robert J. Salzer addressed the contentious area of past belief systems including shamanism; an extremely important, but until now largely ignored area of investigation by archaeologists. Another potentially contentious but important area of archaeological investigation was the attempt to glean insights into past social and political organization as detailed by Peter A. Timmins and John Paul Staeck. Most of the foregoing sampling of papers, as well as many of the other presentations at the Conference, had little or nothing to do with establishing a new taxonomy that could replace current archaeological classifications. In short, it was an interesting and useful archaeological conference, but it did not really address problems relating to taxonomy or any other aspect of archaeological classification.

It was apparent that my expectations of this Symposium were operating at a different level than that of most of the participants. Being odd-man-out, however, does not necessarily mean being irrelevant to the issue of archaeological classification. I am, therefore, taking this opportunity to immodestly propose a national archaeological classification system. It is undoubtedly more practical for one scholar to outline such a classification system which can then act as a gadfly and target for criticism in the hope that the process will eventually result in a scheme that is agreeable to the majority of archaeologists. For the purposes of the exercise it is most appropriate to consider a national archaeological classification system rather than limit considerations to any particular area like the Great Lakes.

In the following classification of archaeological evidence in Canada, a number of assumptions are made. It is taken as given that the archaeological phenomena to be classified are the products of innumerable societies organized into various bands or tribes. These large groupings of people shared, with varying degrees of intensity, a similar cultural pattern in terms of technology, settlement patterns, subsistence, and cosmology. Each cultural pattern also maintains continuity through both time and space. In Canada, such broad cultural patterns are associated with particular environmental zones and, thus, can be demarcated rather sharply in space, albeit allowing for environmental change through time (Harris and Matthews 1987). In planning the structure of *A History of the Native People of Canada* (Wright 1995) it was a prerequisite to organize these broad environment-specific archaeological patterns into a national classification system. It was also

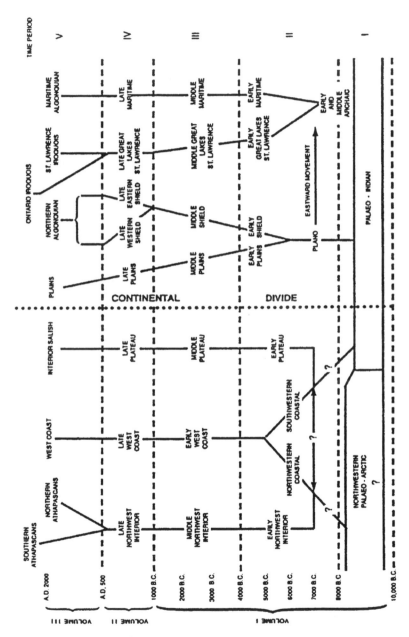

Figure 21.1: A schematic and simplified chronology of the archaeological history of Canada (Reproduced from Wright 1995: Chart 1).

necessary to control the temporal dimension by establishing five absolute time periods across the country. This very broad archaeological classification scheme is reproduced in Figure 21.1. Figure 21.1 does not include the Palaeo-Eskimo and proto-Inuit developments of the north and some marginal cultural manifestations like Midwestern culture in the extreme western portion of Southern Ontario. It will be noted that the names of cultural constructs are essentially environmentally based. Further, each culture in this three volume work, in addition to sections that include a précis and limitations in the evidence, are considered under the following descriptive sections: cultural origins and descendants; technology; subsistence; settlement patterns; cosmology; external relationships; human biology; and inferences on society. These topics are among those regarded as being of classificatory concern by many of the participants in the Symposium.

As was noted in this first attempt at a national synthesis of the archaeological history of Canada, archaeological taxonomy and nomenclature as they pertain to broad cultural patterns are poorly developed in Canada. Archaeological terms tend to be regional in nature and based upon differing criteria rather than being broadly equivalent and systematic (Wright 1995:3). The details of the underlying organizing principles of this upper level of archaeological cultural classification in Canada were presented in the Introduction to Volume I (Wright 1995:1-22). It is important to point out that the term "prehistory" was abandoned in these volumes. Years ago an Iroquois friend, John Dockstader, asked me why only Whitemen have history and Indians prehistory. I went through the usual literate-preliterate explanation, to which John replied "It still sounds to me like a put-down". He was right. There is no question that placing a prefix on the word "history" demeans archaeological history to something that is somehow not real history. It is argued here that there are two major branches of human history, one with a limited geographical distribution and a comparatively short time depth called documentary history based upon written records, and another that encompasses most of human history around the world based upon archaeological evidence and which can be logically designated archaeological history. For similar reasons I abandoned the use of demonstrably Eurocentric expressions like "New World".

It remains to be seen what acceptance the foregoing national archaeological classification scheme will receive. Archaeologists, like most people, prefer the status quo and cherish their old, familiar cultural constructs no matter how inaccurate or narrow in scope. Laurentian Archaic, for example, has nothing to do with the Laurentian Shield and while Plano culture did originate in the Plains it ended up occupying territories as far east as the Atlantic, westward into the Canadian Plateau, and north to the barren grounds of the Arctic. Regardless of the limitations of the classification system outlined in Figure 21.1, it does permit people to speak of archaeological cultures or cultural patterns across the country in equivalent terms of time and space and level of archaeological cultural abstraction. But such a scheme only pertains to an upper level of archaeological cultural abstraction. Throughout the volumes of *A History of the Native People of Canada* it is continuously emphasized that the broad archaeological patterns called "cultures" were each composed of numerous independent societies, many of which would have undoubtedly objected to being lumped with "those strangers of the Land of the Big Rocks". From such a broad national level of archaeological classification one moves downward in ever increasing levels of regional specificity until the individual archaeological site or component is reached. How to classify this hierarchy of levels of classificatory relationships in as objective and systematic a manner as possible is a difficult but essential task. It will also have to be accepted that the boundaries between classification levels will be "fuzzy" rather than precise. After all, it is cultural continua through time and space that are being artificially forced into abstract categories in order to permit some degree of consistency in the level of communication involving masses of archaeological minutiae.

A major step in archaeological classification has been taken by James W. Helmer of the University of Calgary in his effort to systematize the regional and temporal dimensions of Palaeo-Eskimo culture (Helmer 1994). His scheme, with some modification, could be profitably applied across the country. At the upper level, the Helmer classification involves a descending hierarchy of Technological Tradition to Technological Sub-tradition to Cultural Tradition to time-bracketed Cultural Horizons (Figure 21.2).

The Cultural Horizon time-bracketed unit is then refined in a descending order that goes from Cultural Sub-tradition to Regional phase to Complex to Component (Figure 21.3).

By incorporating elements from both the archaeological cultural classification system used in *A History of the Native People of Canada* and Helmer's classification established for Palaeo-Eskimo culture it is possible to arrive at a framework within which any regional

Technological Tradition | Technological Sub-Tradition | Cultural Tradition | Cultural Horizon

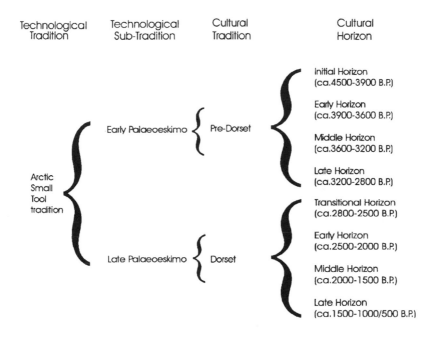

Figure 21.2: A culture-historical framework for the Eastern Arctic (Reproduced with permission from Helmer 1994: Figure 1).

archaeological culture in Canada can be accommodated. For example, Figure 21.4 incorporates a portion of the Great Lakes-St. Lawrence cultural tradition in Canada, a cultural tradition that subsumes earlier archaeological cultural constructs such as Laurentian, Meadowood, Point Peninsula, and Saugeen. In order to simplify the figure pertinent regional phases from New Brunswick, New York, and the northern New England states have been excluded. Helmer's "Cultural Horizon" has been replaced with "Cultural Complex" in order to accommodate both time differentiated horizons and contemporaneous but geographically differentiated cultural manifestations.

The advantage of the classification scheme outlined in Figure 21.4 is that it is sufficiently flexible to adjust to the additions, deletions, and modifications inherently required by the accretionary nature of archaeological evidence. For those who believe, for example, that the cultural developments of the lower Great Lakes and upper St.Lawrence continue unbroken into Period V (A.D. 500 - European contact) and the

James V. Wright

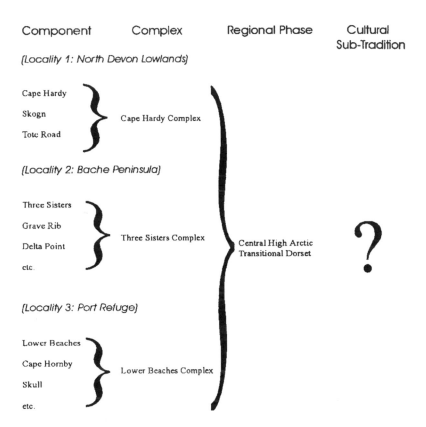

Figure 21.3: A tentative example of a culture-historical framework relating to the Dorset Cultural Tradition and the Transitional Cultural Horizon (Reproduced with permission from Helmer 1994: Figure 2).

northern Iroquoian-speaking peoples (e.g., Wright 1984), the appropriate cultural developments can simply be added onto the figure. If the Susquehanna Archaic manifestation late in Period III should turn out to be an actual intrusion of people into the region and not a product of technological diffusion then an addition can be made to expand the accuracy of the classification. Being hierarchical, such a scheme accommodates research interests that range from the very general to the very specific. This permits consideration of regional archaeological constructs while being capable of incorporating such regional variation within increasingly broader cultural taxa. Thus, the criticism of some

298

researchers, with more particularist and regional concerns, that certain general classificatory schemes, such as the Ontario Iroquoian tradition, somehow inhibit the advancement of knowledge (e.g., MacDonald and Williamson 1995:10) are irrelevant. Such a stance appears to stem from a faulty view that archaeological cultural classification is a monolithic structure rather than being multi-layered with each successive layer complementing the next. Indeed, even the massive Iroquoian community study by William D. Finlayson of numerous Iroquoian villages and hamlets in the Niagara Escarpment area (Finlayson 1998) could be incorporated into Figure 21.4 although, given the number of sites involved, some innovative chart construction would be required.

Technological Tradition	Cultural Tradition	Cultural Complex	Regional Phase	Component	Period
Eastern Archaic/ Woodland Tradition	Late Great Lakes / St. Lawrence	Saugeen (600 BC - ?)	SW S. Ontario	Donaldson Boresma	IV
					1000 BC - AD 500
		Point Peninsula (600 BC - AD 500)	SE S. Ontario SW P.Q.	Serpent Mounds Ault Park Pt.-du-Buisson	
		Meadowood (1,000 BC - ?)	St. Lawrence Valley P.Q. Niagara Peninsula	Batiscan Lambert ?	
	Middle Great Lakes / St. Lawrence	Terminal (2000 - 1000 B.C.)	SW S. Ont.	Knechtel Innes	III
		Brewerton (3500 - 2000 BC)	Rice Lake E. Twp. P.Q. Ottawa Valley	Percy Reach McIntyre Morrison 1 - 6	4000 - 1000 BC
		Vergennes (4000 - 3500 BC)	Ottawa / St. Lawrence	Allumette - 1 Coteau-du-Lac	
	Early Great Lakes / St. Lawrence	Proto-Laurentian	Upper St. Lawrence	Thompson Island	II
					8000 - 4000 BC

Figure 21.4: A classification scheme for archaeological cultural description in the lower Great Lakes and upper St. Lawrence Valley of Ontario and Québec during the time span 5500 B.C. to A.D. 500.

As stated at the beginning, this paper is a response to the papers presented in the symposium titled *Taming the Taxonomy: Toward a New Understanding of Great Lakes Archaeology*. Rather than taming the taxonomy, I would suggest that the task is to develop and test a taxonomy and to perfect it in order to best meet the unique needs of archaeological classification in Canada. The archaeological classification system advocated here possesses the necessary requirements to meet these needs. The uppermost level is based upon environmental regions that in Canada clearly correlate with archaeological cultural patterns. The classification is composed of a series of hierarchical levels and proceeds from the very general to the very specific, thus accommodating a wide range of needs relative to the various levels of archaeological knowledge which have to be addressed. These various levels of archaeological cultural abstraction should be as equivalent internally as possible, while still recognizing that the boundaries between levels will be imprecise given the nature of the phenomena being classified. The system is based upon evidence from habitation sites, recognizing that certain archaeological cultural phenomena, such as mortuary practices, can cross-cut a number of different cultural traditions. Perhaps the most important characteristic is the flexibility inherent in the system which permits new findings to be incorporated, discredited elements discarded, and expansion of the classification structure both vertically and horizontally, while still maintaining the core integrity of the classification. Finally, the proposed classification system is not so esoteric that it cannot be readily understood by the increasingly large audience of nonarchaeologists who, for whatever reasons, require knowledge of the human history of Canada prior to European domination.

Section IV: Synthesis

MASTER AND SERVANT: A CONFERENCE OVERVIEW

22

Bruce G. Trigger
Department of Anthropology, McGill University

I will begin trying to set what has been said at this conference into a broader historical and theoretical perspective by making what I believe is a fairly non-controversial prediction: that classification, no less than chronology, will remain crucial to archaeology for as long as the discipline survives, which should be until a new, budgetarily-induced dark age terminates our civilization. However much some theoretically-oriented archaeologists may profess to despise classification as being too elementary to deserve their attention, classification remains essential for doing archaeology and will occur implicitly if it is not done explicitly. Progress in archaeology results to no small degree from finding ways to classify things better. Chronology and typology are, I need not remind you, historically linked, inasmuch as seriation, which remains an important means for deriving fine-grained, relative chronologies, depends upon classification.

The classic study of what can happen to archaeology when it ignores typology is found in Bulkin et al.'s courageous paper "Attainments and Problems of Soviet Archaeology" (1982). As a result of Russian archaeologists being forced, on ideological grounds, to abandon basic formal classifications and devote themselves entirely to functional studies in the late 1920s, they were unable to develop an adequate understanding of temporal and geographical variation in the archaeological record. Intensive field work and even the eventual introduction of ^{14}C dating was inadequate to help remedy this situation. Only as a result of classification, are archaeologists able to recognize much of the patterning in the archaeological record that it is their business to explain.

Yet, if typology is a good servant, it can be a very bad master. Useful typology, or classification, is not something that stands apart from what is being studied and that, once formulated, is valid for all time. Instead, it changes and (dare I suggest it in this postmodern era?) becomes more insightful as the archaeological record is better understood. The relationship between archaeological interpretation and typology is a dialectical one, in the precise meaning of that much abused term. We have been concentrating at this conference on the uses and impact of classification, rather than on more formal issues such as the distinctions between classifications and taxonomies and under what circumstances categories are better defined in terms of boundaries or of central tendencies (Adams and Adams 1991; Clarke 1968; Dunnell 1971b; Rouse 1972).

Most of today's papers have realized the session's goal of breaking free from formal periodizations and viewing the precontact history of the Great Lakes region processually, using that term in its older, more generic sense, rather than simply as a label for the neoevolutionary, ecologically-determinist archaeology of the 1960s. This change is very striking in Lovis and MacDonald's discussion of Great Lakes paleoecology, which treats the past not as a succession of hotter and colder, drier and wetter periods but as a series of changes brought about by the long term interaction of a complex set of environmental variables. This approach brings us much closer to the *Tao*, or way, of nature than did the periodizations of the past. A similar sense of continuity and agency characterized the cultural papers that followed, all of which addressed problems of change in ways that have relevance for understanding the specific past of the Great Lakes region as well as more general problems of socio-cultural change.

I can vividly remember first sensing this deeper potential for understanding archaeological data when, under Professor William Mayer-Oakes' direction, I read Gordon Willey's (1953) *Prehistoric Settlement Patterns in the Virú Valley, Peru* while I was an undergraduate at the University of Toronto in 1958. In this book the traditional succession of archaeological cultures, each explained as a product of traditions, diffusion, and migrations, was replaced by the portrayal of settlement patterns continuously changing as a result of alterations in population size, technology, subsistence patterns, the natural environment, and social and political organization. I was equally impressed when I read Joseph Caldwell's *Trend and Tradition in the Prehistory of the Eastern United States* (1958). Instead of interpreting major cultural patterns as being introduced by successive waves of immigrants from Siberia and specific cultures as shaped by more local patterns of diffusion and migration, Caldwell argued that ecological adjustments to the disappearance of big game at the end of the last Ice Age had led to more complex and intensive patterns of food production that increased the carrying capacity of most areas and promoted denser and more sedentary populations. These developments, in turn, encouraged the acquisition of heavier and more varied types of equipment than had been useful previously, including soapstone, and later ceramic, cooking vessels. Caldwell stressed the capacity for internally initiated change among the aboriginal cultures of the Eastern Woodlands and the need for archaeologists to understand artifacts, such as pottery vessels, in relation to the functional roles they had once played within adaptive systems. As alternatives to culture-historical archaeology, with its largely classificatory preoccupations, both settlement archaeology and Binfordian New Archaeology sought to promote processual views of the past.

To a considerable degree both settlement and Binfordian archaeology abandoned the concern with cultural classification and chronology building that had characterized culture-historical archaeology. It was fashionable in the 1960s to argue that in many parts of the world a culture-historical framework had already been worked out and that it was now the business of archaeologists to move on to explaining why change had happened. The introduction of ^{14}C dating had also made it possible for archaeologists to determine the rate as well as the direction of change in precontact times and for the first time to align and compare trends in cultural change on different continents (Clark 1961). Change almost everywhere turned out to have occurred more slowly than archaeologists had hitherto believed and this, combined with a more comparative perspective, helped to encourage processual and evolutionary tendencies in archaeology. These developments made the construction of cultural chronologies seem outmoded, except in places such as Canada, where in the 1960s basic culture-historical sequences remained to be worked out.

I adopted a processual approach in my doctoral thesis, which was a study of key variables that accounted for general population trends and changing distributions of population in Lower Nubia between 5950 and 750 B.P. (Trigger 1965). Research done more recently has considerably refined the cultural chronology of Lower Nubia and also has revealed more complex ethnic situations than were recognized in the early 1960s. Hence it could be argued that in preparing my thesis I should have devoted more time to revising the cultural chronology. Yet, had I done so, it is unlikely I would have got around to studying population trends. Moreover, had growing interest in population trends and other processual concerns not stimulated the need for a more fine-grained culture-history of Lower Nubia in pharaonic times, it is unlikely that archaeologists would have used data collected in the early 1960s to refine existing chronologies.

Typologies, as discussed at this conference, can be divided into two broad categories. The first consists of classifications of artifacts, especially ones made of stone and ceramics, as well as classifications of cultural units. The second embraces classifications of various types of social organization and behaviour. The first category of classifications is older and more closely associated with archaeology and often is regarded as the only true form of archaeological classification. A third category could be added: Adams and Adams' (1991:215-17) basic type, which seeks to learn something about the material being classified, rather than to assist archaeologists in some other purpose, such as reconstructing cultures or dating sites. We are discussing what Adams and Adams term "instrumental" typologies.

Artifact typologies were systematically employed in Europe beginning in the early nineteenth century and at first involved a search for artifacts that would distinguish successive époques of cultural development in the same way that index fossils distinguished different geological periods. In the late nineteenth century a growing awareness of regional variation in distributions of artifacts encouraged more precise classifications of artifact types as well as the definition of archaeological cultures in an effort to delineate synchronic cultural variation. This sort of research was more systematically theorized in the United States in the early and mid-twentieth century in the course of debates which dealt with questions such as whether types were real or arbitrary, whether it was more profitable to study types or attributes, and whether the types archaeologists created might have had specific meanings in precontact cultures. Cultures were defined as assemblages of specific artifact types and units such as traditions, horizons, culture areas, and stages of development were used to group cultures that, as a result of historical connections or convergent development, shared various traits (Willey and Sabloff 1993:117-25).

In general, both artifact types and the concept of the archaeological culture were linked to that of ethnicity. Culture-historical anthropology was a product of late eighteenth century German romanticism, which celebrated cultural diversity and viewed each culture as the expression of the creativity and unique achievements of a specific people. Some archaeologists included classifications of graves and house types in their reports and artifact classifications regularly incorporated information relating to function (shape), technology (method of construction), and origin (constituency attributes such as clay and temper) (Adams and Adams 1991:161). Yet almost invariably these elements were viewed from a culture-historical, rather than a functional, point of view. Archaeological cultures were thus viewed as material expressions of a single dimension of variability: ethnicity. Ethnicity, it must be observed, is a wholly cultural and hence wholly subjective concept. One can only know for certain in what groups people claim membership by asking them.

Even in culture-historical terms this unidimensional understanding of variation created numerous difficulties. Lower and Middle Palaeolithic cultures often were found spread over several continents and hence could not be the work of a single social group. Such entities were sometimes called industries in order to de-ethnicize them. In a similar fashion, more recent hunter-gatherer cultures, such as Thule in arctic North America, often were distributed over large areas and associated with numerous hunting bands whose members frequently switched from one band to another. On the other hand, in complex societies the differences between the artifacts associated with the upper and lower classes were often as great as those between any two tribal groups, while a single elite might dominate a number of linguistically and culturally distinctive peasantries. The concept of the archaeological culture seemed to apply best to small, sedentary, socially homogeneous, and strongly bounded middle-range societies (Trigger 1968a:17-18).

Finally, Franz Boas (1940) had demonstrated that there was no inherent correlation between race, language, and culture. In the American Southwest, as a consequence of diffusion, speakers of at least four totally unrelated language families shared a Puebloan cultural pattern. In Ontario, during the culture-historical era, archaeologists did not distinguish between the Hurons and the Petuns or among the four or five tribes that made up the Huron confederacy and they interpreted the Frank Bay site as Iroquoian rather than Nipissing (Wright 1966). While the concept of ethnicity prevailed during the period of culture-historical archaeology, it was clear even then that this concept did not account for all similarities and differences in archaeological finds. For this reason, I repeat my classificatory proposal, which was very poorly received when I first made it in 1968, that it is potentially confusing and therefore methodologically unsound to name any historical, let alone any precontact, archaeological culture after a historical ethnic group (Trigger 1970a:43-4).

One of the major accomplishments of the New Archaeology was to entrench new dimensions of meaning into the interpretation of American archaeological data. In particular, Binford and his adherents stressed the ecological and social significance of archaeological finds. Not only were archaeologists challenged to look for "technomic" and "sociotechnic" meaning in artifacts that hitherto had been considered mainly from the perspectives of chronology and ethnicity, but systematic attention began to be paid to floral and faunal remains that also had largely been ignored; a process that required the adoption of much systematic nomenclature from botany and zoology. In this way, Binford sought to remedy some of the shortcomings that Walter Taylor (1948) had noted in American culture-historical archaeology.

While Binford severely criticized existing terminologies, he continued to employ many conventional artifact types and cultural units (Adams and Adams 1991:9-10), although he sometimes reinterpreted and put them to new uses. On the other hand, a growing interest in the economic, social, and political interpretation of archaeological data led to the proliferation of new terminologies relevant to these problems. Willey's study of settlement patterns in the Virú Valley involved the construction of a typology of the kinds of sites he had encountered in his survey; a process that became an essential part of settlement analysis everywhere. Widespread use was also made of unilinear evolutionary terminologies borrowed from social anthropology, such as Elman Service's (1962) and Marshall Sahlins's (1968) sequence of band, tribe, chiefdom, and state or Morton Fried's (1967) egalitarian, ranked, stratified, and state societies. Archaeologists have also employed Richard Fox's (1977) distinction between regal-ritual, administrative, and mercantile cities. As early as 1955, archaeologists had devised a comprehensive sequence of community patterning, which embraced seven primary types from Free Wandering through Restricted Wandering, Central-Based Wandering, Semi-Permanent Sedentary, Simple Nuclear Central, Advanced Nuclear Central, to Nuclear Integrated. These now largely forgotten types classified all societies according to their degree of sedentariness and complexity, which were assumed to co-vary (Beardsley et al. 1956). Binford's (1980) distinction between forager and collector hunter-gatherer adaptations has enjoyed more lasting popularity. Whether or not their creators were archaeologists, these typologies are less purely archaeological than are those relating to attributes, artifact types, and cultural configurations, and they are usually closely linked to, if not derived from, social anthropology. They are also generally less widely accepted and more controversial than are more purely archaeological typologies. This is evident in David Clarke's (1968) very different treatment of material relating to these two classes in *Analytical Archaeology*, the most systematic survey of archaeological typology ever written.

While these social developmental typologies were accepted relatively easily by neoevolutionists, who believed in a high degree of cross-cultural regularity, they have been heavily criticized by those who believe that they operate at too high a level of abstraction and hence conceal critical synchronous and diachronic variation, as well as intragroup diversity and conflict. It is objected that such typologies both reflect and reinforce unilinearity. These typologies assume that, if one feature is present, other specific features must be present also, which is frequently not the case. Such typologies thus obscure the nature of the very phenomena being studied (Emerson 1997b:168-9). One alternative, as Peter Timmins and John Staeck observed with respect to their Complexity Model, is to study social, political, and economic organization, not as discrete types but as bundled continua of variation. This approach was pioneered by David Easton (1959) and has been implemented in archaeology by Randall McGuire (1983), Olivier De Montmollin (1989), and others. This does not mean that types are not also useful in behavioural research; indeed, as someone currently studying early civilizations, I would be the first to deny such a claim. But to remain useful, definitions of types need to be flexible and able to embrace variation; not Procrustean entities into which data are merely fitted.

Although it is currently unfashionable to say so, I believe that to be useful a typology must be ontologically grounded; that is, it must reflect some aspect of the reality that it seeks to describe. That reality is not necessarily something of which precontact peoples were aware, nor need it be a reality that is properly understood by modern archaeologists. One of the most enduring typologies is the Linnaean classification of biological species, which was initially formulated in the eighteenth century. Linnaeus did not share our current understanding of the nature of biological variation. He believed that the members of each species approximated an ideal existing in the mind of God, that each species was reproductively isolated and unchanging, and that all species together formed a Great Chain of Being that stretched from the simplest unicellular organism to humanity and provided evidence of a divine plan for all living creatures. In the nineteenth century this idealist view of species was shattered by

Darwinian evolution, which showed that species were internally randomly variable and had arisen as a result of descent through modification leading to reproductive isolation. Even today, biologists disagree among themselves about the extent to which species should be defined on the basis of general morphological criteria or in terms of reproductive isolation. In a palaeontological context, reproductive isolation is not easy to determine and distinctions within single lines of descent are of necessity arbitrary. These problems have not, however, prevented Linnaean classification from playing an important role in the biological sciences. Even if Linnaeus did not understand the origin of species, his system was useful as a general classification because it unwittingly approximated the underlying phylogenetic relations that had given rise to different living species. A system of similar utility could not have been based on animals' eating habits or limb shape.

Precontact archaeology must cope with a dual ontology. The first relates to what there is to be known in the archaeological record; the second to what can be learned from archaeological and nonarchaeological data about the behaviour that produced the archaeological record and shaped the course of precontact history. Experimental archaeology, inspired by the New Archaeology, has, as Toby Morrow pointed out, revealed that various stone tool categories, once thought to represent separately conceived and manufactured types, came into existence as a result of reductions that occurred in the course of retouching. Many scrapers began as projectile points. This type of observation is not new; in the nineteenth century William Holmes refuted claims that there was evidence of a Lower Palaeolithic occupation in North America by demonstrating that the artifacts being assigned to that culture were quarry debris from a much more recent era (Meltzer 1983). Nevertheless, the impact of recently improving knowledge of stone tool production or understanding morphological variability has been great. It has also been realized, as a result of experimental archaeology, that the extent to which stone tools are reduced may correlate with the availability of lithic material, an observation that can have political as well as geological implications. Analysis of use contexts has also facilitated classification. The forensic examination in the 1960s of a considerable number of individuals who had died from projectile wounds at Site 117 near Jebel Sahaba, a late Palaeolithic site in Lower Nubia, revealed that the projectiles were tipped with numerous stone artifact types, including debitage. This discovery completely altered an understanding of the functional significance of stone tool types in this culture (Wendorf 1968).

In a recent review, Elizabeth Brumfiel (1997) has considered the possibility that the forces that bring about stability and change in human societies alter as societies become more complex; an idea that Marxists have long championed. She suggests that foraging societies may be shaped primarily by ecological factors, intermediate societies by political processes, and states by cultural factors, especially ones that relate to ideological repression. Upon reflection, I think that this scheme is invalid. Religion plays no less important a role, albeit a different one, in the lives of hunter-gatherers than it does in modern industrial societies. Moreover, if hunter-gatherer societies tend to conceptualize relations with other humans and with supernatural powers in terms of kinship relations, this is equally true of intermediate societies that are variously termed chiefdoms or simple states. It is only as societies grow still more complex and impersonal that kinship metaphors give way to holistic understandings of social relations that are expressed first in terms of religious concepts and later in terms of political and economic theories. These changes do not correspond with Brumfiel's scheme. While Brumfiel has correctly delineated the principal ways in which different sorts of precontact societies are currently being studied by archaeologists, I believe that her scheme reflects patterns of research that are being applied to these societies rather than ontologically grounded differences. There is a need to make sure that differences of this sort do not become further entrenched in a self-reinforcing fashion in the terminological systems of archaeology.

While acknowledging the dissident positions of irredentist ecological determinists, Darwinian evolutionists, and extreme idealists, as well as the battles currently being waged between self-styled processual and postprocessual archaeologists, I believe that today there is more informed agreement among archaeologists than ever before about the nature of socio-cultural phenomena and socio-cultural change. This should make possible greater consensus about classifications of socio-cultural organization and change.

Most archaeologists are prepared to accept that the biological capacity for culture has evolved as a flexible and highly successful means of adapting human beings to their natural and social environments. It is also generally agreed that all human behaviour is culturally mediated; as Gordon Childe observed long ago, the world we adapt to is not the world as it is but the world as we imagine it to be (Childe 1949:6-8). Nevertheless, as Childe also observed, for humanity to survive, the world as imagined must reasonably approximate the real world in a variety of essential ways (Childe 1956:58-60). This means that cultural traditions, in the form of knowledge socially inherited from the past, play a major role in shaping human behaviour, but also that such knowledge is susceptible to alteration in response to changing ecological conditions and various forms of intrasocietal competition. If it were not, culture would not be even minimally adaptive.

While social scientists disagree about how easily human beings can alter their beliefs and behaviour, they agree that self-interest, grounded in both pan-human behavioural characteristics and cultural factors, plays a significant role in shaping human behaviour. Humans live in a realm characterized by cultural particularities as well as by cross-cultural uniformities. Both must be accounted for if human behaviour and cultural change are to be understood (Trigger 1998). The challenge is thus not to create and seek to justify social typologies that prematurely assume cross-cultural uniformities in human behaviour, but to establish means that will permit the objective measurement of both similarities and differences in societies at approximately the same level of development. Otherwise, cross-cultural regularities alone may turn out to be merely an accidental lowest common denominator rather than Julian Steward's (1955) processually significant cultural core. This can be done whether we are defining social types or seeking to establish continua of co-variation.

This growing, albeit far from perfect, consensus undermines a simplistic ecological determinist approach to explaining cultural change, without requiring archaeologists to abandon either a materialist perspective or a Darwinian view of human origins. It makes the study of culture and of behaviour mutually complementary. As Childe also indicated, the social and political organization and religious beliefs of precontact history cannot be treated as predictable epiphenomena of ecological adaptations or relations of production, as ecological determinists and vulgar Marxists once assumed (Childe 1965:98). Within the context of cultural traditions, they constitute cultural givens that in many respects are no less substantial than ecological or economic givens. Like ecological factors, they can play roles in resisting or advancing change. The research of Ian Hodder and his students has also demonstrated that material culture not only reflects social organization but also can play an active role in disguising or inverting the reality of such organization and in negotiating social identity (Hodder 1982). Topics relating to religious beliefs, culture, diffusion and migration, and human psychology that were tabooed as being epiphenomenal, and hence inconsequential, by the New Archaeology have once again, and rightly in my estimation, become legitimate objects of archaeological enquiry. This liberation of archaeology has raised a host of new issues and revived others that were long driven underground. Many of these issues have been well covered at this conference and are recognized as being important for understanding precontact change in the Great Lakes region.

It is thus clear that, as a result of recent developments, we have moved much further away than was the case with New Archaeology from the idea that archaeological cultures are primarily material embodiments of ethnicity. Material culture now is viewed as offering the possibility of inferring aspects of technology, subsistence patterns, economic organization, social status, family organization, community relations and alliances, government structure, gender concepts and behaviour, attitudes towards the aged, and religious beliefs and behaviour, as well as of ethnic identity.

To realize this potential, the geographical and temporal distribution of individual artifact types must be ascertained and an attempt made to understand their practical and symbolic significance before archaeological cultures can be knowledgeably defined and their history discussed. Peter Timmins and John Staeck suggest that among the Iroquoians cultural traditions at the community level may be evident only at the level of attributes rather than of types. Childe adumbrated this method of defining cultures in *The Danube in Prehistory* (1929), one of his first culture-historical works. There he argued that, in order to define cultures, ethnically sensitive types of artifacts had to be distinguished from technologically advantageous ones, which tended to spread quickly from one culture to another. Ethnically sensitive artifacts, which he suggested would generally include home-made pottery and burial customs, would tend to persist in cultural traditions and hence were useful for identifying past peoples, while traits that diffused quickly because of their utility were useful for establishing synchronicity among neighbouring cultures (Childe 1929: vii, 248). While Childe's criteria for ethnicity and his view of culture now seem highly simplistic, the general point he made remains valid: the traits that constitute archaeological cultures do not all express a single dimension of variability. Today, defining archaeological cultures requires first decoding, or at least trying to decode, such variability.

This sort of approach is essential for coping responsibly with the questions raised by Stuart Fiedel concerning migration. It is impossible to attribute cultural change to migrations without offering convincing evidence that migrations actually might have occurred. The political unification of ancient Egypt was long attributed to the invasion of a ruling group of Near Eastern origin who were supposed to have conquered Egypt at the beginning of the First Dynasty and imposed their alien culture over that of the indigenous population. Today, as a result of vastly increased archaeological documentation and better chronological controls, it has become evident that the elite culture of dynastic Egypt developed in southern Egypt over a period of several hundred years, in the course of which it became differentiated from that of the peasantry. In southern Egypt this was a period of rapidly increasing social and economic complexity (Wilkinson 1996). In eastern North America many cultural transitions that once were attributed to migrations have turned out to have been rapid local responses to climatic or technological change.

Irving Rouse (1958) suggested that demonstrating a migration requires finding sites that demonstrate the intrusion of an foreign culture, determining where the intrusive culture originated, and tracing the route along which it moved to its new location. Physical anthropological data also must be examined to see if there is evidence of a movement of human beings parallelling that of the intrusive culture. The temporal relationship among all the units involved must be checked to verify that the migration moved in the anticipated direction and finally an attempt should be made to ascertain why the migration took place and what impact it had on existing local cultures. Very few discussions of precontact migrations in the Great Lakes region meet Rouse's tough criteria. Without understanding the distributions and functional significance of the various traits that occur in individual cultures, it is difficult to properly identify intrusive cultures within a region such as the Great Lakes, where trait diffusion has been common.

Less massive and organized population movements have also occurred that may have introduced new cultural traits and even languages to regions but not markedly disturbed the local cultures. Evidence of such movements might show up in the material culture of particular graves, although it would normally be impossible to determine whether an unusual intrusive burial was that of a migrant or of a long-distance trader or diplomat who had chanced to die while travelling. It would also be difficult to detect situations in which foreign captives were adopted in considerable numbers but acculturated sufficiently quickly and thoroughly that little cultural evidence of their presence remained after the first few years. This constitutes an example of Hodder's notion of material culture as a means of negotiating social identity. The best evidence of this sort of process might be modest changes in local physical types that cannot be attributed to changing food or work habits. George Milner and Anne Katzenberg appear sceptical that mtDNA techniques for analysing skeletons will prove effective for detecting this sort of biological movement within the Great Lakes region. Yet, given the rapid advances that are occurring in biochemical analysis, it is possible that in the future physical anthropological evidence of population movements, even within small and relatively homogenous areas, may become available. Until that day arrives, it is important to remember that not all rapid cultural change is produced by population movements and that population change does not always bring about significant changes in material culture. Failure to take account of these caveats creates most of the problems that are involved in inferring ethnicity from the remains of material culture.

Since the 1960s considerable attention has been paid to inferring precontact social structure in the Great Lakes region. Much of this has been done by studying settlement patterns, with inferences about family structure, community organization, and broader political alliances being based on structures, settlement plans, and regional site distributions. Doing such research well requires the careful dating of structures and sites and determining how long they were occupied, during what seasons, and for what purposes. An example of a major step forward has been Gary Warrick's (1990) devising of a way to estimate how long individual houses were inhabited by determining the extent to which decayed wooden support poles had to be replaced.

Iroquoianists are especially fortunate that the frequent relocation of the communities they study has provided them with a temporally fine-grained record of past changes. As the archaeological record has been more fully recovered, the long term development of individual communities that has been documented by these relocations has become an increasingly important focus of Iroquoian research. Economic, demographic, social, and political changes, as well as changes in material culture, can be studied in relation to site plans. Such favourable opportunities are not available for societies where communities remained in the same place continuously for very long periods, blurring the archaeological record, or for collecting groups who returned seasonally to the same locations for centuries, if not millennia. At least part of the disjuncture between Middle Woodland and Late Woodland culture in southern Ontario, to which Fiedel has alluded, may be an artifact of the transition from a collecting economy to a semi-sedentary horticultural one, rather than the indication of an ethnic change. The need to understand that transition better makes Peter Timmins' (1997) studies of Early Iroquoian settlement patterns, the investigation of the Princess Point culture by Gary Crawford and David Smith, and all studies of the late Middle Woodland Period crucial for understanding the culture history of the region. It is also important to recognize that few other cultures present such favourable opportunities for studying short term changes in community organization and relations among neighbouring communities as do Iroquoian ones. This makes Iroquoian archaeology of special general, as well as regional, importance for investigating the spread of agriculture.

Alexander von Gernet's (1985) detailed study of factors influencing the distribution of ceramic pipes at the Draper site convincingly demonstrated that extensive pre- and post-depositional relocation of fragments of broken pipes ruled out the possibility of different pipe styles revealing anything significant about the location of various clans or lineages within communities, even if such a correlation had existed in Iroquoian society. This suggested the futility of once popular research based on the idea that the distribution of pipe types within Iroquoian sites could indicate the location of different clans. Findings of this sort can exert a major positive influence on how artifacts are classified as well as on how classifications are interpreted.

A subject only briefly touched upon in this session but of great importance for understanding the precontact history of the Great Lakes region is that of gender. Acrimonious anthropological controversies concern the extent to which gender roles are biologically grounded, and hence are cross-culturally generalizable, or purely cultural; a situation which, I believe, compels archaeologists to treat gender behaviour as culturally determined until it is demonstrated otherwise (Gero and Conkey [editors] 1991; Ortner and Whitehead 1981; Sanday 1981). The problem with culturally determined behaviour is that inferring it requires non-archaeological substantiation, in the form of contemporary historical documents, oral traditions, or relevant, historically specific ethnographic analogies. Many archaeologists assume that the precontact hunter-gatherer cultures of the Great Lakes region were patrilineally organized, while at least the later precontact Iroquoian horticulturalists were matrilineal. They also assume that pottery was made by women and stone tools by men. Most of these assumptions are derived from historical ethnographic analogies, often based on very little detailed evidence, which are then projected backwards in time. Yet projections of this sort require substantiation if they are to move beyond the stage of being merely hypotheses. In the case of gendered behaviour, I am not certain how much progress can be made. Contextual studies of the use locations of various types of artifacts may provide a way for cross-checking independent assumptions about various types of artifacts. In the 1930s the Soviet archaeologist P. N. Tretyakov tried to discover the sex of precontact pottery makers through the forensic study of finger prints on such pottery (Childe 1943:6). I suspect that it will be a long time before we can produce many gendered classifications of precontact artifacts that are anything more than speculative.

While the capacity for language is clearly biologically grounded, its content is socio-culturally determined. The history of languages has developed its own form of study which involves building family trees and reconstructing protolanguages. Very serious problems have been encountered in relating protolanguages with specific archaeological complexes. Despite the vast amount of study that has been devoted to the comparative investigation of Indo-European languages, major disagreements continue to flourish concerning the family's place of origin and the nature and cause of its expansion (Mallory 1989; Renfrew 1987). Where there is agreement, consensus often seems to play a more important role than rigorous demonstration.

There are also problems with the assumption that each modern language family is related only to a single language that was spoken by one small society several thousand years ago. In the seventh century A.D., Arabic, a Semitic language, spread over large areas of the Near East and North Africa, eventually replacing various indigenous languages. Yet Arabic, despite its religious prestige, did not establish itself as a vernacular language beyond the range where Afroasiatic, the language family to which Arabic belongs, was already spoken. It did not replace Romance languages in Spain, Greek to the north, or Persian to the east. Hence the spread of Arabic did not result in any significant change in the area that had already been occupied by the Afroasiatic languages for thousands of years. Dean Snow (1980:27-8) long ago argued that much the same process might have happened with various North American Aboriginal languages, thus reducing the likelihood that all modern languages are related only to a tiny fraction of the languages that were spoken as recently as 8,000 years ago. It is possible that much of the Great

Lakes region has long been the home of Iroquoian speakers, even if, as a result of linguistic diffusion or population movements, the Iroquoian languages spoken there today appear to date from a relatively recent period.

It seems to me reasonable to associate historically documented languages with precontact archaeological remains, provided that the association can be traced from historical times back through specific communities which clearly exhibit cultural continuity. In Ontario this can be done successfully as far back as the Early Iroquoian period or perhaps the Princess Point culture. Where the linguistic association is with a broader cultural unit, it becomes less certain. If material culture can spread from one language group to another, even if a correlation can be established for the early historical period between a single language and a single culture, that does not ensure that such a correlation existed in earlier times. Historical Algonquian speakers, such as the Nipissing, used Iroquoian pottery and their sites were classified as Huron until the advent of a community-based approach. It would be as dangerous to equate the Point Peninsula culture with Algonquian languages as it would be to assume that all precontact Pueblo cultures were associated with a single language family.

While the correlation of linguistic and archaeological findings is a legitimate endeavour, it is not something that can be done easily. On the contrary, as is the case with most culturally determined phenomena, methodological rigour is essential if research is to progress beyond the realm of speculation. At this point I would not be prepared to commit myself to identifying the people associated with any specific Middle Woodland culture as being Iroquoian- or Algonquian-speakers, or a combination of both, or neither. For these reasons, it is methodologically as essential to keep linguistic and archaeological classifications separate as it is to distance archaeological from biological classifications.

Christopher Hawkes (1954) long ago declared religion (spiritual life) to be the most inaccessible aspect of human behaviour using only archaeological data. As a purely cultural phenomenon, something "specifically human" rather than "generically animal", as Hawkes put it, religion would seem to be as difficult to infer from archaeological data alone as is language or gender behaviour. Yet religious beliefs often appear to be long lived and relatively stable and because of this to be inferable through the application of the direct historical approach. George Hamell's (1983) comparative analysis of the role played by native metals, marine shells, and crystals in the religious beliefs of early historical Iroquoian-, Algonquian-, and Siouan-speaking peoples appears to shed light on the meaning of burial practices in eastern North America that display elements of continuity extending back continuously for 6,000 years. We can never know precisely what a specific Maritime Archaic individual believed about these substances, but it seems likely that her or his beliefs bore some resemblance to Hamell's general reconstructions. Likewise, as William Fox and Robert Salzer have pointed out, cosmic beliefs identified in historical cultures in the Southeast have been used to infer much about the complex iconography of the precontact Southeastern Ceremonial Complex. It has become widely accepted that all Native Americans shared shamanic beliefs that are very old and ultimately of Siberian origin. These beliefs have been used to explain ritual practices encountered in many parts of North America from the Paleo-Indian period into historical times. More recent examples of what appear to be shamanic practices are also interpreted on a regional basis using the direct historical approach (Brown 1997). There is further evidence in eastern North America of a set of beliefs centred on the shedding of human blood to sustain the forces of nature, which in turn were believed to provide human beings with corn and meat. These ideas appear to have evolved from shamanic beliefs as complex societies developed in Mesoamerica, although they might have been reinvented in the Southeast as stratified societies developed there. In the Lower Great Lakes region early European visitors encountered a retribalized version of such beliefs expressed in the prisoner sacrificial cult, alongside flourishing healing and divinatory practices of local shamanic origin (Knowles 1940; Rands and Riley 1958). This complex amalgam of long lasting beliefs, together with the use of the direct historical approach and the identification of various concerns and symbolisms that appear to be common to all religions, provide a basis for inferring more about religious beliefs and practices in precontact times than Hawkes believed possible. It must be remembered, however, that archaeologists are using material remains and ethnographic knowledge of varying degrees of specificity to infer the general nature of past beliefs, not accessing these beliefs directly, which can only be done through verbal communication in their own language with the people who held these beliefs.

We have already suggested that to be useful classifications must be ontologically grounded in some fashion. It is obvious, however, from my preceding remarks and from the papers presented at this conference, that classifications also conform to specific academic and social agendas. They reflect what their creators believe is important at specific points in time. It is clear that taxonomies can limit the ability of archaeologists to transcend existing concepts, although, to the dismay of extreme relativists, in most cases such schemes do not totally prevent them from doing so. The Midwestern Taxonomic Method was described by its creators as a hierarchical scheme that would enable archaeologists to classify in terms of formal similarities numerous artifact assemblages that had been collected mainly by amateur archaeologists in a region where few sites that had been occupied over long periods of time were yet known. It was specifically denied that the scheme had any historical implications (McKern 1939). Yet its originators generally acted on the assumption that foci and aspects were the archaeological equivalents of ethnographic cultures, that higher and more general taxonomic units, such as patterns, were of greater antiquity than were lower level, more specifically similar ones, such as foci, and that all taxonomic units that were assigned to the same pattern expressed varying degrees of ethnic relations and had evolved by descent from a common ancestral culture.

In New York State, the Midwestern Taxonomic Method incorporated and reinforced an earlier notion that what were now called foci belonging to the Woodland Pattern were associated with Algonquian-speakers, while the Mississippian Pattern embraced the cultures of Iroquoian- and Siouan-speaking peoples. It was also assumed that cultures could not evolve from one pattern to another, any more than an Algonquian language could evolve into an Iroquoian one. This reinforced the longstanding belief that Iroquoian migrants had supplanted an earlier Algonquian population in New York State and perpetuated the pessimism about aboriginal peoples' capacity for change that had characterized American archaeology during the nineteenth century. As it became evident, in the course of the 1930s, that local cultures had evolved from one Midwestern Taxonomic Method pattern to another and that throughout most of the eastern United States Archaic, Woodland, and Mississippian patterns represented successive stages of cultural development, the higher levels of the Midwestern Taxonomic Method were quietly abandoned (Ford and Willey 1941).

Typologies and classifications are tools. They are not meant to last forever, but to be refined and even discarded if they prove inadequate and as better tools become available. Where there is continuity in such systems, it is because a typology has captured some aspect of reality that is useful for achieving a science's long term objectives. There is also evidence of slow and unsteady, but nevertheless real, progress in archaeologists developing the critical self-consciousness about their work that enables them to create more useful classifications. The most important development has been the abandonment of the romantic ideal that culture, including material culture, is principally a reflection of ethnicity. Since the 1960s, and indeed much earlier in Europe, archaeologists have come to view culture from more multifaceted perspectives. Culture is also a highly effective adaptive mechanism, a means for providing material necessities, a way of negotiating social identity in innumerable and subtle ways, an ideology that both sustains and opposes the claims of the rich and the powerful, and a source of beliefs and values that sustain societies and individual human beings, who are compelled by their biological constitution to attribute order and meaning to a cosmos that has relatively little order and no inherent meaning. Traditional typologies of artifacts and cultures have grown increasingly elaborate as archaeologists' interpretive ambitions have created the need for more fine-grained relative chronologies, more detailed understanding of spatial variation in the archaeological record, and information about many hitherto only vaguely considered aspects of human behaviour.

The diversification of the questions archaeologists ask and of the factors that they see influencing human behaviour have also led to a need for more elaborate classifications relating to subsistence behaviour, settlement patterns, gender, religious beliefs and practices, and the nature of cultural change. These behavioural classifications, although they have become vital for the archaeological mission, have not been accorded the respect traditionally reserved for artifact and cultural typologies, which in the past have often been accepted as ends in themselves by archaeologists. Behavioural classifications tend to be hotly debated, altered frequently, and often abandoned. There is no tendency to fetishize such typologies. In broadening the range of topics that it is once more permissible for them to discuss, archaeologists have had to relearn Boasian anthropology's realization that what were once called races, languages, and cultures, are distinct entities that must be treated as such; which means their typologies must be kept separate.

I believe that this conference and today's session have advanced the cause of archaeology in this part of the world by demonstrating that approaches that some archaeologists would like us to regard as mutually exclusive and antithetical are in fact complementary. An appreciation of the roles played by subjectivity and relativism in daily life and in our research is enriching and empowering; it does not have to draw us into a fantasy world in which archaeology, and knowledge itself, become irrelevant. At the same time we must accept our traditional duty to evaluate interpretations rigorously against the traditional criteria of logical coherence and correspondence with available data (Lowther 1962). There are no questions that we can or should deny other archaeologists the right to ask, even if it turns out that some of these questions do not have answers and if, as the great philosopher of science Mario Bunge (1996:105) reminds us, "we shall never attain an exhaustive knowledge of the past...because most facts are never recorded [and others] are destroyed or lost". Human reality in its linked cognitive and behavioural aspects is deep and rich and can never totally be reduced to ecological adaptation, biology, or physics. It is characterized by cultural idiosyncracies no less than by cross-cultural regularities and archaeologists must account for both. Typologies are not eternal; they are at best expedient devices. Numerous typologies are needed to help us try to understand human complexity. We must welcome the creation of new typologies and be prepared to evaluate both old and new ones on their merits. In this way we do our best to ensure that classifications, which we cannot get along without, remain our servants and do not become our masters.

References Cited

Adams, W.Y., and E.W. Adams
1991   *Archaeological Typology and Practical Reality.* Cambridge University Press, New York.

Adovasio, J., and D.R. Pedler
1994   A Tisket, a Tasket: Looking at the Numic Speakers Through the Lens of a Basket. In *Across The West, Human Population Movement and the Expansion of the Numa*, edited by D.B. Madsen and D. Rhode, pp. 114-123. University of Utah Press, Salt Lake City.

Anaya, S.J.
1997   The Indigenous are Peoples: A Reality and a Challenge. *Native Americas* 14:64.

Anderson, D.G.
1995   Paleoindian Interaction Networks in the Eastern Woodlands. In *Native American Interactions: Multiscalar Analyses and Interpretations in the Eastern Woodlands*, edited by M.S. Nassaney and K.E. Sassaman, pp. 3-26. University of Tennessee Press, Knoxville.

Anderson, J.E.
1968   Skeletal Anomalies as Genetic Indicators. In *The Skeletal Biology of Earlier Human Populations*, edited by D.R. Brothwell, pp. 135-147. Pergamon Press, London.

Anderson, T.W., and C.F.M. Lewis
1985   Postglacial Water-Level History of the Lake Ontario Basin. In *Quaternary Evolution of the Great Lakes*, edited by P.F. Karrow and P.E. Calkin. pp. 231-253. Special Paper 30. Geological Association of Canada, St. John's.

Anthony, D.W.
1990   Migration in Archaeology: The Baby and the Bathwater. *American Anthropologist* 92:895-914.

Arnold, J.E.
1996   Understanding the Evolution of Intermediate Societies. In *Emergent Complexity*, edited by J.E. Arnold, pp. 1-12. Archaeological Series 9. International Monographs in Prehistory, Ann Arbor.

Arnold, J.E. (editor)
1996   *Emergent Complexity.* Archaeological Series 9. International Monographs in Prehistory, Ann Arbor.

Baerreis, D.A., H. Daifuku, and J.E. Lundsted
1954 The Burial Complex at the Reigh site, Winnebago County, WI. *The Wisconsin Archeologist* 35:1-36.

Baker, S.W.
1988 Neale's Landing Site Ceramics: A Perspective on the Protohistoric Period from Blennerhasset Island. *West Virginia Archaeologist* 40:40-53.

Bamforth, D.B.
1986 Technological Efficiency and Tool Curation. *American Antiquity* 51:38-50.

Barbeau, C.M.
1912 On Huron Work, 1911. *Geological Survey of Canada, Anthropological Division*, pp. 381-386. Geological Survey of Canada, Ottawa.
1913 On Iroquoian Field Work, 1912. *Geological Survey of Canada, Anthropological Division*, pp. 454-560. Geological Survey of Canada, Ottawa.
1917 Iroquoian Clans and Phraties. *American Anthropologist* 19:392-403.

Barnett, P.J.
1985 Glacial Retreat and Lake Levels, North Central Lake Erie Basin, Ontario. In *Quaternary Evolution of the Great Lakes*, edited by P.F. Karrow and P.E. Calkin, pp. 185-194. Special Paper 30. Geological Association of Canada, St. John's.
1992 Quaternary Geology of Ontario. In *Geology of Ontario*, edited by P.C. Thurston, H.R. Williams, R.H. Sutcliffe, and G.M. Stott, pp. 1010-1088. Ontario Geological Survey Special Volume 4(2). Ontario Ministry of Northern Development and Mines, Toronto.

Barth, F.
1969 Introduction. In *Ethnic Groups and Boundaries*, edited by F. Barth, pp. 9-38. Little, Brown and Company, Boston.

Barth, F. (editor)
1969 *Ethnic Groups and Boundaries*. Little and Brown, Boston.

Bastian, T.J.
1963 *Prehistoric Copper Mining in Isle Royale National Park, Michigan.* Unpublished M.A. thesis, Department of Anthropology, University of Utah, Salt Lake City.

Bateman, R., I. Goddard, R. O'Grady, V.A. Funk, R. Mooi, W.J. Dress, and P. Cannell
1990 The Feasibility of Reconciling Human Phylogeny and the History of Language. *Current Anthropology* 31:1-24.

326

Beardsley, R.K., P. Holder, A.D. Kreiger, R.J. Meggars, J.B. Rinaldo, and P. Kutche
1956   Functional and Evolutionary Implications of Community Patterning. In *Seminars in Archaeology: 1955*, edited by R. Wauchope, pp. 129-57. Society for American Archaeology Memoir 11. Society for American Archaeology, Washington, D.C.

Beauchamp, W.M.
1894   The Origin of the Iroquois. *American Antiquarian* 16: 61-69.
1897   Aboriginal Chipped Stone Implements of New York. *New York State Museum Bulletin* 16.
1898   Earthenware of the New York Aborigines. *New York State Museum Bulletin* 22:75-146.
1900   Iroquois Women. *Journal of American Folklore* 8:81-91.
1905   The Perch Lake Mounds: With Notes on Other New York Mounds and Some Accounts of Indian Trails. *New York State Museum Bulletin* 87.

Bekerman, A.
1995   *Relative Chronology of Princess Point Sites*. Unpublished M.Sc. thesis, Department of Anthropology, University of Toronto, Toronto.

Beld, S.
1991   *Two Terminal Archaic/Early Woodland Sites in Central Michigan*. Technical Report of the University of Michigan Museum of Anthropology 22. University of Michigan, Ann Arbor.

Bell, C.N.
1928   An Implement of Prehistoric Man. *Annual Archaeological Report, Appendix to the Report of the Minister of Education, Ontario* 36:51-54.

Benn, D.W.
1990   Introduction to the Rainbow Site Excavations. In *Woodland Cultures on the Western Prairies: The Rainbow Site Investigations*, edited by D.W. Benn, pp. 1–20. Report 18. Office of the State Archaeologist, University of Iowa, Iowa City.

Benn, D.W., and W. Green
1997   Late Woodland Cultures in Iowa. Paper presented at the Urbana Late Woodland Conference, University of Illinois, Urbana.

Bernabo, J.C.
1981   Quantitative Estimates of Temperature Changes over the Last 2700 Years in Michigan Based on Pollen Data. *Quaternary Research* 15:143-159.

Bettinger, R.L.
1991   *Hunter-Gatherers: Archaeological and Evolutionary Theory.*
        Plenum Press, New York.
Betts, C.
1997   *Lane Enclosure Oneota Ceramics: Form, Function, and Diet.*
        Unpublished M.A. thesis, Department of Anthropology,
        University of Illinois at Urbana-Champaign.
Beukens, R.P., L.A. Pavlish, R.G.V. Hancock, R.M. Farquhar, G.C. Wilson,
P.J. Julig, and W. Ross
1992   Radiocarbon Dating of Copper-Preserved Organics. *Radiocarbon*
        34:890-897.
Bideaux, M.
1986   *Jacques Cartier, Relations.* Presses de l'Université de Montréal,
        Montréal.
Biggar, H.P. (editor)
1922-36 *The Works of Samuel de Champlain.* 6 vols. The Champlain
        Society, Toronto.
1924   *Voyages of Jacques Cartier.* Public Archives of Canada,
        Publication 2. Public Archives of Canada, Ottawa.
Binford, L.R.
1962a   Archaeology as Anthropology. *American Antiquity* 28:217-225.
1962b   Radiometric Analysis of Bone Material from the Oconto Site.
        Wisconsin Archeologist 43:31-41.
1972   *An Archaeological Perspective.* Seminar Press, New York.
1979   Organization and Formation Processes: Looking at Curated
        Technologies. *Journal of Anthropological Research* 35:255-273.
1980   Willow Smoke and Dogs' Tails: Hunter Gatherer Settlement
        Systems and Archaeological Site Formation. *American Antiquity*
        45:4-20.
Birdsell, J.B.
1968   Some Predictions for the Pleistocene Based on Equilibrium
        Systems among Recent Hunter-Gatherers. In *Man the Hunter*,
        edited by R. B. Lee and I. De Vore, pp. 229-240. Aldine,
        Chicago.
Bishop, C.A.
1981   Territorial Groups before 1821: Cree and Ojibwa. In *Handbook
        of North American Indians Volume 6 (Subarctic)*, edited by J.
        Helm, pp. 158-160. Smithsonian Institution, Washington DC.
Blitz, J.H.
1993   Big Pots for Big Shots. *American Antiquity* 58:80-95.
Blondin, G.
1997   *Yamoria The Lawmaker: Stories of the Dene.* NuWest Press.

Boas, F.
1940   *Race, Language and Culture*. Macmillan, New York.
Boserup, E.
1965   *The Conditions of Agricultural Growth*. Aldine, Chicago.
Bowen, J.E.
1980   The Sandusky Tradition. *Toledo Area Aboriginal Research Bulletin* 9:39-58.
1994   *The Sandusky River Area of North-Central Ohio: 1300-1600*. Sandusky Valley Chapter, Archaeological Society of Ohio, Upper Sandusky.
Bradley, J.W., and S.T. Childs
1991   Basque Earrings and Panthers' Tails: The Form of Cross-Cultural Contact in 16th Century Iroquoia. In *Metals in Society: Theory Beyond Analysis*, edited by R. M. Ehrenreich, pp. 7-17. MASCA Research Papers in Science and Archaeology 8 (2). University Museum of Archaeology and Anthropology, University of Pennsylvania, Philadelphia.
Brain, J.P.
1978   The Archaeological Phase: Ethnographic Fact or Fancy? In *Archaeological Essays in Honor of Irving B. Rouse*, edited by R.C. Dunnell and E. S. Hall, pp. 311–318. Mouton, The Hague.
Brainard, G.W.
1950   The Place of Chronological Ordering in Archaeological Analysis. *American Antiquity* 16: 293-301.
Brashler, J.
1973   *A Formal Analysis of Prehistoric Ceramics from the Fletcher Site*. Unpublished M.A. thesis, Department of Anthropology, Michigan State University, Lansing.
1981   *Early Late Woodland Boundaries and Interaction: Indian Ceramics of Southern Lower Michigan*. Publications of the Museum, Anthropological Series 3(3). Michigan State University, East Lansing.
Brashler, J., and M. Holman
1985   Late Woodland Continuity and Change in the Saginaw Valley of Michigan. *Arctic Anthropology* 22:141-152.
Brasser, T.J.
1978   Mahican. In *Handbook of North American Indians Volume 15 (Northeast)*, edited by B.G. Trigger, pp. 198-212. Smithsonian Institution, Washington D.C.
Braun, D.
1991   Why Decorate a Pot? Midwestern Household Pottery, 200 B.C. - A.D. 600. *Journal of Anthropological Archaeology* 10:360-397.

Braun, D. and S. Plog
1982   Evolution of Tribal Social Networks: Theory and Prehistoric North American Evidence. *American Antiquity* 47:504-525.

Brew, J.O.
1946   The Uses and Abuses of Taxonomy. *Archaeology of Alkali Ridge, Southeastern Utah.* Papers of the Peabody Museum, 21:44-66. Peabody Museum, Cambridge, Mass.

Brose, D.S.
1966   The Valley Sweets Site, 20-Sa-24, Saginaw County, Michigan. *Michigan Archeologist* 12:1-21.

1994   *The South Park Village Site and the Late Prehistoric Whittlesey Tradition of Northeast Ohio.* Monographs in World Archaeology 20. Prehistory Press, Madison.

1997a   [Review of] "The Western Basin Tradition: Algonquin or Iroquois?" by David Stothers, and "Culture Continuity and Change: The Western Basin, Ontario Iroquois, and Sandusky Tradition—A 1982 Perspective" by David Stothers and James R. Graves. *North American Archaeologist* 18:151-163.

1997b   Cultural Relationships of the Late Prehistoric Whittlesey and Sandusky Traditions of Northern Ohio: A Response to Stothers, Prufer and Murphy. *North American Archaeologist* 18:177-204.

Brose, D.S. (editor)
1976   *The Late Prehistory of the Lake Erie Drainage Basin: A Symposium.* Cleveland Museum of Natural History, Cleveland.

Brown, C.E.
1904   The Native Copper Implements of Wisconsin. *Wisconsin Archeologist* 3:49-98.

Brown, J.A.
1986   Unresolved Issues in Midwestern Systematics. Paper presented at the 2nd Indianapolis Archaeological Conference, Indianapolis, Indiana.

1997   The Archaeology of Ancient Religion in the Eastern Woodlands. *Annual Review of Anthropology* 26:465-485.

Brown, J.A. (editor)
1961   *The Zimmerman Site: A Report on Excavations at the Grand Village of Kaskaskia, La Salle County, Illinois.* Report of Investigations 9. Illinois State Museum, Springfield.

Brown, J.A., and C. Cleland
1968   The Late Glacial and Early Postglacial Faunal Resources in Biomes Newly Opened to Human Adaptation. In *The Quaternary of Illinois*, edited by R. Bergstrom, pp. 114-122. University of Illinois College of Agriculture Special Publication 14.

References Cited

Brown, J.A. and J. Kelly
1995   *Cahokia and the Southeastern Ceremonial Complex.* In Mounds, Modoc, and Mesoamerica: Papers in Honor of Melvin L. Fowler, edited by S.R. Ahler. State Museum of Science Paper 55. Springfield, Illinois.
Brown, J.A., and J. Willis
1995   Re-Examination of Danner Pottery from the Starved Rock Area. Paper presented at the Midwest Archaeological Conference, Beloit, Wisconsin.
Brown, J.S.H., and R. Brightman
1990   *The Orders of the Dreamed: George Nelson on Cree and Northern Ojibwa Religion and Myth, 1823.* Manitoba Studies in Native History 3. University of Manitoba Press, Winnipeg.
Brown, M.K.
1975   *The Zimmerman Site: Further Excavations at the Grand Village of Kaskaskia.* Reports of Investigations 32. Illinois State Museum, Springfield.
Broyles, B.J.
1971   *Second Preliminary Report: The St. Albans Site, Kanawha County, West Virginia.* Report of Archaeological Investigations 3. West Virginia Geological and Economic Survey, Morgantown, West Virginia.
Brumbach, H.J.
1975   Iroquoian Ceramics in Algonkian Territory. *Man in the Northeast* 10:17-28.
1995a   Introduction to Symposium Papers: Unearthing the Late Woodland, Ethnogenesis and Ceramics in the Northeast. *Northeast Anthropology* 49:1-3.
1995b   Algonquian and Iroquoian Ceramics in the Upper Hudson River Drainage. *Northeast Anthropology* 49:55-66.
Brumfiel, E.M.
1992   Breaking and Entering the Ecosystem — Gender, Class, and Faction Steal the Show. *American Anthropologist* 94:551-67.
1997   Applying Action Theory to Archaeological Research. *American Scientist* 85: 374-375.
Bryson, R.A.
1985   On Climatic Analogs in Paleoclimatic Reconstruction. *Quaternary Research* 23: 275-286.
Bryson, R.A., and F.K. Hare
1974   The Climates of North America. *World Survey of Climatology* 11:1-47. Elsevier, Amsterdam.

Bryson, R.A., and C. Padoch
1981   On the Climates of History. *In Climate and History*, edited by R.
        I. Rotberg and T.K. Rabb, pp. 3-17. Princeton University Press,
        Princeton.
Bryson, R.A., and W.M. Wendland
1967   Tentative Climatic Patterns for Some Late Glacial and Post-
        glacial Episodes in Central North America. In *Life, Land and
        Water: Proceedings of the 1966 Conference on Environmental
        Studies of the Glacial Lake Agassiz Region*, edited by W.J.
        Mayer-Oakes, pp. 271-298. Occasional Papers 1. Department of
        Anthropology, University of Manitoba, Winnipeg.
Buhay, W.M., and T.W.D. Edwards
1995   Climate in Southwestern Ontario, Canada, between AD 1610 and
        1885 Inferred from Oxygen and Hydrogen Isotopic
        Measurements of Wood Cellulose from Trees in Different
        Hydrologic Settings. *Quaternary Research* 44: 438-446.
Buikstra, J.E.
1977   Biocultural Dimensions of Archeological Study: A Regional
        Perspective. In *Biocultural Adaptation in Prehistoric America*,
        edited by R.L. Blakely, pp. 67-84. Southern Anthropological
        Society Proceedings 11. University of Georgia Press, Athens.
1980   Epigenetic Distance: A Study of Biological Variability in the
        Lower Illinois River Region. In *Early Native Americans*, edited
        by D. Bowman, pp.271-299. Mouton, The Hague.
1992   Diet and Disease in Late Prehistory. In *Disease and Demography
        in the Americas*, edited by J.W. Verano and D.H.Ubelaker, pp.
        87-101. Smithsonian Institution Press, Washington, D.C.
1997   Paleodemography: Context and Promise. In *Integrating
        Archaeological Demography: Multidisciplinary Approaches to
        Prehistoric Population*, edited by R.R. Paine, pp. 367-380.
        Occasional Paper 24. Center for Archaeological Investigations,
        Southern Illinois University, Carbondale.
Buikstra J.E., and D.C. Cook
1981   Pre-Columbian Tuberculosis in West-Central Illinois: Prehistoric
        Disease in Biocultural Perspective. In *Prehistoric Tuberculosis
        in the Americas*, edited by J.E. Buikstra, pp. 115-139. Scientific
        Papers 5. Northwestern University Archaeological Program,
        Evanston, Illinois.
Buikstra, J.E., and G.R. Milner
1989   *The Dickson Mounds Site: An Annotated Bibliography*. Reports
        of Investigations 44. Illinois State Museum, Springfield.

Buikstra, J.E., and S. Williams
1991   Tuberculosis in the Americas: Current Perspectives. In *Human Paleopathology: Current Syntheses and Future Options*, edited by D.J. Ortner and A.C. Aufderheide, pp. 161-172. Smithsonian Institution Press, Washington, D.C.

Bulkin, V.A., L.S. Klejn, and G.S. Lebedev
1982   Attainments and Problems of Soviet Archaeology. *World Archaeology* 13: 272-295.

Bunge, M.
1996   *Finding Philosophy in Social Science.* Yale University Press, New Haven.

Burgar, R.W.
1985   *Points to Ponder: A Regional Analysis of the Batten Kill Phase in Southern Ontario.* Unpublished M.A. thesis, Department of Geography, York University, Toronto.

Bursey, J.A.
1997   Lessons from Burlington: A Re-consideration of the Pickering vs. Glen Meyer Debate. *Northeast Anthropology* 53:23-46.

Butler, J.D.
1875-76 Copper Tools Found in the State of Wisconsin. *Transactions of the Wisconsin Academy of Sciences, Arts and Letters* 3:30-36.

Butler, W.B.
1986   *Taxonomy in Northeastern Colorado Prehistory.* Unpublished Ph.D. dissertation. Department of Anthropology, University of Missouri, Columbia.

1988   The Woodland Period in Northeastern Colorado. *Plains Anthropologist* 33:449–465.

Butzer, K.W.
1982   *Archaeology as Human Ecology: Method and Theory for a Contextual Approach.* Cambridge University Press, New York.

Caldwell, J.R.
1958   *Trend and Tradition in the Prehistory of the Eastern United States.* American Anthropological Association, Memoir 88.

Calkin, P.E. and B.H. Feenstra
1985   Evolution of the Erie-Basin Great Lakes. In *Quaternary Evolution of the Great Lakes*, edited by P.F. Karrow and P.E. Calkin, pp. 149-170. Special Paper 30. Geological Association of Canada, St. John's.

Callender, C.
1978a   Fox. In *Handbook of North American Indians Volume 15 (Northeast)*, edited by B.G. Trigger, pp.636-647. Smithsonian Institution, Washington D.C.

1978b   Sauk. In *Handbook of North American Indians Volume 15 (Northeast)*, edited by B.G. Trigger, pp. 648-655. Smithsonian Institution, Washington D.C.

1978c   Miami. In *Handbook of North American Indians Volume 15 (Northeast)*, edited by B.G. Trigger, pp. 681-689. Smithsonian Institution, Washington D.C.

1978d   Illinois. In *Handbook of North American Indians Volume 15 (Northeast)*, edited by B.G. Trigger, pp. 673-680. Smithsonian Institution, Washington D.C.

1978e   Shawnee. In *Handbook of North American Indians Volume 15 (Northeast)*, edited by B.G. Trigger, pp. 622-635. Smithsonian Institution, Washington DC.

Callender, C., R.K. Pope, and S.M. Pope

1978   Kickapoo. In *Handbook of North American Indians Volume 15 (Northeast)*, edited by B.G. Trigger, pp. 656-667. Smithsonian Institution, Washington DC.

Campbell, I.D., and J.H. McAndrews

1991   Cluster Analysis of Late Holocene Pollen Trends in Ontario. *Canadian Journal of Botany* 69:1719-1730.

1993   Forest Disequilibrium Caused by Rapid Little Ice Age Cooling. *Nature* 366: 336-338.

Carr, L.

1887   On the Social and Political Position of Women Among the Huron and Iroquois Tribes. *Reports of the Peabody Museum of American Archaeology and Ethnology* 3:207-232. Harvard University, Cambridge.

1895   The Food of Certain American Indians and Their Methods of Preparing It. *Proceedings of the American Antiquarian Society* 10:155-190.

Carver, J.

1956   *Travels Through the Interior Parts of North America, in the Years 1766, 1767, and 1768.* 3rd Edition. Ross and Haines, Minneapolis.

Chafe, W.L.

1964   Linguistic Evidence for the Relative Age of Iroquois Religious Practices. *Southwest Journal of Anthropology* 20:278-285.

1973   Siouan, Iroquoian, and Caddoan. In *Current Trends in Linguistics Volume 10 (Linguistics in North America)*, edited by T.A. Sebeok, pp. 1164-1209. Mouton, The Hague.

Chafe, W.L., and M.K. Foster

1981   Prehistoric Divergences and Recontacts between Cayuga, Seneca, and the other Northern Iroquoian Languages. *International Journal of American Linguistics* 47:121-142.

Chagnon, N.

1990   Reproductive and Somatic Conflicts of Interest in the Genesis of Violence and Warfare Among Tribesmen. In *The Anthropology of War*, edited by J. Haas, pp. 77-104. Cambridge University Press, New York.

Chalifoux, É., A. Burke, and C. Chapdelaine

1998   *La Préhistoire du Témiscouata. Occupations Amérindiennes dans la Haute Vallée de Wolastokuk.* Paléo-Québec 26. Recherches Amérindiennes au Québec, Montréal.

Chapdelaine, C.

1980   L'Ascendance Culturelle des Iroquoiens du Saint-Laurent. *Recherches Amérindiennes au Québec* 10(3):145-152

1986   La Poterie Amérindienne Préhistorique du Site EbCx-1, Île du Havre de Mingan: Identification Culturelle et Position Chronologique. *Recherches Amérindiennes au Québec* 16 (2-3):95-101.

1989   *Le Site Mandeville à Tracy: Variabilité Culturelle des Iroquoiens du Saint-Laurent.* Collection Signes des Amériques 7. Recherches Amérindiennes au Québec, Montréal.

1993a   La Transhumance et les Iroquoiens du Saint-Laurent. *Recherches Amérindiennes au Québec* 23(4):23-38.

1993b   The Sedentarization of the Prehistoric Iroquoians: A Slow or Rapid Transformation? *Journal of Anthropological Archaeology* 12:173-209.

1995   An Early Late Woodland Pottery Sequence East of Lac Saint-Pierre. *Northeast Anthropology* 49:77-95.

Chapdelaine, C. (editor)

1992   L'Origine des Iroquoiens: un Débat. *Recherches Amérindiennes au Québec* 22(4):3-36.

Chapdelaine, C., and G. Kennedy

1990   The Origin of the Iroquoian Rim Sherd from Red Bay. *Man in the Northeast* 40:41-43.

Chapdelaine, C., G. Kennedy, and É. Chalifoux

1995   Kégashka : de la Poterie Iroquoienne ou Algonquienne? In *Étude du Réseau d'Interactions des Iroquoiens Préhistoriques du Québec Méridional par les Analyses Physicochimiques,* edited by C. Chapdelaine, N. Clermont and R. Marquis, pp. 71-84. Paléo-Québec 24. Recherches Amérindiennes au Québec, Montréal.

Chapman, J.
1976   The Archaic Period in the Lower Little Tennessee River Valley: Radiocarbon Dates. *Tennessee Anthropologist* 1:1-12.

Chapman, R.W.
1996   Problems of Scale in the Emergence of Complexity. In *Emergent Complexity*, edited by J.E. Arnold, pp. 35-49. Archaeological Series 9. International Monographs in Prehistory, Ann Arbor.

Charles, D.K., and J.E. Buikstra
1983   Archaic Mortuary Sites in the Central Mississippi Drainage: Distribution, Structure, and Implications. In *Archaic Hunters and Gatherers*, edited by J. Philips and J. Brown, pp. 117-45. Academic Press, New York.

Charlevoix, P.F. Xavier de
1923   *Journal of a Voyage to North America.* 2 volumes. Caxton Club, Chicago.

Chaumonot, P.
1869   *Le Père Pierre Chaumonot de la Compagnie de Jésus: Autobiographie et Pièces Inédites.* August Carayon, Poitiers.

Childe, V.G.
1929   *The Danube in Prehistory.* Oxford University Press, Oxford.
1936   *Man Makes Himself.* Watts, London.
1939   *The Dawn of European Civilization.* Third Edition. Kegan Paul, London.
1943   Archaeology in the U.S.S.R.: The Forest Zone. *Man* 43:4-9.
1949   *Social Worlds of Knowledge.* Oxford University Press, Oxford.
1951   *Social Evolution.* Schuman, New York.
1956   *Society and Knowledge.* Harper, New York.
1958   *The Prehistory of European Society.* Penguin, Harmondsworth.
1965   *Man Makes Himself.* 4th edition. Watts, London.

CHIN Archaeological Sites Working Group.
1994   *The Archaeological Sites Data Dictionary of the Canadian Heritage Information Network.* Ministry of Supply and Services Canada, Ottawa.

Chrétien, Y.
1995   Les Lames de Cache du Site Lambert et l'influence de la Culture Meadowood dans la Région de Québec. In *Archéologies Québécoises*, edited by C. Chapdelaine, N. Clemont, and F. Duguay, pp.185-201. Paléo-Québec 23. Recherches Amérindiennes au Québec, Montréal.

Clark, J.G.D.
1952   *Prehistoric Europe: The Economic Basis.* Methuen, London.

1954   *Excavations at Star Carr.* Cambridge University Press, New York.

1961   *World Prehistory.* Cambridge University Press, New York.

Clarke, D.L.

1968   *Analytical Archaeology.* Methuen and Company, London.

Clarke, P.D.

1870   *Origin and Traditional History of the Wyandotte and Sketches of Other Indian Tribes of North America.* Hunter Rose, Toronto.

Clayton, L.

1983   Chronology of Lake Agassiz Drainage to Lake Superior. In *Glacial Lake Agassiz*, edited by J.T. Teller and L. Clayton, pp. 291-307. Special Paper 26. Geological Association of Canada, St. John's.

Cleland, C.E.

1966   *The Prehistoric Animal Ecology and Ethnozoology of the Upper Great Lakes Region.* University of Michigan Museum of Anthropology Anthropological Papers 29. University of Michigan, Ann Arbor.

Cleland, C.E., M.B. Holman, and A. Holman.

1998   The Mason-Quimby Line Revisited. In *From the Northern Tier: Papers in Honor of Ronald J. Mason*, edited by C. E. Cleland and R. A. Birmingham, *The Wisconsin Archeologist* 79: 8-27. Milwaukee.

Clermont, N.

1995a   The Meaning of Early Late Woodland Pottery from Southwestern Quebec. *Northeast Anthropology* 49:67-75.

1995b   Réflexions sur Quatre Tessons de Poterie. In *Archéologies Québécoises,* edited by A.-M. Balac, C. Chapdelaine, N. Clermont, and F. Duguay, pp. 69-78. Paléo-Québec 23. Recherches Amérindiennes au Québec, Montréal.

1996   The Origin of the Iroquoians. *The Review of Archaeology* 17:59-62.

Clermont, N., and C. Chapdelaine

1982   *Pointe-du-Buisson 4: Quarante Siècles d'Archives Oubliées.* Collection Signes des Amériques 1. Recherches Amérindiennes au Québec, Montréal.

1992   Au Pied du Cap Diamant : l'Occupation Préhistorique de la Pointe de Québec. In *Cérane Inc.: L'occupation Historique et Péhistorique de la Place-Royale.* Coll. Patrimoines, Dossier 76. Ministère des Affaires Culturelles du Québec, Québec.

Clermont, N., C. Chapdelaine, and R. Ribes
  1986   Regard sur la Préhistoire Trifluvienne: le Site Bourassa. *Recherches Amérindiennes au Québec* 16 (2-3): 5-55.
Clifton, J.A.
  1978   Potawatomi. In *Handbook of North American Indians Volume 15 (Northeast)*, edited by B.G. Trigger, pp. 725-742. Smithsonian Institution, Washington D.C.
CLIMAP Project Members
  1981   Seasonal Reconstructions of the Earth's Surface at the Last Glacial Maximum. *Geological Society of America Map and Chart Series* MC-36:1-18.
Coakley, J.P. and C.F.M. Lewis
  1985   Postglacial Lake Levels in the Erie Basin. In *Quaternary Evolution of the Great Lakes*, edited by P.F. Karrow and P.E. Calkin, pp. 195-212. Special Paper 30. Geological Association of Canada, St. John's.
Cobb, C.R., and M.S. Nassaney
  1995   Interaction and Integration in the Late Woodland Southeast. In *Native American Interactions: Multiscalar Analyses and Interpretations in the Eastern Woodlands*, edited by M.S. Nassaney and K.E. Sassaman, pp. 205-226. University of Tennessee Press, Knoxville.
Cohen, M.N.
  1989   *Health and the Rise of Civilization.* Yale University Press, New Haven, Connecticut.
  1994   The Osteological Paradox Reconsidered. *Current Anthropology* 35:629-631.
  1997   Does Paleopathology Measure Community Health? A Rebuttal of "The Osteological Paradox" and its Implication for World History. In *Integrating Archaeological Demography: Multidisciplinary Approaches to Prehistoric Population*, edited by R.R. Paine, pp. 242-260. Occasional Paper 24. Center for Archaeological Investigations, Southern Illinois University, Carbondale.
Cohen, M.N., and G.J. Armelagos
  1984   Paleopathology at the Origins of Agriculture: Editors Summation. In *Paleopathology at the Origins of Agriculture*, edited by M.N. Cohen and G.J. Armelagos, pp. 585-601. Academic Press, Orlando.
Cohen, R.
  1978   Ethnicity: Problem and Focus in Anthropology. *Annual Review*

of Anthropology 7:379-403.

Collins, J.M.

1989   The Des Moines Rapids and Western Oneota Socio-Political Patterns. *Journal of the Steward Anthropological Society* 18:165-186.

Conkey, M. and C. Hastorf (editors)

1990   *The Uses of Style in Archaeology*. Cambridge University Press, New York.

Conkey, M., and J. Spector

1984   Archaeology and the Study of Gender. *Advances in Archaeological Method and Theory* 7:1-38.

Connelley, W.E.

1900   The Wyandots. *In Annual Archaeological Report for 1899, Being Part of Appendix to the Report of the Minister of Education*, pp. 92-123. Warwick Bros. and Rutter, Toronto.

Converse, H.

1974   *Myths and Legends of the New York Iroquois*. New York State Museum and Science Service, Bulletin 125 (Reprint), Albany.

Courty, M.A., J. MacPhail, and P. Goldberg

1989   *Micromorphology and Archaeology*. Cambridge University Press, New York.

Crawford, G.W., and D.G. Smith

1996   Migration in Prehistory: Princess Point and the Northern Iroquoian Case. *American Antiquity* 61:782-790.

Crawford, G.W., D.G. Smith, and V.E. Bowyer

1997   Dating the Entry of Corn (*Zea Mays*) into the Lower Great Lakes Region. *American Antiquity* 62:112-119.

Creamer, W., and J. Haas

1985   Tribe Versus Chiefdom in Lower Central America. *American Antiquity* 50:738-754.

Cremin, W.M.

1996   The Berrien Phase of Southwest Michigan: Proto-Potawatomi? In *Investigating the Archaeological Record of the Great Lakes State: Essays in Honor of Elizabeth Baldwin Garland*, edited by M.B. Holman, J.G. Brashler, and K.E. Parker, pp. 383-413. New Issues Press, Western Michigan University, Kalamazoo.

Crumley, C. L.

1987   A Dialectical Critique of Hierarchy. In *Power Relations and State Formation*, edited by T.C. Patterson and C.W. Gailey, pp. 155-159. American Anthropological Association, Washington, D.C.

Custer, J.
1981   Comments on David Meltzer's "Paradigms and the Nature of Change in American Archaeology". *American Antiquity* 46:660-661.

D'Annibale, C., and B.D. Ross
1994   After Point Peninsula: Pickering vs. Owasco in the St. Lawrence Valley. *The Bulletin: Journal of the New York State Archaeological Association* 107: 9-16.

Davis, D.D.
1983   Investigating the Diffusion of Stylistic Innovations. In *Advances in Archaeological Method and Theory Volume 6*, edited by M. Schiffer, pp. 53-89. Academic Press, New York.

Davis, M.B.
1986   Climatic Instability, Time Lags, and Community Disequilibrium. In *Community Ecology*, edited by J. Diamond and T.J. Case, pp. 269-284. Harper and Row, New York.

Davis, M.B., and D.B. Botkin
1985   Sensitivity of Cool-Temperate Forests and Their Fossil Pollen Record to Rapid Temperature Change. *Quaternary Research* 23: 327-340.

Davis, W.
1990   Style and History in Art History. In *The Uses of Style in Archaeology*, edited by M. Conkey and C. Hastorf, pp. 18-31. Cambridge University Press, New York.

DeBoer, W.
1990   Interaction, Imitation, and Communication as Expressed in Style: the Ucayali Experience. In *The Uses of Style in Archaeology*, edited by M. Conkey and C. Hastorf, pp. 82-104. Cambridge University Press, New York.

DeLaurier, A., and M.W. Spence
1998   Moatfield Ossuary Discrete Cranial Traits: Implications for Postmarital Residence Patterns. In *Bones of the Ancestors: The Archaeology and Osteobiography of the Moatfield Ossuary*, edited by R.F. Williamson and S. Pfeiffer. Ms. on file, Archaeological Services Inc., Toronto.

De Montmollin, O.
1989   *The Archaeology of Political Structure*. Cambridge University Press, New York.

Deetz, J.
1965   *The Dynamics of Stylistic Change in Arikara Ceramics*. Illinois Studies in Anthropology 4. University of Illinois Press, Urbana.

1967   *Invitation to Archaeology.* Natural History Press, Garden City, New York.

Delcourt, P.A., and H.R. Delcourt

1987   *Long-term Forest Dynamics of the Temperate Zone: A Case Study of Late-Quaternary Forests In Eastern North America.* Springer-Verlag, New York.

Deller, D.B.

1989   Interpretation of Chert Type Variation in Paleoindian Industries, Southwestern Ontario. In *Eastern Paleoindian Lithic Resource Use*, edited by C.J. Ellis and J.C. Lothrop, pp. 191-220. Westview Press, Boulder.

Deller, D.B., and C.J. Ellis

1992   *Thedford II: A Paleo-Indian Site in the Ausable River Watershed of Southwestern Ontario.* Museum of Anthropology Memoir 24. University of Michigan, Ann Arbor.

Deuel, T.

1935   Basic Cultures of the Mississippi Valley. *American Anthropologist* 37:424-445.

Didier, M.E.

1967   A Distributional Study of the Turkey-Tail Point. *The Wisconsin Archeologist* 48:3-73.

Dincauze, D., and R. Hasenstab

1989   Explaining the Iroquois: Tribalization on a Prehistoric Periphery. In *Centre and Periphery: Comparative Studies in Archaeology*, edited by T.C. Champion, pp. 67-87. Unwin and Hyman, London.

Divale, W.

1984   *Matrilocal Residence in Pre-Literate Society.* University Microfilms Inc., Ann Arbor.

Dodd, C.F., D.R. Poulton, P.A. Lennox, D.G. Smith, and G. Warrick

1990   The Middle Ontario Iroquoian Stage. In *The Archaeology of Southern Ontario to A.D. 1650,* edited by C.J. Ellis and N. Ferris, pp. 321-360. Occasional Publication 5. London Chapter, Ontario Archaeological Society, London, Ontario.

Dole, G.

1968   Tribes as the Autonomous Unit. In *Essays in the Problem of Tribe*, edited by J. Helm, pp. 83-100. University of Washington Press, Seattle.

Donaldson, W.S., and S. Wortner

1995   The Hind Site and the Glacial Kame Burial Complex in Ontario. *Ontario Archaeology* 59:5-95.

Drennan, R.D.
1991   Prehispanic Chiefdom Trajectories in Mesoamerica, Central America, and Northern South America. In *Chiefdoms: Power, Economy, and Ideology*, edited by T. Earle, pp. 263-87. Cambridge University Press, New York.
1996   One for All and All for One: Accounting for Variability without Losing Sight of Regularities in the Development of Complex Society. In *Emergent Complexity*, edited by J.E. Arnold, pp. 25-34. Archaeological Series 9. International Monographs in Prehistory, Ann Arbor.

Drennan, R.D., and C.A. Uribe (editors)
1987   *Chiefdoms in the Americas*. University Press of America, Lanham, Maryland.

Drexler, C.W., W.R. Farrand, and J.D. Hughes
1983   Correlation of Glacial Lakes in the Superior Basin with Eastward Discharge Events from Lake Agassiz. In *Glacial Lake Agassiz*, edited by J.T. Teller and L. Clayton, pp. 309-329. Special Paper 26. Geological Association of Canada, St. John's.

Droessler, J.
1981   *Craniometry and Biological Distance*. Center for American Archaeology Research Series 1. Northwestern University, Evanston, Illinois.

Drooker, P.B.
1996   Madisonville Metal and Glass Artifacts: Implications for Western Fort Ancient Chronology and Interaction Networks. *Midcontinental Journal of Archaeology* 21:1-46.
1997   *The View from Madisonville: Protohistoric Western Fort Ancient Interaction Patterns*. Museum of Anthropology Memoir 31. University of Michigan, Ann Arbor.
1998   Zoom In to Madisonville. CD-ROM to accompany *The View from Madisonville: Protohistoric Western Fort Ancient Interaction Patterns*. Museum of Anthropology Memoir 31. University of Michigan, Ann Arbor.

Duke, P.G.
1988   Models of Cultural Process During the Avonlea Phase. In *Avonlea Yesterday and Today: Archaeology and Prehistory*, edited by L.B. Davis, pp. 265–271. Saskatchewan Archaeological Society, Saskatoon.

Dunnell, R.C.
1971a   Sabloff and Smith's The Importance of Both Analytic and Taxonomic Classification in the Type-Variety System. *American*

Antiquity 36:115-118.

1971b   *Systematics in Prehistory.* Free Press, New York.

Dustin, F.

1957   An Archaeological Reconnaissance of Isle Royale. *Michigan History* 41:1-34.

Earle, T.

1978   *Economic and Social Organization of a Complex Chiefdom: The Halelea District, Kaua'i, Hawaii.* Museum of Anthropology, Anthropology Papers 63. University of Michigan, Ann Arbor.

1987   Chiefdoms in Archaeological and Ethnohistorical Perspective. *Annual Review of Anthropology* 16:279-303.

1989   The Evolution of Chiefdoms. *Current Anthropology* 30:84-88.

1991   The Evolution of Chiefdoms. In *Chiefdoms: Power, Economy, and Ideology,* edited by T. Earle, pp. 1-15. Cambridge University Press, New York.

Earle, T. (editor)

1991   *Chiefdoms: Power, Economy, and Ideology.* Cambridge University Press, New York.

Easton, D.

1959   Political Anthropology. In *Biennial Review of Anthropology,* edited by B.J. Siegel, pp. 210-262. Stanford University Press, Stanford.

Edens, C.

1992   Dynamics of Trade in the Ancient Mesopotamian World System. *American Anthropologist* 94:118-139.

Edwards, T.W.D., R. Aravena, P. Fritz, and A.V. Morgan

1985   Interpreting Paleoclimate from ^{18}O and ^{2}H in Plant Cellulose: Comparison with Evidence from Fossil Insects and Relict Permafrost in Southwestern Ontario. *Canadian Journal of Earth Sciences* 22: 1720-1726.

Edwards, T.W.D., and W.M. Buhay

1994   Isotope Paleoclimatology in Southern Ontario. In *Great Lakes Archaeology and Paleoecology: Exploring Interdisciplinary Initiatives for the Nineties,* edited by R.I. MacDonald, pp. 197-208. Quaternary Sciences Institute Publication 10. University of Waterloo, Waterloo, Ontario.

Eliade, M.

1974   *Shamanism: Archaic Techniques of Ecstasy.* Princeton University Press, Princeton.

Ellen, R.

1982   *Environment, Subsistence and System: The Ecology of Small-*

Scale Social Formations. Cambridge University Press, New York.

Ellis, C.J.
1989   The Explanation of Northeastern Paleoindian Lithic Procurement Patterns. In *Eastern Paleoindian Lithic Resource Use*, edited by C.J. Ellis and J.C. Lothrop, pp. 139-164. Westview Press, Boulder.
1994   Miniature Early Paleo-Indian Stone Artifacts from the Parkhill, Ontario Site. *North American Archaeologist* 15:253-267.

Ellis, C.J., and D.B. Deller
1990   Paleo-Indians. In *The Archaeology of Southern Ontario to A.D. 1650*, edited by C.J. Ellis and N. Ferris, pp. 37-63. Occasional Publication 5. London Chapter, Ontario Archaeological Society, London, Ontario.
1997   Variability in the Archaeological Record of Northeastern Early Paleoindians: a View from Southern Ontario. *Archaeology of Eastern North America* 25: 1-30.

Ellis C.J., and N. Ferris (editors)
1990   *The Archaeology of Southern Ontario to A.D. 1650.* Occasional Publication 5. London Chapter, Ontario Archaeological Society, London, Ontario.

Ellis, C.J., I.T. Kenyon, and M.W. Spence
1990   The Archaic. In *The Archaeology of Southern Ontario to A.D. 1650*, edited by C. J. Ellis and N. Ferris, pp. 65-124. Occasional Publication 5. London Chapter, Ontario Archaeological Society, London, Ontario.

Ellis, C.J., and M.W. Spence
1997   Raw Material Variation and the Organization of Small Point Archaic Lithic Technologies in Southwestern Ontario. In *Preceramic Southern Ontario*, edited by P.J. Woodley and P.G. Ramsden, pp. 119-140. Occasional Papers in Northeastern Archaeology 9. Copetown Press, Dundas, Ontario.

Ellis, C.J., S. Wortner, and W.A. Fox
1991   Nettling: An Overview of an Early Archaic Kirk Corner-Notched Cluster Site in Southwestern Ontario. *Canadian Journal of Archaeology* 15:1-34.

Emberling, G.
1997   Ethnicity in Complex Societies: Archaeological Perspectives. *Journal of Archaeological Research* 5:295–344.

Emerson, J.N.
1954   *The Archaeology of the Ontario Iroquois.* Unpublished Ph.D.

dissertation, Department of Anthropology, University of Chicago.

1959   A Rejoinder Upon the MacNeish-Emerson Theory. *Pennsylvania Archaeologist* 29:98.

1961   Problems of Huron Origins. *Anthropologica* 3:181- 201.

1966   *The Payne Site: An Iroquoian Manifestation in Prince Edward County.* National Museum of Canada Bulletin 206:126-257. National Museum of Canada, Ottawa.

Emerson, J.N., and R.E. Popham

1952   Comments on the Huron and Lalonde Occupations of Ontario. *American Antiquity* 18:162-164.

Emerson, T.E.

1989   Water, Serpents, and the Underworld: An Exploration into Cahokian Symbolism. In *The Southeastern Ceremonial Complex: Artifacts and Analysis*, edited by P. Galloway, pp. 45-92. University of Nebraska Press, Lincoln.

1997a   *Cahokia and the Archaeology of Power.* University of Alabama Press, Tuscaloosa.

1997b   Reflections From the Countryside on Cahokian Hegemony. In *Cahokian: Domination and Ideology in the Mississippian World*, edited by T. R. Pauketat and T. E. Emerson, pp. 167-189. University of Nebraska Press, Lincoln.

Engelbrecht, W.

1978   Ceramic Patterning Between New York Iroquois Sites. In *The Spatial Organisation of Culture*, edited by I. Hodder, pp. 141- 152. Duckworth, London.

1980   Methods and Aims of Ceramic Description. In *Proceedings of the Iroquois Pottery Conference*, edited by C. F. Hayes, pp. 27-30. Research Records 13. Rochester Museum and Science Center, Rochester, New York.

1985   New York Iroquois Political Development. In *Cultures in Contact: The Impact of European Contacts on Native American Cultural Institutions A.D. 100 -1800*, edited by W. Fitzhugh, pp. 163-183. Smithsonian Institution Press, Washington.

1991   Erie. *The Bulletin: Journal of the New York State Archaeological Association* 102:2-12.

1995   The Case of the Disappearing Iroquoians: Early Contact Period Superpower Politics. *Northeast Anthropology* 50:35-59.

Eschman, D.F., and P.F. Karrow

1985   Huron Basin Glacial Lakes: A Review. In *Quaternary Evolution of the Great Lakes*, edited by P.F. Karrow and P.E. Calkin, pp.

79-93. Special Paper 30. Geological Association of Canada, St. John's.

Esuary, D., and T.R. Pauketat
1992   *The Lohman Site: An Early Mississippian Center in the American Bottom.* American Bottom Archaeology FAI 270 Site Report 25. University of Illinois, Urbana.

Farrand, W., and C. Drexler
1985   Late Wisconsinan and Holocene History of the Lake Superior Basin. In *Quaternary Evolution of the Great Lakes*, edited by P.F. Karrow and P. Calkin, pp. 17-32. Special Paper 30. Geological Association of Canada, St. John's.

Farrand, W.R., R. Zahner, and W.S. Benninghoff
1969   *Cary-Port Huron Interstade — Evidence from a Buried Bryophyte Bed, Cheboygan County, Michigan.* Special Paper 123: 249-262. Geological Society of America, Boulder.

Feest, C.F.
1986   Indians of Northeastern North America. In *Iconography of Religions, Section X: North America*, edited by T.H. vanBaaren, L.P. van den Bosch, H.G. Kippenberg, L. Leertouwer, F. Leemhuis, H. te Velde, H. Witte, and H. Buning, pp. 1-49. E.J. Brill, Leiden.

Feinman, G.
1995   The Emergence of Inequality. In *Foundations of Social Inequality*, edited by T.D. Price and G.M. Feinman, pp. 255-279. Plenum Press, New York.

Feinman, G., and J. Neitzel
1984   Too Many Types: An Overview of Prestate Societies in the Americas. In *Advances in Archaeological Method and Theory Volume 7*, edited by M.B. Schiffer, pp. 39-102. Academic Press, New York.

Fenton, M.M., S.R. Moran, J.T. Teller, and L. Clayton
1983   Quaternary Stratigraphy and History in the Southern Part of the Lake Agassiz Basin. In *Glacial Lake Agassiz*, edited by J.T. Teller and L. Clayton, pp. 49-74. Special Paper 26. Geological Association of Canada , St. John's.

Fenton, W.N.
1940   Problems Arising from the Historic Northeastern Position of the Iroquois. In *Essays in the Historical Anthropology of North America*, pp. 159-251. Smithsonian Miscellaneous Collections 100. Smithsonian Institution, Washington, D.C.
1941   *Tonawanda Longhouse Ceremonies: Ninety Years after Lewis*

Henry Morgan. Bureau of American Ethnology Bulletin 128:139-166. Smithsonian Institution, Washington, D.C.

Fenton, W., and G. Kurath
1951   *The Feast of the Dead, or Ghost Dance at Six Nations Reserve, Canada.* Bureau of American Ethnology Bulletin 149:139-165. Smithsonian Institution, Washington, D.C.
1953   *The Iroquois Eagle Dance, an Offshoot of the Calumet Dance.* Bureau of American Ethnology, Bulletin 156. Smithsonian Institution, Washington, DC.

Ferris, N.
1998   The Milton Heights Site: Artifact Analysis of a Seventeenth Century Neutral Ossuary Pit. *Kewa* 98(1-2):2-35.

Ferris, N., and M.W. Spence
1995   The Woodland Traditions in Southern Ontario. *Revista de Arqueologia Americana* 9:83-138.

Fiedcl, S.J.
1987   Algonquian Origins: A Problem in Linguistic-Archaeological Correlation. *Archaeology of Eastern North America* 15:1-13.
1990   Middle Woodland Algonquian Expansion: A Refined Model. *North American Archaeologist* 11:209-230.
1991   Correlating Archaeology and Linguistics: The Algonquian Case. *Man in the Northeast* 41:9-32.
1994   Some Inferences Concerning Proto-Algonquian Economy and Society. *Northeast Anthropology* 48:1-11.
1999   Older than We Thought: Implications of Corrected Dates for Paleoindians. *American Antiquity* 64:95-116.

Finlayson, W.D.
1998   *Iroquoian Peoples of the Land of Rocks and Water, A.D. 1000-1650: A Study in Settlement Archaeology Volume 1.* London Museum of Archaeology, London, Ontario.

Fischer, F.W.
1972   Schultz Site Ceramics. In *The Schultz Site at Green Point*, edited by J. Fitting, pp. 137-190. Museum of Anthropology Memoirs 4. University of Michigan, Ann Arbor.

Fisher, A.K.
1997   Origin of the Midwestern Taxonomic Method. *Midcontinental Journal of Archaeology* 22:117–122.

Fitting, J.E.
1965a   Middle Woodland Manifestations in Eastern Michigan. Paper presented at 30th Annual Meeting of Society for American Archaeology, Urbana.

1965b   *Late Woodland Cultures of Southeastern Michigan.* Museum of Anthropology Anthropological Papers 24. University of Michigan, Ann Arbor.

1970   *The Archaeology of Michigan.* Natural History Press, Garden City.

1975   *The Archaeology of Michigan: A Guide to the Prehistory of the Great Lakes Region.* Cranbrook Institute of Science, Bloomfield Hills, Michigan.

Fitzgerald, W.R.

1982a   A Refinement of Historic Neutral Chronologies: Evidence from Shaver Hill, Christianson, and Dwyer. *Ontario Archaeology* 38:31-47.

1982b   *Lest the Beaver Run Loose: The Early 17th Century Christianson Site and Trends in Historic Neutral Archaeology.* Archaeological Survey of Canada, Mercury Series Paper 111. National Museum of Man, Ottawa.

1986   Is the Warminster Site Champlain's Cahiague? *Ontario Archaeology* 45:3-8.

1990   *Chronology to Cultural Process: Lower Great Lakes Archaeology, 1500-1650.* Unpublished Ph.D. dissertation, Department of Anthropology, McGill University, Montreal.

1993   *The Cache (DaEh-1) Site: The 1993 Archaeological Investigations at Aire 4.* Ms. on file, Ministère de la Culture et des Communications du Québec, Québec.

Fitzgerald, W.R., L. Turgeon, R.H. Whitehead, and J.W. Bradley

1993   Late Sixteenth-Century Basque Banded Copper Kettles. *Historical Archaeology* 27:44-57.

Flannery, R.

1939   *An Analysis of Coastal Algonquian Culture.* Anthropological Series 7. Catholic University of America, Washington, D.C.

Flannery, K.V.

1972   The Cultural Evolution of Civilizations. *Annual Review of Ecology and Systematics* 3:399-426.

1982   The Golden Marshalltown: A Parable for the Archeology of the 1980s. *American Anthropologist* 84:265–278.

Fogel, I.L.

1963   The Dispersal of Copper Artifacts in the Late Archaic Period of Prehistoric North America. *The Wisconsin Archeologist* 44:129-180.

Ford, J.A.
1954   The Type Concept Revisited. *American Anthropologist* 56:42-53.

Ford, J.A., and G.R. Willey
1941   An Interpretation of the Prehistory of the Eastern United States. *American Anthropologist* 43:325-363.

Fowler, M.L.
1991   Mound 72 and Early Mississippian at Cahokian. In *New Perspectives on Cahokian*, edited by J. Stoltman, pp. 1-28. Monographs in World Prehistory 2. Prehistory Press, Madison.

Fox, R.G.
1977   *Urban Anthropology*. Prentice Hall, Englewood Cliffs.

Fox, W.A.
1985   The Couture Site (AdHl-1): Salvaging Kent County Prehistory. *Kewa* 85(8):11-19.

1986a   The Elliott Villages (AfHc-2) — An Introduction. *Kewa* 86(1):11-17.

1986b   The Breaks on the Elliott Site. *Kewa* 86(2):28-29.

1988   The Elliott Village: Pit of the Dead. *Kewa* 88(4):2-9.

1990a   The Middle Woodland to Late Woodland Transition. In *The Archaeology of Southern Ontario to A.D. 1650*, edited by C. J. Ellis and N. Ferris, pp. 171-188. Occasional Publication 5. London Chapter, Ontario Archaeological Society, London, Ontario.

1990b   The Odawa. In *The Archaeology of Southern Ontario to A.D. 1650*, edited by C. J. Ellis and N. Ferris, pp. 457-474. Occasional Publication 5. London Chapter, Ontario Archaeological Society, London, Ontario.

1997   Constructing Archaeological Expectations from Meskwaki Ritual. *The Michigan Archeologist* 43(1):3-24.

Fox, W.A,. and J.E. Molto
1994a   A Special Child: The Monarch Knoll Burial *Midcontinental Journal of Archaeology* 19: 99-136.

1994b   The Shaman of Long Point. *Ontario Archaeology* 57:23-44.

Fox, W.S., and W. Jury
1949   *St. Ignace, Canadian Altar of Martyrdom*. McClelland and Stewart, Toronto.

Freilich, M. (editor)
1972   *The Meaning of Culture: A Reader in Cultural Anthropology*. Xerox College Publishing, Lexington, Massachusetts.

Fried, M.
1967   *The Evolution of Political Society: An Essay in Political Economy.* Random House, New York.

Frison, G.C.
1978   *Prehistoric Hunters of the High Plains.* Academic Press, New York.

Funk, R.E.
1983   The Northeastern United States. In *Ancient North Americans,* edited by J. D. Jennings, pp. 303-371. W. H. Freeman, New York.
1997   An Introduction to the History of Prehistoric Archaeology in New York State. *The Bulletin: Journal of the New York State Archaeological Association* 113:4-59.

Furst, P.T.
1974   Roots and Continuities; Stones, Bones and Skin: Ritual and Shamanic Art. *artscanada* 30:33-60.

Gadacz, R.R.
1978   Towards a Diffusion Paradigm. In *Diffusion and Migration: Their Roles in Cultural Development,* edited by P.G. Duke, J. Ebert, G. Langemann, and A.P. Buchner, pp.14-21. University of Calgary Archaeological Association, Calgary, Alberta.

Gagné, M.
1993   Une Incursion dans l'Univers des Iroquoiens du Saint-Laurent au Sud du Lac Saint-François, *À Fleur de Siècles* 7, pp. 28-36.

Galloway, P.
1997   Where Have all the Menstrual Huts Gone? The Invisibility of Menstrual Seclusion in the Late Prehistoric Southeast. In *Women in Prehistory: North America and Mesoamerica,* edited by C. Classen and R. Joyce, pp.47-62. University of Pennsylvania Press, Philadelphia.

Gartner, W.G.
1993   The Geoarchaeology of Sediment Renewal Ceremonies at the Gottschall Rockshelter, Wisconsin. Unpublished M.A. thesis, Department of Geography, University of Wisconsin, Madison.
1996   Archaeoastronomy as Sacred Geography. In "The Ancient Skies and Sky Watchers of Cahokia: Woodhenges, Eclipses, and Cahokian Cosmology", edited by M.L.Fowler, pp. 128-150. *The Wisconsin Archeologist 77(3/4).*

Gates St-Pierre, C.
1999   La Production Céramique du Sylvicole Moyen Tardif au Québec Méridional: Indices d'une Stase Technologiqe et d'une Tradition

Régionale. *Archéologiques* 11-12: 175-186

Geary, J.
1997   Speaking in Tongues. *Time*, July 7, 1997: 36-42.

Gendron, F.
1868   *Quelques Particularitez du Pays des Hurons en la Nouvelle France, Remarquées par le Sieur Gendron, Docteur en Medecine qui a Demeuré dans ce Pays-la Fort Longtemps*. Shea, Albany.

Gerin, L.
1990   The Hurons of Lorette. *British Association for the Advancement of Science* 70:549-568.

Gero, J.M., and M.W. Conkey (editors.)
1991   *Engendering Archaeology: Women and Prehistory*. Blackwell, Oxford.

Gibbon, G.E.
1972   Cultural Dynamics and the Development of the Oneota Life-Way. *American Antiquity* 37:166-85.
1998   Old Copper in Minnesota: A Review. *Plains Anthropologist* 43:27-50.

Giesen, M.J.
1992   *Late Prehistoric Populations in the Ohio Area: Biological Affinities and Stress Indicators*. Unpublished Ph.D. dissertation, Department of Anthropology, Ohio State University, Columbus.

Gifford, J.C.
1960   The Type-Variety Method of Ceramic Classification as an Indicator of Cultural Phenomena. *American Antiquity* 25:341-347.

Giguère, G.É.
1973   *Oeuvres de Champlain*. 3 volumes. Éditions du Jour, Montréal.

Goddard, I.
1978a   Mascouten. In *Handbook of North American Indians Volume 15 (Northeast)*, edited by B.G. Trigger, pp. 668-672. Smithsonian Institution, Washington D.C.
1978b   Eastern Algonquian Languages. In *Handbook of North American Indians Volume 15 (Northeast)*, edited by B.G. Trigger, pp. 70-77. Smithsonian Institution, Washington D.C.

Goldenweiser, A.A.
1912   On Iroquois Work. *Geological Survey of Canada Annual Report*, pp. 386-387. Geological Survey of Canada, Ottawa.
1913   On Iroquois Work. *Geological Survey of Canada Annual Report*, pp.464-475. Geological Survey of Canada, Ottawa.
1914   On Iroquois Work. *Geological Survey of Canada Annual Report*,

pp.365-372. Geological Survey of Canada, Ottawa.

Goldstein, L.
1998   Editor's Corner. *American Antiquity* 63:5-6.

Goodman, A. H.
1993   On the Interpretation of Health from Skeletal Remains. *Current Anthropology* 34:281-288.

Goodman, A.H., J. Lallo, G.J. Armelagos, and J. C. Rose
1984   Health Changes at Dickson Mounds, Illinois (A.D. 950-1300). In *Paleopathology at the Origins of Agriculture*, edited by M. N. Cohen and G. J Armelagos, pp. 271-305. Academic Press, Orlando.

Gould, S.J.
1983   *Hens' Teeth and Horses' Toes: Further Reflections on Natural History*. W.W. Norton, New York.

Graham, R.W., E.L. Lundelius, Jr., and FAUNMAP Working Group
1994   *FAUNMAP: A Database Documenting Late Quaternary Distributions of Mammal Species in the United States*. Illinois State Museum, Scientific Papers, 25(1,2).

Granger, J.
1978   *Meadowood Phase Settlement Pattern in the Niagara Frontier Region of Western New York*. Museum of Anthropology, Anthropological Papers 65. University of Michigan, Ann Arbor.
1981   The Steward Site Cache and a Study of the Meadowood Phase "Cache Blade" in the Northeast. *Archaeology of Eastern North America* 9:63-103.

Grantham, L.
1993   The Illini Village of the Marquette and Jolliet Voyage of 1673. *Missouri Archaeologist* 54:1-20.

Graves, M.
1991   Pottery Production and Distribution Among the Kalinga: A Study of Household and Regional Organization and Differentiation. In *Ceramic Ethnoarchaeology*, edited by W. Longacre, pp.112-143. University of Arizona Press, Tucson.

Greber, N.
1983   Recent Excavations at the Edwin Harness Mound, Liberty Works, Ross County, Ohio. *Midcontinental Journal of Archaeology,* Special Paper 5.

Green, W., and D. Nolan
1997   Late Woodland Peoples in West-Central Illinois. Paper presented at the Urbana Late Woodland Conference, University of Illinois, Urbana.

Green, W., J.B. Stoltman, and A.B. Kehoe (editors)
1986   Introduction to Wisconsin Archaeology: Background for Cultural Resource Planning. *The Wisconsin Archeologist* 67(3-4):163-395.

Greenberg, J.H.
1987   *Language in the Americas*. Stanford University Press, Stanford.

Greenman, E.F.
1937   *The Younge Site: An Archaeological Record from Michigan*. Occasional Contributions from the Museum of Anthropology 6. University of Michigan, Ann Arbor.
1939   *The Wolf and Furton Sites, Macomb County, Michigan*. Occasional Contributions from the Museum of Anthropology 8. University of Michigan, Ann Arbor.

Grieder, T.
1982   *Origins of Pre-Columbian Art*. University of Texas Press, Austin.

Griffin, J.B.
1943   *The Fort Ancient Aspect: Its Cultural and Chronological Position in Mississippi Valley Archaeology*. University of Michigan, Ann Arbor.
1945   The Pedestal Vessels of the Madisonville Site. *American Antiquity* 10:386-387.
1964   The Northeast Woodlands Area. In *Prehistoric Man in the New World*, edited by J.D. Jennings and E. Norbeck, pp. 223–258. University of Chicago Press, Chicago.
1983   The Midlands. In *Ancient North Americans*, edited by J.D. Jennings, pp. 243-301. W.H. Freeman, New York.

Griffin, J.B. (editor)
1961   *Lake Superior Copper and the Indians: Miscellaneous Studies of Great Lakes Prehistory*. Anthropological Papers 17. Museum of Anthropology, University of Michigan, Ann Arbor.

Grove, J.M.
1988   *The Little Ice Age*. Methuen, New York.

Guimond, J.
1994   Des Grains de Maïs d'une Valeur Inestimable. *Mémoires Vives* 6-7:49.

Haas, J.
1990   Warfare and the Evolution of Tribal Polities in the Prehistoric Southwest. In *The Anthropology of War*, edited by J. Haas, pp. 171-189. Cambridge University Press, New York.

Haas, M.R.
1966   Historical Linguistics and the Genetic Relationship of Languages. In *Current Trends in Linguistics Volume 3*, edited by T.A. Sebeok, pp. 113-153. Mouton, The Hague.

Hale, H.
1895   An Iroquois Condoling Council. *Proceedings and Transactions of the Royal Society of Canada* 1:45-65.

Hall, R.L.
1977   An Anthropocentric Perspective for Eastern United States Prehistory. *American Antiquity* 42:449-518.
1979   In Search of the Ideology of the Adena-Hopewell Climax. In *Hopewell Archaeology: The Chillicothe Conference*, edited by D. Brose and N. Greber, pp. 258-265. Kent State University Press, Kent.
1983   A Pan-Continental Perspective on Red Ochre and Glacial Kame Ceremonialism. In *Lulu Linear Punctated: Essays in Honor of George Irving Quimby*, edited by R.C. Dunnell and D.K. Grayson, pp. 75-103. Museum of Anthropology Anthropological Papers 72. University of Michigan, Ann Arbor.
1993   Red Banks, Oneota, and Winnebago: Views from a Distant Rock. *The Wisconsin Archaeologist* 74:10-79.

Halsey, J.R.
1976   *The Bussinger Site. A Multicomponent Site in the Saginaw Valley of Michigan, with a Review of Early Late Woodland Mortuary Complexes in the Northeastern Woodlands*. Unpublished Ph.D. dissertation, Department of Anthropology, University of North Carolina, Chapel Hill, North Carolina.

Hammond, J.H.
1904   The Ojibwas of Lakes Huron and Simcoe. *Annual Archaeological Report 1904, Being Part of Appendix to the Report of the Minister of Education, Ontario*, pp. 71-73. Warwick Bros. and Rutter, Toronto.

Hamell, G.R.
1983   Trading in Metaphors: The Magic of Beads. In *Proceedings of the 1982 Glass Trade Bead Conference*, edited by C.F. Hayes III, pp. 5-28. Research Records 16. Rochester Museum and Science Center, Rochester.
1987   Mythical Realities and European Contact in the Northeast During the Sixteenth and Seventeenth Centuries. *Man in the Northeast* 33:63-87.

Hansel, A.K., D.M. Mickelson, A.F. Schneider, and C.E. Larsen
1985   Late Wisconsin and Holocene History of the Lake Michigan Basin. In *Quaternary Evolution of the Great Lakes*, edited by P.F. Karrow and P.E. Calkin, pp. 39-53. Special Paper 30. Geological Association of Canada, St. John's.

Harris, M.
1968   *The Rise of Anthropological Theory.* Harper & Row, Publishers, New York.

Harris, R.C., and G.J. Matthews
1987   *Historical Atlas of Canada, Volume I (From the Beginning to 1800).* University of Toronto Press, Toronto.

Hawkes, C.F.
1954   Archeological Theory and Method: Some Suggestions from the Old World. *American Anthropologist* 56:155-68.

Hayden, B.
1981   Research and Development in the Stone Age: Technological Transitions Among Hunter-Gatherers. *Current Anthropology* 22:519-548.
1995   Pathways to Power: Principles for Creating Socio-economic Inequalities. In *Foundations of Social Inequality*, edited by T.D. Price and G.M. Feinman, pp. 15-86. Plenum Press, New York.
1996   Thresholds of Power in Emergent Complex Societies. In *Emergent Complexity*, edited by J.E. Arnold, pp. 50-58. Archaeological Series 9. International Monographs in Prehistory, Ann Arbor.

Headland, T.N., and L.A. Reid
1989   Hunter-Gatherers and Their Neighbors from Prehistory to the Present. *Current Anthropology* 30:43-66.

Heathcote, G.M.
1978   Problems in Interpreting Migrations Through Osteometry. In *Diffusion and Migration: Their Roles in Cultural Development*, edited by P.G. Duke, J. Ebert, G.Langemann, and A.P. Buchner, pp.45-54. University of Calgary Archaeological Association, Calgary, Alberta.

Hedican, E.J., and J. McGlade
1993   A Taxometric Analysis of Old Copper Projectile Points. *Man in the Northeast* 45:21-38.

Heidenreich, C.E.
1978   Huron. In *Handbook of North American Indians Volume 15 (Northeast)*, edited by B.G. Trigger, pp.368-388. Smithsonian Institution, Washington DC.

1990   History of the St. Lawrence-Great Lakes Area to A.D. 1650. In *The Archaeology of Southern Ontario to A.D. 1650*, edited by C.J. Ellis and N. Ferris, pp. 475-492. Occasional Publication 5. London Chapter, Ontario Archaeological Society, London, Ontario.

Helmer, J.W.

1994   Resurrecting the Spirit(s) of Taylor's Carlsberg Culture: Cultural Traditions and Cultural Horizons in Eastern Arctic Prehistory. In *Threads of Arctic Prehistory: Papers in Honour of William E. Taylor Jr.*, edited by D. Morrison and J.-L. Pilon, pp. 15-34. Archaeological Survey of Canada, Mercury Series Paper 149. Canadian Museum of Civilization, Hull.

Hemmings, E.T.

1977   *Neale's Landing: An Archaeological Study of a Fort Ancient Settlement on Blennerhassett Island, West Virginia.* Ms. on file, West Virginia Geological and Economic Survey, Morgantown, West Virginia.

Henderson, A.G., C.E. Jobe, and C.A. Turnbow

1986   *Indian Occupation and Use in Northern and Eastern Kentucky during the Contact Period (1540-1795): An Initial Investigation.* Ms. on file, Kentucky Heritage Council, Frankfort.

Herold, E.B., P.J. O'Brien, and D.J. Wenner Jr.

1990   Hoxie Farm and Huber: Two Upper Mississippian Archaeological Sites in Cook County, Illinois. In *At the Edge of Prehistory: Huber Phase Archaeology in the Chicago Area*, edited by J.A. Brown and P.J. O'Brien, pp. 1-119. Center for American Archaeology, Kampsville, Illinois.

Hewitt, J.

1907   Huron. *Bureau of American Ethnology Bulletin* 30(1): 584-591

1932   Status of Women in Iroquois Polity Before 1784. *Board of Regents Annual Report*, pp. 475-488. Smithsonian Institution, Washington DC.

Hill, R.

1997   Personal Reflections on the Meaning of the Longhouse. Paper presented at the Longhouse Conference, Rochester Museum and Science Center, Rochester.

Hockett, C.F.

1964   The Proto-Central Algonquian Kinship System. In *Explorations in Cultural Anthropology: Essays in Honor of George Peter Murdock*, edited by W.H. Goodenough, pp. 239-257. Harper and Row, New York.

Hodder, I.
1979   Economic and Social Stress and Material Culture Patterning. *American Antiquity* 44:446-454.
1982   *Symbols in Action.* Cambridge University Press, New York.
1990   Style as Historical Quality. In *The Uses of Style in Archaeology*, edited by M. Conkey and C. Hastorf, pp. 44-52. Cambridge University Press, New York.

Hoffman, C.M.
1985   Projectile Point Maintenance and Typology: Assessment with Factor Analysis and Canonical Correlation. In *For Concordance in Archaeological Analysis,* edited by C. Carr, pp. 566-612. Westport Publishers, Kansas City.

Hollinger, R.E.
1995   Residence Patterns and Oneota Cultural Dynamics. In *Oneota Archaeology: Past, Present, and Future*, edited by W. Green. Office of the State Archaeologist Report 20. University of Iowa, Iowa City.

Holmes, W.H.
1901   Aboriginal Copper Mines of Isle Royale, Lake Superior. *American Anthropologist* 3:684-696.

Hooton, E.A., and C.C. Willoughby
1920   *Indian Village Site and Cemetery near Madisonville, Ohio.* Papers of the Peabody Museum of American Archaeology and Ethnology, 8(1). Peabody Museum, Harvard University, Cambridge.

Horvath, S.
1973   A Computerized Study of Princess Point Complex Ceramics: Some Implications of Late Prehistoric Social Organization in Ontario. *Toledo Area Aboriginal Research Club Bulletin* 2(2):5-12.

Howie-Langs, L.
1998   *The Praying Mantis Site: A Study of Ceramic Variability and Cultural Behaviour at an Early Iroquoian Village.* Unpublished M.A. thesis, Department of Anthropology, University of Western Ontario, London, Ontario.

Hoxie, R.D.
1980   *A Formal Analysis of the Prehistoric Ceramics from Draper Park (20-Sc-40): A Wayne Tradition Occupation on the St. Clair River in Southeastern Michigan.* Unpublished M.A. thesis, Department of Anthropology, Western Michigan University, Kalamazoo, Michigan.

Hruska, R.
1967   The Riverside Site: A Late Archaic Manifestation in Michigan. *The Wisconsin Archeologist* 48:145-260.

Hulin, L.C.
1989   The Diffusion of Religious Symbols Within Complex Societies. In *The Meanings of Things: Material Culture and Symbolic Expression*, edited by I. Hodder, pp. 90-96. Unwin Hyman, London.

Hunn, E.
1994   Place Names, Population Density and the Magic Number 500. *Current Anthropology* 35:81-85.

Hurley, W.M.
1975   *An Analysis of Effigy Mound Complexes in Wisconsin.* Anthropological Papers 59. Museum of Anthropology, University of Michigan, Ann Arbor.

Irwin-Williams, C., H.T. Irwin, G.A. Agogino, and C.V. Haynes, Jr.
1973   Hell Gap: Paleoindian Occupation on the High Plains. *Plains Anthropologist* 18:40-53.

Jackson, D.K.
1990   The Willoughby Site (11-MS-610). In *Selected Early Mississippian Household Sites in the American Bottom*, edited by D.K. Jackson and N.H. Hanenberger, pp. 17-90. American Bottom Archaeology FAI 270 Site Reports 22. University of Illinois, Urbana.

Jackson, L.J.
1978   *Late Wisconsin Environments and Paleo-Indian Occupation in the Northeastern United States and Southern Ontario.* Unpublished M.A. thesis, Department of Anthropology, Trent University, Peterborough, Ontario.

Jamieson, J.B.
1990   The Archaeology of the St. Lawrence Iroquoians. In *The Archaeology of Southern Ontario to A.D. 1650,* edited by C.J. Ellis and N. Ferris, pp. 385-404. Occasional Publication 5. London Chapter, Ontario Archaeological Society, London, Ontario.

Jamieson, S.M.
1981   Economics and Ontario Iroquoian Social Organization. *Canadian Journal of Archaeology* 5:19-30.
1984   *Neutral Iroquois Lithics: Technological Process and its Implications.* Unpublished Ph.D. dissertation, Washington State University. University Microfilms International, Ann Arbor.

1989   Precepts and Percepts of Northern Iroquois Households and Communities: The Changing Past. In *Households and Communities: Proceedings of the 21st Annual Chacmool Conference*, edited by S. MacEachern, D.J.W. Archer, and R. Garvin, pp. 307-314. Archaeological Association of the University of Calgary, Calgary.

1991   A Pickering Conquest? *Kewa* 91(5):2-18.

1992   Regional Interaction and Ontario Iroquois Evolution. *Canadian Journal of Archaeology* 16:70-88.

1996   The Documented Past: An Historic Neutral Iroquois Chiefdom? In *Debating Complexity: Proceedings of the 25th Annual Chacmool Conference*, D.A. Meyer, P.C. Dawson and D.T. Hanna. University of Calgary Archaeological Association, Calgary.

Jenkins, N.J., and R.A. Krause

1986   *The Tombigbee Watershed in Southeastern Prehistory.* University of Alabama Press, University, Alabama.

Jennings, F.

1984   *The Ambiguous Iroquois Empire.* W.W. Norton, New York.

Jochim, M.A.

1981   *Strategies for Survival: Cultural Behavior in an Ecological Context.* Academic Press, New York.

1991   Archeology as Long-Term Ethnography. *American Anthropologist* 93: 308-321.

1994   An Ecological Agenda for Archaeological Research. In *Great Lakes Archaeology and Paleoecology: Exploring Interdisciplinary Initiatives for the Nineties*, edited by R.I. MacDonald, pp. 5-23. Quaternary Sciences Institute Publication 10. University of Waterloo, Waterloo, Ontario.

Johnson, A.E.

1973   Archaeological Investigations at the Budenbender Site, Tuttle Creek Reservoir, North-Central Kansas, 1957. *Plains Anthropologist* 18:271–299.

Johnson, G.A.

1982   Organizational Structure and Scalar Stress. In *Theory and Explanation in Archaeology: The Southampton Conference*, edited by C. Renfrew, M.J. Rowlands, and B.A. Seagraves, pp 389-421. Academic Press, New York.

Johnson, L., Jr.

1986   A Plague of Phases. *Bulletin of the Texas Archeological Society* 57:1–26.

Johnson, W., and D.S. Speedy
1992   Cultural Complexity and Change in the Middle and Late Woodland Periods in the Upper James Estuary, Prince George County, Virginia. *Journal of Middle Atlantic Archaeology* 8:91-106.
Johnson, W.C.
1994   The Protohistoric Monongahela and the Case for an Iroquois Connection. In *Societies in Eclipse: Eastern North America at the Dawn of History*, edited by D.S. Brose. Smithsonian Institution, Washington, D.C.
Jones, A.E.
1910   Huron Indians. *Catholic Encyclopedia* 7:545-583.
Jones, S.
1997   *The Archaeology of Ethnicity: Constructing Identities in the Past and Present*. Routledge, London.
Justice, N.D.
1987   *Stone Age Spear and Arrow Points of the Midcontinental and Eastern United States.* Indiana University Press, Bloomington.
Jury, W. and E.M. Jury
1954   *Sainte-Marie Among the Hurons*. Oxford University Press, Toronto.
Kapches, M.
1990   The Spatial Dynamics of Ontario Iroquoian Longhouses. *American Antiquity* 55:49-67.
1994   Hydrogeographics and Transportation Network Modelling. Paper presented at the 1994 Chacmool Conference, University of Calgary Archaeological Association, Calgary.
1995   Chaos Theory and Social Movements: A Theoretical View of the Formation of the Northern Iroquoian Longhouse Cultural Pattern. In *Origins of the People of the Longhouse: Proceedings of the 21st Annual Symposium of the Ontario Archaeological Society*, edited by A. Bekerman and G. Warrick, pp.86-96. Ontario Archaeological Society, Toronto.
Karrow, P.F.
1989   Quaternary Geology of the Great Lakes Subregion. In *Quaternary Geology of Canada and Greenland*, edited by R.J. Fulton, pp. 326-350. Geological Survey of Canada, Ottawa.
1994   Geomorphology and Glacial History: The Archaeological Implications of Quaternary Geology. In *Great Lakes Archaeology and Paleoecology: Exploring Interdisciplinary Initiatives for the Nineties*, edited by R.I. MacDonald, pp. 219-

235. Quaternary Sciences Institute Publication 10. University of Waterloo, Waterloo, Ontario.

Katzenberg, M.A.
1992   Changing Diet and Health in Pre- and Protohistoric Ontario. In *Health and Lifestyle Change*, edited by R. Huss-Ashmore, J. Schall, and M. Hediger, pp. 23-31. MASCA Research Papers in Science and Archaeology 9. Museum of Archaeology and Anthropology, University of Pennsylvania, Philadelphia.

Katzenberg, M.A., H.P. Schwarcz, M. Knyf, and F.J. Melbye
1995   Stable Isotope Evidence for Maize Horticulture and Paleodiet in Southern Ontario, Canada. *American Antiquity* 60:335-350.

Keeley, L.H.
1996   *War Before Civilization*. Oxford University Press, New York.

Keener, C.
1995   Warfare as the Evolutionary Mechanism for Iroquoian Tribalization: A Selectionist View. In *Origins of the People of the Longhouse: Proceedings of the 21st Annual Symposium of the Ontario Archaeological Society*, edited by A. Bekerman and G. Warrick, pp.97-105. Ontario Archaeological Society, Toronto.

Keenlyside, D.
1977   *Late Prehistory of Point Pelee, Ontario and Environs*. Manuscript 227. Parks Canada, National Sites Branch, Ottawa.
1978   *Late Prehistory of Point Pelee, Ontario and Environs*. Archaeological Survey of Canada, Mercury Series Paper 80. National Museum of Man, Ottawa.

Kehoe, A.B.
1990   The Monumental Midwestern Taxonomic Method. In *The Woodland Tradition in the Western Great Lakes: Papers Presented to Elden Johnson*, edited by G.E. Gibbon, pp. 31–36. Publications in Anthropology 4. University of Minnesota, Minneapolis.

Kelly, J.E.
1991   The Evidence for Prehistoric Exchange and Its Implications for the Development of Cahokia. In *New Perspectives on Cahokia: Views from the Periphery*, edited by J.B. Stoltman, pp. 65-92. Monographs in World Archaeology 2. Prehistory Press, Madison, Wisconsin.

Kelly, K.M.
1994   On the Magic Number 500: An Expostulation. *Current Anthropology* 35:435-438.

Kennedy, C.C.
1966   Preliminary Report on the Morrison's Island-6 Site. *National Museum of Canada Bulletin* 206:100-125.
Kent, B.C.
1984   *Susquehanna's Indians*. Anthropological Series 6. Pennsylvania Historical and Museum Commission, Harrisburg.
Kenyon, I.T.
1980   The Satchell Complex in Ontario: A Perspective from the Ausable Valley. *Ontario Archaeology* 34:17-43.
1983   Late Archaic Stemmed Points from the Adder Orchard Site. *Kewa* 83(2):7-14.
1984   Sagard's Rassade Rouge of 1624. *Kewa* 84(4):2-14.
1989   Terminal Archaic Projectile Points in Southwestern Ontario: An Exploratory Study. *Kewa* 89(1):2-21.
Kenyon, W.A.
1981   *The Grimsby Site: A Historic Neutral Cemetery*. Royal Ontario Museum, Toronto.
Kershaw, A.C.
1978   Diffusion and Migration Studies in Geography. In *Diffusion and Migration: Their Roles in Cultural Development*, edited by P.G. Duke, J. Ebert, G. Langemann, and A.P. Buchner, pp. 6-13. University of Calgary Archaeological Association, Calgary.
Kertzer, D.I.
1988   *Ritual, Politics, and Power*. Yale University Press, New Haven.
Kidd, K.E.
1949   *The Excavation of Ste. Marie I*. University of Toronto Press, Toronto.
Killan, G.
1983   *David Boyle: From Artisan to Archaeologist*. University of Toronto Press, Toronto.
Kimball, L.R.
1992   Early Archaic Settlement and Technology: Lessons from Tellico. In *Paleoindian and Early Archaic Period Research in the Lower Southeast: A South Carolina Perspective*, edited by D.G. Anderson, K.E. Sassaman, and C. Judge, pp. 143-180. Council of South Carolina Professional Archaeologists.
Kinsey, A.C., W.B. Pomeroy, and C.E. Martin
1948   *Sexual Behavior in the Human Male*. W.B. Saunders, Philadelphia.
Knowles, N.
1940   The Torture of Captives by the Indians of Eastern North

America. *Proceedings of the American Philosophical Society* 82:151-225.

Konigsberg, L.
1988   Migration Models of Prehistoric Postmarital Residence. *American Journal of Physical Anthropology* 77:471-482.

Konigsberg, L., and J.E. Buikstra
1995   Regional Approaches to the Investigation of Past Human Biocultural Structure. In *Regional Approaches to Mortuary Analysis*, edited by L. Beck, pp.191-219. Plenum Press, New York.

Konrad, V.
1981   An Iroquois Frontier: The North Shore of Lake Ontario During the Late Seventeenth Century. *Journal of Historical Geography* 7:129-144.

Krakker, J.A.
1983   *Changing Sociocultural Systems During the Late Prehistoric Period in Southeast Michigan.* Unpublished Ph.D. dissertation, Department of Anthropology, University of Michigan, Ann Arbor.

Krause, R.A.
1969   Correlation of Phases in Central Plains Prehistory. In *Two House Sites in the Central Plains: An Experiment in Archaeology*, edited by W.R. Wood, pp. 82–96. Plains Anthropologist Memoir 6. Plains Anthropological Society, Lincoln, Nebraska.

1977   Taxonomic Practice and Middle Missouri Prehistory: A Perspective on Donald J. Lehmer's Contributions. In *Trends in Middle Missouri Prehistory: A Festschrift Honoring the Contributions of Donald J. Lehmer*, edited by W.R. Wood, pp. 5–13. Plains Anthropologist Memoir 13. Plains Anthropological Society, Lincoln, Nebraska.

1989   Toward a History of Great Plains Systematics. *Plains Anthropologist* 34:281–292.

1998   A History of Great Plains Prehistory. In *Archaeology on the Great Plains*, edited by W.R. Wood, pp. 48–86. University Press of Kansas, Lawrence.

Kroeber, A.L., and C. Kluckhohn
1952   *Culture: A Critical Review of Concepts and Definitions.* Papers of the Peabody Museum of American Archaeology and Ethnology 47 (1). Harvard University, Cambridge.

Kuhn, T.
1970   *The Structure of Scientific Revolutions*. University of Chicago Press. Chicago.
Lackowicz, R.
1996   *An Attribute and Spatial Analysis of Several Ground Stone Artifact Types from Southern Ontario, in Relation to Their Patterning and Context in the Northeast*. Unpublished M.A. thesis, Department of Anthropology, Trent University, Peterborough, Ontario.
Lafitau, J.F.
1724   *Moeurs des Sauvages Amériquains, Comparées aux Moeurs des Premiers Temps*. Saugrain l'Aine, Paris.
Lamb, H.H.
1982   Reconstruction of the Course of Postglacial Climate over the World. In *Climatic Change In Later Prehistory*, edited by A. Harding, pp. 11-32. University of Edinburgh Press, Edinburgh.
Lane, R., and A. Sublett
1972   Osteology of Social Organization: Residence Pattern. *American Antiquity* 37:186-201.
Langdon, S. P.
1995   Biological Relationships Among the Iroquois. *Human Biology* 67:355-374.
Larsen, C.E.
1985   Lake Level, Uplift, and Outlet Incision, the Nipissing and Algoma Great Lakes. In *Quaternary Evolution of the Great Lakes*, edited by P.F. Karrow and P.E. Calkin, pp. 63-77. Special Paper 30. Geological Association of Canada, St. John's.
1987   Geological History of Glacial Lake Algonquin and the Upper Great Lakes. *U.S. Geological Survey Bulletin* 1801. U.S. Government Printing Office, Washington, D.C.
Larsen, C.S.
1995   Biological Changes in Human Populations with Agriculture. *Annual Review of Anthropology* 24:185-213.
1997   *Bioarchaeology*. Cambridge University Press, New York.
Lasker, G.W., and C.G.N. Mascie-Taylor
1988   The Framework of Migration Studies. In *Biological Aspects of Human Migration*, edited by C.G.N. Mascie-Taylor and G.W. Lasker, pp.1-13. Cambridge University Press, New York.
Latta, M.A.
1985   Identification of 17th Century French Missions in Eastern Huronia. *Canadian Journal of Archaeology* 9:147-171.

1987   Iroquoian Stemware. *American Antiquity* 52:717-724.
1988   The Search for St Ignace II. *Ontario Archaeology* 48:3-16.
1990   The Stem of the Matter: Reply to Ramsden and Fitzgerald. *American Antiquity* 55:162-165.
1991   The Captive Bride Syndrome: Iroquoian Behaviour or Archaeological Myth? In *The Archaeology of Gender: Proceedings of the 22nd Annual Chacmool Conference*, edited by D. Walde and N.D. Willows, pp. 375-382. University of Calgary Archaeological Association, Calgary.

Latta, M.A., H. Martelle-Hayter, and P. Reed
1998   Women in Early Ontario Archaeology: Reclaiming Voices. In *Bringing Back the Past: Historical Perspectives on Canadian Archaeology*, edited by P.J. Smith and D. Mitchell, pp. 25-38. Archaeological Survey of Canada, Mercury Series Paper 158. Canadian Museum of Civilization, Hull.

Legge, A.J., and P.A. Rowley-Conwy
1988   *Starr Carr Revisite*d. Centre for Extra-Mural Studies. University of London, London.

Lehmer, D.J.
1971   *Introduction to Middle Missouri Archeology*. Anthropological Papers 1. National Park Service, Washington, D.C.

Lehmer, D.J., and W.W. Caldwell
1966   Horizon and Tradition in the Northern Plains. *American Antiquity* 31:511–516.

Lenius, B.J., and D.M. Olinyk
1990   The Rainy River Composite: Revisions to Late Woodland Taxonomy. In *The Woodland Tradition in the Western Great Lakes: Papers Presented to Elden Johnson*, edited by G.E. Gibbon, pp. 77–112. Publications in Anthropology 4. University of Minnesota, Minneapolis.

Lennox, P.A.
1981   *The Hamilton Site: A Late Historic Neutral Town*. Archaeological Survey of Canada, Mercury Series Paper 103:211-403. National Museum of Man, Ottawa.

1984a   *The Hood Site: A Historic Neutral Town of 1640 A.D.* Archaeological Survey of Canada, Mercury Series Paper 121:1-183. National Museum of Man, Ottawa.

1984b   *The Bogle I and Bogle II Sites: Historic Neutral Hamlets of the Northern Tier*. Archaeological Survey of Canada, Mercury Series Paper 121:184-289. National Museum of Man, Ottawa.

Lennox, P.A. and W.R. Fitzgerald
1990   The Culture History and Archaeology of the Neutral Iroquoians. In *The Archaeology of Southern Ontario to A.D. 1650*, edited by C.J. Ellis and N. Ferris, pp. 405-456. Occasional Publication 5. London Chapter, Ontario Archaeological Society, London, Ontario.

Lennox, P.A., and J.E. Molto
1995   The Archaeology and Physical Anthropology of the E.C. Row Site: A Springwells Phase Settlement, Essex County, Ontario. *Ontario Archaeology* 60:5-39.

Leverett, F. and F. Taylor
1915   *The Pleistocene of Indiana and Michigan and the History of the Great Lakes*. Monograph 53. U.S. Geological Survey, Washington, D.C.

Lewis, G.J.
1982   *Human Migration: A Geographical Perspective*. St. Martin's Press, New York.

Lizee, J.
1995   Cross-Mending Northeastern Ceramic Typologies. Paper presented at the 1994 Annual Meeting of the Northeastern Anthropological Association, Genesco, New York.

Longacre, W.
1991   Sources of Ceramic Variability Among the Kalinga of Northern Luzon. In *Ceramic Ethnoarchaeology*, edited by W. Longacre, pp.95-111. University of Arizona Press, Tucson.

Loring, S.
1985   Boundary Maintenance, Mortuary Ceremonialism, and Resource Control in the Early Woodland: Three Cemetery Sites in Vermont. *Archaeology of Eastern North America* 13:93-127.

Lounsbury, F.G.
1961   Iroquois-Cherokee Linguistic Relations. In *Symposium on Cherokee and Iroquois Culture*, edited by W.N. Fenton and J. Gulick. Bureau of Ethnology, Bulletin 180. Smithsonian Institution, Washington, D.C.

1978   Iroquoian Languages. In *Handbook of North American Indians Volume 15 (Northeast)*, edited by B.G. Trigger, pp. 334-344. Smithsonian Institution, Washington D.C.

Lovis, W.A.
1990   Accelerator Dating the Ceramic Assemblage From the Fletcher Site: Implications of a Pilot Study for the Interpretation of the Wayne Period. *Midcontinental Journal of Archaeology* 15:37-50.

Lovis, W.A., M.B. Holman, G.W. Monaghan, and R.K. Skowronek
1994   Archaeological, Geological, and Paleoecological Perspectives on Regional Research Design in the Saginaw Bay Region of Michigan. In *Great Lakes Archaeology and Paleoecology: Exploring Interdisciplinary Initiatives for the Nineties*, edited by R.I. MacDonald, pp. 81-94. Quarternary Science Institute Publication 10. University of Waterloo, Waterloo, Ontario.

Lovis, W., and J. O'Shea
1994   A Reconsideration of Archaeological Research Design in Michigan: 1993. *The Michigan Archaeologist* 39(3-4): 107-126.

Lowther, R.
1962   Epistemology and Archaeological Theory. *Current Anthropology* 3: 495-509.

Lugenbeal, E.
1978   The Blackduck Ceramics of the Smith Site (21Kc3) and Their Implications for the History of Blackduck Ceramics and Culture in Northern Minnesota. *Midcontinental Journal of Archaeology* 3:45-68.

Lyman, R.L., M.J. O'Brien, and R.C. Dunnell
1997   *The Rise and Fall of Culture History*. Plenum Press, New York.

MacDonald, R.I.
1988   Ontario Iroquoian Sweat Lodges. *Ontario Archaeology* 48:17-26.
1992   Ontario Iroquoian Semisubterranean Sweatlodges. In *Ancient Images, Ancient Thought, The Archaeology of Ideology*, edited by A.S. Goldsmith, S. Garvfie, D. Selin, and J. Smith, pp. 323-330. Proceedings of the 23rd Annual Conference of the Archaeological Association of the University of Calgary. University of Calgary, Calgary.

MacDonald, R.I., and R.H. Pihl
1994   Prehistoric Landscapes and Land Uses: The Role of Predictive Modelling in Cultural Resource Management. In *Great Lakes Archaeology and Paleoecology: Exploring Interdisciplinary Initiatives for the Nineties*, edited by R.I. MacDonald, pp. 25-59. Quaternary Sciences Institute Publication 10. University of Waterloo, Waterloo, Ontario.

MacDonald, R.I., and R.F. Williamson
1995   The Hibou Site (AlGo-50): Investigating Ontario Iroquoian Origins in the Central North Shore Area of Lake Superior. In *Origins of the People of the Longhouse, Proceedings of the 21st Annual Symposium of the Ontario Archaeological Society*, edited by A. Bekerman and G. Warrick, pp. 9-42. Ontario

Archaeological Society, Toronto.

MacDonald, R.I., and M.S. Cooper
1997   Environmental Context. In *In the Shadow of the Bridge: The Archaeology of the Peace Bridge Site (AfGr-9), 1994-1996 Investigations*, edited by R.F. Williamson and R.I. MacDonald, pp. 9-36. Occasional Publications 1. Archaeological Services Inc., Toronto.

MacDonald, R.I., B. Welsh, and M. Cooper
1997   Ground Stone Tools. In *In the Shadow of the Bridge: The Archaeology of the Peace Bridge Site (AfGr-9), 1994-1996 Investigations*, edited by R.F. Williamson and R.I. MacDonald, pp. 372-375. Occasional Publications 1. Archaeological Services Inc., Toronto.

MacEachern, S.
1994   "Symbolic Reservoirs" and Inter-Group Relations: West African Examples. *The African Archaeological Review* 12:205-224.
1998   Scale, Style, and Cultural Variation: Technological Traditions in the Northern Mandara Mountains. In *The Archaeology of Social Boundaries*, edited by M.T. Stark, pp. 107–131. Smithsonian Institution Press, Washington, D.C.

MacNeish, R S.
1952   *Iroquois Pottery Types: A Technique for the Study of Iroquois Prehistory*. National Museum of Canada Bulletin 124. National Museum of Canada, Ottawa.
1959   A Speculative Framework of Northern North American Prehistory as of April 1959. *Anthropologica* 1:7-23.
1976   The In Situ Iroquois Revisited and Rethought. In *Cultural Change and Continuity: Essays in Honor of James Bennett Griffin*, edited by C.E. Cleland, 79-98. Academic Press, New York.

Majumder, P.P.
1991   Recent Developments in Population Genetics. In *Annual Review of Anthropology* 20, edited by B.J. Siegel, pp. 97-117. Annual Reviews Inc., Palo Alto.

Mallory, J.P.
1989   *In Search of the Indo-Europeans: Language, Archaeology, and Myth*. Thames and Hudson, London.

Marois, R.J.M.
1975   *Quelques Techniques de Décoration de la Céramique Impressionnée: Correspondance des Termes Français et Anglais*. Commission Archéologique du Canada, Collection Mercure 40.

Musée National de l'Homme, Ottawa.
1984   *La Céramique Préhistorique Canadienne: Essai de Systématisation de l'analyse de la Décoration.* Commission Archéologique du Canada, Collection Mercure 127. Musée National de l'Homme, Ottawa.

Martijn, C.A.
1969   Île aux Basques and the Prehistoric Iroquois Occupation of Southern Quebec. *Cahiers d'Archéologie Québécoise* 3:55-114.
1986   Voyages des Micmacs dans la Vallée du Saint-Laurent, sur le Côte-Nord et à Terre-Neuve. In *Les Micmacs et la Mer*, edited by C.A. Martijn, pp. 197-223. Recherches Amérindiennes au Québec, Montréal.
1990   The Iroquoian Presence in the Estuary and Gulf of the Saint-Lawrence River Valley: A Reevaluation. *Man in the Northeast* 40:45-63.
1991   Gepèg (Québec), un Toponyme d'origine Micmaque. *Recherches Amérindiennes au Québec* 21:51-64.

Martin, L.
1965   *The Physical Geography of Wisconsin.* University of Wisconsin Press, Madison.

Martin, S.R. (editor)
1993   20KE20: Excavations at a Prehistoric Copper Workshop. *The Michigan Archaeologist* 39:127-193.

Mason, R.J.
1958   *Late Pleistocene Geochronology and the Paleo-Indian Penetration of the Lower Michigan Peninsula.* Anthropological Papers 1. Museum of Anthropology, University of Michigan, Ann Arbor.
1963   Two Late Paleo-Indian Complexes in Wisconsin. *The Wisconsin Archeologist* 44:199-211.
1970   Hopewell, Middle Woodland, and the Laurel Culture: A Problem in Archaeological Classification. *American Anthropologist* 72:802–815.
1976   Ethnicity and Archaeology in the Upper Great Lakes. In *Cultural Change and Continuity: Essays in Honor of James Bennett Griffin*, edited by C.E. Cleland, pp. 349–361. Academic Press, New York.
1981   *Great Lakes Archaeology.* Academic Press, New York.
1986   *Rock Island: Historical Indian Archaeology in the Northern Lake Michigan Basin.* Midcontinental Journal of Archaeology Special Paper 6. The Kent State University Press, Kent, Ohio.

1993   Oneota and Winnebago Ethnogenesis: An Overview. *The Wisconsin Archeologist* 74(1-4):400-421.
1997   Archaeoethnicity and the Elusive Menominis. *Midcontinental Journal of Archaeology* 22:69–94.

Mason, C.I., and R.J. Mason
1961   The Age of the Old Copper Culture. *The Wisconsin Archeologist* 42(4):143-155.

Mayer Heritage Consultants Inc. (MHCI)
1996   Archaeological Mitigative Excavation (Stage 4) Silverman Site (AbHr-5), Registered Plan 12R-13025, Town of St. Clair Beach, Essex County, Ontario. Ms. on file, Ontario Ministry of Citizenship, Culture, and Recreation, London, Ontario.

McAndrews, J.H.
1981   Late Quaternary Climate of Ontario: Temperature Trends from the Fossil Pollen Record. *In Quaternary Paleoclimate*, edited by W. C. Mahaney, pp. 319-333. GeoAbstracts, Norwich.

McAndrews, J.H., and L. Jackson
1988   Age and Environment of Late Pleistocene Mastodont and Mammoth in Southern Ontario. In *Late Pleistocene and Early Holocene Paleoecology and Archeology of the Eastern Great Lakes Region*, edited by R. Laub, N. Miller and D. Steadman, pp. 161-172. Bulletin 33. Buffalo Society of Natural Sciences, Buffalo.

McConaughy, M.A.
1993   Weaver Phase Occupation(s) Summarized and Defined. In *Rench: A Stratified Site in the Central Illinois River Valley*, edited by M.A. McConaughy, pp. 338–354. Reports of Investigations 49. Illinois State Museum, Springfield.

McGarry, K.
1997   *The Relationship Between Ontario Iroquoian Material Culture (ca. 1580-1650 A.D.), Cultural Stress, and Revitalization.* Unpublished M.A. thesis, Department of Anthropology, Trent University, Peterborough, Ontario.

McGhee, R.
1996   *Ancient People of the Arctic.* University of British Columbia Press, Vancouver.

McGuire, R.H.
1983   Breaking Down Cultural Complexity: Inequality and Heterogeneity. In *Advances in Archaeological Method and Theory Volume 6*, edited by M.B. Schiffer, pp. 91-142. Academic Press, New York.

McIlwraith, T.F.
1947   On the Location of Cahiague. *Royal Society of Canada Transactions* 41:99-102.
McHugh, W.P.
1973   New Archaeology and the Old Copper Culture. *The Wisconsin Archeologist* 54(2)70-83.
McKern, W.C.
1939   The Midwestern Taxonomic Method as an Aid to Archaeological Culture Study. *American Antiquity* 4: 301-313.
1942   The First Settlers of Wisconsin. *Wisconsin Magazine of History* 826(2):153-169.
McPherron, A.
1967   *The Juntunen Site and the Late Woodland Prehistory of the Upper Great Lakes Area.* Anthropological Papers 30. Museum of Anthropology, University of Michigan, Ann Arbor.
Meltzer, D.J.
1979   Paradigms and the Nature of Change in American Archaeology. *American Antiquity* 44: 644-657
1981   Paradigms Lost – Paradigms Found? *American Antiquity* 46: 662-664
1983   The Antiquity of Man and the Development of American Archaeology. In *Advances in Archaeological Method and Theory 6*, edited by M.B. Schiffer, pp. 1-51. Academic Press, New York.
1989   Was Stone Exchanged Among Eastern North American Paleoindians? In *Eastern Paleoindian Lithic Resource Use*, edited by C.J. Ellis and J.C. Lothrop, pp. 11-39. Westview Press, Boulder.
Meltzer, D., and R.C. Dunnell (editors)
1992   *The Archaeology of William Henry Holmes.* Smithsonian Institution, Washington, D.C.
Merriwether, D.A., Reed, D.M., and R.E. Ferrell
1997   Ancient and Contemporary Mitochondrial DNA Variation in the Maya. In *Bones of the Maya*, edited by S.L. Whittington and D.M. Reed, pp. 208-217. Smithsonian Institution, Washington, D.C.
Meyer, D., and D. Russell
1987   The Selkirk Composite of Central Canada: A Reconsideration. *Arctic Anthropology* 24(2):1–31.
Mikell, G.A.
1992   The Fort Walton Mississippian Variant on the Northwest Florida Gulf Coast. *Southeastern Archaeology* 11:51–65.

Milner, G.R.
  1995   An Osteological Perspective on Prehistoric Warfare. In *Regional Approaches to Mortuary Analysis*, edited by L.A. Beck, pp. 221-244. Plenum, New York.
  1999   Warfare in Prehistoric and Early Historic Eastern North America. *Journal of Archaeological Research*, 7(2): 105-151.
Milner, G.R., E. Anderson, and V.G. Smith
  1991   Warfare in Late Prehistoric West-Central Illinois. *American Antiquity* 56:581-603.
Milner, G.R., and V.G. Smith
  1990   Oneota Human Skeletal Remains. In *Archaeological Investigations at the Morton Village and Norris Farms 36 Cemetery*, edited by S.K. Santure, A.D. Harn, and D. Esarey, pp. 111-148. Reports of Investigations 45. Illinois State Museum, Springfield.
Mithun, M.
  1984   The Proto-Iroquoians: Cultural Reconstruction from Lexical Materials. In *Extending the Rafters: Interdisciplinary Approaches to Iroquoian Studies*, edited by M.K. Foster, J. Campisi, and M. Mithun, pp. 259-281. State University of New York Press, Albany.
Molnar, J.S.
  1997   *Interpreting Fishing Strategies of the Odawa.* Unpublished Ph.D. Dissertation, Department of Anthropology, State University of New York, Albany.
Molto, J.E.
  1983   *Biological Relationships of Southern Ontario Woodland Peoples: The Evidence of Discontinuous Cranial Morphology.* Archaeological Survey of Canada, Mercury Series Paper 117. National Museum of Man, Ottawa.
Monaghan, G.W., and D. Hayes.
  1997   Archaeological Site Burial: A Model for Site Formation within the Middle-to-Late Holocene Alluvial Settings of the Great Lakes Basin. Paper presented at the Joint 1997 Annual Meeting of the Ontario Archaeological Society and the Midwest Archaeological Conference. Toronto.
Moore, J.A.
  1983   The Trouble with Know-It-Alls: Information as a Social and Ecolgical Resource. In *Archaeological Hammers and Theories*, edited by J.A. Moore and A.S. Keene, pp. 173-191. Academic Press, New York.

1994   Putting Anthropology Back Together Again: The Ethnogenetic Critique of Cladistic Theory. *American Anthropologist* 96:925-948.

Moratto, M.J.
1984   *California Archaeology*. Academic Press, New York.

Moreau, J.-F.
1995   The Eastern Subarctic: Assessing the Transition from the Middle to Late Woodland Periods. *Northeast Anthropology* 49: 97-108.

Moreau, J.-F., É. Langevin, and L. Verreault
1991   Assessment of the Ceramic Evidence for Woodland Period Cultures in the Lac Saint-Jean Area, Eastern Québec. *Man in the Northeast* 41:33-64.

Morgan, L.H.
1901   *League of the Ho-de-no-sau-nee or Iroquois*. Mead, New York.

Morin, E.
1998   *The Early Late Woodland (A.D. 1000-A.D. 1300) in the Upper St Lawrence: Proposition of a Ceramic Sequence* Paper presented at the 82nd annual meeting of the New York State Archaeological Association, Alexandria Bay, New York.

Morrow, J.E.
1996   *The Organization of Early Paleoindian Lithic Technology in the Confluence Region of the Mississippi, Illinois, and Missouri Rivers*. Unpublished Ph.D. dissertation, Department of Anthropology, Washington University, St. Louis, Missouri.

Morrow, T.A.
1997   A Chip Off the Old Block: Alternative Approaches to Debitage Analysis. *Lithic Technology* 22: 51-69.

Moxley, R.W.
1988   The Orchard Site: A Proto-Historic Fort Ancient Village Site in Mason County, West Virginia. *West Virginia Archaeologist* 40:33-41.

Muir, J.
1997   The Faunal Remains of the Praying Mantis Longhouses. Paper presented to the London Chapter, Ontario Archaeological Society.

Muller, E.H., and V.K. Prest
1985   Glacial Lakes in the Ontario Basin. In *Quaternary Evolution of the Great Lakes*, edited by P.F. Karrow and P.E. Calkin, pp. 213-229. Special Paper 30. Geological Association of Canada, St. John's.

Murdock, G.P.
1960   *Social Structure*. Macmillan, New York.
Murphy, C., and N. Ferris
1990   The Late Woodland Western Basin Tradition in Southern
          Ontario. In *The Archaeology of Southern Ontario to A.D. 1650*,
          edited by C.J. Ellis and N. Ferris, pp. 189-278. Occasional
          Publication 5. London Chapter, Ontario Archaeological Society.
          London, Ontario.
Nagata, J.
1981   In Defense of Ethnic Boundaries: The Changing Myths and
          Charters of Malay Identity. In *Ethnic Change*, edited by C. F.
          Keyes, pp. 88-116. University of Washington Press, Seattle.
Nassany, M.S., and K. Pyle
1999   The Adoption of the Bow and Arrow in Eastern North America:
          A View from Central Arkansas. *American Antiquity* 64: 243-264.
Needs-Howarth, S.J.
1999   *Native Fishing in the Great Lakes – A Multidisciplinary*
          Approach to Zooarchaeological Remains from Precontact
          Iroquoian Villages near Lake Simcoe, Ontario. Biologisch-
          Archaeologisch Instituut, University of Groningen, Groningen.
Nelson, R.
1997   Cluster and Discriminant Function Analyses of Human Skeletal
          Material in the Collections of the Public Museum of Grand
          Rapids and Grand Valley State University. Private Ms.
Neumann, G.K.
1952   Archeology and Race in the American Indian. In *Archeology of*
          Eastern United States, edited by J.B. Griffin, pp. 13-34.
          University of Chicago Press, Chicago.
Nichols, J.
1997   Modelling Ancient Population Structures and Movement in
          Linguistics. *Annual Review of Anthropology* 26:359-384.
Niemczycki, M.A.P.
1984   *The Origin and Development of the Seneca and Cayuga Tribes*
          of New York State. Research Records 17. Rochester Museum and
          Science Center, Rochester.
1988   Seneca Tribalization: An Adaptive Strategy. *Man In the*
          Northeast 36:77-87.
1995   Ceramics and Ethnicity in West-Central New York: Exploring
          Owasco-Iroquois Connections. *Northeast Anthropology* 49:43-
          54.

Noble, W.C.
1979   Ontario Iroquois Effigy Pipes. *Canadian Journal of Archaeology* 3:69-90.
1980   Thorold: An Early Historic Niagara Neutral Town. In *Villages in the Niagara Peninsula*, edited by J. Burtniak and W.B. Turner, pp. 43-55. Brock University, St. Catharines.
1984   Historic Neutral Iroquois Settlement Patterns. *Canadian Journal of Archaeology* 8:3-27.
1985   Tsouharissen's Chiefdom: An Early Historic 17th Century Neutral Iroquoian Ranked Society. *Canadian Journal of Archaeology* 9(2):131-146.
O'Gorman, J.
1995   *The Tremaine Site (47-LC-95)*. Archaeology Research Series 3, Museum Archaeology Program, State Historical Society of Wisconsin.
O'Shea, J.M., and A.W. Barker
1996   Measuring Social Complexity and Variation: A Categorical Imperative? In *Emergent Complexity*, edited by J.E. Arnold, pp. 13-24. Archaeological Series 9. International Monographs in Prehistory, Ann Arbor.
Odell, G.H. (editor)
1996   *Stone Tools: Theoretical Insights into Human Prehistory*. Plenum Press, New York.
Orr, B.
1914   Accessions to the Museum. *Annual Archaeological Report for Ontario for 1914, Being Part of Appendix to the Report of the Minister for Education*, pp. 80-99. L.K. Cameron, Toronto.
1915   The Mississaugas. *Annual Archaeological Report for Ontario for 1915, Being Part of Appendix to the Report of the Minister of Education*, pp. 7-19. A.T. Wilgress, Toronto.
1917   The Nippisings. *Annual Archaeological Report for Ontario for 1917, Being Part of Appendix to the Report of the Minister of Education*, pp. 9-23. A.T. Wilgress, Toronto.
1921   The Hurons. *Annual Archaeological Report for Ontario for 1920, Being Part of Appendix to the Report of the Minister of Education*, pp. 9-23. Clarkson W. James, Toronto.
Ortner, D.J.
1991   Theoretical and Methodological Issues in Paleopathology. In *Human Paleopathology: Current Syntheses and Future Options*, edited by D.J. Ortner and A.C. Aufderheide, pp. 5-11. Smithsonian Institution Press, Washington, D.C.

Ortner, S.B., and H. Whitehead
1981   *Sexual Meanings: The Cultural Construction of Gender and Sexuality.* Cambridge University Press, New York.

Overstreet, D.F.
1993   McCauley, Astor, and Hanson—Candidates for the Provisional Dandy Phase. *The Wisconsin Archeologist* 74(1-4):120-196.

Overstreet, D.F., and P.B. Richards (editors)
1992   *Archaeology at Lac des Puans: The Lake Winnebago Phase – A Classic Horizon Expression of the Oneota Tradition in East-Central Wisconsin.* Great Lakes Archaeological Research Center, Inc., Milwaukee.

Papworth, M.L.
1967   *Cultural Traditions in the Lake Forest Region During the Late High-Water Stages of the Post-Glacial Great Lakes.* Unpublished Ph.D. dissertation, Department of Anthropology, University of Michigan, Ann Arbor.

Parker, A.C.
1909   Secret Medicine Societies of the Seneca. *American Anthropologist* n.s. 11:161-185.
1910   Iroquois Uses of Maize and Other Plant Foods. *New York State Museum Bulletin 144.*
1916   The Origins of the Iroquois as Suggested by Their Archaeology. *American Anthropologist* 18:479-507.
1922   The Archaeological History of New York. *New York State Museum Bulletin* 235-238.
1923   *Seneca Myths and Folk Tales.* Buffalo Historical Society Publications 27. Buffalo.

Parr, R.L., S.W. Carlyle, and D.H.O'Rourke
1996   Ancient DNA Analysis of Fremont Amerindians of the Great Salt Lake Wetlands. *American Journal of Physical Anthropology* 99:507-518.

Parry, W.J., and R.L. Kelly
1988   Expedient Core Technology and Sedentism. In *The Organization of Core Technology,* edited by J. Johnson and C. Morrow, pp. 285-304. Westview Press, Boulder, Colorado.

Pauketat, T.R. and T.E. Emerson
1991   The Ideology of Authority and the Power of the Pot. *American Anthropologist* 93(4):919-941.

Pendergast, J.F.
1975   An In-Situ Hypothesis to Explain the Origin of the St. Lawrence Iroquoians. *Ontario Archaeology* 25:47-55.

1991   The Massawomeck: Raiders and Traders into the Chesapeake Bay in the Seventeenth Century. *Transactions of the American Philosophical Society* 81(2).

Pengelly, J.W., K.J. Tinkler, W.G. Parkins, and F.M. McCarthy
1997   12,600 Years of Lake Level Changes, Changing Sills, Ephemeral Lakes and Niagara Gorge Erosion in the Niagara Peninsula and Eastern Lake Erie Basin. *Journal of Paleolimnology* 17: 377-402.

Penman, J.T.
1977   The Old Copper Culture: An Analysis of Old Copper Artifacts. *The Wisconsin Archeologist* 58(1):3-23.

Penney, D.W.
1987   The Origins of an Indigenous Ontario Arts Tradition: Ontario Art from the Late Archaic Through the Woodland Periods, 1500 B.C.-A.D. 600. *Journal of Canadian Studies* 21(4):37-55.

Perttula, T.K.
1992   *The Caddo Nation: Archaeological and Ethnohistoric Perspectives*. University of Texas Press, Austin.

Petersen, J.B.
1990   Evidence of the Saint-Lawrence Iroquoians in Northern New England : Population Movement, Trade, or Stylistic Borrowing? *Man in the Northeast* 40:31-39.

1993   *Iroquoian Ceramics in New England: A Reconsideration of Ethnicity, Evolution and Interaction*. Paper presented at the 57th Annual Congress of the Society of American Archaeology, Pittsburg, Pennsylvania.

1995   Preceramic Archaeological Manifestations in the Far Northeast: A Review of Recent Research. *Archaeology of Eastern North America* 23:207-230.

Petersen, J.B., and D. Sanger
1991   An Aboriginal Ceramic Sequence for Maine and the Maritime Provinces, In *Prehistoric Archaeology in the Maritime Provinces: Past and Present Research*, edited by M. Deal and S. Blair, pp. 121-178. Reports in Archaeology 8. The Council of Maritime Premiers, Maritime Committee on Archaeological Cooperation, Fredericton.

Pettipas, L.
1997   Ethnic Markers in Precontact Manitoba: A Review. *Manitoba Archaeological Journal* 7(2):64–72.

Pfeiffer, S.
1984   Paleopathology in an Iroquoian Ossuary, with Special Reference to Tuberculosis. *American Journal of Physical Anthropology* 65:181-189.

Phillips, P.
1970   *Archaeological Survey in the Lower Yazoo Basin, Mississippi, 1949–1955*. Papers of the Peabody Museum of Archaeology and Ethnology 60. Harvard University, Cambridge.

Phillips, P., and J.A. Brown
1978   *Pre-Columbian Shell Engravings from the Craig Mound at Spiro, Oklahoma, Part 1*. Peabody Museum Press, Harvard University, Cambridge.

1984   *Pre-Columbian Shell Engravings from the Craig Mound at Spiro, Oklahoma, Part 2*. Peabody Museum Press, Harvard University, Cambridge.

Phillips, P., J. Ford, and J. Griffin
1951   *Archaeological Survey in the Lower Mississippi Alluvial Valley, 1940-1947*. Papers of the Peabody Museum of Archaeology and Ethnology 25, Harvard University, Cambridge.

Phillips, R.B.
1989   Dreams and Designs: Iconographic Problems in Great Lakes Twined Bags. In *Great Lakes Indian Art*, edited by D. Penny, pp. 52-68. Wayne State University Press and the Detroit Institute of Arts, Detroit.

Piddington, R.
1965   Editor's Introduction. In *Kinship and Geographical Mobility*, edited by R. Piddington, pp. xi-xiv. E.J. Brill, Leiden.

Pleger, T.C.
1992   A Functional and Temporal Analysis of Copper Implements from the Chautauqua Grounds Site (47-MT-71): A Multicomponent Site Near the Mouth of the Menominee River. *The Wisconsin Archeologist* 73(3-4):160-176.

1998   *Social Complexity, Trade, and Subsistence During the Archaic / Woodland Transition in the Western Great Lakes: A Diachronic Study of Copper-Using Cultures at the Oconto and Riverside Cemeteries*. Unpublished Ph.D. dissertation, Department of Anthropology, University of Wisconsin, Madison.

Plog, S.
1978   Social Interaction and Stylistic Similarity: A Reanalysis. In *Advances in Archaeological Method and Theory Volume 1*, edited by M. Schiffer, pp. 143-182. Academic Press, New York.

1983   Analysis of Style in Artifacts. In *Annual Review of Anthropology* 12, edited by B. Siegel, pp. 125-42. Annual Reviews, Palo Alto.

1990   Socio-Political Implications of Stylistic Variation in the American Southwest. In *The Uses of Style in Archaeology*, edited by M.W. Conkey and C.A. Hastorf, pp. 61-72. Cambridge University Press, New York.

Plourde, M.

1990   Un Site Iroquoien à la Confluence du Saguenay et du Saint-Laurent, au XIIIe siècle. *Recherches Amérindiennes au Québec* 20 (1):47-61.

1993   Iroquoians in the St. Lawrence Estuary: The Ouellet Site Seal Hunters. In *Essays in St. Lawrence Iroquoian Archaeology*, edited by J.F. Pendergast and C. Chapdelaine, pp.101-119. Occasional Papers in Northeastern Archaeology 8. Copetown Press, Dundas, Ontario.

1994   *Préhistoire des Iroquoiens sur la Haute-Côte-Nord du Saint-Laurent : Ré-évaluation des Sites DaEk-19, DbEj-7, DbEj-1, DbEi-2 et DcEi-1.* Ms. on file, Ministère de la Culture et des Communications du Québec, Québec.

1995   *Fouilles Aarchéologiques au Site de Pointe à Crapaud (DbEi-2),* Été 1994. Ms. on file, Ministère de la Culture et des Communications du Québec, Québec.

Popham, R.E., and J.N. Emerson

1954   Manifestations of Old Copper Industry in Ontario. *Pennsylvania Archaeologist* 24:1-19

Powell, M.L.

1991   Endemic Treponematosis and Tuberculosis in the Prehistoric Southeastern United States: Biological Costs of Chronic Endemic Disease. In *Human Paleopathology: Current Syntheses and Future Options*, edited by D.J. Ortner and A.C. Aufderheide, pp. 173-180. Smithsonian Institution Press, Washington, D.C.

Prahl, E., D. Brose, and D. Stothers

1976   A Preliminary Synthesis of Late Prehistoric Phenomena in the Western Basin of Lake Erie. In *The Late Prehistory of the Lake Erie Drainage Basin: A 1972 Symposium Revisited*, edited by D. Brose, pp. 251-282. Cleveland Museum of Natural History, Cleveland.

Prevec, R.

1987   The Elliott Site (AfHc-2) 1987 Faunal Report. Ms. on file, Ontario Ministry of Citizenship, Culture and Recreation, Toronto.

Price, T.D
1981   Complexity in "'Non-Complex" Societies. *In Archaeological Approaches to the Study of Complexity*, edited by S.E. van der Leeuw, pp. 53-97. Institut voor Pre-en Protohistorie, Amsterdam.

Price, T.D., and J.A. Brown
1985   Aspects of Hunter-Gatherer Complexity. In *Prehistoric Hunter-Gatherers: The Emergence of Cultural Complexity*, edited by T.D. Price and J.A. Brown, pp. 3-20. Academic Press, New York.

Price, T.D., and G.M. Feinman (editors)
1995   *Foundations of Social Inequality*. Plenum Press, New York.

Quimby, G.I.
1952   The Archaeology of the Upper Great Lakes Area. In *The Archaeology of the Eastern United States*, edited by J.B. Griffin, pp. 99-107. University of Chicago Press, Chicago.

Radin, P.
1923   *The Winnebago Tribe*. Thirty-Seventh Annual Report of the United States Bureau of American Ethnology:35-550, Washington, D.C.

1948   Winnebago Hero Cycles: A Study in Aboriginal Literature. *Indiana University Publications in Anthropology and Linguistics, Memoir 2*. Bloomington.

1954   *The Evolution of an American Indian Prose Epic: A Study in Comparative Literature, Part 1*. Special Publication of the Bollingen Foundation 3.

Rajnovich, G.
1994   *Reading Rock Art Interpreting The Indian Rock Paintings of the Canadian Shield*. Natural Heritage Press, Toronto.

Ramsden, P.G.
1990   Death in Winter: Changing Symbolic Patterns in Southern Ontario Prehistory *Anthropologica* 32:167-182

1977   *A Refinement of Some Aspects of Huron Ceramic Analysis*. Archaeological Survey of Canada, Mercury Series Paper 63. National Museum of Man, Ottawa.

Ramsden, P.G., and W.R. Fitzgerald
1990   More (or Less) on Iroquoian Stemware. *American Antiquity* 55:159-161.

Rands, R.L,. and C.L. Riley
1958   Diffusion and Discontinuous Distribution. *American Anthropologist* 60:274-97.

Read, D.W.
1982   Toward a Theory of Archaeological Classification. In *Essays on Archaeological Typology*, edited by R. Whallon and J.A. Brown, pp. 56-92. Center For American Archaeology Press, Kampsville, Illinois.

Reid, C.S., and G. Rajnovich
1991   Laurel: A Re-evaluation of the Spatial, Social and Temporal Paradigms. *Canadian Journal of Archaeology* 15:193–234.

Renfrew, C.
1968   Models in Prehistory. *Antiquity* 62: 132-134.
1986   Introduction: Peer Polity Interaction and Socio-Political Change. In *Peer Polity Interaction and Socio-Political Change*, edited by C. Renfrew and J. Cherry, pp. 1-18. Cambridge University Press, New York.
1987   *Archaeology and Language: The Puzzle of Indo-European Origins*. Jonathan Cape, London.
1994   The Archaeology of Religion. In *The Ancient Mind*, edited by C. Renfrew and E. Zubrow, Cambridge University Press, New York.
1997   The Three Dimensions of Human History: A Talk with Colin Renfrew. In *Edge 24*. John Brockman.

Renfrew, C., and P. Bahn
1996   *Archaeology: Theories, Methods, and Practice*. Thames and Hudson, New York.

Renfrew, C., and J. Cherry (editors)
1986   *Peer Polity Interaction and Socio-Political Change*. Cambridge University Press, New York.

Reynolds, T.
1856   Discovery of Copper and other Indian Relics, Near Brockville. *The Canadian Journal* n.s.1(4):329-334.

Ridley, F.
1952   The Huron and Lalonde Occupations of Ontario. *American Antiquity* 17:197-210.
1954   The Frank Bay Site, Lake Nipissing, Ontario. *American Antiquity* 20:40-50.
1958   Did the Huron Really Migrate North from the Toronto Area? *Pennsylvania Archaeologist* 28:2-4.
1961   *Archaeology of the Neutral Indians*. Etobicoke Historical Society, Etobicoke, Ontario.
1963   The Ontario Iroquoian Controversy. *Ontario History* 55:49-59.
1966   Archaeology of Lake Abitibi: Ontario-Quebec. *Anthropological*

Journal of Canada 4(2):2-50.

Rioux, S,. and R. Tremblay
1999   Cette Irréductible Préférence : la Chasse au Mammifères Marins
          par les Iroquoiens de la Région de Québec. *Archéologiques* 11-
          12:191-198

Ritchie, J.C.
1986   Climate Change and Vegetation Response. *Vegetatio* 67:65-74.

Ritchie, W.A.
1932   The Algonkin Sequence in New York. *American Anthropologist*
          34:406-415.
1938   A Perspective of Northeastern Archaeology. *American Antiquity*
          4: 94-112.
1944   *The Pre-Iroquoian Occupations of New York State.* Rochester
          Museum of Arts and Sciences Memoir 1:115-186.
1947   Archaeological Evidence for Ceremonialism in the Owasco
          Culture. *Researches and Transactions of the New York State
          Archaeological Association* 11(2):55-75.
1949   *An Archaeological Survey of the Trent Waterway in Ontario,
          Canada, and its Significance for New York State Prehistory.*
          Research Records 9. Rochester Museum of Arts and Sciences,
          Rochester.
1955   *Recent Discoveries Suggesting an Early Woodland Burial Cult
          in the Northeast.* Circular 40. New York State Museum and
          Science Service, Albany, New York.
1961   *A Typology and Nomenclature for New York State Projectile
          Points.* Bulletin 284. New York State Museum and Science
          Service, Albany, New York.
1965   *The Archaeology of New York State.* Natural History Press, New
          York.
1969   *The Archaeology of New York State (2nd Edition).* Natural
          History Press, New York.
1980   *The Archaeology of New York State (Revised Edition).* Harbor
          Hill Books, New York.

Ritchie, W.A., and R.S. MacNeish
1949   The Pre-Iroquoian Pottery of New York State. *American
          Antiquity* 20:40-50.

Ritzenthaler, R.E. (editor)
1957   The Old Copper Culture of Wisconsin. *Wisconsin Archeologist*
          38(4):185-329.
1978   Southwestern Chippewa. In *Handbook of North American
          Indians Volume 15 (Northeast)*, edited by B.G. Trigger, pp. 743-

759. Smithsonian Institution, Washington D.C.

Ritzenthaler, R.E., and G.I. Quimby
1962   The Red Ochre Culture of the Upper Great Lakes and Adjacent Areas. *Fieldiana: Anthropology* 36(11):243-75.

Ritzenthaler, R.E. , and W.L. Wittry
1952   The Oconto Site – An Old Copper Manifestation. *The Wisconsin Archeologist* 33(4):199-223.

Robert, D.L.
1996   *King's Forest Park (AhGw-1) and Pergentile (AhGw-2): Early Ontario Iroquoian Settlement at the Head of Lake Ontario.* Unpublished M.A. thesis, Department of Anthropology, Trent University, Peterborough, Ontario.

Roberts, A.
1985   *Preceramic Occupations Along the North Shore of Lake Ontario.* Archaeological Survey of Canada, Mercury Series Paper 132, National Museum of Canada, Ottawa.

Robertson, D.A., R.F. Williamson, R.I. MacDonald, R.H. Pihl and M.S. Cooper
1997   Interpretations and Conclusions. In *In the Shadow of the Bridge: The Archaeology of the Peace Bridge Site (AfGr-9), 1994-1996 Investigations*, edited by R.F. Williamson and R.I. MacDonald, pp. 493-510. Occasional Publications 1. Archaeological Services Inc., Toronto.

Rodgers, M.B.
1972   The 46th Street Site and the Occurrence of Allegan Ware in Southwestern Michigan. *Michigan Archaeologist* 18:47-108.

Roe, P.
1980   Art and Residence Among the Shipibo Indians of Peru: A Study in Micro-acculturation. *American Anthropologist* 82:42-71.

Rogers, E.S., and E. Leacock
1981   Montagnais-Naskapi. In *Handbook of North American Indians Volume 6 (Subarctic)*, edited by J. Helm, pp. 169-189. Smithsonian Institution, Washington D.C.

Roosa, W.B.
1965   Some Great Lakes Fluted Point Types. *Michigan Archaeologist* 11:89-102.

Root, D.
1983   Information Exchange and the Spatial Configuration of Egalitarian Societies. In *Archaeological Hammers and Theories*, edited by J.A. Moore and A.S. Keene, pp. 193-219. Academic Press, New York.

Ross, W.
1995   The Interlakes Composite: A Re-definition of the Initial Settlement of the Agassiz-Minong Peninsula. *The Wisconsin Archeologist* 76:244-268.
Rouse, I.B.
1958   The Inference of Migrations From Anthropological Evidence. In *Migrations in New World Culture History*, edited by R.H. Thompson, pp. 63-68. Social Science Bulletin 27. University of Arizona, Tucson.
1972   *Introduction to Prehistory.* McGraw-Hill, New York.
Royce, A.P.
1982   *Ethnic Identity: Strategies of Diversity.* Indiana University Press, Bloomington.
Rutsch, E.S.
1973   *Smoking Technology of the Aborigines of the Iroquois Area of New York State.* Associated University Presses, Cranbury, New Jersey.
Sackett, J.R.
1977   The Meaning of Style in Archaeology. *American Antiquity* 42:369-380.
1986a   Style, Function and Assemblage Variability: A Reply to Binford. *American Antiquity* 51:628-634.
1986b   Isochrestism and Style: A Clarification. *Journal of Anthropological Archaeology* 5:266-77.
1990   Style and Ethnicity in Archaeology: The Case for Isochrestism. In *The Uses of Style in Archaeology*, edited by M.W. Conkey and C.A. Hastorf, pp. 32-43. Cambridge University Press, New York.
Sagard, G.
1866   *Histoire du Canada et Voyages que les Frères Mineurs Recollects y ont Faicts pour la Conversion des Infidelles.* 4 volumes. Librairie Tross, Paris.
Sahlins, M.D.
1968   *Tribesmen.* Prentice-Hall, Englewood Cliffs.
Sahlins, M.D., and E.R. Service
1960   *Evolution and Culture.* University of Michigan Press, Ann Arbor.
Salzer, R.J.
1974   The Wisconsin North Lakes Project: A Preliminary Report. In *Aspects of Upper Great Lakes Prehistory: Papers in Honor of Lloyd A. Wilford*, edited by E. Johnson, pp. 40-54. Minnesota Prehistoric Archaeology Series 11. Minnesota Historical Society, St. Paul.

1987   Preliminary Report on the Gottschall Site (47Ia80). *The Wisconsin Archeologist* 68(4): 419- 472.

1993   Oral Literature and Archaeology. *The Wisconsin Archeologist* 74(1-4):80-119.

n.d.   Wisconsin Rock Art. *The Wisconsin Archeologist.* In press.

Sampson, K.W.

1988   Conventionalized Figures on Late Woodland Ceramics. *The Wisconsin Archeologist* 69(3):163-188.

Sanday, P.R.

1981   *Female Power and Male Dominance: On the Origins of Sexual Inequality.* Cambridge University Press, New York.

Santure, S.K., A.D. Harn, and D. Esarey (editors)

1990   *Archaeological Investigations at the Morton Village and Norris Farms 36 Cemetery.* Reports of Investigations 45. Illinois State Museum, Springfield.

Sassaman, K.E.

1993   *Early Pottery in the Southeast: Tradition and Innovation in Cooking Technology.* University of Alabama Press, Tuscaloosa.

Schortman, E.M.

1989   Interregional Interaction in Prehistory: the Need for a New Perspective. *American Antiquity* 54:52-65.

Schortman, E.M., and P.A. Urban

1987   Modelling Interregional Interaction in Prehistory. In *Advances in Archaeological Method and Theory Volume 11,* edited by M. Schiffer, pp. 37-95. Academic Press, San Diego.

1992   Current Trends in Interaction Research. In *Resources, Power, and Interregional Interaction,* edited by E. Schortman and P. Urban, pp. 235-249. Plenum Press, New York.

Sciulli, P.W., S. Lozanoff, and K.N. Schneider

1984   An Analysis of Diversity in Glacial Kame and Adena Skeletal Samples. *Human Biology* 56:603-616.

Sears, W.H.

1961   The Study of Social and Religious Systems in North American Archaeology. *Current Anthropology* 2(3):223-246.

Seeman, M.F.

1981   A Late Woodland Steatite Pipe from the Catlin Site, Vermillion Co., Indiana: The Implications for East-West Trade. *Archaeology of Eastern North America* 9:103-109.

1994   Inter-Cluster Lithic Patterning at Nobles Pond: A Case for "Disembedded" Procurement Among Early Paleoindian Societies. *American Antiquity* 59:273-288.

1996 The Ohio Hopewell Core and Its Many Margins: Deconstructing Upland and Hinterland Relations. In *A View from the Core: A Synthesis of Ohio Hopewell Archaeology*, edited by P. J. Pacheco, pp. 304–315. Ohio Archaeological Council, Columbus.

Seeman, M.F., G. Summers, E. Dowd, and L. Morris

1994 Fluted Point Characteristics at Three Large Sites: The Implications for Modelling Early Paleoindian Settlement Patterns in Ohio. In *The First Discovery of America: Archaeological Evidence of the Earliest Inhabitants of the Ohio Area,* edited by W.S. Dancey, pp. 77-93. Ohio Archaeological Council, Columbus.

Semken, H.A., Jr.

1983 Holocene Mammalian Biogeography and Climatic Change in the Eastern and Central United States. In *Late-Quaternary Environments of the United States Volume 2*, edited by H.E. Wright, Jr., pp. 182-207. University of Minnesota Press, Minneapolis.

Sempowski, M.L.

1997 The Metaphor of the Iroquois Longhouse: Its Role in the Expansion of the League of the Iroquois. Paper Presented at the Longhouse Conference, Rochester Museum and Science Center, Rochester.

Sempowski, M.L., L.P. Saunders, and G.C. Cervone

1988 The Adams and Culbertson Sites: A Hypothesis for Village Formation. *Man in the Northeast* 35:95-108.

Service, E.R.

1962 *Primitive Social Organization: An Evolutionary Perspective.* Random House, New York.

1971 *Cultural Evolutionism: Theory in Practice.* Holt, Rinehart, and Winston, New York.

1975 *Origins of the State and Civilization: The Process of Cultural Evolution.* Norton, New York.

Sharrock, S.R.

1974 Crees, Cree-Assiniboines and Assiniboines: Interethnic Social Organization on the Far Northern Plains. *Ethnohistory* 21:95-122.

Shoshani, J., A.R. Pilling, and H.T. Wright

1989 Kessell Side-Notched Point: First Record from Michigan. *Current Research in the Pleistocene* 6:22-24.

Shoshani, J., H.T. Wright, and A.R. Pilling

1990 Ecological Context of Two Early Archaic Projectile Points from

Michigan: A LeCroy and a Kessell Point Recovered at 200K394. *Michigan Archaeologist* 36:1-20.

Shott, M.J.
1989   Bipolar Industries: Ethnographic Evidence and Archaeological Implications. *North American Archaeologist* 10(1): 1-24.
1996   Innovation and Selection in Prehistory: A Case Study from the American Bottom. In *Stone Tools: Theoretical Insights into Human Prehistory*, edited by G.H. Odell, pp. 279-309. Plenum Press, New York.

Shryock, A.J.
1987   The Wright Mound Reexamined: Generative Structures and the Political Economy of a Simple Chiefdom. *Midcontinental Journal of Archaeology* 12:243-268.

Siebert, F.T.
1967   The Original Home of the Proto-Algonquian People. *National Museum of Canada Bulletin* 214, Anthropology Series 78:13-45.
1975   Resurrecting Virginia Algonquian from the Dead: the Reconstituted and Historical Phonology of Powhatan. In *Studies in Southeastern Indian Languages*, edited by J.M. Crawford, pp. 285-453. University of Georgia Press, Athens, Georgia.

Skinner, A.
1925   Traditions of the Ioway Indians. *Journal of American Folklore* 38:425-506.

Skinner, A., and J. V. Satterlee
1915   *Menomini Folklore*. Anthropological Papers 13, American Museum of Natural History. New York.

Smith, B.A.
1996   *Systems of Subsistence and Networks of Exchange in the Terminal Woodland and Early Historic Periods in the Upper Great Lakes*. Unpublished Ph.D. disseration, Department of Anthropology, Michigan State University, Lansing.

Smith, B.D.
1989   Origins of Agriculture in Eastern North America. *Science* 246:1566-1571.

Smith, D.G.
1983   *An Analytical Approach to the Seriation of Iroquoian Pottery*. Research Report 12. Museum of Indian Archaeology, London, Ontario.
1987   Archaeological Systematics and the Analysis of Iroquoian Ceramics: A Case Study from the Crawford Lake Area, Ontario. Bulletin 15. Museum of Indian Archaeology, London.

1990   Iroquoian Studies in Southern Ontario: Introduction and Historic Overview. In *The Archaeology of Southern Ontario to A.D. 1650*, edited by C. J. Ellis and N. Ferris, pp. 279-290. Occasional Publication 5. London Chapter, Ontario Archaeological Society, London, Ontario.

1997   Radiocarbon Dating the Middle to Late Woodland Transition and Earliest Maize in Southern Ontario. *Northeast Anthropology* 54:37-73.

Smith, D.G., and G.W. Crawford

1995   The Princess Point Complex and the Origins of Iroquoian Societies in Ontario. In *Origins of the People of the Longhouse: Proceedings of the 21st Annual Symposium of the Ontario Archaeological Society*, edited by A. Bekerman and G. Warrick, pp. 55-70. Ontario Archaeological Society, Toronto.

1997   Recent Developments in the Archaeology of the Princess Point Complex of Southern Ontario. *Canadian Journal of Archaeology* 21(1):9-32.

Snow, D.R.

1980   *The Archaeology of New England*. Academic Press, New York.

1992a   L'Augmentation de la Population Chez les Groupes Iroquoiens et ses Consequences sur L'Etude de leurs Origines. *Recherches Amerindiennes au Quebec* 22(4):5-12.

1992b   La Démographie des Iroquoiens. *Recherches Amérindiennes au Québec* 22(4):32-36.

1994   Paleoecology and the Prehistoric Incursion of Northern Iroquoians into the Lower Great Lakes Region. In *Great Lakes Archaeology and Paleo-ecology: Exploring Interdisciplinary Initiatives for the Nineties*, edited by R.I. MacDonald, pp. 283-293. Quaternary Sciences Institute Publication 10. University of Waterloo, Waterloo, Ontario.

1995a   Migration in Prehistory: The Northern Iroquoian Case. *American Antiquity* 60:59-79.

1995b   Population Movements During the Woodland Period: The Intrusion of Iroquoian Peoples. In *Origins of the People of the Longhouse: Proceedings of the 21st Annual Symposium of the Ontario Archaeological Society*, edited by A. Bekerman and G. Warrick, pp.5-8. Ontario Archaeological Society, Toronto.

1996   More on Migration in Prehistory: Accommodating New Evidence in the Northern Iroquoian Case. *American Antiquity* 61: 791-796.

Spaulding, A.C.

1953   Statistical Techniques for the Discovery of Artifact Types.

References Cited

American Antiquity 18:305-313.

Spence, M.W.

1986   Band Structure and Interaction in Early Southern Ontario. *Canadian Journal of Anthropology* 5(2):83-95.

1988   The Human Skeletal Material of the Elliott Site. *Kewa,* 88(4):10-20.

1994   Mortuary Programmes of the Early Ontario Iroquoians. *Ontario Archaeology* 58:6-20.

Spence, M.W., and W.A. Fox

1986   The Early Woodland Occupations of Southern Ontario. In *Early Woodland Archaeology,* edited by K.B. Farnsworth and T.E. Emerson, pp. 4-46. Center for American Archaeology Press, Kampsville, Illinois.

Spence, M.W., R. H. Pihl, and J.E. Molto

1984   Hunter-Gatherer Social Group Identification: A Case Study from Middle Woodland Southern Ontario. In *Exploring the Limits: Frontiers and Boundaries in Prehistory,* edited by S. De Atley and F. Findlow, pp. 117-142. International Series 223. British Archaeological Reports, Oxford.

Spence, M.W., R.H. Pihl, and C. Murphy

1990   Cultural Complexes of the Early and Middle Woodland Periods. In *The Archaeology of Southern Ontario to A.D. 1650,* edited by C.J. Ellis and N. Ferris, pp. 125-169. Occasional Publication 5. London Chapter, Ontario Archaeological Society, London, Ontario.

Spence, M.W., R. Williamson, and J. Dawkins

1978   The Bruce Boyd Site: An Early Woodland Component in Southwestern Ontario. *Ontario Archaeology* 29:33-46.

Spencer, C.S.

1987   Rethinking the Chiefdom. In *Chiefdoms in the Americas,* edited by R.D. Drennan and C.A. Uribe, pp. 369-390. University Press of America, Lanham, Maryland.

1990   On the Tempo and Mode of State Formation: Neoevolutionism Considered. *Journal of Anthropological Archaeology* 9:1-30.

Spielmann, K.A.

1986   Interdependence Among Egalitarian Societies. *Journal of Anthropological Archaeology* 5:279-312.

Spindler, L S.

1978   Menominee. In *Handbook of North American Indians Volume 15 (Northeast),* edited by B.G. Trigger, pp. 708-724. Smithsonian Institution, Washington D.C.

389

Squier, E.G., and E.H. Davis
1848   Ancient Monuments of the Mississippi Valley. *Smithsonian Contributions to Knowledge* 1, Smithsonian Institution, Washington D.C.

Staeck, J.P.
1994   Archaeology, Identity and Oral Traditions. Unpublished Ph.D. dissertation, Department of Anthropology, Rutgers University, New Brunswick, N.J.

Stanislawski, M.
1969   The Ethno-Archaeology of Hopi Pottery Making. *Plateau* 42:27-33.

Starna, W.A., and R.E. Funk
1994   The Place of the In Situ Hypothesis in Iroquoian Archaeology. *Northeast Anthropology* 47:45-54.

Steadman, D.W.
1997   *Population Genetic Analysis of Regional and Interregional Prehistoric Gene Flow in West-Central Illinois*. Unpublished Ph.D. dissertation, Department of Anthropology, University of Chicago, Chicago.

Steinbring, J.H.
1975   *Taxonomic and Associational Considerations of Copper Technology During the Archaic Tradition*. Unpublished Ph.D. dissertation, Department of Anthropology, University of Minnesota, Minneapolis.

Steponaitis, V.P.
1978   Location Theory and Complex Chiefdoms: A Mississippian Example. In *Mississippian Settlement Patterns*, edited by B.D. Smith, pp. 417-454. Academic Press, New York.

Sterner, J.
1989   Who is Signalling Whom? Ceramic Style, Ethnicity and Taphonomy Among the Sirak Bulahay. *Antiquity* 63:451-459.

Stevenson, K.P., R.F. Boszhardt, C.R. Moffat, P.H. Salkin, T.C. Pleger, J.L. Theler, and C.M. Arzigian
1997   The Woodland Tradition. In "Wisconsin Archaeology," edited by R. A. Birmingham, C.I. Mason, and J.B. Stoltman, pp. 140-201. *The Wisconsin Archeologist* 78(1-2).

Steward, J.H.
1955   *Theory of Culture Change: The Methodology of Multilinear Evolution*. University of Illinois, Urbana.

Stites, S.
1905   *Economics of the Iroquois*. Lancaster, Pennsylvania

Stoltman, J.B.
1986   The Archaic Tradition. In "Introduction to Wisconsin Archaeology: Background for Cultural Resource Planning," edited by W. Green, J.B. Stoltman, and A.B. Kehoe. *The Wisconsin Archeologist* 67(3-4):207-238.
1997   The Archaic Tradition. In "Wisconsin Archaeology," edited by R.A. Birmingham, C.. Mason, and J.B. Stoltman, pp. 112-139. *The Wisconsin Archeologist* 78(1-2).
Stoltman, J.B. and K. Workman
1969   A Preliminary Study of Wisconsin Fluted Points. *The Wisconsin Archaeologist* 50(4):189-214.
Stone, A.C.
1996   *Genetic and Mortuary Analyses of a Prehistoric Native American Community.* Unpublished Ph.D. dissertation, Department of Anthropology, Pennsylvania State University, University Park.
Stone, A.C., and M. Stoneking
1993   Ancient DNA from a Pre-Columbian Amerindian Population. *American Journal of Physical Anthropology* 92:463-471.
1998   mtDNA Analysis of a Prehistoric Oneota Population: Implications for the Peopling of the New World. *American Journal of Human Genetics* 62:1153-1170.
Storck, P.J., and A.E. Spiess
1994   The Significance of New Faunal Identifications Attributed to an Early Paleoindian (Gainey Complex) Occupation at the Udora Site, Ontario, Canada. *American Antiquity* 59:121-142.
Stothers, D.M.
1977   *The Princess Point Complex.* Archaeological Survey of Canada, Mercury Series Paper 58, National Museum of Man, Ottawa.
1978   The Western Basin Tradition: Algonquin or Iroquois? *The Michigan Archaeologist* 24(1):11-36.
1994a   The Wayne Taxonomic Construct in Michigan Prehistory. *North American Archaeologist* 15(1):1-15.
1994b   *The Protohistoric Time Period in the Southwestern Lake Erie Region: European-Derived Trade Material, Population Movement and Cultural Realignment.* Paper presented at Cultures Before Contact: A Conference on the Late Prehistory of the Ohio Region. Ohio Archaeological Council, Cincinnati.
1996   Resource Procurement and Band Territories: A Model for Lower Great Lakes Paleoindian and Early Archaic Settlement Systems. *Archaeology of Eastern North America* 24:173-216.

Stothers, D.M., and T. Abel
  1990   Filling the Gap: Baker I and the Green Creek Phase in Northcentral Ohio. *Ohio Archaeologist* 40(1):36-49.
  1991   Beads, Brass, and Beaver: Archaeological Reflections of Protohistoric Fire Nation Trade and Exchange. *Archaeology of Eastern North America* 19: 121-134
  1993   Archaeological Reflections of the Late Archaic and Early Woodland Time Periods in the Western Lake Erie Region. *Archaeology of Eastern North America* 21:25-109.
Stothers, D.M., and J.R. Graves
  1983   Cultural Continuity and Change: The Western Basin, Ontario Iroquois and Sandusky Traditions – A 1982 Perspective. *Archaeology of Eastern North America* 11:109-142.
  1985   The Prairie Peninsula Co-Tradition: An Hypothesis for Hopewellian to Upper Mississippian Continuity. *Archaeology of Eastern North America* 13:153-175.
  1992   Archaeology, Linguistics, and Ethnicity: A Conjunctive Approach. Paper presented at 57th Annual Meeting of Society for American Archaeology, Urbana.
Stothers, D.M., J.R. Graves, S.K. Bechtel, and T.J. Abel
  1994   Current Perspectives on the Late Prehistory of the Western Lake Erie Region and a Reply to Murphy and Ferris. *Archaeology of Eastern North America* 21:135-196.
Stothers, D.M., J.R. Graves, and S. Conway
  1984   The Weiser Site: A Sandusky Village in Transition. *Michigan Archaeologist* 26(4):59-89.
Stothers, D.M., J.R. Graves, and B. Redmond
  1984   The Sandusky and Western Basin Traditions: A Comparative Analysis of the Settlement-Subsistence Systems. *Toledo Area Aboriginal Research Bulletin* 13:1-39.
Stothers, D.M., and G.M. Pratt
  1981   New Perspectives on the Late Woodland Cultures of the Western Lake Erie Region. *Midcontinental Journal of Archaeology* 6:92-121.
Struiver, M., and P.J. Reimer
  1993   Extended ^{14}C Data Base and Revised CALIB 3.0 ^{14}C Age Calibration. *Radiocarbon* 35(1): 215-230
Styles, B.W., and F.B. King
  1990   Faunal and Floral Remains from the Bold Counselor Phase Village. In *Archaeological Investigations at the Morton Village and Norris Farms 36 Cemetery*, edited by S.K. Santure, A.D.

Harn, and D. Esarey, pp. 57-65. Reports of Investigations 45. Illinois State Museum, Springfield.

Swadesh, M.
1955   Toward Greater Accuracy in Lexicostatistic Dating. *International Journal of American Linguistics* 21:121-137.

Swain, A.M.
1978   Environmental Changes During the Past 2000 Years in North-Central Wisconsin in Analysis of Pollen, Charcoal, and Seeds from Varved Lake Sediments. *Quaternary Research* 10: 55-68.

Swartz, B.K.
1977   A Cycle of North American Archaeologies. *Archaeology of Eastern North America* 5: 138-143.

Syms, E.L.
1977   *Cultural Ecology and Ecological Dynamics of the Ceramic Period in Southwestern Manitoba.* Plains Anthropologist Memoir 12. Plains Anthropological Society, Lincoln, Nebraska.

Taillon, H.
1995   *Évaluation Archéologique du Site Paléohistorique de Cap-de-Bon-Désir.* Ms. on file, Parcs Canada, Québec.

Tanton, T.L.
1931   *Fort William and Port Arthur, and Thunder-Cape Map Areas, Thunder Bay District, Ontario.* Memoir 167:1-222. Geological Survey of Canada, Ottawa.

Taylor, R.E., C.V. Haynes, Jr., and M. Stuiver
1996   Clovis and Folsom Age Estimates: Stratigraphic Context and Radiocarbon Calibration. *Antiquity* 70:515-525.

Taylor, W.W.
1948   A Study of Archaeology. Memoir Number 69, *American Anthropologist* 50(3:2).

Thomas, Chief Jacob
1994   *Teachings From The Longhouse.* With Terry Boyle. Stoddart Publishing, Toronto.

Thwaites, R.G. (editor)
1896-1901   *The Jesuit Relations and Allied Documents.* 73 volumes. Burrows Brothers, Cleveland.

1959   *The Jesuit Relations and Allied Documents: Travels and Explorations of the Jesuit Missions in New France 1610-1791.* 73 volumes. Pageant Book Company, New York.

Tiffany, J.A.
1983   An Overview of the Middle Missouri Tradition. In *Prairie Archaeology: Papers in Honor of David A. Baerreis*, edited by

G.E. Gibbon, pp. 87–108. Publications in Anthropology 3. University of Minnesota, Minneapolis.

1986 Ceramics from the F-518 Project. In *Archaeological Investigations along the F-518 Corridor*, edited by S.C. Lensink, pp. 227–245. Iowa Quaternary Studies Contribution 9. University of Iowa, Iowa City.

Timmins, P.A.

1994 Alder Creek: A Paleo-Indian Crowfield Phase Manifestation in the Region of Waterloo, Ontario. *Midcontinental Journal of Archaeology* 19(2):170-197.

1997 *The Calvert Site: An Interpretive Framework for the Early Iroquoian Village*. Archaeological Survey of Canada, Mercury Series Paper 156. Canadian Museum of Civilization, Hull.

Torrence, R.

1989 Retooling: Towards a Behavioral Theory of Stone Tools. In *Time, Energy and Stone Tools*, edited by R. Torrence, pp. 57-66. Cambridge University Press, Cambridge.

Tratebas, A.M.

1992 Stylistic Chronology Versus Absolute Dates for Early Style Rock Art on the North American Plains. Paper presented at the 2nd AURA Congress, Cairns, Queensland, Australia.

Tremblay, R.

1993a *Les Outils en Os de la Préhistoire Récente dans l'estuaire du Saint-Laurent*. Paper presented at the 26th annual congress of the Canadian Archaeological Association, Montréal.

1993b Iroquoian Beluga Hunting on Ile Verte. In *Essays in St. Lawrence Iroquoian Archaeology*, edited by J.F. Pendergast and C. Chapdelaine, pp. 121-137. Occasional Papers in Northeastern Archaeology 8. Copetown Press, Dundas, Ontario.

1994 Des Grains de Maïs Révélateurs d'Ancienneté Culturelle. *Recherches Amérindiennes au Québec* 24(4):85-86.

1995a L'île aux Corneilles : Deux Occupations du Sylvicole Supérieur entre la Province de Canada et le Saguenay. In *Archéologies Québécoises*, edited by A.-M. Balac, C. Chapdelaine, N. Clermont, and F. Duguay, pp. 271-306. Paléo-Québec 23. Recherches Amérindiennes au Québec, Montréal.

1995b *Rapport des Activités Archéologiques Menées à l'île Verte, Été 1994*. Ms. on file, Ministère de la Culture et des Communications du Québec, Québec.

1997 La Connexion Abénaquise : Quelques Éléments de Recherche sur la Dispersion des Iroquoiens du Saint-Laurent Orientaux.

Archéologiques 10:77-86.

1998a   Présence du Noyer Cendré dans l'Estuaire du Saint-Laurent durant la Préhistoire. *Recherches Amérindiennes au Québec* 27(3-4):99-106.

1998b   Le Site de l'anse à la Vache et le Mitan du Sylvicole Supérieur dans l'Estuaire du Saint-Laurent. In *L'Éveilleur et l'Ambassadeur. Essais Archéologiques et Ethnohistoriques en Hommage à Charles A. Martijn*, edited by R. Tremblay, 91-125, Paléo-Québec 27. Recherches Amérindiennes au Québec, Montréal.

Tremblay, R., and J.-B. Vaillancourt

1994   *Rapport des Activités Archéologiques Menées sur les Îles du Bas-Saint-Laurent, Été 1993*. Ms. on file, Ministère de la Culture et des Communications du Québec, Québec.

Trigger, B.G.

1965   *History and Settlement in Lower Nubia.* Yale University Publications, New Haven.

1968a   *Beyond History: The Methods of Prehistory.* Holt Rinehart and Winston. New York.

1968b   Archaeological and Other Evidence: A Fresh Look at the Laurentian Iroquois. *American Antiquity* 33: 429-440.

1969   More on Models. *Antiquity* 63: 59-61.

1970a   The Strategy of Iroquoian Prehistory. *Ontario Archaeology* 14:3-48.

1970b   Aims in Prehistoric Archaeology. *Antiquity* 44:26-37.

1976   *The Children of Aataentsic: A History of the Huron People to 1660.* McGill-Queen's University Press, Montreal.

1977   Comments on Archaeological Classification and Ethnic Groups. *Norwegian Archaeological Review* 10:20–23.

1978a   *Time and Traditions: Essays in Archaeological Interpretation.* Columbia University Press. New York.

1978b   The Development of the Archaeological Culture in Europe and America. In *Time and Traditions: Essays in Archaeological Interpretation*, pp. 75–95. Columbia University Press, New York.

1978c   The Strategy of Iroquoian Prehistory. In *Archaeological Essays in Honor of Irving B. Rouse*, edited by R. C. Dunnell and E. S. Hall, pp. 275–310. Mouton, The Hague.

1978d   Ethnohistory and Archaeology. *Ontario Archaeology* 30:17-24

1980   Archaeology and the Image of the American Indian. *American Antiquity* 45:662-676.

1986   *Natives and Newcomers: Canada's "Heroic Age" Reconsidered.*

McGill-Queen's University Press, Montreal.

1989   *A History of Archaeological Thought.* Cambridge University Press, New York.

1990a   *The Huron: Farmers of the North.* 2nd edition. Holt, Rinehart and Winston, Toronto.

1990b   Maintaining Economic Equality in Opposition to Complexity: An Iroquoian Case Study. In *The Evolution of Political Systems: Sociopolitics in Small-Scale Sedentary Societies,* edited by S. Upham, pp. 119-145. Cambridge University Press, New York.

1998   Archaeology and Epistemology: Dialoguing Across the Darwinian Chasm. *American Journal of Archaeology.* In press.

Tschauner, H.

1994   Archaeological Systematics and Cultural Evolution: Retrieving the Honour of Culture History. *Man* (n.s.) 29:77–93.

Tuck, J.A.

1971   *Onondaga Iroquois Prehistory: A Study in Settlement Archaeology.* Syracuse University Press, Syracuse.

Turgeon, L., W. Fitzgerald, et R. Auger

1992   Les Objets des Échanges entre Français et Amérindiens au XVIe Siècle. *Recherches Amérindiennes au Québec* 22(2-3):152-167.

Turner, R.L., Jr.

1978   The Tuck Carpenter Site and its Relation to Other Sites within the Titus Focus. *Bulletin of the Texas Archeological Society* 49:1-110.

Upham, S.

1990   Analog or Digital: Toward a Generic Framework for Explaining the Development of Emergent Political Systems. In *The Evolution of Political Systems: Sociopolitics in Small-scale Sedentary Societies,* edited by S. Upham, pp. 87-115. Cambridge University Press, New York.

Upham, S. (editor)

1990   *The Evolution of Political Systems: Sociopolitics in Small-scale Sedentary Societies.* Cambridge University Press, New York.

Vastokas, J.

1987   Native Art as Art History: Meaning and Time from Unwritten Sources. *Journal of Canadian Studies* 21(4):7-37.

Voget, F.

1984   Anthropological Theory and Iroquois Ethnology: 1850-1970. *Extending the Rafters: Interdisciplinary Approaches to Iroquoian Studies,* edited by M. Foster, J. Campisi and M. Mithun, pp. 343-357. State University of New York Press, Albany.

von Gernet, A.
1985   *Analysis of Intrasite Artifact Spatial Distributions: The Draper Site Smoking Pipes.* Research Report 16. Museum of Indian Archaeology, London, Ontario.
1992   New Directions in the Construction of Prehistoric Amerindian Belief Systems. In *Ancient Images, Ancient Thought: The Archaeology of Ideology*, edited by A. Goldsmith, S. Garvie, D. Selin and J. Smith, pp. 133-140. Proceedings of the 23rd Annual Chacmool Conference. University of Calgary, Archaeological Association, Calgary.
1994   Editorial: Four Studies in Ontario Iroquoian Prehistory. *Ontario Archaeology* 58:3-5.
1995   The Date of Time Immemorial: Politics and Iroquoian Origins. In *Origins of the People of the Longhouse: Proceedings of the 21st Annual Symposium of the Ontario Archaeological Society*, edited by A. Bekerman and G. Warrick, pp. 119-128. Ontario Archaeological Society, Toronto.

von Gernet, A. and P.A. Timmins
1987   Pipes and Parakeets: Constructing Meaning in an Early Iroquoian Context. In *Archaeology As Long-Term History*, edited by I, Hodder, pp.31-42. Cambridge University Press, New York.

Wallbridge, T.C.
1860   On Some Ancient Mounds upon the Shores of the Bay of Quinte. *The Canadian Journal* 5:408-417.

Warrick, G.A.
1990   *A Population History of the Huron-Petun, A.D. 900-1650.* Unpublished Ph.D. dissertation, Department of Anthropology, McGill University, Montreal.

Watts, C.M.
1997   *A Quantitative Analysis and Chronological Seriation of Riviere au Vase Phase Ceramics From Southwestern Ontario.* Unpublished M.Sc. thesis, Department of Anthropology, University of Toronto, Toronto.

Waugh, F.W.
1916   *Iroquois Foods and Food Preparation.* Memorandum 86. Geological Survey of Canada, Ottawa.

Webb, T., III
1985   Holocene Palynology and Climate. In *Paleoclimate Analysis and Modelling*, edited by A. D. Hecht, pp. 163-195. John Wiley and Sons, Toronto.
1986   Is Vegetation in Equalibrium with Climate? How to Interpret

Late-Quaternary Pollen Data. *Vegetatio* 67: 75-91.

Weintraub, B.
1993   Going Head-to-Head with Indian Prehistory. *National Geographic* 184(6).

Wendorf, F.
1968   Site 117: A Nubian Final Paleolithic Graveyard Near Jebel Sahaba, Sudan. In *The Prehistory of Nubia*, edited by F. Wendorf, pp. 954-995. Southern Methodist University Press, Dallas.

Whallon, R.
1968   Investigations of Late Prehistoric Social Organization in New York State. In *New Perspectives in Archeology*, edited by S. Binford and L. Binford, pp.223-244. Aldine Press, Chicago.

Wheat, J.B., C. Gifford, and W. Wasley
1958   Ceramic Variety, Type Cluster, and Ceramic System in Southwestern Pottery Analysis. *American Antiquity* 24:34-47.

White, M.E.
1978   Erie. In *Handbook of North American Indians Volume 15 (Northeast)*, edited by B.G. Trigger, pp. 412-417. Smithsonian Institution, Washington, D.C.

Whittlesey, C.
1863   Ancient Mining on the Shores of Lake Superior. *Smithsonian Contributions to Knowledge* 13(4):1-32.

Wiessner, P.
1983   Style and Social Information in Kalahari San Projectile Points. *American Antiquity* 49:253-76.

1984   Reconstructing the Behavioural Basis for Style: A Case Study Among the Kalahari San. *Journal of Anthropological Archaeology* 3:190-234.

1988   Style and Changing Relations Between the Individual and Society. In *The Meaning of Things: Material Culture and Symbolic Expression*, edited by I. Hodder, pp. 56-63. Unwin Hyman, London.

1990   Is There a Unity to Style? In *The Uses of Style in Archaeology*, edited by M.W. Conkey and C.A. Hastorf, pp. 105-112. Cambridge University Press, New York.

Wilkinson, R.G.
1971   *Prehistoric Biological Relationships in the Great Lakes Region*. Museum of Anthropology Anthropological Papers 43. University of Michigan, Ann Arbor.

Wilkinson, T.A.H.
1996 *State Formation in Egypt.* Tempus Reparatum, Oxford.
Willey, G.R.
1953 *Prehistoric Settlement Patterns in the Virú Valley, Peru.* Bureau of American Ethnology Bulletin 155. Smithsonian Institution, Washington, D.C.
1966 *An Introduction to American Archaeology Volume 1 (North America).* Prentice-Hall, Englewood Cliffs, New Jersey.
1968 *An Introduction to American Archaeology Volume 2 (Central and South America).* Prentice-Hall, Englewood Cliffs, New Jersey.
Willey, G.R. (editor)
1956 Prehistoric Settlement Patterns in the New World. *Viking Fund Publications In Anthropology,* New York.
Willey, G.R., and P. Phillips
1958 *Method and Theory in American Archaeology.* University of Chicago Press, Chicago.
Willey, G.R., and J.A. Sabloff
1982 *A History of American Archaeology.* W.H. Freeman and Company, San Francisco.
1993 *A History of American Archaeology* (3rd ed.). Freeman, New York.
Willey, P.
1990 *Prehistoric Warfare on the Great Plains: Skeletal Analysis of the Crow Creek Massacre Victims.* Garland, New York.
Williams, B.J.
1974 *A Model of Band Society.* American Antiquity Memoir 29. Society for American Archaeology, Washington, D.C.
Williamson, R.F.
1985 Glen Meyer: People in Transition. Unpublished Ph.D. dissertation, Department of Anthropology, McGill University, Montreal.
1986 The Mill Stream Cluster: The Other Side of the Coin. In *Studies in Southwestern Ontario Archaeology,* edited by W.A. Fox, pp. 25-31. Occasional Publication 1. London Chapter, Ontario Archaeological Society, London, Ontario.
1990 The Early Iroquoian Period of Southern Ontario. In *The Archaeology of Southern Ontario to A.D. 1650,* edited by C.J. Ellis and N. Ferris, pp. 291-320. Occasional Publication 5. London Chapter, Ontario Archaeological Society, London, Ontario.

Williamson, R.F., and D.A. Robertson

1994a   Peer Polities Beyond the Periphery: Early and Middle Iroquoian Regional Interaction. *Ontario Archaeology* 58:27-44.

1994b   Reply to Jamieson's Comment. *Ontario Archaeology* 58:47-48.

Willis, J.

1998   Early Historic Ceramics of the Zimmerman Site (11LS13) and Starved Rock (11LS12) of Illinois: A Review of Previous Descriptions and a Re-Analysis of Some of the Materials These Descriptions Were Based On. Paper presented at the 43rd Midwest Archaeological Conference, Muncie, Indiana.

Wilson, D.

1856   The Ancient Miners of Lake Superior. *The Canadian Journal*, n.s. 1(3):227-37.

1885   The Huron-Iroquois of Canada, a Typical Race of American Aborigines. *Royal Society of Canada, Proceedings and Transactions, Series I* 2(2):55-106.

Wintemberg, W.J.

1940   *Lawson Prehistoric Village Site, Middlesex County, Ontario.* Bulletin 94. National Museum of Canada, Ottawa.

1942   The Geographical Distribution of Aboriginal Pottery in Canada. *American Antiquity* 8: 129-141.

1946   The Sidey-MacKay Village Site. *American Antiquity* 11: 154-182.

1948   *The Middleport Prehistoric Village Site.* Bulletin 109. National Museum of Canada, Ottawa.

Witthoft, J.

1949   *Green Corn Cermonialism in the Eastern Woodlands.* Occasional Contributions from the Museum of Anthropology Papers 13. University of Michigan, Ann Arbor.

Wittry, W.L.

1951   A Preliminary Study of the Old Copper Culture. *The Wisconsin Archeologist* 32(1)311-329.

Wittry, W.L., Arnold, J.C., C.O. Witty, and T.R. Pauketat

1994   *The Holdener Site: Late Woodland, Emergent Mississippian, and Mississippian Occupations in the American Bottom Uplands.* American Bottom Archaeology, FAI 270 Site Report 26. University of Illinois, Urbana.

Wittry, W.L., and R.E. Ritzenthaler

1956   The Old Copper Complex: An Archaic Manifestation in Wisconsin. *American Antiquity* 21(3):244-254.

Wobst, H.M.

1968   The Butterfield Site, 20 By 29, Bay County, Michigan. In *Contributions to Michigan Archaeology*, edited by J.E. Fitting, pp. 173-275. Museum of Anthropology Papers 32. University of Michigan, Ann Arbor.

1976   Locational Relationships in Paleolithic Society. *Journal of Human Evolution* 5:49-58.

1977   Stylistic Behavior and Information Exchange. In *Papers for the Director: Research Essays in Honor of James B. Griffin*, edited by C.E. Cleland, pp. 317-342. Museum of Anthropology Papers 61. University of Michigan, Ann Arbor.

1978   The Archaeo-Ethnology of Hunter-Gatherers, or The Tyranny of the Ethnographic Record in Archaeology. *American Antiquity* 43:303-309.

Wood, J.W.

1998   A Theory of Preindustrial Population Dynamics: Population, Economy, and Well-Being in Malthusian Systems. *Current Anthropology* 39:99-135.

Wood, J.W., and G.R. Milner

1994   Reply. *Current Anthropology* 35:631-637.

Wood, J.W., G.R. Milner, H.C. Harpending, and K.M. Weiss

1992   The Osteological Paradox: Problems of Inferring Prehistoric Health from Skeletal Samples. *Current Anthropology* 33:343-370.

Worster, D.

1977   *Nature's Economy: A History of Ecological Ideas.* Cambridge University Press, New York.

Wray, C.F., M.L. Sempowski, L.P. Saunders, and G. Carlo Cervone

1987   *The Adams and Culbertson Sites.* Research Records 19. Rochester Museum and Science Center, Rochester.

Wright, J.V.

1960   *A Distributional Study of Some Archaic Traits in Southern Ontario.* Bulletin 180. National Museum of Canada, Ottawa.

1965   A Regional Examination of Ojibwa Culture History. *Anthropologica* 7:189–227.

1966   *The Ontario Iroquois Tradition.* Bulletin 210. National Museum of Canada, Ottawa.

1967a   *The Laurel Tradition and the Middle Woodland Period.* Bulletin 217. National Museum of Canada, Ottawa.

1967b   Type and Attribute Analysis: Their Application to Iroquois Culture History. In *Iroquois Culture History and Prehistory*, edited by E. Tooker, pp. 99-100. New York State Museum and Science Service.

1972   *The Shield Archaic.* Publications in Archaeology 3. National Museum of Canada, Ottawa.

1974   Archaeological Taxonomy: Apples and Oranges. *Canadian Archaeological Association Bulletin* 6:206–209.

1978   The Implications of Probable Early and Middle Archaic Projectile Points from Southern Ontario. *Canadian Journal of Archaeology* 2:59-78.

1980   The Role of Attribute Analysis in the Study of Iroquoian Prehistory. In *Proceedings of the 1979 Iroquois Pottery Conference*, edited by C.F. Hayes III, pp. 21-26. Research Records 13. Rochester Museum and Science Center, Rochester.

1981   Prehistory of the Canadian Shield. In *Handbook of North American Indians Volume 6 (Subarctic)*, edited by J. Helm, pp. 86-96. Smithsonian Institution, Washington D.C.

1984   The Cultural Continuity of the Northern Iroquoian-Speaking Peoples. In *Extending the Rafters: Interdisciplinary Approaches to Iroquoian Studies*, edited by M.K. Foster, J. Campisi, and M. Methun, pp. 283-299. State University of New York Press, Albany.

1985   The Development of Prehistory in Canada, 1935-1985. *American Antiquity* 50(2):421-433.

1990   Archaeology of Southern Ontario to A.D. 1650: A Critique. In *The Archaeology of Southern Ontario to A.D. 1650*, edited by C.J. Ellis and N. Ferris, pp. 493-503. Occasional Publication 5. London Chapter, Ontario Archaeological Society, London, Ontario.

1992   The Conquest Theory of the Ontario Iroquois Tradition: A Reassessment. *Ontario Archaeology* 54:3-16.

1995   *A History of the Native People of Canada, Volume I (10,000-1,000 BC).* Archaeological Survey of Canada, Mercury Series Paper 152. Canadian Museum of Civilization, Hull.

Wright, M.

1981   *The Walker Site.* Archaeological Survey of Canada, Mercury Series Paper 103:1-209. National Museum of Canada, Ottawa.

Wrong, G.M. (editor)

1939   *Father Gabriel Sagard: The Long Journey to the Country of the Hurons.* The Champlain Society, Toronto.

Wylie, A.

1985   The Reaction Against Analogy. In *Advances In Archaeological*

Method and Theory Volume 8, edited by M. Schiffer, pp. 63-111. Academic Press, New York.

1989a   The Interpretive Dilemma. In *Critical Traditions In Contemporary Archaeology: Essays in the Philosophy, History and Socio-politics of Archaeology*, edited by V. Pinsky and A. Wylie, pp. 18-27. Cambridge University Press, New York.

1989b   Matters of Fact and Matters of Interest. In *Archaeological Approaches to Cultural Identity*, edited by S. Shennan, pp. 94-109. Unwin Hyman, Boston.

Zeder, M.

1997   The American Archaeologist: Results of the 1994 SAA Census. *Society for American Archaeology Bulletin* 15(2):12-17.